ALGORITHMICS

ALGORITHMICS
The Spirit of Computing

DAVID HAREL
The Weizmann Institute of Science, Rehovot, Israel

Not by might, nor by power, but by my spirit
Zechariah 4: 6

for the spirit of the . . . creature was in the wheels
When those moved, these moved;
and when those stood still, these stood still
Ezekiel 1: 20, 21

ADDISON-WESLEY PUBLISHING COMPANY
Wokingham, England · Reading, Massachusetts · Menlo Park, California
New York · Don Mills, Ontario · Amsterdam · Bonn · Sydney
Singapore · Tokyo · Madrid · Bogota · Santiago · San Juan

The programs presented in this book have been included for their instructional value. They have been tested with care but are not guaranteed for any particular purpose. The publisher does not offer any warranties or representations, nor does it accept any liabilities with respect to the programs.

Cover design by John Gibbs from an idea suggested by the author.
Illustrations by Chartwell Illustrators.
Typeset by MCL Computerset Ltd., Ely, Cambs.
Printed in Great Britain by T J Press (Padstow) Ltd., Cornwall.

First printed 1987.
Reprinted 1987.

British Library Cataloguing in Publication Data
Harel, David
    Algorithmics : the spirit of computing.
    1. Electronic data processing
    2. Computers
    I. Title
    004   QA76

    ISBN 0–201–19240–3

QA
76
, H2833
1987

Library of Congress Cataloging in Publication Data
Harel, David, 1950-
    Algorithmics : the spirit of computing.

    Bibliography; p.
    Includes index.
    1. Electronic data processing.   2. Algorithms.
I. Title.
QA76 . H2833   1987   004   86-32038
ISBN 0–201–19240–3

To my dear parents,
Joyce and Harold Fisch,
for the first 20 years

and to Varda,
for all the rest

Preface

This book tells a story. The story concerns the concepts, ideas, methods and results fundamental to computer science. It is not specifically about computer technology, nor is it about computer programming, though obviously it is heavily influenced by both.

The book is intended to fill a crucial gap in the literature related to the computer revolution. Scores of excellent books can be found on computers themselves, with details of their structure, workings and operation. There are also numerous books about the act of writing programs for computers in any of a growing number of languages. These books come at a wide range of levels, some aimed at people with no computer-related background at all, and some aimed at the most computer-literate professionals. In addition, there are many books on subjects peripheral to the technology, such as the social and legal aspects of the revolution, as well as books describing the relevance of computers to a variety of application areas. All this comes as no surprise. People are curious about computers, and want to learn how to put them to use. They are typically interested in specific kinds of computers, and often for specific purposes too.

Then there are textbooks. Indeed, computer science is a fast-growing academic discipline, with ever-larger numbers of potential students knocking at the doors of admission offices. Well-established academic disciplines have a habit of yielding excellent textbooks, and computer science is no exception. Over the years many comprehensive and clearly written textbooks have appeared, containing detailed technical accounts of the subjects deemed appropriate to students of computer science. However, despite the dizzying speed with which some of the *technological* innovations become obsolete and are replaced by new ones, the fundamentals of the *science* of computation, and hence many of the basic concepts that are considered important in a computer science curriculum, change slowly, if at all. Of course, new technologies and new languages require revisions in scientific emphasis, which are eventually reflected in the scientific literature. However, by and large, there is almost universal agreement on a core of fundamental topics that computer science students should be taught.

It would appear that anyone associated with computers ought to be aware of these topics, and not only those who have decided to spend three or four years getting a particular kind of academic diploma. Moreover, given that a revolution is indeed taking place before our very eyes, many of these topics, and the special ways of thinking that go with them, ought to be available to the enquiring person even if that person is not directly associated with a computer at all.

Books concerned primarily with computers or programming are intended to fulfil quite different needs. Computers are made of bits and bytes, and programming is carried out using languages with rigid rules of grammar and punctuation. Consequently, computer books often suffer from the 'bit/byte syndrome' and programming books from the 'semicolon syndrome'. In other words, the reader becomes predominantly involved in the principles of a particular computer or a particular programming language (or both). It would seem that things cannot be explained without first describing, in detail, either a machine or a medium for communicating with one (or both).

Many advanced textbooks *do* treat the fundamentals, but by their very nature they concentrate on specific topics, and do so at an advanced technical level that is usually unsuitable for the general reader. Even professional programmers and systems analysts might lack the background or motivation required to get through books aimed at full-time computer science students.

Curiously, there appears to be very little written material devoted to the *science* of computing and aimed at the technically oriented general reader as well as the computer professional. This fact is doubly curious in view of the abundance of precisely this kind of literature in most other scientific areas, such as physics, biology, chemistry and mathematics, not to mention humanities and the arts. There appears to be an acute need for a technically detailed, expository account of the fundamentals of computer science; one that suffers as little as possible from the bit/byte or semicolon syndromes and their derivatives, one that transcends the technological and linguistic whirlpool of specifics, and one that is useful both to a sophisticated layperson and to a computer expert. It seems that we have all been too busy with the revolution to be bothered with satisfying such a need.

This book is an attempt in this direction. Its objective is to present a readable account of some of the most important and basic topics of computer science, stressing the fundamental and robust nature of the science in a form that is virtually independent of the details of specific computers, languages, and formalisms.

*   *   *

This book grew out of a series of lectures given by the author on 'Galei Zahal', one of Israel's national radio channels, between October 1984 and January 1985. It is about what shall be called **algorithmics** in this book – that is, the study of algorithms. An algorithm is an abstract recipe, prescribing a process that might be carried out by a human, by a computer, or by other means. It thus represents a very general concept, with numerous applications. Its principal interest and use, however, is in those cases where the process is to be carried out by a computer.

The book can be used as the basis of a one-semester introductory course in computer science or as a text for a general computer science literacy course in science and engineering schools. Moreover, it can be used as supplementary reading in many kinds of computer-related educational activities, from basic programming courses to advanced graduate or undergraduate degree programs in computer science. The material covered herein, while not directly aimed at producing better programmers or system analysts, can aid people who work with computers by providing an overall picture of some of the most fundamental issues relevant to their work.

*   *   *

The preliminary chapters discuss the concept of an **algorithmic problem** and the **algorithm** that solves it, followed by cursory discussions of the **structure** of algorithms, the **data** they manipulate, and the languages in which they are programmed. With the ground thus set, Part Two of the book turns to some general methods and paradigms for algorithmic design. This is followed by two chapters on the analysis of algorithms, treating, respectively, their **correctness** and **efficiency** (mainly time efficiency), including techniques for establishing the former and estimating the latter. Part Three of the book is devoted to the **inherent limitations** of effectively executable algorithms, and hence of the computers that implement them. Certain precisely defined problems, including important and practical ones, are shown to be **provably** not solvable by any computers of reasonable size in any reasonable amount of time (say, the life time of a person), and never will be. Worse still, it is shown that some problems are provably not solvable by computers at all, even with unlimited time! In Part Four of the book the requirements are relaxed – for example, by employing concurrent activities or coin tossing, in order to overcome some of these difficulties. Finally, the relationship of computers to human intelligence is discussed, emphasizing the 'soft' *heuristic*, or intuitive, nature of the latter, and the problems involved in relating it to the 'hard' scientific subject of algorithmics.

The book is intended to be read sequentially, not to be used as a reference. It is organized so that each chapter depends on the previous ones, but with smooth readability in mind. Most of the material in the preliminary

Part One should be familiar to people with a background in programming. Thus, Chapters 1 and 2 and parts of Chapter 3 can be browsed through superficially by such readers. Starting with Chapter 4, however, the material becomes increasingly harder as it proceeds, until Chapter 12 is reached, which is of somewhat lighter nature.

** Certain sections contain relatively technical material and can be skipped by the reader without too much loss of continuity. They are set in smaller type and are enclosed between asterisks. It is recommended, however, that even those sections be skimmed, at least to get a superficial idea of their contents. **

Whenever appropriate, brief discussions of the research topics that are of current interest to computer scientists are included. The text is followed by a section of detailed bibliographic notes for each chapter, with 'backward' pointers connecting the discussions in the text with the relevant literature.

*   *   *

It is hoped that this book will facilitate communication between the various groups of people who are actively involved in the computer revolution, and between them and those who, for the time being, are observers only.

David Harel
Pittsburgh
February 1987

Write the vision, and make it plain upon tablets,
that he[†] who reads it may run
Habakkuk 2: 2

[†] Relying on no less an authority than The Bible itself, the masculine forms 'he', 'him', 'his', etc., will be used whenever the more precise, but far more awkward, forms 'she/he', 'her/him', 'hers/his', etc., are intended.

Acknowledgements

Therefore will I give thanks to thee
Psalm 18: 50

Parts of this book were written while I was visiting Digital Equipment Corporation's Systems Research Center in Palo Alto in the Summer of 1985 and Carnegie-Mellon University's Computer Science Department for the 1986/7 academic year. I would like to express my deepest gratitude for these opportunities to work on the book undisturbed.

T. Yuval, Managing Editor of the *Broadcast University* programs on the Israeli radio channel 'Galei Zahal', deserves special thanks for convincing me to prepare the lecture series out of which this book grew.

I am indebted to my colleagues at the Weizmann Institute, A. Pnueli, A. Shamir and S. Ullman, for discussions related to the material appearing herein. It is amazing how one's whole approach can benefit from being surrounded by researchers of such calibre.

I am most grateful to M. Ben-Ari, S. D. Brookes, A. Fiat and M. Vardi, as well as to the three anonymous reviewers commissioned by Addison-Wesley, who read significant parts of the manuscript, identified errors, and provided helpful and insightful feedback. I would also like to thank the following people, who all took time to read and comment on parts of the manuscript: H. Berliner, A. K. Chandra, N. Dershowitz, A. Heydon, C. A. R. Hoare, Z. Reisel, E. Roberts, S. Safra, D. Sherman, R. Sherman, B. Simons, D. Sleator, D. Tygar, P. Wegner and L. Zuck. In addition, collective thanks go to the many people I have pestered recently with questions pertaining to the bibliography.

I would like to thank Y. Barbut for his superb graphical work on the figures, and S. Fliegelman and C. Weintraub for helping me to struggle with the task of TEXing the draft manuscript. I am grateful to Addison-Wesley's S. Troth and A. King for being such effective sponsoring editors, and to D. Myson-Etherington for the endless hours she has devotedly spent on the project throughout its production.

As usual, my wife Varda and our children, Sarit, Hadas, Efrat and Yair, put up with everything in the best imaginable way, and provided the warm and loving environment that is so important for such an endeavour.

Table of Contents

Declare the things that are to come hereafter
Isaiah 41: 23

PART THREE   LIMITATIONS AND ROBUSTNESS

PART FOUR   RELAXING THE RULES

PART ONE

PRELIMINARIES

Now, these are the foundations
II Chronicles 3: 3

1

Introduction and Historical Review

OR

What's It All About?

Computers are amazing machines. They seem to be able to do anything. They fly aircraft and spaceships, and control power stations and hazardous chemical plants. Companies can no longer be run without them, and a growing number of sophisticated medical procedures cannot be performed in their absence. They serve lawyers and judges who seek judicial precedents in scores of documented trials, and help scientists in performing immensely complicated and involved mathematical computations. They route and control millions of telephone calls in networks that span continents, and are used for map reading, typesetting, graphical picture processing and integrated circuit design. They can relieve us of many boring chores, such as keeping a meticulous track of home expenses, and at the same time provide us with exciting alternatives, such as realistic computer games or computerized music. Also, computers of today are hard at work helping design the even more powerful computers of tomorrow.

In short, computers are awesome and fascinating, but at the same time indispensable. For many of us they are also intimidating, and for others threatening. Whatever the case, we cannot afford to be indifferent to them. They are here to stay, and the remarkable growth in their rate of

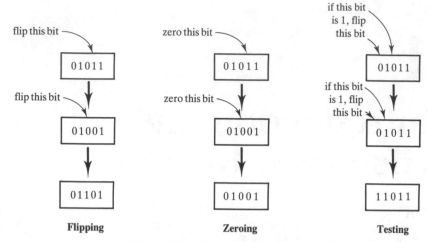

Figure 1.1   Operations on bits.

performance and range of applications shows no signs of coming to a halt.

It is all the more remarkable, therefore, that the digital computer, even the most modern and complex one, can be thought of as merely a large collection of switches. These switches, or **bits** as they are called in technical jargon, are not 'flipped' by the user, but are special, internal switches that are 'flipped' by the computer itself. Each bit can be in one of two positions, or, to put it another way, can take on one of two **values**, 0 or 1. Typically, the value of a bit is determined by some electronic characteristic, such as whether a certain point has a positive or negative charge.

Any computer can directly execute only a small number of extremely trivial operations, like flipping, zeroing, or testing a bit. Flipping changes the bit's value, zeroing makes sure that the bit ends up in the 0 position, and testing does one thing if the bit is already in the 0 position, and another if it is not (see Figure 1.1). Different computers differ in their size (i.e., the number of available bits), in the types of elementary operations they can perform, in the speed in which these operations are performed, in the physical media that embody the bits and their internal organization, and, significantly, in their external environment. This last item means that two computers, which are otherwise identical, might seem very different to an observer: one might be similar in appearance to a television set with a keyboard, and the other might be buried under the dials and knobs of an automatic knitting machine. In a sense, such peripheral but highly visible objects are far less important as components of the computer than the bits and their internal arrangement. It is the bits that 'sense' the external stimuli arriving from the outside world via buttons, levers, keys on a keyboard, electronic communication lines, and even microphones and cameras. It is the bits that 'decide' how to react to these stimuli, ultimately causing other stimuli to be sent back outside via displays, screens, printers, and even loudspeakers, beepers, levers and cranks.

How do they do it? What is it that spans the immense distance between such trivial operations on bits and the incredible feats that computers are capable of? The answer lies in the central concepts treated in this book: the **process**, and the **algorithm** that controls it and causes it to take place.

Some Gastronomy

Imagine a kitchen, containing a supply of ingredients, an array of baking utensils, an oven, a (human) baker, etc. Baking a delicious raisin cake is a process that is carried out *from* the ingredients, *by* the baker, *with* the aid of the oven, and, most significantly, *according* to the recipe. The ingredients are the **inputs** to the process, the cake is its **output**, and the recipe is the **algorithm**. In other words, the algorithm prescribes the activities that constitute the process. The recipes, or algorithms, relevant to a set of processes under discussion are often gathered under the general term **software**, whereas the utensils and oven are generally called **hardware**. The baker, in this case, can also be considered part of the hardware (see Figure 1.2).

In analogy with the simplicity of the bit operations that a computer

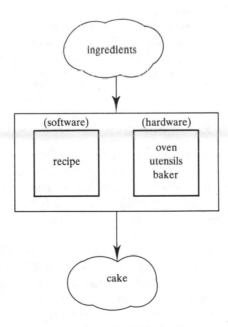

Figure 1.2   Baking a cake.

is capable of, the baker/oven/utensils constellation can also be said to have very limited direct abilities. This cake baking hardware can pour, mix, spread, drip, light-the-oven, open-the-oven-door, measure-time, measure-quantities, etc. It cannot directly bake cakes. Recipes, those magical objects that serve to convert the limited abilities of kitchen hardware into cakes, will be the subject of this book, not ovens or bakers.

Recipes, as just mentioned, are called algorithms here, while the area of human study, knowledge and expertise that concerns algorithms will be called **algorithmics**. The analogy drawn here has been made as exact as possible: the recipe, which is in a sense an abstract entity, is the algorithm; the formal written version of the recipe, such as the one found in a cook book, is analogous to a computer **program**. Software actually refers more to programs – precise representations of algorithms written in special computer-readable languages – than to the algorithms themselves. However, until we discuss programming languages in Chapter 3, this distinction will be quite immaterial.

We confront algorithms wherever we go. Many everyday processes are governed by algorithms: changing a flat tire, constructing a do-it-yourself cabinet, knitting a sweater, dividing numbers, looking up a telephone number, updating a list of expenses, and filling out an income tax form. Some of these might be immediately related in our minds to computers (division, for example), and others less so (cabinet construction, for example), but this is of less concern to us here. Although computers are fundamental to the topic of this book, we shall not concentrate on their physical aspects at all, except implicitly in parts of Chapters 3 and 9, and we shall definitely not be talking about any specific type or brand of computer. It is with their *spirit* that we are concerned; with the recipes that make them tick – with their algorithms.

Algorithmics vs. Computer Science

Algorithmics is more than a branch of computer science. It is central to all areas of computer science, and, in all fairness, can be said to be relevant to most of science, business and technology. The very nature of algorithmics, however, renders it particularly applicable to those disciplines that benefit from the use of computers, and these are fast becoming an overwhelming majority.

Sometimes people ask: 'What really *is* computer science? Why don't we have submarine science, dishwasher science or telephone science?' Telephones, it might be argued, are as important to modern life as computers are, perhaps even more so, and likewise dishwashers. A slightly more focussed question is whether computer science is not covered by such classical disciplines as mathematics, physics, electrical engineering, linguistics, logic and philosophy.

We would do best to avoid this issue here, as we might appear pretentious in claiming to be able to answer these questions here and now. The hope, however, is that the book will implicitly convey something of the uniqueness and universality of algorithmics, and hence something of the importance of computer science as an autonomous (albeit, young) field of study. Since computers could conceivably restrict the generality of algorithmics, some people view the unavoidable link between the two as unfortunate. In fact, terming the field 'computer science', someone once said, is like referring to surgery as 'knife science'. Be that as it may, it is clear that algorithmics would never have developed the way it has without that link. However, it is generally agreed that the term 'computer science' is misleading, and that something like 'information science', 'process science', or 'the science of the discrete' might be better. Again, we can pass the buck by claiming that our subject matter, algorithmics, only forms the underpinnings of computer science, not that it replaces it.

Some of the topics we discuss in the sequel, such as the existence of problems that computers *cannot* solve, have philosophical implications, not only on the limits of the wonderful machines we are able to build, but also on our own limits as mortals with finite mass and a finite life span. The profound nature of such implications notwithstanding, the emphasis in this book is on the more pragmatic goal of acquiring a deep understanding of the fundamentals of machine-executable processes, and the recipes, or algorithms, that govern them.

*   *   *

Some History

Let us now review several important milestones in the development of computers and computer science, mainly to illustrate that as a scientific discipline the field is extremely young.

Somewhere between 400 and 300 BC, the great Greek mathematician Euclid invented an algorithm for finding the greatest common divisor (gcd) of two positive integers. The gcd of X and Y is the largest integer that exactly divides both X and Y. For example, the gcd of 80 and 32 is 16. The details of the algorithm itself are of no concern here, but the Euclidian algorithm, as it is called, is considered to be the first non-trivial algorithm ever devised. The word *algorithm* is derived from the name of the Persian mathematician Mohammed al-Khowârizmî who lived during the ninth century and who is credited with providing the step-by-step rules for adding, subtracting, multiplying and dividing ordinary decimal numbers. When written in Latin, the name became Algorismus, from which *algorithm* is but a small step. Clearly, Euclid and al-Khowârizmî were algorithmicians *par excellence*.

Turning from software to hardware, one of the earliest machines to carry out a process controlled by what might be called an algorithm was a weaving loom invented in 1801 by a Frenchman, Joseph Jacquard. The pattern woven was determined by cards with holes punched at various locations. These holes, which were sensed by a special mechanism, controlled the selection of threads and other actions of the machine. It is interesting that Jacquard's loom had nothing to do with the narrow numerical connotation of the term 'computation'.

One of the most important and colorful figures in the history of computer science was Charles Babbage. This English mathematician, after having partially built a machine in 1833, called 'the difference engine', for evaluating certain mathematical formulae, conceived and planned a remarkable machine that he called 'the analytical engine'. In contrast to the difference engine, which was designed to carry out a specific task, the analytical engine was to have been capable of executing algorithms, or programs, encoded by the user as holes punched in cards. Had the analytical engine been built, it would have been the mathematical analogue of Jacquard's loom, which was in fact its inspiration. Needless to say, Babbage's machines were mechanical in nature, based on levers, cogs and gears, rather than on electronics and silicon. Nevertheless, the ideas present in his design of the analytical engine form the basis of the internal structure and workings of today's computers. Babbage is generally considered to have lived well before his time, and his ideas were not really appreciated until much later.

An American engineer by the name of Herman Hollerith invented a machine, also based on punched cards, that was used by the American Census Bureau to help tabulate the 1890 national census. However, the first general-purpose computers were built only in the 1940s, partly as a response to the computational needs of physicists and astronomers, and partly as a natural outgrowth of the availability of the appropriate electromechanical and electronic devices. Ironically, the Second World War, with its bomb building and code cracking activities, also helped. Some of the key figures in this crucial and exciting period were the Englishman Alan Turing, the Americans Howard Aiken, John Mauchly, J. Presper Eckert, and Herman Goldstine, and the famous mathematician John von Neumann.

Returning to software and algorithmics, the mid 1930s witnessed some of the most fundamental work on the theory of algorithms, which yielded results concerning the capabilities and limitations of machine-executable algorithms. It is remarkable that this work, parts of which will be described later in the book, predated the actual materialization of the computer. Nevertheless, it is of universal and lasting importance. Some of the key figures here, all mathematicians, are, again, Alan Turing, the German Kurt Gödel, the Russian Andrei A. Markov, and the Americans Alonzo Church, Emil Post and Stephen Kleene.

The 1950s and 1960s witnessed far-reaching and rapid technological advancements in computer design and construction. This can be attributed to the arrival of the era of nuclear research and space exploration on the one hand, and to the boom in large businesses and banks, and diverse government activity on the other. Precise prediction of various nuclear phenomena required very heavy computing power, as did the planning and simulation of space missions. Space exploration also required advances in computer-supported communication, facilitating reliable analysis and filtering, and even improvement of data that was communicated to and from satellites and spaceships. Business, banking, and government activity required computers to help in the storage, manipulation and retrieval of information concerning very large numbers of people, inventory items, fiscal details, etc.

Interesting evidence of the importance of the technological machine-oriented developments during that period can be found in the names of the world's largest computer company, IBM, and one of the world's largest computer-related professional organizations, the ACM. The former name was coined around 1920 and the latter in the late 1940s. In both cases the 'M' comes from the word 'machine': International Business Machines, and the Association for Computing Machinery. (As an aside, IBM evolved from a company formed in 1896 by the aforementioned Herman Hollerith to produce his tabulating machines.)

The recognition of computer science as an independent academic discipline came about around the mid 1960s, when several universities formed computer science departments. In 1968, the ACM published a widely acclaimed recommendation for a curriculum of courses in computer science, which forms the basis of most current computer science programs of study at the undergraduate level. This curriculum is revised periodically. Today, almost every academic institution has a department of computer science, or a computer science group within its mathematics or electrical engineering departments. The 1960s showed a renewed interest in the 1930s work on algorithmics, and the field has been the subject of extensive and far-reaching research ever since.

We shall not dwell any further on the present technological situation: computers are simply everywhere. Children request, and get, personal computers for their birthdays; students of computer science in several universities are required to purchase their own computers for homework assignments; and there is almost no industrial, scientific, or commercial activity that is not crucially assisted by computers.

A Strange Dichotomy

Despite all of this (or possibly as a result) the general public is strangely divided when it comes to computer literacy. There are those who know absolutely nothing about computers, and then there are the members of the ever-growing class of computer literates, starting with the 12-year-old owners of personal computers, through managers, engineers, bankers, and technicians, who use computers on a day-to-day basis, and all the way to professional programmers, system analysts, and members of the computer industry itself.

Why is this strange? Well, here is a science, computer science, about which some people know nothing, but about which a rapidly increasing number of people apparently know everything! As it happens, however, the really unusual phenomenon is that large and important parts of the science of computing are not sufficiently known, not only to members of the first group, but to members of the second group as well.

It is one of the purposes of this book to try to illuminate an important facet of the computer revolution, by presenting some of the fundamental concepts, results and trends underlying the *science* of computation. It is aimed at both populations. A reader with no knowledge of computers will (it is hoped) learn about their 'spirit' here, and the kind of thinking that goes into making them work, but will have to look elsewhere in order to supplement this information with material concerning their 'flesh'. The computer-knowledgeable reader, who might find the first couple of chapters rather slow going, will (it is hoped) be able to learn much from the later ones.

Some Limitations of Computers

Before embarking on our tour, let us contrast the opening paragraph of this chapter with some feats that current computers are of yet incapable of performing. We shall leave this contrast lingering until the final chapter of the book, which deals with the relationship between computers and human intelligence, but it might help to keep the examples in mind throughout.

Currently computers are capable of on-the-spot analysis of an enormous quantity of data resulting from many X-ray pictures of a human patient's brain, taken from gradually increasing angles. The analyzed data is then used by the computer to generate a cross-cut picture of the brain, providing information about the brain's tissue structure, and thus enabling precise location of such irregularities as tumors or excess fluids. In striking contrast, no currently available computer can analyze a single, ordinary picture of the very same patient's face and determine the patient's age with an error margin of, say, five years. However, most 12-year-old kids can! Even more striking is the ability of a one-year-old baby to recognize its mother's face in a photograph it has never seen, a feat computers are nowhere near imitating (this is not merely because they have no mothers . . .).

Computers are capable of controlling, in the most precise and efficient way imaginable, extremely sophisticated industrial robots used to construct complex pieces of machinery consisting of hundreds of components. In contrast, today's most advanced computers are incapable of directing a robot to construct a bird's nest from a pile of twigs, a feat any 12-month-old bird can perform!

Today's computers can play chess on the level of an international master, and hence can beat the vast majority of human players. However, on changing the rules of the game very slightly (for example, by allowing a knight two moves at a time, or by limiting the queen's moves to five squares), the best of these computers will not be able to adapt without being reprogrammed or reconstructed by humans. In contrast, a 12-year-old amateur chess player will be able to play a reasonably good game with the new rules in a very short time, and will become better and better as experience is gained.

As mentioned, these dissimilarities are related to the difference between human and computerized intelligence. After having learnt more about algorithms and their properties we shall be in a better position to discuss these matters further.

٭   ٭   ٭

A Recipe

Here is a recipe for chocolate mousse, taken from Sinclair and Malinowski's *French Cooking* (Weathervane Books, 1978, p. 73). The ingredients (i.e., the inputs) include 8 ounces of semisweet chocolate pieces, 2 tablespoons of water, $\frac{1}{4}$ cup of powdered sugar, 6 separated eggs, etc. The outputs are six to eight servings of delicious *mousseline au chocolat*. Here is the recipe; that is, the algorithm:

> "*Melt chocolate and 2 tablespoons water in double boiler. When melted, stir in powdered sugar; add butter bit by bit. Set aside. Beat egg yolks until thick and lemon-colored, about 5 minutes. Gently fold in chocolate. Reheat slightly to melt chocolate, if necessary. Stir in rum and vanilla. Beat egg whites until foamy. Beat in 2 tablespoons sugar; beat until stiff peaks form. Gently fold whites into chocolate-yolk mixture. Pour into individual serving dishes. Chill at least 4 hours. Serve with whipped cream, if desired. Makes 6 to 8 servings.*"

This is the 'software' relevant to the preparation of the mousse; this is the algorithm that controls the process that produces the mousse from the ingredients. The process itself is carried out by the 'hardware', in this case the person preparing the mousse together with the various utensils: the double boiler, the heating apparatus, beater, spoons, timer, etc.

Levels of Detail

Let us take a closer look at the most elementary instructions present in this recipe. Consider the instruction 'stir in powdered sugar.' Why does the recipe not say 'take a little powdered sugar, pour it into the melted chocolate, stir it in, take a little more, pour, stir, . . .?' Even more specifically, why does it not say 'take 2365 grains of powdered sugar, pour them into the melted chocolate, pick up a spoon and use circular movements to stir it in, . . .?' Or, to be even more precise, why not 'move your arm towards the ingredients at an angle of 14°, at an approximate velocity of 18 inches per second, . . .?' The answer, of course, is obvious. The 'hardware' *knows* how to stir powdered sugar into melted chocolate, and does not need further details. Well, how about turning things around and asking whether it is possible that the hardware knows how to prepare sugared and buttered chocolate mixture, in which case the entire first part of the recipe could be replaced by the simple instruction 'prepare chocolate mixture.' Taking this to the extreme, maybe the hardware knows how to prepare chocolate mousse. This would make it possible to replace the entire recipe by 'prepare chocolate mousse.' Given such a level of hardware expertise, this is a perfect recipe for obtaining *mousseline au chocolat*; it is short and clear, contains no mistakes, and is guaranteed to produce the desired outputs.

Such thought experiments make it clear that the *level of detail* is very important when it comes to an algorithm's elementary instructions. It must be tailored to fit the hardware's particular capabilities, and should also be appropriate for the comprehension level of a potential reader or user of the algorithm.

Consider another example, learnt early in our lives, and which is somewhat closer to computation – the orderly multiplication of numbers. Suppose we are asked to multiply 528 by 46. We know exactly what to do. We multiply the 8 by the 6, yielding 48, write down the units digit of the result, 8, and remember the tens digit, 4; we then multiply the 2 by the 6 and add the 4, yielding 16; we write down the units digit 6 to the left of the 8 and remember the tens digit 1; etc.

Here the very same questions can be asked. Why 'multiply the 8 by the 6?' Why not 'look up the entry appearing in the eighth row and sixth column of a multiplication table,' or 'add 6 to itself 8 times,' etc. Similarly, why can't we solve the entire problem in one stroke by the simple and satisfactory algorithm 'multiply the two numbers?' This last question is rather subtle: why are we allowed to multiply 8 by 6 directly, but not 528 by 46? Again, it is clear that the level of detail is a crucial feature of our acceptance of the multiplication algorithm. We assume that the relevant hardware (in this case, we ourselves) is capable of carrying out 8 times 6 but not 528 times 46, and that we can do so in our heads, or at least we know of some other way of doing it, so that we do not have to be told how to look up the result in a table.

These examples show the need for agreeing right at the start on the *basic actions* that an algorithm is to be capable of prescribing. Without doing so there is no point in trying to find algorithms for anything. Furthermore, different problems are naturally associated with different kinds of basic actions. Recipes entail stirring, mixing, pouring, and heating; multiplying numbers entails addition, digit multiplication, and, significantly, remembering a digit; looking up a telephone number might entail turning a page, moving a finger down a list, and comparing a given name to the one being pointed at.

In the precise kinds of algorithms we shall be discussing in the sequel, these agreed on basic instructions must be stated clearly and precisely. We cannot accept things like 'beat egg whites until foamy,' since one person's idea of foam might be quite unlike another's! Instructions must be adequately distinguishable from non-instructions such as 'makes 6 to 8 servings.' Fuzzy phrases, such as 'about 5 minutes,' have no place in an algorithm suited for computer execution, as is the case with ambiguities like 'serve with whipped cream, if desired.' (Is it the actual serving, or the addition of whipped cream, that depends on the person's desires?) Recipes for mousse, in contrast with the algorithms that will be of interest to us, take too many things for granted, the most notable of which is the fact that a human being is part of the hardware. We cannot depend on that kind of luxury, and hence have to be far more demanding. The overall quality of an algorithm depends crucially on the selection of allowed basic actions and their appropriateness to the matter at hand.

The reader might be puzzled by the contrast between the present discussion and that on bit operations earlier. Here, the recommendation is that different algorithms be designed using basic actions of varying levels of detail, whereas earlier it was stated that real computers can only carry out extremely simple operations on extremely simple objects. Well, there is indeed a contrast, but one that will be cleared up when we discuss how algorithms are linked to actual computers in Chapter 3.

Short Algorithms for Long Processes

Suppose we are given a list of personnel records, one for each employee in a certain company, each containing the employee's name, personal details, and salary. We are interested in the total sum of all salaries of all employees. Here is an algorithm for carrying out this task:

(1)   make a note of the number 0;
(2)   proceed through the list, adding each employee's salary to the noted number;
(3)   having reached the end of the list, produce the noted number as output.

Before proceeding, we should first convince ourselves that this simple algorithm does the job. The 'noted' number, which can be thought of as being memorized or written down on a piece of paper, starts out as having the value zero. After carrying out the addition in clause (2) for the first employee, this number actually has the value of that employee's salary. After the second employee, its value is the sum of the salaries of the first two employees, etc. At the end, its value is clearly the sum of all salaries (see Figure 1.3).

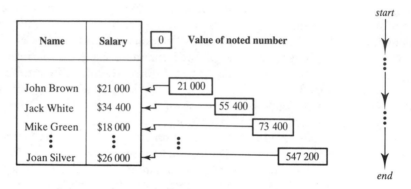

Figure 1.3   Summing salaries.

It is interesting that the *text* of this algorithm is short and fixed in length, but the *process* it describes and controls varies with the length of the employee list, and can be very, very long. Two companies, the first with one employee and the second with a million, can both feed their employee list into the same algorithm, and the salary summation problem will be solved equally well for each. Of course, the process will not take long for the first company, whereas for the second it will be quite lengthy. The algorithm, however, is fixed.

Not only is the text of the algorithm short and of fixed size, but both the small and large company require only a single noted number in order to do the job, so that the quantity of 'utensils' here is also small and fixed. Of course, the potential *value* of the noted number will presumably have to be greater for larger companies, but there will be only one number all along.

*   *   *

The Algorithmic Problem

And so, we have a fixed algorithm prescribing many processes of varying lengths, the precise duration and nature of the process depending on the inputs to the algorithm. Indeed, even the simple example of salary summation shows a variety of possible inputs: one-person companies, companies with a million people, companies in which some of the salaries are zero, ones in which all salaries are equal, etc. At times an algorithm must also work with bizarre inputs, such as companies with no employees at all, or those that employ people receiving negative salaries (i.e., employees who pay the company for the pleasure of working for it).

Actually, the salary algorithm is supposed to perform satisfactorily for an *infinite* number of inputs. There is an infinite number of perfectly acceptable lists of employees, and the algorithm should be able to sum the salaries in any one of them when given as an input.

This issue of infinitely many potential inputs does not quite fit the recipe analogy, since although a recipe should work perfectly no matter how many times it is used, its ingredients arc usually described as being fixed in quantity, and hence in essence the recipe has only one potential input. However, the chocolate mousse recipe could have been made *generic*; that is, its list of ingredients could have read something like 'X ounces of chocolate pieces, $X/4$ tablespoons of water, $X/32$ cups of powdered sugar, etc.,' and its final line could have been 'makes $3X/4$ to X servings.' This would be more in line with the real notion of an algorithm. In its present form, the recipe is an algorithm of somewhat trivial nature, as it is tailored for one specific set of ingredients. It might be carried out (or, in algorithmic terminology, it might be **run** or **executed**) several times, but with essentially the same input, since one cup of flour is considered exactly the same as any other.

The input itself has to be *legal* relative to the purpose of the algorithm. This means, for example, that the New York Times list of bestsellers would not be acceptable as input to the salary summation, any more than peanut butter and jelly would be accepted as ingredients for the mousse recipe. This entails some kind of **specification** of the allowed inputs. Someone must specify precisely which employee lists are legal and which are not; where exactly in the list the salary occurs; whether it is given in longhand (for example, $32 000) or perhaps in some abbreviated form (for example, $32K); where an employee record ends and another begins, etc.

To put it in the most general terms, recipes, or algorithms, are *solutions* to certain kinds of problems, called **computational** or **algorithmic problems**. In the salary example, the problem can be specified as asking for a certain number to be produced from a list of employees of any length, organized in such and such a fashion, and that the number is the sum of the salaries of all employees on the list. This problem can be viewed as the search for the contents of a 'black box', which is specified by a precise definition of the legal inputs and a precise definition of the required outputs as a function of those inputs; that is, the way in which each output depends on the input (see Figure 1.4). An algorithmic problem has been solved when an appropriate algorithm has been found. The black box has then actually been provided with contents; it 'works' according to the algorithm A. Given A, the black box can produce the appropriate output from any legal input by executing the process that is prescribed and governed by A.

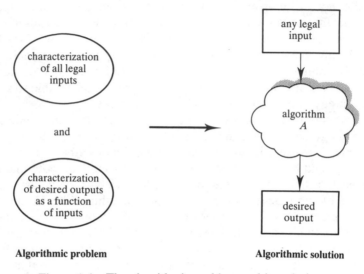

Algorithmic problem   **Algorithmic solution**

Figure 1.4   The algorithmic problem and its solution.

The word 'any' in the previous sentence is very important. We are not interested in solutions that do not work for all specified inputs. A solution that works well for only some of the legal inputs is easy to come by. As an extreme example, the trivial algorithm:

(1)   produce 0 as output.

works extremely well for several interesting lists of employees: those with no employees at all, those in which everyone earns $0.00 (or multiples thereof), as well as those with a payroll that reflects a perfect balance between positive and negative salaries.

Later we shall address such issues as the efficiency and practicality of algorithms. Here we make the minimal requirement that the algorithm does, in fact, solve the problem, even though it might do so inefficiently. Of course, the problem itself can specify the required behavior of a potential algorithm on *undesirable* inputs, but then these inputs, although undesirable, are still legal. For example, the salary summation problem could conceivably contain the requirement that for an employee whose record does not show a number in the salary area (but, say, a question mark, or some other nonsensical data) the algorithm should add that employee's name to a special list, which will be forwarded to the payroll office for further action. Such an unorthodox list of employees is nevertheless legal; it just is not dealt with in the standard way, but is given some special treatment that befits its abnormal nature. Thus, keeping illegal inputs separate is the responsibility of the algorithmic problem, while treating special classes of unusual or undesirable inputs is that of the algorithm.

Bounds on Basic Actions

There is one other important matter that we need to address at this point concerning the execution of the basic actions, or operations, prescribed by an algorithm. It is obvious that each of these actions must be carried out in a finite amount of time, otherwise, of course, the algorithm will never reach an end. Thus, infinitely long actions are bad. Actions that can take infinitesimally small amounts of time are outlawed too, a fact that needs little justification. It is unthinkable that a machine will ever be able to perform actions in diminishing amounts of time. The speed of light, for one, would always be a lower bound on the speed of any machine. Similar bounds on the resources (i.e., utensils) used to perform basic actions have to be enforced too, but we shall not discuss the reasons here.

Clearly, all our assumptions about basic actions also hold for real computers. The basic bit manipulation actions, for example, are precise and unambiguous, and take bounded amounts of time and resources. Thus, as promised, the theory of algorithmics described herein will be directly applicable to problems intended for computer-based solution.

The Problem and Its Solution: Summary

To summarize, an algorithmic problem consists of:

(1)   a characterization of a legal, possibly infinite, collection of potential input sets, and

(2)   a specification of the desired outputs as a function of the inputs.

It is assumed that either a description of the allowed basic actions or a hardware configuration, together with its built-in basic actions, are also provided in advance. A solution to an algorithmic problem consists of an algorithm, composed of elementary instructions prescribing actions from the agreed on set. This algorithm, when executed for any legal input set, solves the problem, producing the output as required. In Chapters 10 and 11 we shall be generalizing these notions somewhat, but until then the present definition will suffice.

It is important to recognize the considerable difficulty involved in solving algorithmic problems satisfactorily. By starting out with a mousse recipe and then giving a simple summation algorithm, a certain amount of injustice has been done to the field of algorithmics at large, as it might appear that things are easy. Nothing is further from the truth. Algorithmic problems, in practice, can be incredibly complex, and can take years of work to solve successfully. Worse still, as we shall see later, many problems do not admit satisfactory solutions, while others do not admit any solutions at all. For many problems the status, as far as good algorithmic solutions are concerned, is as yet unknown, despite extensive work by many talented people.

Obviously, we shall not be able to illustrate the issues treated in this book with overly lengthy and complex examples, but we can get a feel for the difficulty of designing algorithms by thinking about the following (informally described) algorithmic problems. The input to the first problem is a legal chess position (i.e., a description of the situation reached at some point during a chess game), while the output is the best move for White (i.e., the description of a move that maximizes White's chances of winning the game). The second problem concerns newspaper distribution. Suppose 20 000 papers are to be distributed to 1000 locations in 100 towns using 50 trucks. The input contains the road distances between the towns and between the locations within each town, the number of papers required at each location, the present location of each truck, each truck's newspaper carrying ability, as well as its gasoline capacity and miles-per-gallon performance, details of available drivers, including their present whereabouts, etc. The output is to be a list, matching drivers to trucks, and containing detailed itineraries for each of the trucks, so that the total number of miles driven is minimized. Actually, the problem calls for an algorithm that works for any number of newspapers, locations, towns and trucks, so that the numbers of these also vary and form part of the inputs.

Before we can discuss issues of correctness and efficiency, or deeper questions concerning the nature or very existence of solutions to certain algorithmic problems, we have to learn more about the structure of algorithms, and the structure of the objects they manipulate.

I have declared the former things from the beginning
Isaiah 48: 3

2

Algorithms and Data

OR

Getting It Done

> *And this is the fashion of which thou shalt make it*
> Genesis 6: 15

We already know that algorithms contain carefully selected elementary instructions that prescribe the basic actions to be performed. We have not yet discussed the way these instructions are arranged in the algorithm, so that one can figure out (in particular, a computer can figure out) the precise order in which the actions are to be performed. Nor have we discussed the objects manipulated by these actions.

The execution of an algorithm can be thought of as being carried out by a little robot, or **processor** (who might appropriately be named Runaround). The processor receives orders to run around doing this and that, where the 'this and thats' are the basic actions of the algorithm. In the salary summation algorithm of the previous chapter little Runaround is told to make a note of 0 and then to start working its way through the employee list, finding salaries and adding them to the noted number. It should be quite obvious that the order in which the basic actions are carried out is crucial. It is of paramount importance not only that the elementary instructions of the algorithm be clear and unambiguous, but that the same should apply to the mechanism that controls the *sequence* in which those instructions are carried out. The algorithm must therefore contain **control instructions** to 'push' the processor in this or that direction, telling it what to do at each step and when to stop and say 'I'm done.'

Control Structures

Sequence control is usually carried out with the aid of various combinations of instructions called **control-flow structures**, or simply **control structures**. Even the chocolate mousse recipe contains several typical ones, such as the following:

- **Direct sequencing**, of the form 'do A followed by B,' or 'do A and then B.' (In the recipe, every semicolon or period hides an implicit 'and then' phrase; e.g., 'gently fold in chocolate [and then] reheat slightly . . .')

- **Conditional branching**, of the form 'if Q then do A otherwise do B,' or just 'if Q then do A,' where Q is some condition. (For example, in the recipe 'reheat slightly to melt chocolate, if necessary,' or 'serve with whipped cream, if desired.')

As it happens, these two control constructs, sequencing and branching, do not explain how an algorithm of fixed (maybe even short) length can describe processes that can become longer and longer depending on the particular input. An algorithm containing only sequencing and branching can prescribe processes of at most some fixed length, since no part of such an algorithm is ever executed more than once. Control constructs that are responsible for prescribing ever-longer processes are indeed hidden even in the mousse recipe, but they are far more explicit in algorithms that deal with many inputs of different sizes, such as the salary summation algorithm. They are generically called **iterations**, or **looping constructs**, and come in many flavors. Here are two:

- **Bounded iteration**, of the general form 'do A exactly N times,' where N is a number.

- **Conditional iteration**, sometimes called **unbounded iteration**, of the form 'do A until Q,' or 'while Q do A,' where Q is a condition. (For example, in the recipe 'beat egg whites until foamy.')

When describing the salary summation algorithm in Chapter 1, we were quite vague about the way the main part of the algorithm was to be carried out; we said 'proceed through the list, adding each employee's salary to the noted number,' and then 'having reached the end of the list, produce the noted number as output.' We should really have used an iteration construct, making the way in which the processor is to proceed through the list more precise, in addition to the way the list's end becomes apparent. Let us assume then that the input to the problem includes not only the list of employees, but also its *length*; i.e., the total number of employees, call it N. It is now possible to use a bounded iteration construct, yielding the following algorithm:

    (1)   make a note of 0; point to the first salary on the list;

    (2)   do the following $N-1$ times:
        (2.1)   add the salary pointed at to the noted number;
        (2.2)   point to the next salary;

    (3)   add the salary pointed at to the noted number;

    (4)   produce the noted number as output.

The phrase 'the following' in clause (2) refers to the segment consisting of subclauses (2.1) and (2.2). This convention, coupled with textual indentation to emphasize the 'nested' nature of (2.1) and (2.2), will be used freely in the sequel.

The reader is encouraged to seek the reason for using $N-1$ and adding the final salary separately, rather than simply using N and then producing the output and halting. Notice that the algorithm fails if the list is empty (i.e., if $N=0$), since the second part of clause (1) makes no sense.

If the input does not include N, the total number of employees, we must use a conditional iteration, and to do so precisely would require us to provide a way to tell when we have reached the end of the list. The resulting algorithm would look very much like the version given, but would use the form 'do the following until end of list reached' in clause (2). The reader is encouraged to write down the full algorithm for this case.

Notice how iteration constructs make it possible for a short portion of an algorithm's text to prescribe very long processes, the length being dictated by the size of the inputs, in this case the length of the employee list. Iteration, therefore, is the key to the seeming paradox of a single fixed algorithm performing tasks of ever-longer duration.

Combining Control Structures

An algorithm can contain many control-flow constructs in nontrivial combinations. Sequencing, branching, and iteration can be interleaved and nested within each other. As an example, algorithms can contain **nested iterations**, or, more commonly, **nested loops**. A loop inside a loop can take on the form 'do A exactly N times,' where A itself is, say, of the form 'do B until Q.' The processor executing such a segment has to work quite hard; each of the N times it carries out A – that is, each time the **outer** loop is traversed – the **inner** loop must be traversed repeatedly, until Q becomes true. Here the outer loop is bounded and the inner one conditional, but other combinations are possible too. The A part of the outer loop can contain many further segments, each of which can, in turn, employ additional sequencing, branching, and iteration constructs. Thus, there is no limit to the potential intricacy of one's algorithms.

Let us consider a simple example of the power of nested iterations. Suppose that the problem was to sum salaries, but not of *all* employees, only of those who earn more than their direct managers. Of course it is assumed that an employee's record contains the name of that employee's manager. An algorithm that solves this problem might be constructed so that an outer loop runs down the list as before, but for each employee 'pointed at' an inner loop searches the list for the record of that employee's direct manager. When the manager has finally been found, a conditional construct is used to determine whether or not the employee's salary should be accumulated in the 'noted number', a decision that requires comparing the two salaries. Upon completing this 'internal' activity, the outer loop resumes control, proceeding to the next employee, whose manager is then sought for, etc. (See Figure 2.4 for a diagrammatic version of this algorithm.)

Bubblesort: An Example

To further illustrate control structures, let us examine a sorting algorithm. Sorting is one of the most interesting topics in algorithmics, and many important developments are connected with it in one way or another. The input to a sorting problem is an *unordered* list of elements, say numbers. Our task is to produce the list sorted in ascending order. The problem can be phrased more generally, admitting, say, lists of words instead of numbers, with the intention that they be sorted by their lexicographic ordering (i.e., as in a dictionary or telephone book). One of the many known sorting algorithms is called **bubblesort**. Actually, bubblesort is considered to be a bad sorting algorithm, for reasons explained in Chapter 6. It is used here only to illustrate control structures.

It is assumed that the list of elements is preceded by its length, N, and that the only way to obtain information concerning the magnitude of these elements is to perform binary comparisons; that is, to compare two elements and act according to the outcome of the comparison.[†]

The bubblesort algorithm is based on the following observation. If the jumbled list is traversed in sequence, one element at a time, and whenever two adjacent elements are found to be in the wrong order (i.e., the first is larger than the second) they are exchanged, then when the traversal is over the largest element is in its rightful place; namely, at the end of the

---

[†] There is some subtlety to this. If we knew in advance, for example, that the input list consisted of the numbers 1, 2, 3, . . . , N jumbled in some unknown way, a trivial algorithm could be written that simply prepared a new list of length N, initially containing nonsensical elements, and then directly inserted each number encountered in the input list into its proper place in the new list. The reader should be able to appreciate the difference between this situation and the present one, which can be exemplified by a jumbled telephone book that has to be put in order. There is no way an algorithm can simply 'look' at a name in the book and 'know' where its right place in the new list should be.

list. Figure 2.1(a) illustrates such a traversal for a simple five-element list. (The list has been drawn from bottom to top: the first element is the lowest in the picture. The arrows show only the elements exchanged, not those compared.) Clearly, the traversal might correct other incorrect orderings besides placing the maximal element in its final position. However, Figure 2.1(a) shows that one traversal does not necessarily sort the list. Now, a second traversal will bring the *second* largest element to its proper resting point, the penultimate position in the list, as can be seen in Figure 2.1(b). This leads to an algorithm that carries out $N-1$ such traversals (why not N?), resulting in the sorted list. The name 'bubblesort' stems from the way in which large elements 'bubble up' to the top of the list as the algorithm proceeds, exchanging places with smaller elements that remain lower down.

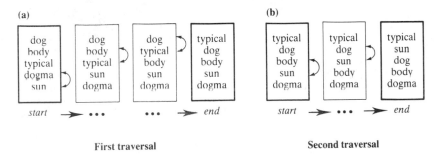

First traversal   Second traversal

Figure 2.1   Two bubblesort traversals on five elements. (Arrows indicate elements exchanged, not elements compared.)

Before writing down the algorithm in more detail, it should be pointed out that the second traversal need not extend to the last element, since by the time the second traversal starts, the last position in the list already contains its rightful tenant – the largest element in the list. Similarly, the third traversal need not go any further than the first $N-2$ elements, etc. This means that a more efficient algorithm would traverse only the first N elements in its first traversal, the first $N-1$ in its second, $N-2$ in its third, and so on. We shall return to the bubblesort algorithm and this improvement in Chapter 6, but for now the unimproved version will suffice:

(1)   do the following $N-1$ times:
    (1.1)   point to the first element;
    (1.2)   do the following $N-1$ times:
        (1.2.1)   compare the element pointed to with the next element;
        (1.2.2)   if the compared elements are in the wrong order, exchange them;
        (1.2.3)   point to the next element.

Notice how two-level indentation is used here. The first 'following', on line (1), involves all lines starting with 1, and the second, on line (1.2), involves those starting with 1.2. In this way the looping constructs are clearly seen to be nested within each other.

The main steps taken by the algorithm on an eight-item list are illustrated in Figure 2.2, where the situation is depicted just prior to each execution of clause (1.2). The elements appearing above the line are in their final positions. Notice that in this particular example the last two traversals (not shown) are redundant; the list becomes sorted after five, not seven, traversals. However, observe that if, for example, the smallest element happens to be last in the original list (i.e., at the top in our illustrations), then all $N-1$ traversals are in fact necessary, since elements that are to be 'bubbled down' (elbbubed?...) cause more trouble than those which 'bubble up'.

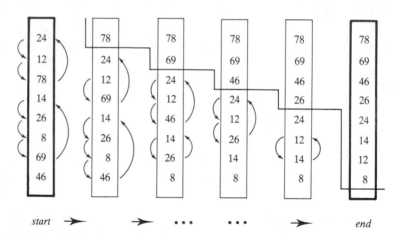

Figure 2.2   The main stages in bubblesort of eight elements. (Arrows indicate elements changing places.)

The 'Goto' Statement

There is another important control instruction that is generally called the **goto** statement. It has the general form 'goto G', where G marks some point in the text of the algorithm. In our examples we could write, say, 'goto (1.2)', an instruction that causes the processor Runaround to literally go to line (1.2) of the algorithm and resume execution from there. This construct is controversial for a number of reasons, the most obvious of which is pragmatic in nature. An algorithm that contains many 'goto' statements directing control backwards and forwards in a tangled fashion quickly becomes very difficult to understand. Clarity, as we shall argue later, is a very important consideration in algorithmic design.

Besides potentially reducing our ability to understand an algorithm, 'goto' statements can also introduce technical difficulties. What happens if a 'goto' statement directs the processor into the midst of a loop? Inserting the instruction 'goto (1.2.1)' between (1.1) and (1.2) in the bubblesort algorithm is an example of this. Is the processor to execute (1.2.1) through (1.2.3) and then halt, or should these be executed $N - 1$ times? What if the same instruction appears *within* the (1.2.1)–(1.2.3) sequence? This kind of problem is rooted in the ambiguity resulting from an attempt to match the text of an algorithm with the process it prescribes. Clearly, there *is* such a match, but since fixed algorithms can prescribe processes of varying length, a single point in the text of the algorithm can be associated with *many* points in the execution of the corresponding process. Consequently, 'goto' statements are in a sense inherently ambiguous creatures, and many researchers are opposed to using them freely in algorithms.

Diagrams for Algorithms

Visual, diagrammatic techniques are one way of presenting the control flow of an algorithm in a clear and readable fashion. There are various ways of 'drawing' algorithms, as opposed to writing them down. One of the best known of these involves writing the elementary instructions in rectangular boxes and the tests in diamond-shaped ones, and using arrows to describe how the processor Runaround runs around executing the algorithm. The resulting objects are called **flowcharts**. Figure 2.3 shows a flowchart of the regular salary summation algorithm, and Figure 2.4 shows one for the more sophisticated version that involves only employees earning more than their direct managers.

Notice the way an iteration shows up visually as a cycle of boxes, diamonds and arrows, and nested iterations show up as cycles within cycles. This explains the use of the term 'looping'. The flowcharts in Figures 2.3 and 2.4 also illustrate the appropriateness of the term 'branching' that was associated with conditional instructions.

*   *   *

Subroutines, or Procedures

Suppose we are given a lengthy text and we are interested in finding out how avaricious its author is, by counting the number of sentences that contain the word 'money'. It is not the number of occurrences of 'money' that we need, but the number of sentences in which it occurs. An algorithm

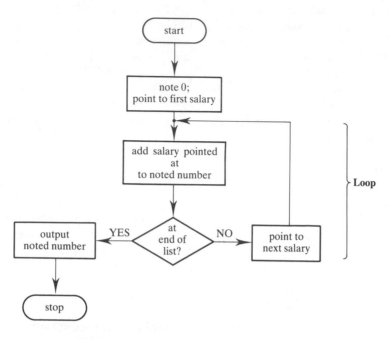

Figure 2.3   Flowchart for salary summation.

can be designed that runs through the text looking for 'money'. Upon finding such an occurrence, it proceeds to run ahead looking for the end of a sentence, which for our purposes is assumed to be a period followed by a space; that is, the '. ' combination. When the end of a sentence is found, the algorithm adds 1 to a counter (i.e., a 'noted number', as in the salary summation algorithm), which was initialized to 0. It then resumes its search for 'money' from the beginning of the next sentence; that is, from the letter following the '. ' combination. Of course, the algorithm must keep looking out for the end of the text, so that it can output the value of the counter when it is reached.

The algorithm takes the form of an external loop whose duty it is to count the relevant sentences. Within this loop there are two searches, one for 'money' and one for the '. ' combination, each constituting a loop in itself (see the schematic flowchart of Figure 2.5). The point is that the two internal loops are very similar; in fact, they both do exactly the same thing – searching for a sequence of symbols in the text. Having both loops appear explicitly in the algorithm clearly works, but we can do better.

The idea is to write the searching loop only *once*, with a **parameter** that is assumed to contain the particular combination of symbols searched for. This algorithmic segment is called a **subroutine,** or a **procedure**, and it is activated (or *invoked*, or *called*) twice in the main algorithm, once with

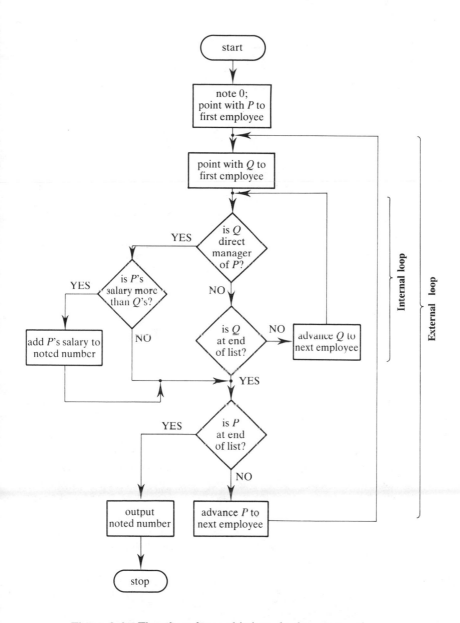

Figure 2.4 Flowchart for sophisticated salary summation.

'money' as its parameter, and once with the '. ' combination. The text of
the subroutine is provided separately, and it refers to the varying parameter
by a name, say X. The subroutine assumes that we are pointing to some

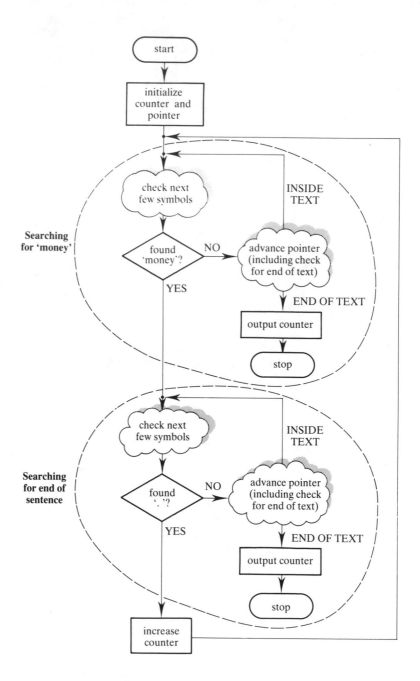

Figure 2.5   Schematic flowchart for sentences with 'money'.

place in the input text, and it might look as follows:

subroutine **search-for** X:

(1) do the following until either the combination X is being pointed at, or
the end of the text is reached:
(1.1) advance the pointer one symbol in the text;

(2) if the end of the text is reached, output the counter's value and stop;

(3) otherwise return to the main algorithm.

The main part of the algorithm will utilize the search subroutine twice, by
instructions of the form 'call **search-for** 'money'' and 'call **search-for** '. ''.
Contrast Figure 2.5 with Figure 2.6, in which the version with the subroutine
is shown schematically.

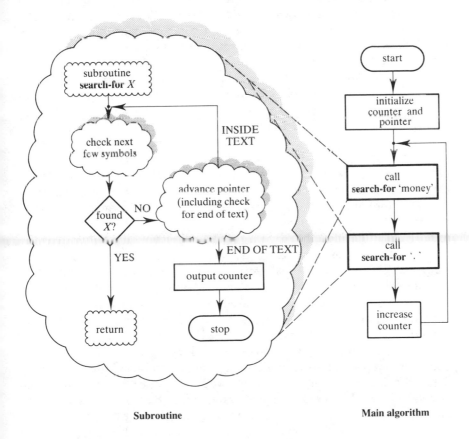

Subroutine   Main algorithm

Figure 2.6   Sentences with 'money' using a subroutine.

The processor which runs around doing things, will now have to be slightly more sophisticated. When told to 'call' a subroutine, it will stop whatever it has been doing, remember where it was, pick up the parameter(s), so to speak, and move over to the text of the subroutine. It will then do whatever the subroutine tells it to do, using the current value of a parameter wherever the subroutine refers to that parameter by its internal name (X, in our example). If and when the subroutine tells it to return, it will do just that; namely, it will return to the point following the 'call' that led it to the subroutine in the first place, and will resume its duties from there.

The Virtues of Subroutines

Obviously, subroutines can be very economical as far as the size of an algorithm is concerned. Even in this simple example, the searching loop is written once but is used twice, whereas without it, of course, the algorithm would have had to include two detailed versions of that loop. This economy becomes considerably more significant for complex algorithms with many subroutines called from various places. Also, an algorithm can contain subroutines that call other subroutines, etc. Thus, algorithmic structure is given a new dimension; there are not only nested loops but nested subroutines. Moreover, loops, conditional statements, sequential constructs, 'goto' statements, and now subroutines, can all be interleaved, yielding algorithms of increasing structural complexity.

Economy, however, is not the only advantage of subroutines. A subroutine can be viewed as a 'chunk' of algorithmic material, some kind of building block, which, once formed, can be used in another algorithmic chunk by a single instruction. This is just like saying that we have extended our repertoire of allowed elementary instructions. In the 'money' counting example, once the search routine is there (and even beforehand, as long as it has been decided that such a routine will eventually be written) the instruction 'call **search-for** 'abc'' is, for every practical purpose, a new elementary instruction. This is a very powerful idea, as it not only shortens algorithms but also makes them clear and well structured. Clarity and structure, as is repeatedly emphasized, are of the utmost importance in algorithmics, and many an effort is devoted to finding ways of imposing them on algorithm designers.

Using subroutines, it is possible to develop a complex algorithm gradually, step by step. A typical algorithmic problem calls for a fully detailed solution that utilizes the allowed elementary actions only. The designer can work towards that goal gradually, by first devising a **high-level algorithm**, which uses 'elementary' instructions that are not in the book. These are actually calls to subroutines that the designer has in mind, which are written later. These subroutines, in turn, might use other instructions, which, not being elementary enough, are again regarded as calls to subroutines that are eventually written. At some point, all elementary instructions are at a sufficiently low level to be among those explicitly allowed. It is then that the gradual development process ends. This approach gives rise either to a 'top-down' design, which, as just described, goes from the general to the specific, or to a 'bottom-up' design, whereby one prepares the subroutines that will be needed, and then designs the more general routines that call them, thus working from the detailed to the general. There is no universal agreement as to which of these is the better approach to algorithmic design. The common feeling is that some kind of mixture should be used.

Returning for a moment to gastronomy, preparing a 'chocolate mixture' might be a good candidate for a subroutine within the chocolate mousse recipe of Chapter 1. This would enable us to describe the recipe in the following way, where each of the four instructions is treated as a call to a subroutine (or should we say, a subrecipe) whose text would then be written separately:

(1) prepare chocolate mixture;

(2) mix to produce chocolate-yolk mixture;

(3) prepare foam of egg-whites;

(4) mix both to produce the mousse.

It is worth pointing out that the book from which the mousse recipe was taken employs subroutines quite extensively. For example, pages 72–77 therein describe a number of recipes whose ingredients contain items such as Sweet Pastry Dough, Croissants or Puff Pastry, for which the user is referred to previously given recipes dedicated to these very items.

It is fair to say that the power and flexibility provided by subroutines cannot be overestimated.

Recursion

One of the most useful aspects of subroutines, which to many people is also one of the most confusing, is **recursion**. By this we mean simply the ability of a subroutine, or procedure, to call itself. Now, this might sound absurd, since how on earth does our processor come any closer to solving a problem by being told, in the midst of trying to solve that problem, to leave everything and start solving the *same* problem all over again?

The following example should aid us in resolving this paradox, and it might help if we say at the start that the resolution is based on the very same property of algorithms mentioned earlier: the same text (in this case, that of the recursive subroutine) can correspond to many portions of the process described by it. Iterative constructs are one way of mapping lengthy processes on to short texts; recursive subroutines are another.

The example is based on a rather ancient puzzle known as the Towers of Hanoi, originating in a monastery in Tibet. Suppose we are given three towers, or to be more humble, three pegs, A, B and C. On the first peg, A, there are three rings piled in descending order of magnitude, while the others are empty (see Figure 2.7). We are interested in moving the rings from A to B, perhaps using C in the process. By the rules of the game, rings are to be moved one at a time, and at no instant may a larger ring be placed atop a smaller one. This simple puzzle can be solved as follows, where $X \rightarrow Y$ represents the action of moving the top ring from peg X to peg Y:

$$A \rightarrow B; \quad A \rightarrow C; \quad B \rightarrow C; \quad A \rightarrow B; \quad C \rightarrow A; \quad C \rightarrow B; \quad A \rightarrow B.$$

Before proceeding, we should first convince ourselves that these seven actions really do the job, and we should then try the same puzzle with four rather than three rings on peg A (the number of pegs does not change). A moderate amount of work by the reader should suffice to discover a sequence of fifteen $X \rightarrow Y$ actions that solve the four-ring version.

A B C

Figure 2.7   The Towers of Hanoi with three rings.

Such puzzles are intellectually challenging, and those who enjoy puzzles may like to consider the original Tibetan version which involves the same three pegs, but with no less than 64 rings on A. As we shall see in Chapter 7, the inventors of the puzzle were not completely detached from reality when they stated that the world will end when all 64 rings are correctly piled on peg B. However, we are not dealing with puzzles here but with algorithmics, and consequently we are more interested in the general algorithmic problem associated with the Towers of Hanoi. The input is a positive integer N, and the desired output is a list of $X \rightarrow Y$ actions, which, if followed, solve the puzzle involving N rings. Clearly, a solution to this problem must be an algorithm that works for every N, producing a list of actions that satisfy the constraints; in particular, following them never causes a larger ring to be placed atop a smaller one.

This is the problem we should really be trying to solve, since once an algorithm is available, every instance of the puzzle, be it the three-, four-, or 3078-ring version, can be solved simply by running the algorithm with the desired number of rings as input. Well, how is it done? The answer is simple: by the magic of recursion.

The Towers of Hanoi: An Example

The algorithm presented here accomplishes the task of moving N rings from A to B via C in the following way. It first checks to see whether $N=1$, in which case it simply moves the one ring it was asked to deal with to its destination (or, more precisely, it outputs a description of the one move that will do the job), and then returns immediately. If N is greater than 1, it first moves the top $N-1$ rings from A to the 'accessory' peg C using the *same* routine recursively; it then picks up the only ring left on A, which has to be the largest ring (why?), and transfers it to its final destination, B; it then, recursively again, moves the $N-1$ rings it had previously 'stored' on C to their final destination, B. That this algorithm abides by the rules of the game is a little difficult to see, but on the assumption that the two processes involving the $N-1$ rings contain only legal moves, it is fairly easy to see that so does the overall process of moving the N rings.

Here then is the algorithm. It is written as a recursive routine whose title and parameters (there are four of them) speak for themselves:

subroutine **move** N **from** X **to** Y **using** Z:

(1)   if $N=1$ then output '$X \rightarrow Y$';
(2)   otherwise (i.e., if $N>1$) do the following:
    (2.1)   call **move** $N-1$ **from** X **to** Z **using** Y;
    (2.2)   output '$X \rightarrow Y$';
    (2.3)   call **move** $N-1$ **from** Z **to** Y **using** X;
(3)   return.

To illustrate the workings of this routine, which might look rather ridiculous at first sight, we could try running it with $N=3$; that is, simulating the processor's work when there are three rings. This should be done by executing a 'main algorithm' consisting of the single instruction:

call **move** 3 **from** A **to** B **using** C

The simulation should be carried out carefully, since the parameter names X, Y and Z start out innocently enough as being A, B and C, but change each time the processor re-enters the routine. As if to make things more confusing, they resume their old values when the 'call' is over and the processor returns to where it came from. Figure 2.8 helps illustrate the sequence of actions for the $N = 3$ case. Notice that the processor (and us too, if indeed we are trying to simulate the routine) now has to remember not only where it came from in order to return to the right place, but also what the values of the parameter names were prior to its new errand, in order to resume its work properly. Figure 2.8 is organized to reflect the *depth of recursion* and the corresponding way the parameters change values. The arrows represent the processor's trips: downward arrows correspond to calls, upward arrows to returns, and horizontal arrows to simple sequencing. As if by magic, the final sequence of actions is found to be identical to the one arrived at earlier by trial and error.

As it turns out, the Towers of Hanoi problem admits another algorithmic solution, which employs a simple iteration and no subroutine calls at all, and can be carried out by a small child! This algorithm will be presented in Chapter 5.

The Expressive Power of Control Structures

Can we do with only a few simple control structures? The answer is yes. Various **minimal sets** of control structures have been identified, meaning that in certain technical senses other control structures can be replaced by appropriate combinations of those in the minimal set, so that in practice these are the only ones needed. A well-known minimal set consists of sequencing (*and–then*), conditional branching (*if–then*), and some kind of unbounded loop construct (e.g., *while–do*). It is not too difficult, for example, to show that an instruction of the form 'do A until Q is true,' can be replaced by 'do A, and then while Q is false do A,' so that in the presence of 'while' constructs one can do without 'until' constructs. In a similar vein, it is possible to completely eliminate 'goto' statements from any algorithm, albeit at the expense of expanding the algorithm somewhat, and changing its original structure considerably.

Similarly, there is a precise mathematical sense, in which anything that can be done with subroutines and recursion can be done using only simple loops. However, using this result to rid a given algorithm of its subroutines involves adding considerable 'machinery' (in the form of new elementary instructions) to the algorithm. It is possible to show that if such machinery is not allowed, then recursive subroutines are more powerful than iteration, so that certain things can be done with the former only. These topics are touched upon here only in the most superficial way in order to give the reader some feel for the relevant questions of interest.

*   *   *

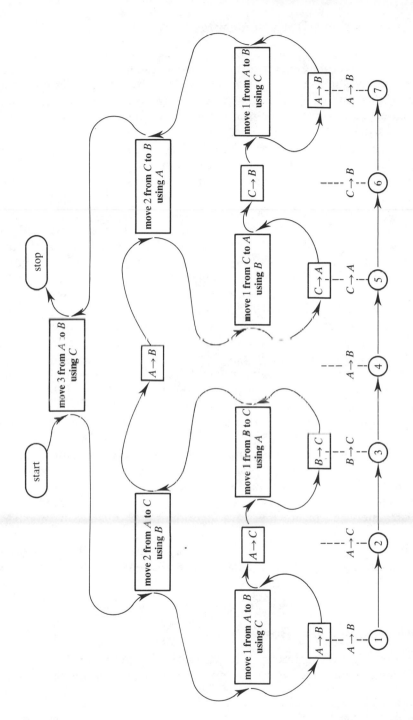

Figure 2.8   Structured run of the recursive solution to the Towers of Hanoi.

Data Types and Data Structures

So we now know what an algorithm looks like and how, given inputs, the processor runs around executing the process it describes. However, we have been quite vague as to the objects manipulated by an algorithm. We had lists, words, and texts, as well as funny things like 'noted numbers' that increased, and 'pointers' that made progress. If we wish to go to extremes, we can also say we had flour, sugar, cakes, and chocolate mousse, as well as towers, pegs, and rings. These objects constituted not only the algorithm's inputs and outputs, but also intermediate accessories that were constructed and used during its life time, such as the counters ('noted numbers') and the pointers. For all of these we use the generic term **data**.[†]

Data comes in various flavors, or can be of various types. Some of the most common **data types** present in algorithms that are executed by computers are **numbers** of various kinds (integers, decimals, binary numbers, etc.), and **words** written in various alphabets. Actually, numbers can be construed as words too; decimal integers, for example, are 'words' over an alphabet consisting of the digits $0, 1, 2, \ldots, 9$, and binary numbers use the alphabet consisting of 0 and 1 only. It is beneficial, however, to keep such types separate, not only for clarity and good order, but also because each type admits its own special set of allowed operations, or actions. It makes no more sense to list the vowels in a number than it does to multiply two words! And so, our algorithms will have to be told what objects they can manipulate and precisely which manipulations are allowed. Manipulation includes not only carrying out operations but also asking questions, such as testing whether a number is even or whether two words start with the same letter.

These observations seem quite natural in view of our discussion of elementary operations in Chapter 1, and are reminiscent of the facts about the bit-manipulation capabilities of computers. Here we take basic data types and the operations and tests associated with them for granted. What we are interested in are the ways algorithms can organize, remember, change, and access *collections* of data. While control structures serve to tell the processor where it should be going, **data structures**, and the operations upon them, organize the data items in ways that enable it to do whatever it should do when it gets there.

Variables, or Little Boxes

The first objects of interest are **variables**. In the salary summation algorithm, for example, we used a 'noted number', which was first initial-

---

[†] The singular form is **datum**, but we shall mostly use the terms **data item** and **data element** here.

ized to 0 and was then used to accumulate the sum of the employee's salaries. We were actually using a variable. A variable is not a number, a word, or some other item of data. Rather, it can be viewed as a small box, or cell, in which a single item can be kept. We can give the variable a name, say X, and then use instructions like 'put 0 in X,' or 'increase the contents of X by 1.' We can also ask questions about the contents of X, such as 'does X contain an even number?' Variables are very much like hotel rooms; different people can occupy a room at different times, and the person in the room can be referred to by the phrase 'the occupant of room 326.' The term '326' is the name of the room, just as X is the name of the variable. (There are differences, however. Two hotel rooms cannot have the very same contents, whereas two variables can.)

Algorithms typically utilize many variables with different names, and for very different purposes. In the bubblesort algorithm, for example, a detailed version might use one variable to count the number of times the outer loop is performed, another for the inner loop, and a third to help in exchanging two elements in the list. To perform the exchange, one element is 'put in the box' for a moment, the other is put in its place, and the 'boxed' element is then put in the second element's original place. Without using the variable there would appear to be no way to keep the first element around without losing it. This illustrates the use of variables as **memory** or **storage** in an algorithm. Of course, the fact that elements are exchanged many times in one run of bubblesort does not mean that we need many variables – the same 'box' can be used each time. This is a result of the fact that all exchanges in the bubblesort algorithm are disjoint; no exchange starts before the previous one has ended. Variables can thus be reused.

When variables are used in practice the phrase 'contents of' is usually omitted, and we write things like $X \leftarrow 0$ (read 'X gets 0' or 'set X to 0') to set the initial *value* of (i.e., contents of) X to 0, and $X \leftarrow X + 1$ (read 'X gets $X + 1$') to increase the value of X by 1. This last instruction, for example, tells the processor to 'read' the number found in X, increase it by one, and replace it with the result. More about such instructions and the way to formally write them down can be found in Chapter 3.

Vectors, or Lists

Let us take a closer look at our employee list. Such a list might be viewed simply as a multitude of data elements, which we might decide to keep, or **store**, in a multitude of variables, say $X, Y, Z, \ldots$. This clearly would not enable an algorithm of finite fixed size to 'run' through the list, whose length can vary, since each element in the list would have to be referred to in the algorithm by a unique name. Lengthier lists would require more variable names and hence longer algorithms. What we need is a way of referring to many elements in a *uniform* manner. We need **lists** of variables that can be 'run through', or accessed in some other way, but without the need to name each of their elements explicitly. We want to be able to 'point' to elements in these lists, to refer to the 'next' element or the 'previous' one, and so on. For these purposes we use **vectors**, also called **one-dimensional arrays**.

If a variable is like a hotel room, then a vector can be thought of as an entire corridor, or floor, in the hotel. Rooms 301, 302, ..., 346 might be the individual 'variables'; each can be referred to separately, but in contrast to a simple collection of variables, the entire corridor or floor also has a name (say 'floor 3'), and the rooms therein can be accessed by their **index**. The 15th room along that corridor is 315, and the Xth room is $3X$. This means that we can use a variable to index the vector. Changing the value of X can be used to refer to the contents of different elements in the vector. The notation that is used in practice separates the name of the vector from its index by parentheses; we write $V(6)$ for the sixth element of vector V, and similarly $V(X)$ for the element of V whose index is the current value of the variable X. We might even write $V(X+1)$, which refers to the element following $V(X)$ in the list. (Notice that $V(X+1)$ and $V(X)+1$ denote two completely different things!)

In the bubblesort algorithm, for example, we can use a variable X to control the inner loop, and at the very same time it can double as a pointer to the vector V of elements being sorted. Here is what the resulting (more concise, and also more precise) version of the algorithm might look like, with '$<$' standing for 'is smaller than':

(1)   do the following $N-1$ times:
    (1.1) $X \leftarrow 1$;
    (1.2)   while $X < N$ do the following:
        (1.2.1)   if $V(X+1) < V(X)$ then exchange them;
        (1.2.2) $X \leftarrow X + 1$.

The reader is encouraged to modify this algorithm, incorporating the observation mentioned earlier, to the effect that with each traversal of the outer loop the number of elements inspected in the inner loop can be decreased by 1.

Vectors that represent lists of elements have numerous applications. A telephone book is a list, and so are dictionaries, personnel files, inventory descriptions, course requirements, etc.

In a way, a vector as a data structure is closely related to a loop as a control structure. Traversing a vector (for the purpose of inspection, search, summation, etc.) is typically carried out with a single iterative construct. Just as the loop is a control structure for describing lengthy processes, so is a vector a data structure for representing lengthy lists of data items. There are also special 'indexed' versions of iterative control constructs, tailored towards vector traversal. For example, we can write:

   for X going from 1 to 100 do the following

which is similar to:

   do the following 100 times

except that with the former we can refer directly to the Xth element in a vector within the repeated segment, whereas with the latter we cannot.

Arrays, or Tables

In many cases it is convenient to arrange the data not in a simple, one-dimensional list, but in a **table**. The corresponding algorithmic data structure is called a **matrix**, or a **two-dimensional array**, or simply an **array** for short. Here too, applications are plentiful. The standard second-grade multiplication table is a 10×10 array in which the data item at each point is the product of the row and column indices; a list of students plotted against a list of courses can be thought of as an array, where the data items are the student's grade in the course; the earth's latitude/longitude grid can be the basis of an array giving the altitudes at each intersection point, and so on.

   Referring to an array element is typically achieved using *two* indices, row and column. We write $A(5, 3)$ for the element located at row 5 and column 3, so that, for example, if A is the multiplication table, then the value of $A(5, 3)$ is 15. As before, we may write $A(X, Y)$, as well as $A(X + 4, 17 - Y)$, and the like.

   If a variable is like a hotel room and a vector is like a hotel corridor/floor, then a matrix, or an array, is like an entire hotel. Its 'rows' are the various floors, and its 'columns' represent the locations along the floor/corridor. If a vector as a data structure corresponds to a loop as a control structure, then an array corresponds to nested loops (see Figure 2.9). Running through the entire array of students' grades can be achieved by an outer loop running through all students and an inner one running through all of a particular student's grades, or vice versa.

   It is not always the case that data can be arranged in a precise rectangular format. Take the students and courses example; different students might be associated not only with different courses, but also with a different *number* of them. We might still use an array (wide enough to contain the maximal number of possible courses), but leaving parts of it empty, wherever the student in question has not taken the course in question. Alternatively, we can use a new data structure, consisting of a vector whose elements themselves point to vectors of varying length. The difference is illustrated in Figure 2.10.

Figure 2.9   Data structures, control structures, and hotels.

Algorithms can use more elaborate arrays, such as ones with higher dimensionality. A three-dimensional array is like a cube, with three indices needed to point to an element.[†] If so desired, we can utilize only special

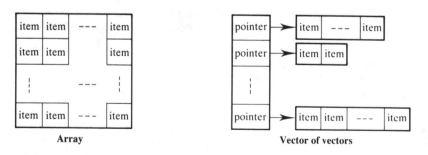

Figure 2.10   An array vs. a vector of vectors.

[†] Stretching the hotel metaphor becomes difficult here. Is a three-dimensional array not a single hotel but a whole resort area?

portions of arrays, such as the upper triangular portion of a two-dimensional array, obtained by restricting the indices in $A(X, Y)$ to satisfy the inequality $X < Y$.

Queues and Stacks

An interesting variation on the vector/array theme follows from the observation that in many applications of vectors and arrays, we do not need the full power provided by indices. Sometimes a list is used just to model a **queue**, in which case all the algorithm needs in way of interaction with the list is the ability to add elements to its 'back' and remove them from its 'front'. Other times the list is to model a **stack**, like those used in a restaurant for storing plates. Here the algorithm needs adding and removing abilities only at one end of the list, its 'top'. A queue is sometimes referred to as a FIFO list (First-In–First-Out), and a stack as a LIFO list (Last-In–First-Out). Elements are *pushed* on to a stack, the topmost element being the only one exposed for inspection, and then the stack can be *popped*, meaning that the topmost element is removed (see Figure 2.11). The point in these special cases is that it is worthwhile, at least for reasons of algorithmic clarity, to think of queues and stacks as being in themselves data structures, rather than being merely special kinds of lists. We can then use specially devised elementary instructions such as 'add X to queue Q,' or 'push X on stack S,' rather than obscure looking formulations that explicitly involve indices.

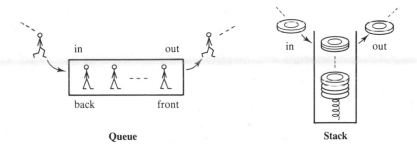

Queue   Stack

Figure 2.11   A queue and a stack.

**   When discussing recursion earlier, we implicitly came across the need for a vector that is really used only as a stack. The details will not be presented here, but the reader is invited to think about the way the processor goes about remembering where it really is when executing a recursive algorithm. Remembering its whereabouts in the *text* of the algorithm does not pose a problem. What does require some bookkeeping is managing the list of recursive calls that have not yet been completed, and figuring out where to return to when each call is completed. It is not too difficult to see – and we can use the Towers of Hanoi algorithm to illustrate this – that we actually need a stack. Whenever it is asked to re-enter the routine by a recursive call, the processor 'pushes' its return 'address' and the current values of the parameters on to the stack. (In the Towers example there is a choice of two such possible addresses, corresponding to the two call instructions in the algorithm.) When it completes an execution of the recursive routine, it reads the 'pushed' information from the top of the stack, restores the old values to the parameters, and returns to the specified address in the algorithm's text. In the process, it also 'pops' that information off the top of the stack and discards it.   **

Another example of the use of stacks involves traversing a labyrinth by exhausting all possibilities. Such a traversal requires that we keep a list of crossroads already visited, adding new ones to the stack as they are reached, and deleting the ones whose paths have all been traversed. In this way the stack can be seen to contain at all times a path from the start to the presently visited point in the labyrinth.

Trees, or Hierarchies

One of the most important and prominent data structures in existence is the **tree**. This is not a tree in the botanic sense of the word, but one of more abstract nature. We have all seen such trees used to describe family connections. The two most common kinds of family trees are the 'ancestor tree', which starts at an individual and works back through parents, grandparents, etc., and the 'descendant tree', which works forward through children, grandchildren, etc.

A tree is essentially a hierarchical arrangement of data. One item resides in a special place called the **root**, and the others are organized as the root's **offspring**, or its offspring's offspring, etc. In computer science, trees are visualized 'upside down' – the root at the top, and the rest of the tree spread out below. The terminology used is a strange mixture of terms from mathematics, botany, and mono-parental family life. We talk about the root, about a tree's **nodes** (points in the tree), its **leaves** (nodes at the 'bottom' of the tree, having no offspring), its **paths**, or **branches** (sequences of nodes corresponding to downward traversals in the direction from the root to a leaf), as well as about parents, ancestors, descendants, and siblings (two nodes are siblings if they have the same parent). Figure 2.12 shows a tree, deliberately constructed with no particular explanation in mind for its contents or arrangement. Nevertheless, 'blink' is its root, or to use different terminology, it is a node on level 1 of the tree; the chair and the number 173 are the root's offspring, or, equivalently, they are the nodes on level 2 of the tree, and so on.

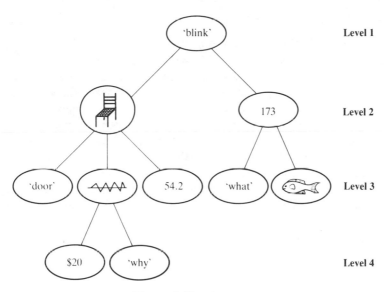

Figure 2.12   A tree.

Trees are to be found elsewhere in everyday life. The organizational charts of most companies are trees, as are schematic descriptions of the breakup of complex machines. Even algorithms themselves can often be described in a tree structure; roughly speaking, the levels of the tree correspond to the levels represented by the sequences of numbers we use in this book for labelling instructions.

Another important example concerns **game trees**. The root of a chess tree, for example, contains a description of the opening board configuration in chess, together with an indication that it is White's turn to move. The root's offspring represent the 20 possible board configurations resulting from White making a first move, and the offspring of each of them would represent the results of all possible responses on Black's part, etc. Most two-person game trees, like that of chess, have a number of interesting properties. Odd-numbered levels correspond to the first player's turn to move, whereas even-numbered ones correspond to the other player's turn. Paths correspond to actual games, and *any possible* game appears as a path in the tree. Finally, leaves represent game endings (e.g., in chess by checkmate or a three-fold repetition). We shall have occasion to return to game trees later on in the book.

Trees are used in numerous diverse applications, and more than any other structural method for combining parts into a whole they can be said to represent the special kind of structuring that abounds in algorithmics.

Treesort: An Example

To give some kind of feel for the usefulness of trees, let us now consider another sorting routine, based on **binary** trees. A binary tree is one in which each node has at most two offspring. (The ancestor family tree, for example, is binary.) A binary tree can also be defined as a tree whose **outdegree** is bounded by 2. The advantage of the latter term is in its generality; we can talk about trees with outdegree 17 or 938, or even of those with *infinite* outdegree.[†] Returning to binary trees, since the outdegree at each node is at most 2, it is convenient to distinguish between the two offspring, referring to them as the left-hand and right-hand ones, respectively.

Treesort, as we shall call it, consists of two main steps:

(1)   transform the input list into a binary search tree T;

(2)   traverse T in a left-first fashion, and output each element on the second visit.

Some explanation is in order here. To sort a list of elements (say numbers), the algorithm first organizes the elements as a binary tree, every node of which enjoys a very special property: all of its 'left descendants' (i.e., *all* elements in its left-hand subtree, not only its immediate left-hand offspring) are smaller in value than the node itself, and all of its right descendants are larger than it. Figure 2.13 shows an example of such a **binary search tree**. This tree can be constructed by appointing the first element in the list to be the root, and then attaching each element in turn to the tree as a new leaf, possibly 'unleafing' previously inserted leaves in the process. Finding a new element's rightful place as a leaf in the tree is done by comparing it repeatedly with the nodes arrived at, turning left or right according to the outcome of the comparison. The reader should use Figure 2.13 to become acquainted with this procedure, and should then try writing down the subroutine representing step (1).

Now comes the interesting part. Having constructed the search tree T, the second stage of treesort calls for traversing it in the following manner. The processor starts at the root and moves downwards, always keeping to the left. Whenever it tries to move left but cannot (e.g., when there is no left-hand offspring) it reluctantly moves right. Having exhausted both left and right, either by virtue of the absence of offspring, or by virtue of having already visited those offspring, it **backtracks**; that is, it moves upwards to the current node's parent. If this upwards move completes the trip from the

---

[†] Notice that a tree with outdegree 1 is simply a list, or a vector.

parent node to its *left* offspring, the processor turns right and plunges downwards once more; but if it has just returned from the *right*ward trip, it has actually exhausted both possibilities of the parent node, and so it moves up to *its* parent. This process continues until both downwards directions of the tree's root have been exhausted, having thus traversed the entire tree. Figure 2.14 shows the left-first traversal of the tree of Figure 2.13.

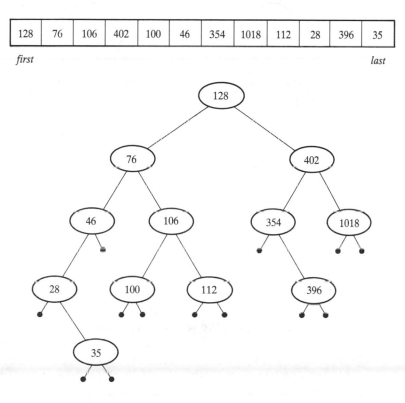

| 128 | 76 | 106 | 402 | 100 | 46 | 354 | 1018 | 112 | 28 | 396 | 35 |

first   *last*

Figure 2.13   A list and its resulting binary search tree.

Why do we carry out this strange traversal? Well, first observe that each node in the tree is 'visited' precisely three times, if we consider the absence of an offspring to cause a short 'stump', or 'dead end', to be present, which also has to be traversed. Now, if, when traversing the tree in this fashion, we consistently output the data element found at a node when visiting it precisely for the *second* time, the list will eventually be sent to the output in its entirety, sorted in ascending order! This might sound like magic, but it can be easily illustrated by following the twisted traversal arrows in Figure 2.14, jotting down the numbers as they are visited, and then marking the second appearance of each in the resulting list. These marks form the sorted list (see Figure 2.15).

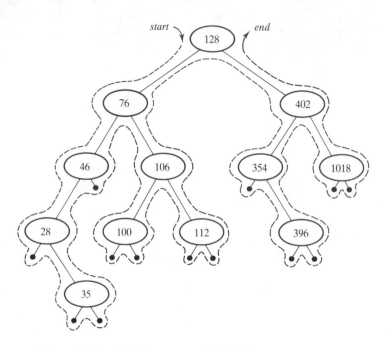

Figure 2.14   Left-first traversal of a binary search tree.

Both stages of the treesort algorithm can be described in more detail as recursive subroutines. Here is the second stage, where we use '*left(T)*' to denote the left-hand subtree of *T*, and similarly for '*right(T)*'. By our convention regarding the presence of stumps when offspring do not exist, '*left(T)*', for a tree that has no left subtree, will be the special **empty tree**; that is, the tree containing nothing, not even a root.

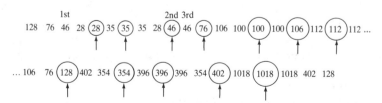

Figure 2.15   Second-visit marking in a left-first traversal.

subroutine **second-visit-traversal-of** *T*:

(1) if *T* is empty then return;

(2) otherwise (i.e., if *T* is not empty) do the following:
    (2.1) call **second-visit-traversal-of** *left*(*T*);
    (2.2) output the data element found at the root of *T*;
    (2.3) call **second-visit-traversal-of** *right*(*T*);

(3) return.

The observation used in the construction of this routine is that the second time a node is visited is always just after the traversal of its entire left-hand subtree has been completed, and just before that of its right-hand subtree has begun. Thus, we first call the subroutine recursively in order to complete the entire traversal for the left-hand subtree. When that call has terminated (meaning that the traversal of that subtree has been completed), we output the element at the root, since it is now visited for the second time, the first time being when we proceeded downwards to its left-hand subtree. We then recursively proceed downwards to the right to carry out the right-hand traversal.

The 'left-first' characteristic of the traversal becomes quite obvious in this recursive formulation, since for every subtree (that is, for every recursive call) the routine can easily be seen to go first to the left and then to the right. Incidentally, it is interesting to see what happens in terms of the output list when we turn this around, going consistently first to the right and then to the left. (What does happen, and how do we change the subroutine accordingly?)

The structure of this routine is reminiscent of the **move** routine for the Towers of Hanoi. In fact, if we apply this routine to a sample tree and then draw the picture of the processor's toils, as was done in Figure 2.8, the picture will precisely reflect the shape of the sample tree. Figure 2.8 itself forms a tree which, being of uniform depth (or height, depending on our point of view), is sometimes called a **full** tree.

One conclusion from this is that if vectors and arrays as data structures correspond, respectively, to loops and nested loops as control structures, then trees correspond to recursive routines. A tree is an inherently recursive object, consisting of nothing, or of a root attached (recursively) to some number of trees. This explains why tree traversals, such as the one just considered, are so easy to describe recursively.

There are some interesting ways to introduce flexibility into existing data structures. A good example is the concept of **self-adjustment**. By this we mean that each time an element is inserted or deleted from a data structure, the structure executes an adjustment routine that makes simple changes, intended to retain certain 'nice' properties. For example, in many applications of trees it is possible that, due to some sequence of insertions/deletions, the tree becomes thin and long, whereas for reasons of efficiency (see Chapter 6) it might be desirable that it be wide and short. It is possible to make small local changes to a tree whenever an operation is performed on it, which will guarantee the property of being wide and short.

*   *   *

Databases and Knowledge Bases

For many computer applications data structures are not enough. It is not always a question of merely pondering an algorithmic problem and finding, or defining, nice and useful data structures for its solution. At times there is a need for a very large 'pool' of data, which many algorithms treat as (part of) their inputs, and which must therefore be of fixed structure, and readily available for retrieval and manipulation. Examples include the financial and personnel data of a company, the reservations and flight information of an airline, and the volume indexing data of a library. Such masses of data are called **databases**.

Typically, databases are very large, and contain many different kinds of data, ranging from names and addresses to obscure codes and symbols, and in some cases even free text. They are usually subject to numerous kinds of insertion, deletion, and retrieval procedures, utilized for different purposes and by different people. Now, while the addition of a new student to a university database, or the removal of an old one, are relatively easy tasks, when it comes to **querying** a database, with the purpose of retrieving information from it, intricacy seems to have no bounds. Just for perspective, here are a few queries that might be addressed to a flight reservation database:

- list all passengers confirmed on flight X;

- list all seats on flight Y occupied by passengers with no checked baggage;

- find the number of passengers who have reserved seats on two identically numbered flights scheduled for consecutive days in March of this year;

- list the names and seat numbers of all first-class passengers on Paris-bound flights on day Z who have ordered vegetarian food, and who have intercontinental continuation flights upon which first-class service does not provide special meals, and whose stopover points are either Zurich or Rome.

These examples illustrate the importance of a 'good' organization of the database. If continuation flights are listed in the database in some obscure place, and if there is no easy way to gather the information concerning a given passenger's itinerary, then writing an algorithm to solve the last-listed retrieval problem will become a difficult task indeed. As with data structures, good database design is important not only for reasons of clarity and ease in writing; it can be of the utmost importance when it comes to questions of efficiency, and to the feasibility of constructing a database system which can respond to such queries in a reasonable amount of time.

Various general **models** for database organization have been proposed and are used in real databases. These models are designed to maintain large quantities of data, while capturing, faithfully and efficiently, the relationships between the data items. Many methods and languages for manipulating and querying databases have been developed. One of the most popular database models, the **relational** model, caters for the arrangement of the data in large tables, which are reminiscent of the array data structure. Others call for certain kinds of tree-like, or network-like arrangements such as the **hierarchical** model, which organizes data in multiple-layer tree-like form (cf. Figure 3.3). However, there is little consensus as to the preferable models for particular applications.

Certain kinds of data are better viewed as fragments of *knowledge*, rather than just as numbers, names or codes. In addition to a large database describing the inventory of a manufacturing company, we might want to have a large **knowledge base** containing information relevant to the running of that company. Its **knowledge items** might have to somehow encode information such as 'Our company is currently the third largest of its kind in the world,' 'Mr Smith is a better manager than Ms Brown when it comes to personnel problems, but not when technical issues are concerned,' or 'If the price of oil goes up we shall have to lower all salaries within the following month.'

It is obvious that such fragments of information require more complex organization than data items of more or less fixed format, especially if we are interested in efficient retrieval. Knowledge bases are thus becoming the natural next step after databases, and are a rich source of interesting questions related to representation, organization, and algorithmic retrieval. We shall have more to say about knowledge in Chapter 12.

And thou shalt make loops
Exodus 26: 4

And he spoke of trees
I Kings 5: 13

3

Programming Languages

OR

Getting It Done by Computer

Thinking about algorithmic problems and their solutions is fine, and in fact, as should be obvious by now, it is beneficial not only in computer related problem solving, but also in the realms of cake baking, tire changing, cabinet making, and telephone book lookup. However, clearly our main concern is with algorithms that are intended for computer execution, and hence before we continue with our account of the scientific aspects of algorithmics, we should spend some time relating algorithms to real computers.

As mentioned in Chapter 1, even the most sophisticated computer is really only a large, well-organized volume of bits, and moreover it can normally carry out only a small number of extremely simple operations on them, such as zeroing, flipping, and testing (see Figure 1.1). How do we present an algorithm to a *real* computer and get it to carry out the corresponding process as intended? Let us put it more bluntly. How do we get a dumb machine, capable of so little, to impressively perform our subtle and carefully worked-out algorithms? Of course, this question becomes all the more pressing when we look around and see computers carrying out not only our toy examples of salary summation and word searching, but incredibly complex feats such as automatic flight control, graphical simulation of chemical reactions, and the orderly maintenance of communication networks with millions of subscribers.

The first observation is that our algorithms must be written in an unambiguous and formal fashion. Before trying to understand how playing around with bits can be made to accomplish even a simple task such as 'proceed through the list, adding each salary to the noted number,' that task itself has to be precisely specified: Where does the computer find the list? How does it proceed through it? Where does it find the salary and the 'noted number?' and so on. 'Beat egg whites until foamy' is not much worse in terms of precision and unambiguity than 'proceed through a list.'

To describe an algorithm for a computer's benefit, rather than just for human comprehension, we use a **programming language**, in which we write **programs**. A program is an official and formal rendition of the algorithm, suitable for computer execution. A programming language consists of the notation and rules by which one writes programs, and the person writing the program is called a **programmer**. (This person need not be the one who devised the algorithm upon which the program is based.)

Programs Require Precise Syntax

A programming language is typically associated with a rigid **syntax**, allowing the use of only special combinations of selected symbols and keywords. Any attempt at stretching this syntax might turn out to be disastrous; for example, if **input** X is written in a language whose input commands are of the form **read** X, the chances are that the result will be a blunt '$SYNTAX$ $ERROR$ $E4514$ ON $LINE$ 108.' This, of course, precludes even such polite but imprecise requests such as 'please read a value for X from the input,' or 'how about getting me a value for X.' These might result in a long string of obscure error messages. It is true that nice, talkative instructions are more pleasant for a human reader and for him are perhaps less ambiguous than their terse and impersonal equivalents, and it also true that we would like computers to be as 'user friendly' as possible. However, these facts should be contrasted with the current inability of computers to understand freely spoken (or freely typed) natural languages like English (see Chapter 12). A formal, concise, and rigid set of syntactic rules is therefore a must.

The formal syntax of a typical programming language includes orderly versions of several control structures, orderly ways of defining various data structures, and orderly formats for the basic instructions supported by the language. The difference is that now our imaginary little robot Runaround is less imaginary, since the computer is doing the work, and it will not carry out any instruction, however clear and unambiguous, if that instruction is not among those allowed by the programming language.

An algorithm for summing the numbers from 1 to N might be written in a typical (hypothetical) programming language PL as follows:

```
input N;
X := 0;
for Y from 1 to N do
    X := X + Y
end; output X.
```

Here $X := 0$ is the **assignment** statement that sets variable X to initial value 0 (in our algorithms we write $X \leftarrow 0$ for this). Notice the boldface keywords; they are part of the syntax of PL, meaning that the formal definition of that syntax most probably contains a clause to the effect that one of the legal kinds of **statements** in the language is a *for-statement*, whose general format consists of the keyword **for**, followed by a legal *for-header*, followed by **do**, followed by a legal statement, followed by **end**.[†] Syntax definitions can be written symbolically, in a form termed BNF (standing for Backus–Naur Form, after its inventors), as follows, where '|' denotes 'or':

⟨*statement*⟩ *is* :   ⟨*for-statement*⟩ | ⟨*assignment-stmt*⟩ | . . .
⟨*for-statement*⟩ *is:*   **for** ⟨*for-header*⟩ **do** ⟨*statement*⟩ **end**

The description of a header clause might read:

⟨*for-header*⟩ *is:*   ⟨*variable*⟩ **from** ⟨*value*⟩ **to** ⟨*value*⟩

The ⟨*value*⟩ might then be specified to be a variable, an explicit number, or some other object. Figure 3.1 shows a diagrammatic way of presenting such syntax rules. The example shows how the language enforces a special format for a particular kind of bounded-loop control construct.

Formats for defining data structures are similarly enforced. For example, a two-dimensional array AR of size 50 by 100, whose values can be integers, might be defined in the hypothetical language PL by the statement:

define AR **array** $[1 . . 50, 8 . . 107]$ **of integers**

and the language might allow reference to elements of AR by expressions of the form:

AR(value, value)

[†] Notice that this definition is recursive. Statements are defined in terms of themselves! To resolve this apparent cyclicity there must be an 'escape clause', whereby certain statements, such as assignments, do not recursively refer to statements in their definition, only, say, to values and variables.

Notice how we have not only specified the dimensions of *AR*, but also its *subscript values*; its rows are numbered 1, 2, ..., 50, but its columns are (for some reason) numbered 8, 9, ..., 107.

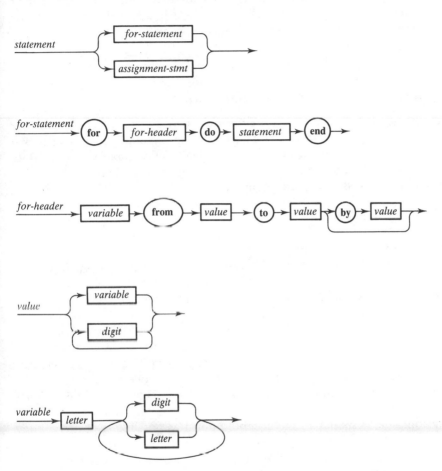

Figure 3.1   Syntax diagrams for programming language definition.

Actually, the syntax prescribes much more than the available control and data structures and the allowed elementary operations. Usually a language has rigid rules even for such petty issues as the legal strings of symbols that may be used to name variables or data structures, and the maximal number of digits allowed in numeric values. Some languages restrict variable names to be at most, say, eight symbols long, the first being alphabetical. Here *punctuation* does not get overlooked either; it is not atypical for a programming language to require a semicolon to follow some kinds of statements, a space to follow others, comments to be enclosed in special brackets, and so on, all with penalties for violators. This is the reason for our use of the term 'semicolon syndrome' in the preface to this book. In order to make readers knowledgeable enough to bend computers to their will, many computer books start out with a meticulous description of the syntax of a specific programming language, semicolon rules and all.

Programs Require Precise Semantics

Providing the language with a precise syntax is only part of a programming language designer's job. Without a formal and unambiguous **semantics** – that is, without a *meaning* for each syntactically allowed phrase – the syntax is all but worthless. If meanings for instructions in the language have not been provided, the program segment:

for Y **from** 1 **to** N **do**

in the hypothetical language PL might, for all we know, mean 'subtract Y from 1 and store the result in N'. Worse still, who says that the keywords **from**, **to**, **do**, etc., have anything at all to do with their meaning in conventional English? Maybe the very same program segment means 'erase all of the computer's memory, change the values of all variables to 0, output "TO HELL WITH PROGRAMMING LANGUAGES", and stop!' Who says that ':=' stands for 'assign to' and '+' stands for 'plus'? Who says that instructions are carried out in their written order? Maybe ';' means '*after* doing the following' rather than 'and *then* do the following.'

Of course, we might be able to guess what is meant, since the designer of PL probably chose keywords and special symbols intending that their meaning be as similar to the accepted norm as possible. But a *computer* cannot be made to act on such assumptions. Even if it could somehow reason about the conventional meaning of English words and of symbols like '+', how, without being told explicitly, would it know what to do with the loop header:

for Y **from** 1 **to** N **do**

when the value of N is, say, -314.1592? Is the body of the loop to be carried out 316 times, with Y working its way through the values 1, 0, -1, -2, ..., -313, and -314? Maybe it is carried out 317 times, including the case -315; or 634 times, running through 1, $\frac{1}{2}$, 0, $-\frac{1}{2}$, -1, ..., -315? Maybe it is not carried out at all, the rationale being that N's value is smaller than 1, and **for** loops must *in*crease their built-in counters, not *de*crease them.

Maybe arriving at the **for** statement with such a bizarre value in N should be treated as '*LOOP INDEX ERROR Z3088 ON LINE 365.*'

It seems clear, therefore, that a programming language requires not only rigid rules for defining the *form* of a legal program, but also rules, just as rigid, for defining its *meaning*.

It might come as a surprise to some people that for many modern programming languages a satisfactory semantics has not been worked out at all. Wherever such a semantic definition exists, it was usually prepared, not by the language designer or the computer manufacturer, but by independent researchers interested in the semantical problems raised by specific languages and their powerful features.

Designers and manufacturers do supply detailed **documentation** to go along with the language – volumes of it. These **language manuals**, as they are sometimes called, contain a wealth of information concerning both syntax and semantics, but the semantical information is usually not sufficient for the user to figure out what will happen in each and every syntactically legal program. The problem is a real one, and evidence for this can be found in the deep and intricate work of programming language semanticists. It is very tempting to add a new and powerful feature to a language, and to specify how to deal with it in a natural context. However, it is the unpredictability of the interaction of such a feature with all others supported by the language that can cause things to get out of hand.

Routines as Parameters: An Example

Let us assume that a language supporting recursive routines is to allow, not only variables whose values are numbers or words (= symbol strings), but also special variables whose values are the very names of routines. Once such features are allowed, it should also be possible to use routine variables as parameters to other routines. In this way if a routine P is defined as:

> *subroutine* P-**with-parameter-**V

where V is a routine variable, and somewhere inside P there is an instruction of the form:

> call V

then if P is invoked with the value of V being the routine Q, this instruction will effect a call to Q inside P, whereas if P is invoked with V being some other routine R, it will effect a call to R inside P. This is quite a powerful feature, enabling external control over the routines that P calls, simply by changing V's value. However, serious semantical problems arise. What if V is also a routine whose parameter is a routine variable?

** To sharpen the question, here is an example of such a P:

subroutine P-**with-parameter**-V,

(1) call V-**with-parameter**-V, placing returned value in X;

(2) if $X = 1$ then return with 0; else return with 1

But what will our confused processor do when asked to carry out the following initial call to P:

call P-**with-parameter**-P

Syntactically, everything is fine; the routines are all called with the right syntax and the right kinds of parameters. Nevertheless, there is a paradox embodied in the very question. It is impossible that the call returns 0, because by the definition of the body of P, the value returned is 0 if a call to V-**with-parameter**-V (which is now really a call to P-**with-parameter**-P) returns 1. So, the call can return 0 only if it returns 1, which is ridiculous! A similar argument shows that the P-**with-parameter**-P call cannot return 1 either, but by the text of P it cannot return anything *other* than 0 or 1. So what *does* it do? Does this strange call entail an endless 'see-saw' process? Is it simply forbidden by the language? Neither of these suggestions sounds quite right. With the first we would expect to see some kind of infinite execution reflected in the text, and with the second it is not clear how to characterize the forbidden programs syntactically. Clearly, a formal semantics to such a language must imply precise and unambiguous answers to such questions. **

*   *   *

From High-Level Languages to Bit Manipulation

So here we are, with a programming language PL, syntax, semantics and all, and we have just finished devising an algorithm A for the solution of some algorithmic problem. We now proceed to program the algorithm in the language PL, an action sometimes referred to as the **coding** of A into PL, and we would like to present the resulting program, call it A_P, to our computer. What happens next? The answer is that basically there are two possibilities, depending on the language and computer used. Here is the first.

The program A_P is entered into the computer's memory, by typing it in from a keyboard, reading it in from a recording device such as a magnetic disk, receiving it along an electronic communication channel from another computer, or by some other means. While these physical media and how they are used are of no concern here, what happens next is. The program A_P goes through a number of **transformations**, which gradually bring it 'down' to a level the computer can deal with. The final product of these transformations is a program A_M on the **machine level** (it is also said to be written in **machine language**), meaning that its basic operations are those which the computer 'understands', such as bit manipulation instructions. The number of such downward transformations varies from language to language and from one machine to another, but is typically between two and four. The intermediate objects are usually legal programs in increasingly more primitive programming languages. Their repertoire of control and data structures gradually becomes more humble, and hence also the basic instructions, until finally only the most elementary bit capabilities remain. It is after this final transformation stage that the computer can really *run*, or execute, the original program, or at least can give the user the impression that it is doing just that, by asking for a set of legal inputs and running the transformed version A_M. For reasons that should now be obvious, languages of the kind the user's original program A_p is written in are termed **high-level** programming languages (see Figure 3.2).

The downward transformations are somewhat reminiscent of replacing subroutines by their bodies. An instruction in a high-level language can be thought of as a call to a routine, or as a basic instruction that is not basic enough for the computer. As a consequence, it has to be refined and brought down to the computer's level of competence.

Compilation and Assembly Languages

Let us talk about the first transformation, called **compilation**, in which the high-level program A_p is translated into a program A_s in a lower-level language, called **assembly language**. Assembly languages differ from machine to machine, but, as a rule, they employ rather simple control structures, that resemble **goto** statements and **if–then** constructs, and they deal not solely with bits but also with integers and strings of symbols. They can refer directly to locations in the computer's **memory** – that large area containing acres upon acres of bits – they can *read* from those locations whatever numbers and strings they encode, and they can *store* encodings of numbers and strings therein.

A typical high-level loop construct such as:

for Y **from** 1 **to** N **do**
  ⟨body-of-loop⟩
end

might be translated into an assembly language equivalent looking like this (the parenthesized explanations are our own):

```
        MVC 0, Y    (move constant 0 to location Y)
LOOP    CMP N, Y    (compare values at locations N and Y)
```

       JEQ REST   (if equal jump to statement labelled 'REST')
       ADC 1, Y (add constant 1 to value at location Y)

    ⟨translated-body-of-loop⟩

       JMP LOOP   (jump back to statement labelled 'LOOP')
REST   (rest of program)

Prior to (or following) the assembly program itself there would appear additional instructions to associate the symbols Y and N with certain fixed memory locations, but we shall not get into these matters here.

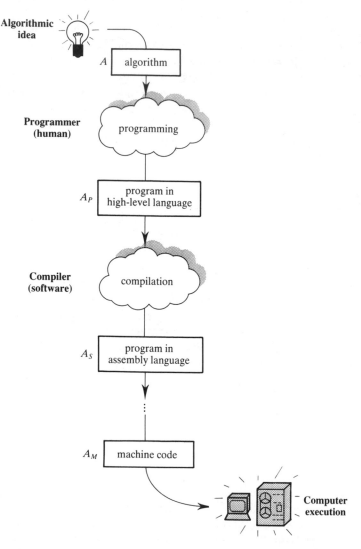

Figure 3.2   Transforming a high-level program into machine code.

Now comes the interesting point. The compilation process that translates high-level computer programs into assembly language is *itself* carried out by a computer program. This lengthy and complex piece of software, called a **compiler**, is usually supplied by the computer manufacturer together with the hardware. Figure 3.2 illustrates the downward transformation process, of which compilation is the first and most intricate part. The remaining steps translate assembly language into machine language. They are somewhat more straightforward than compilation and hence we shall not deal with them here.

As an aside, it is worth pointing out that compilers for the various high-level languages that a particular computer supports are but one kind of a large number of manufacturer-supplied programs, sometimes called generically **system software**. Their general role is to facilitate a variety of high-level modes of operation of the computer, while subtly insulating the user from many of the low-level details involved in doing so. Running user-written programs is one of these modes, communicating with other computers and interfacing with special external equipment is another.

Interpreters and Immediate Execution

There is another way computers execute the programs they are presented with, which does not involve translating the entire program into a lower level language. Rather, each of the program's high-level statements is translated into machine-level instructions immediately on being encountered, and these in turn are promptly executed. In a sense, the computer is playing the role of the robot or processor directly, running around and actually carrying out the high-level instructions one by one precisely as given. The mechanism responsible for this local-translation-and-immediate-execution is also a piece of system software, usually called an **interpreter**.

The interpreter approach has certain obvious advantages, among which are:

(1)   it is usually easier to write a 'quick-and-dirty', but reasonably useful, interpreter, than it is to write a reasonable compiler;

(2)   interpreter-driven execution yields a more traceable account of what is happening, especially when working interactively with the computer through a terminal with a display screen.

There are, however, several disadvantages of interpretation over compilation, which will be hinted at in later chapters.

Whether a particular computer will compile or interpret a given program depends on the computer at hand, the programming language, and the particular package of system software in use. Nevertheless, while some programming languages lend themselves to interpretation more easily than others, all languages can, in principle, be compiled.

*   *   *

Why Not an Algorithmic Esperanto?

Since the time high-level programming languages started to appear in the early 1950s, hundreds have been designed, and compilers and/or interpreters have been written for them. Many are extinct, and probably many more should be, but there are still scores of languages in common day-to-day use. These languages are, for the most part, quite diverse in nature, both in looks and in substance. Moreover, new ones pop up like mushrooms after rain.

Why? Would it not have been better to have a single universal language, some kind of algorithmic Esperanto, in which all algorithms are written, and which anyone can easily learn to use? Why the multitude of languages? What makes them different from one another? Who uses which languages, and for what purposes?

There are basically two reasons for this phenomenon: new technological developments in hardware, and new and diverse application areas, both of which cause the need for new programming languages. A good example of the first is the recent trend towards the development of **parallel** computers. These are machines that employ many distinct but interconnected 'single-track' computers. One of the consequences of these technological developments is the considerable effort devoted to the development of so-called **concurrent** programming languages, which, very briefly, cater for many processors carrying things out simultaneously. Chapter 10 is devoted to the subject of concurrency, hence we shall not dwell on it any further here.

The rest of this chapter is devoted to saying something in turn about each of a number of widespread programming languages. The reasons for this are two-fold: firstly, it gives the reader some feel for several important ones, but, more importantly, it provides evidence of the second reason given for their proliferation – namely, the diversity of application areas. Although some of the languages discussed are not considered general-purpose programming languages, they do illustrate the response of language designers to needs in specific application areas.

It should be noted that no attempt is made to teach the reader any of the languages, nor is the treatment claimed to come anywhere near being a survey of them. Rather, the aim is to present a small sample of the essential features and to give the reader some idea of what the programs look like and wherein their power lies. Many other important languages (most notably ALGOL, BASIC, C, MODULA-2 and ADA[†]) deserve to be mentioned too, but diversity in form and applications is preferred to extensive coverage.

FORTRAN: A Language for Science and Engineering

FORTRAN (FORmula TRANslator) is one of the most widely used high-level programming languages, and strangely enough also one of the first. It was designed and implemented in the mid 1950s and is particularly fitting for numerical computations. It is fair to say that its development was the result of an acute need for such computations in scientific and engineering applications. It is quite difficult to write the software for, say, the personnel management of a company, in FORTRAN, whereas the language is highly appropriate for, say, simulating the effects of a nuclear reaction. Over the years many compilers have been written for FORTRAN, and the language can be used on most modern computers.

FORTRAN was designed with efficient compilation in mind, rather than clarity or readability. As a result, it does not support many features for enhancing good program structure, which are considered important in a high-level language. A typical program consists of a main segment followed by a set of subroutines, with recursion and structural nesting of routines forbidden. Control flow is achieved by **goto** instructions, conditional statements and bounded iteration. FORTRAN supports vectors and multidimensional arrays, but virtually no other data structures. As to its numerical capabilities, these are quite powerful and extensive. The popularity of the language in the scientific and engineering community has resulted in numerous complex mathematical functions that have been preprogrammed as fixed subroutines, and catalogued in various **function libraries**. Such functions, although not an original part of the FORTRAN language, are made available simply by the same kind of subroutine calling that one would normally use in the language. This can significantly extend the programmer's repertoire of available elementary operations.

Here is a short example of a FORTRAN program for computing the average of the maximal and minimal elements of a vector of integers. Note the use of a **real number** (i.e., one that can contain a fraction too) for the computed value.

```
integer I, MX, MN, A(100)
real RS
read (A(I), I = 1, 100)
MX = A(1)
MN = A(1)
```

[†] ADA is a trademark of the US Department of Defense.

```
       do 10 I = 2, 100
       if (A(I).gt.MX) MX = A(I)
       if (A(I).lt.MN) MN = A(I)
   10  continue
       RS = (MN + MX)/2
       write RS
       end
```

The lines of this FORTRAN program accomplish the following, respectively:

- introduce three integer variables, and an integer vector $A(1)$ ... $A(100)$;
- introduce the real number variable RS;
- read the contents of A from the input device;
- set MX to the value of first element of A;
- same for MN;
- do everything from here to line number 10 repeatedly, with I running from 2 to 100;
- if Ith element of A is larger than MX, update MX to be current maximum, i.e., $A(I)$;
- if Ith element of A is smaller than MN, update MN to be current minimum, i.e., $A(I)$;
- line number 10: end of the body of the loop 'do 10...';
- set RS to be half the sum of MN and MX;
- write the value of RS on the output device.

COBOL: A Language for Business and Commerce

COBOL (COmmon Business Oriented Language) is antithetical to FORTRAN in almost every aspect. It too is one of the most widely used high-level languages and one of the first, being designed around 1959. But this is where the similarity ends. COBOL was designed in response to the acute need for a language appropriate for the voluminous data-processing requirements of banks, government agencies, and large corporations. Thus, while it is quite natural to write programs for personnel management in COBOL, a typical FORTRAN application, like the numerical simulation of a nuclear reaction, is hopelessly difficult.

COBOL was designed with readability and certain kinds of clarity in mind, and to that end programs look less like terse and cryptic mathematics, and more like human exchanges. This has its disadvantages, of course;

programs are much longer and 'watered down' in COBOL, and therefore rather tedious to write, and it can be quite difficult at times to comprehend a program's basic structure.

The main innovation in the design of COBOL is the facility for defining a file structure, whereby objects resembling arrays crossed with trees are possible. The language supports **goto** statements, a certain kind of conditional, and a general **perform** statement, encompassing both bounded iteration and a restricted form of subroutine call. The subroutines are not written separately, but are part of the regular program text and are referred to by delimiting labels. The entire program typically consists of four divisions, two of which are the **data division** and the **procedure division**, describing, respectively, the program's data organization and its algorithm.

Here is a COBOL definition of a simple university file containing information relevant to student performance and university courses. The structure of the file is illustrated in Figure 3.3. The **pic** parts appearing in the textual definition specify the format of data items: an A stands for an alphabetic character, and a 9 for a digit. Thus, for example, A(5) means five letters and AAAA999 means four letters followed by three digits.

```
data division
   01   UNIVERSITY FILE
      02   STUDENT occurs 100 times
         03   STUDENT-NAME pic A(15)
         03   COURSE occurs 30 times
            04   COURSE-NAME pic AAAA999
            04   SCORE pic 99
         03   STUDENT-ID# pic 99999
      02   DEPARTMENT occurs 20 times
         03   DEPT-NAME pic A(10)
         03   COURSE occurs 80 times
            04   COURSE-NAME pic AAAA999
            04   TEACHER pic A(10)
```

PASCAL: A General-Purpose Language

Following the development of FORTRAN and COBOL and their success as high-level programming languages, the need arose for a good general-purpose language, appropriate both for FORTRAN-like and COBOL-like applications. Over the years several were suggested, the most influential of which were ALGOL and its derivatives, and PL/I. Building on the ideas appearing in these, as well as on ideas from FORTRAN and COBOL, the PASCAL language was designed and implemented in the early 1970s. It has since become *the* programming language for much of the computer science community, in the sense that it is the 'native tongue' of virtually all students and researchers therein; PASCAL is the language taught in the

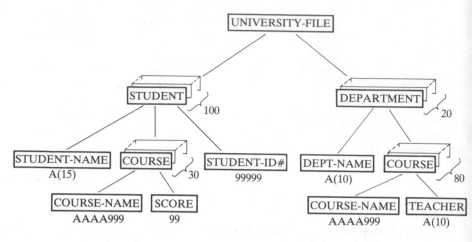

Figure 3.3 Structure of a COBOL university file.

first year of computer science degree programs in most universities and colleges, and it stays with the student as the main programming language throughout his course of study. PASCAL is also fast becoming a standard general-purpose language in a wide range of applications. (In this last respect, ADA, a relatively new and broad-featured language, seems to be PASCAL's main competitor, and in the former another language, MODULA-2.)

FORTRAN and COBOL were widely used at the time PASCAL was created, but were considered by many to be unsatisfactory, especially when it came to readability and modularity. PASCAL is in many senses a much 'cleaner' language. It supports several control constructs which are considered to be 'good'; proper use of them can lead to clear and well-structured programs. A PASCAL program is itself a well-structured object, consisting of subroutines nested inside one another, with various rules governing the **scope** of variables. An example of this concerns variables that are recognized only inside the routines in which they are defined, a feature which provides for a cleaner and less cluttered interface between a subroutine and its calling environment. The language offers a wide range of data structure facilities, including powerful constructs for the definition of new data types. It supports arrays, records, files, sets, and pointers, with which the user can define trees, graphs, and other objects. These can be 'flat' or multilayered, and their basic elements can be numbers of various kinds, symbol strings, or, in turn, other data structures. For example, we can write:

    type color = (blue, red, purple, brown, yellow);
    type color-set = set of color;
    type day-of-year = 1..365;

and then use the names color, color-set, and day-of-year as variables whose possible values are restricted to be, respectively, one of the specified colors, a set thereof, or one of the numbers between 1 and 365. Structures such as the COBOL file shown in Figure 3.3 can also be defined in PASCAL in a straightforward way.

PASCAL's compilers will carry out many kinds of tests for consistency in type definitions and in the ranges of variable values, resulting in a more reliable approach to the programming task. In fact, PASCAL is considered to be one of the first so-called languages for **reliable software**, preventing, by their very nature, many of the semantic errors that tend to appear in programs.

To illustrate the use of pointers in constructing self-defined data structures, here is a PASCAL program that reads in numbers one by one and forms a data structure called a **linked list**. Figure 3.4 shows sample input and a picture of the resulting structure.[†]

```
type thing = record
      contents : integer;
      next : link
end;
type link = ↑ thing;
var TOP, X : link;
begin
new (TOP);
X := TOP;
while not eof do
   begin
      read (X ↑ .contents);
      if not eof then
         begin
         new (X ↑ .next);
         X := X ↑ .next
         end
   end;
X ↑ .next := nil
end.
```

The segment defines a *thing* to be a composite **record** consisting of two **fields**. One, called *contents*, can carry an integer, and the other, called *next*, carries a *link*. A *link* is defined to be a pointer to a *thing*. Having defined the variables *TOP* and *X* to be of type *link*, the PASCAL segment sees to it that a fresh, content-free *thing* is prepared, pointed to by *TOP*. It then

---

[†] As an aside, one of the advantages of a linked list over an ordinary indexed list is in the fact that its length need not be fixed in any way; linked lists can be easily made to grow and shrink during program execution.

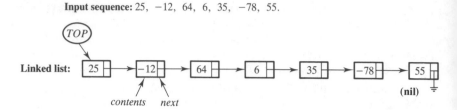

Input sequence: 25, −12, 64, 6, 35, −78, 55.

Figure 3.4   An input sequence and its linked list representation.

makes *X* point to the same *thing* too. The subsequent loop reads input numbers repeatedly until the input file ends (indicated by **eof**, i.e., end of file). Each input number is stored in the *contents* field of the latest *thing*. Then, if we are not yet at the end of the file, the program allocates a fresh *thing* pointed to by the *next* area of the current one, and forwards *X* to point to this new *thing* so that it promptly becomes the current one. Following this loop the final *link* is set to **nil**, the special empty pointer.

   The following is a self-explanatory PASCAL program segment that traverses the *thing* list, summing the numbers it represents. The outcome, if applied to the list of Figure 3.4, would be 107. (The symbol < > stands for 'not equal'.)

```
var SUM : integer;
begin
X := TOP;
while X < > nil do
   begin
      SUM := SUM + X ↑ .contents;
      X := X ↑ .next
   end;
write (SUM)
end.
```

SNOBOL: A Language for String and Text Manipulation

SNOBOL (StriNg Oriented symBOlic Language) was designed in the early 1960s to provide a powerful tool for applications involving symbolic manipulation of texts. The language, like many others, has been since extended and strengthened, culminating in a version called SNOBOL4.

   SNOBOL's main innovative feature is the notion of a programmer definable **pattern**, that can be subsequently matched with a text – that is, a string of symbols. Patterns can involve a variety of features, each representing part of a search through the text in an attempt to find a match.

The language supports a number of operations on patterns, enabling the construction of complex patterns from simpler ones in a manner not unlike the construction of complex arithmetical expressions from simpler ones using the elementary operations of arithmetic. Control flow is to a large extent achieved through **goto** statements that depend on the *success* or *failure* of an attempt to match patterns. The language also features programmer-defined data types that are similar to those allowed in COBOL, subroutines that can be recursive, and standard kinds of arithmetic and logical operations. However, it is fair to say that the main characteristic of the language is to encourage its use in symbol manipulation applications by the very power of the constructs and operations devoted to those ends.

A typical pattern-matching statement consists of a text (or the name of a variable containing one), followed by the sought-for pattern (or a variable containing one), followed by labels specifying the statements to be executed next in case the matching succeeds or fails, respectively.

** Here is a SNOBOL program segment that reads in symbol strings one at a time, and for each one determines whether or not it is of the form $AAA\ldots A\llcorner\!\!\llcorner\!\!\llcorner\ldots\llcorner BBB\ldots B$, where each '$\llcorner$' can be any symbol other than A or B, and the lengths of the three sequences (As, neither-A-nor-Bs, and Bs) are to be all equal. The first two lines set X to the desired pattern as explained below, *TEXT X* is the instruction to try matching *TEXT* with the pattern X. The **f**(*END*) on the right means 'if execution fails goto *END*,' and similarly for **f**(*BAD*), and :(*L*) means simply 'goto *L*'.

```
      X = pos(0) (span('A') @N span(notany('AB'))
   +         pos(*(2 * N)) rpos(*N) span('B') rpos(0))
   L      TEXT = input                    :f(END)
          TEXT X                          :f(BAD)
          output = 'INPUT IS GOOD'        :(L)
   BAD    output = 'INPUT IS BAD'         :(L)
   END
```

In the assignment to X (which is two lines long, the continuation being signified by a '+') **pos**(0) confirms that we are located at the first position in the text; i.e., we have already gone through 0 symbols. **span**('A') matches any sequence consisting solely of As, and, likewise, **span**(**notany**('AB')) matches any sequence consisting of anything but As or Bs. Equal length is enforced in the pattern by pausing between the first two **span** clauses, setting the variable N to the current position in the text (which is the role of @N), and pausing again before **span**('B') to check whether we are now both at position $2N$ from the beginning of the text and, simultaneously, at position N from its end (**rpos** counts symbols still to be encountered, and *N evaluates N only when it is reached). Finally, **rpos**(0) requires that the span of Bs reach the end of the string. The entire working of this SNOBOL segment is dependent upon the fact that the string of symbols read into the *TEXT* variable satisfies the requirements *precisely* when the pattern matching succeeds on all counts; any failure is a sign that *TEXT* does not conform to the requirements and it can therefore be safely labeled *BAD*.   **

LISP: An Applicative Language Based on List Processing

LISP (LISt Processing) was designed in 1960, and has since been extended considerably. The basic ideas, however, are all present in the first version, which is generally referred to as *pure* LISP. Pure LISP was influenced by a mathematical formalism, called the **lambda calculus,** that was invented in the 1930s. LISP is quite different from most other high-level languages in that it is **applicative**, meaning that it is based almost exclusively on the application of functions to arguments, the results being in turn used in other functions.

The language owes its elegance in part to the fact that applicativity is coupled with the decision to base the structure of all objects on a rich kind of list. Lists in LISP are just vectors, but their elements can in turn be other lists, and so on. This gives rise to a recursive concept, of which ordinary vectors, arrays, and trees are all special cases. Figure 3.5 shows how trees can be described as lists in LISP. The application of a function to its arguments is written simply as the list whose first element (its **car** in LISP terminology) is the function name and whose remaining elements (the list's **cdr**) constitute its arguments. Thus, we write (**plus** X Y) instead of $X + Y$, or X **plus** Y. We can define new functions and give them names, to be used later on, as in:

(**define** ($CALC$ (**lambda** (X Y) (**plus** (**times** (X X) Y)))))

This rather cryptic statement defines $CALC$ to be another name for the function of X and Y whose value is $X^2 + Y$. It can then be used in a context such as ($CALC$ 7 3), which evaluates to 52.

In LISP, recursion is really the name of the game; data is defined recursively, programs are constructed recursively, and the main control structure is recursion (though later versions have added more conventional constructs such as **goto**). The following is a remarkable consequence of these basic features: both a LISP program and its data are just lists. This means that programs can be manipulated (e.g., changed) in the way data is, and data, if it is of the proper form, can be executed as a program.

LISP has turned out to be most successful in applications involving **symbolic computation**, such as game playing, natural language processing, learning, decision making, and logical deduction. Many of these fall under

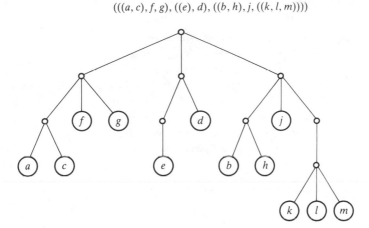

$$(((a, c), f, g), ((e), d), ((b, h), j, ((k, l, m))))$$

Figure 3.5 A LISP list and its corresponding tree.

the general category of problems in **artificial intelligence,** about which we shall have more to say in Chapter 12.

Programs in LISP are usually not compiled but are interpreted and executed statement by statement, a fact that makes LISP very convenient as an interactive language, with the programmer or user having the ability to follow execution as it proceeds.

The following is a LISP definition of a function *FLATTEN*, which accepts a LISP list representing a tree and returns a simple 'flat' list containing all bottom-level elements (**atoms,** in LISP terminology). If applied, say, to the program for defining *CALC* (which, as mentioned, is really just another LISP list), it would return the flat list:

(**define** *CALC* **lambda** *X Y* **plus times** *X X Y*)

Here is the program itself:

```
(define (FLATTEN (lambda (X)
   (cond ((null X) nil)
      ((atom (X)) (X))
      ((atom (car X)) (cons (car X) (FLATTEN (cdr X))))
      (T (append (FLATTEN (car X)) (FLATTEN (cdr X)))) )))  )
```

The program uses the LISP functions **cons, append, nil, null**, and **cond**, and rather than discussing them we shall only say that the program formalizes the following algorithm.

subroutine **flatten** X:

(1) if X is empty then return with nothing;

(2) if X is an atom then return with X itself;

(3) if **car**-of-X is an atom then do the following:
    (3.1) recursively call **flatten** with **cdr**-of-X;
    (3.2) return with **car**-of-X attached to the result of this call;

(4) otherwise (i.e., **car**-of-X is itself a list) do the following:
    (4.1) recursively call **flatten** with **car**-of-X;
    (4.2) recursively call **flatten** with **cdr**-of-X;
    (4.3) return with the list obtained by concatenating the results of both
    these calls.

PROLOG: A Language Based on Clausal Logic

PROLOG (PROgramming in LOGic) was designed in 1970. The language is based on **clauses**, which specify that certain **facts** follow logically from sets of other facts. A fact generally states that certain elements, or expressions denoting elements, are in some relationship to one another. Thus:

    EATS(cats, mice)

is a fact, stating that cats and mice are related via the relationship *EATS*. More subtle, and far more general, is the clause:

    EATS(X, Y) :- *EATS*(X, Z), *EATS*(Z, Y)

which states that if Xs eat Zs and Zs eat Ys, then it can be deduced that Xs in effect eat Ys.

A program consists of a set of 'known' facts, a set of clauses, and a **question**. The question asks whether a certain fact is true, and the program attempts to answer it by figuring out, using the given clauses to repeatedly deduce new facts, whether the fact in question follows logically from the known facts.

PROLOG derives its power from the ability to use variables and functional terms in clauses and facts, and the ability of clauses to be recursive (*EATS*, in the foregoing clause, feeds recursively into itself, in a manner of speaking). In this sense, in PROLOG, as in LISP too, recursion is an essential part of the language, since not only is recursion the main control structure but data structures are also defined and traversed recursively.

Variables can be used in the program's question to signify outputs.

For example, rather than asking if elephants eat frogs, we can ask the following question:

?- *EATS*(*X*, frogs)

to which PROLOG can be made to respond by listing *all* things that eat frogs, or, more precisely, all things with the property that the fact that they eat frogs follows from the known facts. This makes PROLOG a fitting language for querying databases (see Chapter 2). In fact, it is most fitting for querying and manipulating knowledge bases. A clause like the recursive one for *EATS* can itself be thought of as a knowledge item, so that PROLOG programs are in a sense knowledge, and (certain kinds of) knowledge can function as PROLOG programs. With this in mind, PROLOG is a highly **declarative** language. The programmer supplies more 'what's' than 'how's', declaring what the relationships between things are, and not so much how things are computed.

PROLOG has a range of applications similar to that of LISP; namely, those involving symbolic computation, and hence is also regarded as being highly appropriate for artificial intelligence applications. A program works by considering clauses in order, in an attempt to answer the question. In the process, it looks for ways to match the variables and expressions in parts of the clauses with those in the current facts it is trying to establish. This process is called **unification**. If appropriate matches cannot be found, PROLOG **backtracks** to some previous point in its attempts, and decides to try out a different clause.

As in LISP, the central data structure in PROLOG is a general kind of recursively defined list, which is really a tree. A list can be given explicitly, or in the form [*A* | *B*], where *A* is its first element (its **car**), which of course can itself be a list, and *B* consists of its remaining elements (its **cdr**). There follows a PROLOG version of the definition of the flattening function, described previously for LISP, and in it the second parameter of *FLATTEN* signifies the output. Thus, if we add to this segment the question:

?- *FLATTEN*([*n*,[*i*,*c*],[[*e*,*p*,*r*],*o*,[*l*,*o*]],*g*], *X*)

where *X* is a variable, the output will be the flat list [*n*,*i*,*c*,*e*,*p*,*r*,*o*,*l*,*o*,*g*].

FLATTEN([], []).
FLATTEN(*X*, [*X*]) :- **atom** (*X*).
FLATTEN([*X* | *Y*], *Z*) :-
    FLATTEN(*X*, X_1), *FLATTEN*(*Y*, Y_1), **append** (X_1, Y_1, *Z*).

These three PROLOG lines specify the following, respectively:

- empty lists are flat;

- if a list is just an atom, it is flat;
- if, recursively, X_1 is the flattened version of X, and Y_1 is that of Y, then the flattened version of $[X \mid Y]$ is obtained by appending X_1 to Y_1.

APL: The Quintessentially Compact Language

APL (A Programming Language) was designed in the early 1960s, and in all fairness can be said to be the least conventional of commonly used languages. Its design takes compactification to the limit, replacing lengthy program segments, which might have required several nested loops, by single symbols. It is used widely in scientific and engineering applications, and has several fast and efficient implementations.

The language was motivated by the need to supply programmers with a powerful tool that could be used interactively – something of a super desk calculator. The most striking feature of APL is its rich set of operators, which apply equally well to vectors and arrays of higher dimension as they do to single elements. Thus, if A and B are just numbers, then $A + B$ has its standard meaning, whereas if they are, say, two-dimensional arrays of size 20 by 20, the same expression will yield a 20 by 20 array each of whose elements is the sum of the corresponding elements in A and B. In fact, multidimensional arrays are the main data structure in APL, and in a sense the entire language revolves around them. There are operators for restructuring arrays into new dimensions and sizes, for unravelling arrays into linear vectors, for combining arrays into new ones, for chopping parts off arrays, for rotating, reversing and transposing arrays, for testing membership of an element in an array, for applying standard operators to an array in **element-wise** fashion, as in $A + B$ or $A < B$ (which yields a 20 by 20 array containing 1 wherever the A-element is smaller than the B-element, and 0 otherwise), or for applying standard operators in **cumulative** fashion, as in the expression $+/A$, which sums the entire array A, regardless of dimensionality or size.

Since its operators are so powerful, and since they can be 'piled' on top of each other in an applicative manner, APL provides for extremely terse and cryptic-looking programs. In fact, APL specialists delight in writing 'one-liners'; these are symbol-ridden one-line programs, which are capable of the equivalent of many lines of FORTRAN or PASCAL. However, APL also supports subroutines that are allowed to be recursive, **goto** statements, and certain kinds of conditional branching. Hence, if so desired, APL programs can be written in a reasonably readable fashion. APL programs are meant to be interpreted, not compiled, which explains in part why one-liners are so popular: a one-liner gets interpreted and executed immediately.

As an example of operator application, the operator ι applied to a number N generates a vector consisting of the numbers 1, 2, 3, ..., N. The operator ρ, when used as a binary connector, reshapes the array given on its right according to the dimensions of the array given on its left. These two operators combine in the expresssion:

3 4 ρι 12

to yield the 3 by 4 array:

```
1   2   3    4
5   6   7    8
9  10  11   12
```

** Here is a short APL subroutine *FIB* which, when called with parameter N, generates a vector containing the first N Fibonacci numbers. These numbers form a sequence starting with 1, 1, with each subsequent number being the sum of its two precedents.

```
∇ FIB N
[1]   A←1 1
[2]   →2 × N>ρA←A, +/⁻2 ↑ A ∇
```

The first line following the subroutine header sets A to be the vector 1, 1. The second line reads from right to left (a practice typical to APL) as follows: ∇ marks the end of the subroutine. ⁻2 ↑ A yields the last two elements of A, which are summed by the segment +/⁻2 ↑ A. The result is attached to the end of A by the segment $A ← A$, ..., which uses the comma operator denoting array (or vector) concatenation. So far the program has simply computed the next Fibonacci number and has attached it to A. It now has to iterate this until A contains N numbers. This is done by the remaining parts of the second line: ρA, in which ρ is used as a unary operator, stands for the length of A, which is promptly compared to N by the segment $N > ρA$. This comparison yields 1 as its result if the answer is 'yes', and 0 if not. The answer is then multiplied by 2 in the segment $2 × N > ρA$, yielding 2 or 0. This result is the parameter of the '→' symbol, which is a **goto**, specifying that control is to return either to line 2 to calculate the next Fibonacci number, or to the nonexistent line 0, signifying an end to the execution. If called by the expression:

FIB 12

the APL interpreter will respond with:

1 1 2 3 5 8 13 21 34 55 89 144,

which is simply a list of the first 12 Fibonacci numbers.   **

Research on Programming Languages

Programming languages form one of the most active and widely addressed research areas in computer science, and we have only touched upon a few of the issues involved.

People are interested in general-purpose and special-purpose languages, and in their precise definition and efficient implementation. Sophisticated compilation and translation techniques are developed, new control structures and data structures are proposed, and powerful methods for enabling programmers to define their own are established. Languages that encourage 'good' programming style are sought for, and people try to design them to incorporate various recommended ways of thinking about algorithms.

As far as semantics goes, computer scientists are interested in providing tools and methods for producing computer programs with mathematically sound meaning. Obviously, precise syntax is a prerequisite for precise semantics, and therefore the phrase 'semantics of algorithms' is somewhat meaningless. It is only when an algorithm has been programmed in a formal programming language that it can be given a formal and unambiguous meaning.

There are several approaches to semantic definitions. One, called **operational semantics**, describes the meaning of a program by rigorously defining the sequence of steps taken during execution, and the effect of each step on the **program state**. A state is like a snapshot of all that is of relevance in a program at a given instant, and it typically includes the values of all variables, parameters, and data structures, as well as the current location of control (i.e., of the processor) in the program's text.

A more abstract approach, called **denotational semantics**, describes the meaning of a program as a pure mathematical object of some suitable kind. Typically, these objects are certain kinds of **functions** that capture the transformations from the initial start state to the final end state that programs entail. This approach pays less attention to the actual steps in an execution of the program and more to its overall externally observable effects. Whatever the approach, getting such definitions right is not easy even for simple languages, and for ones including tricky features it can become a formidable task indeed.

We mentioned databases in Chapter 2. Query and data manipulation languages for databases can actually be viewed as special-purpose programming languages. People are interested in developing ones that are powerful, flexible, and efficient, and in this particular case design teams also have to be sensitive to the fact that many database users are not professional programmers, so that the languages should be extra easy to use.

Researchers are interested in developing **programming environments**; namely, user-friendly interactive systems that enable a programmer to write, edit, change, execute, analyze, correct, and simulate programs. Some of these involve visual techniques (made possible by modern graphical computer terminals and workstations), such as the animation of program execution using flowcharts coupled with pictures of the data structures as they change. A somewhat new and exciting direction is that of **visual programming languages**, with which it is possible to *draw* programs rather than write them. The idea is not merely to draw a flowchart capturing the control visually, but to somehow introduce new diagrammatic modes of algorithmic thought. Here too there are problems of precise syntax and semantics, as well as efficient implementation. (How, for example, can recursion be visualized?)

A final remark here concerns the **universality** of programming languages. In a certain technical sense, all the programming languages discussed here, and for that matter virtually all others too, are *equivalent* in their expressive power. Any algorithmic problem solvable in one language is, in principle, solvable in any other language too. The differences between languages are pragmatic, and involve appropriateness for certain applications, clarity and structure, efficiency of implementation, and algorithmic ways of thinking. Given the significant differences between programming languages this might come as something of a surprise. In actuality, it is one of the most fundamental facts of algorithmics, and will be discussed in detail in Chapter 9.

people of a strange speech and of a hard language
Ezekiel 3: 5

PART TWO

METHODS AND ANALYSIS

Come now, and let us reason together

Isaiah 1: 18

4

Algorithmic Methods

OR

Getting It Done Methodically

*And he strictly raises it
according to the method prescribed*
Isaiah 28: 26

It seems that we can now proceed happily with our algorithmic chores. We know how algorithms are structured and how to arrange the objects they manipulate, and we also know how to write them up for computer execution. We can therefore tell our processor what it should be doing and when. However, this is an overly naive assessment of the situation, and we shall see various reasons for this as we proceed.

One of the problems is rooted in the fact that we have not provided any methods that can be used to *devise* an algorithm. It is all very well talking about the *constructs* that an algorithm may use – that is, the pieces it might be composed of – but we must say something more about the ways of going about using these pieces to make a whole. In this chapter we shall review a number of quite general **algorithmic methods** that a designer can employ in order to find a solution to an algorithmic problem.

It must be noted, however, that there are no good recipes for devising recipes. Each algorithmic problem is a challenge for the algorithm designer. Some problems are straightforward, some are complicated, and even others are tantalizing, and the present chapter shows only that certain algorithms follow certain general paradigms quite nicely. As a moral, the algorithm designer might benefit from trying these out first. By and large, however, algorithmic design is a creative activity, which at times can require real ingenuity.

Searches and Traversals

Many algorithmic problems give rise to the need to **traverse** certain structures. At times the structure is simply one of the data structures explicitly available in the algorithm, and at times it is some implicit structure that perhaps cannot be actually 'seen', but that exists under the surface. At times one is looking for something special within the structure ('who is the director of the public relations department?'), and at times some work has to be done at each point ('compute the average grades of all students'). The straightforward salary summation problem of Chapter 1, for example (cf. Figure 2.3), is readily seen to require a simple traversal of the given list of employees. On the other hand, the problem that involved only employees earning more than their managers (cf. Figure 2.4) can be thought of as requiring the traversal of an imaginary two-dimensional array, in which employees are plotted against employees, and the search is for certain employee/manager pairs.

In such cases the task is to find the most natural way of traversing the data structure at hand (whether explicit or implicit) and thus devise the algorithm. When vectors or arrays are involved, loops and nested loops typically appear, as explained in Chapter 2 (cf. Figure 2.9), and in quite the same vein, when trees are involved recursion appears, as indeed was the case in the treesort example. It is true that the idea behind the treesort algorithm is quite subtle and cannot be found by simply figuring out the best control structure for traversing the given data structure. However, once the idea has been hit upon, it is a small thing to realize that the second visit trip, in which the elements are output in order, is nothing more than a certain traversal of a binary tree, from which it is not too difficult to reach the conclusion that recursion should be used.

The traversal induced by the recursive left-first trip of Figure 2.14 is sometimes called **depth-first** search with backtracking, as the processor 'dives' into the tree trying to get as deep down as possible, and when it cannot go any further it backtracks reluctantly, always striving to resume its diving. The only additional feature here is the requirement that diving be performed as much to the left as possible. There are several other ways of traversing trees, one of which, the dual of depth-first search, is termed **breadth-first** search. Traversing in a breadth-first manner means that the levels of the tree (see Figure 2.12) are exhausted in order; first the root, then all of its offspring, then *their* offspring, etc.

Maximal Polygonal Distance: An Example

Many interesting algorithmic problems involve geometric concepts such as points, lines, and distances, and are thus part of the subject matter known as **computational geometry**. Many of the problems in this area are deceptively easy to 'solve' using the human visual system, but are often a real challenge for algorithm designers. Here is a very simple one.

Suppose we are given a simple convex polygon[†] of the kind appearing in Figure 4.1, and suppose we are interested in finding two points of maximal distance on its borderline. The polygon is assumed to be represented by a sequence of the $\langle X, Y \rangle$ coordinates of the vertices, in clockwise order. As the maximum distance will occur for two of the *vertices*, there is no need to look at any points along the polygon's edges other than the vertices.

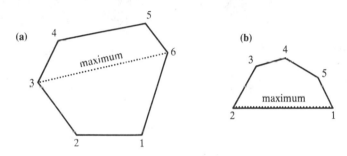

Figure 4.1   Two convex polygons.

A trivial solution would involve considering *all* pairs of vertices in some order, keeping the current maximum and the pair achieving this maximum in variables. Each new pair considered is subjected to a simple distance computation, the new distance is compared with the current maximum and the variables are updated if the new distance is found to be larger, which means that it is actually a new maximum. If we ponder this solution for a moment, it becomes clear that we are actually traversing an imaginary array in which vertices are plotted against vertices. The imaginary data item at point $\langle I, J \rangle$ of this array is the distance between the vertices I and J. The traversal can then be easily carried out by two nested loops, and the reader is indeed encouraged to write down the resulting algorithm.

This solution, however, considers far too many potential pairs; should it not be possible to consider only 'opposite' pairs of points, such as $\langle 1, 4 \rangle$, $\langle 2, 5 \rangle$, and $\langle 3, 6 \rangle$ in Figure 4.1(a)? This would mean traversing only a vector of 'special' pairs, rather than the array of all pairs, clearly resulting

---

[†] A convex polygon is one with no angles greater than 180°.

in a more efficient algorithm that requires only a single loop. Now, this is not quite as simple as it sounds, since the desired opposite pairs are not necessarily those which have an equal number of vertices on either side; Figure 4.1(b) shows a polygon in which the maximum occurs in *neighboring* vertices, which would have been missed by an algorithm that considered only oppositely numbered ones. The better solution, which indeed employs a single loop and considers only the 'right' kind of opposite pairs, is illustrated in Figure 4.2.

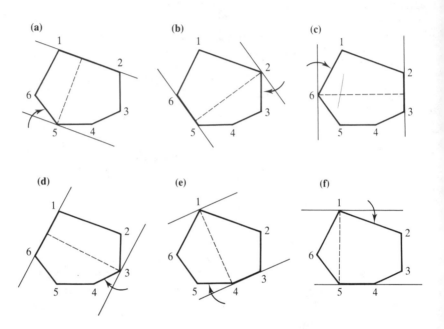

Figure 4.2   Finding maximal distance by clockwise traversal.

* *   It works as follows. First, a line is 'drawn' along edge $\langle 1, 2 \rangle$, the edge between vertex 1 and 2. Next, a line parallel to it is gradually brought towards the polygon from beyond it until one of the vertices is hit; cf. Figure 4.2(a). The initial approximation to the maximum is taken to be the larger of the distances between that vertex and vertices 1 and 2. Then, a clockwise movement is started, each step of which involves rotating one of the two lines until it lies along the next edge in clockwise order, and adjusting the other to be parallel to it. Exactly which of the lines is rotated and which is adjusted is determined by comparing the efforts needed for rotation; the line with the smaller angle to the next edge is the one rotated. Upon completing a rotation there is a new vertex that resides on the line just rotated. The distance between that vertex and the one on the adjusted line is computed, and is compared to the current maximum as before, and all this is carried out around the entire polygon. All the actions required by this algorithm involve simple numerical manipulations of the coordinates of the vertices, which follow from elementary analytic geometry. Figure 4.2 illustrates the sequence of transformations on the lines.   * *

This example was chosen to further illustrate that recognizing the need for a traversal, and figuring out what really is to be traversed, is important and can be of considerable help, but it does not always suffice when it comes to solving tricky algorithmic problems; some insight and a good deal of knowledge of the relevant subject matter can do no harm.

Divide-and-Conquer

Often a problem can be solved by reducing it to smaller problems of the same kind and solving them, and then, with some additional work, combining the partial solutions to form a final solution to the original problem. If the smaller problems are *precisely* the same problem at hand but applied to 'smaller' or 'simpler' inputs, then obviously recursion can be used in the algorithm. The method is called **divide-and-conquer** for obvious reasons.

Several algorithms in this book embody this 'split-and-hit' idea. We have already seen it implicitly in the Towers of Hanoi example: the algorithm solved the problem for N rings by solving two problems for $N-1$ rings in the proper order and context. Other cases appear later. Here are two additional applications of dividing and conquering.

Imagine being given a jumbled telephone book, or, to sound more profound, an unordered list L. We are not interested in sorting L, but merely in finding the largest and smallest elements appearing therein. Clearly we can simply traverse the list once, keeping the current minimum and current maximum in variables, comparing each element to both as we proceed.

The following algorithm utilizes the divide-and-conquer strategy in a simple way, and is actually slightly better than the naive algorithm considered in the last section (see Chapter 6). Schematically it reads:

(1)   if L consists of one element, then that element is both the minimum and the maximum; if it consists of two elements, then the smaller is its minimum and the larger is its maximum;

(2)   otherwise do the following:
  (2.1)   split L into two halves, L_1 and L_2;
  (2.2)   find their extremal elements *MIN1*, *MAX1*, *MIN2*, and *MAX2*;
  (2.3)   select the smaller of *MIN1* and *MIN2*; it is the minimal element of L;
  (2.4)   select the larger of *MAX1* and *MAX2*; it is the maximal element of L.

(Obviously, the splitting in line (2.1) should be defined in such a way as to cover the case of a list L of odd length.) Line (2.2) begs to be carried out recursively, as the problems to be solved there are precisely the **min&max** problem on the smaller lists L_1 and L_2. One slight difficulty with a simple-minded attempt at going ahead with this recursion, is that here, in contrast with the Towers of Hanoi routine, the recursive call has to produce results, to be used in the sequel. Somehow, the processor must not only remember its return address and how to restore the environment to the situation prior to embarking on the present recursive endeavor, but it must also be capable of bringing certain items back from its toils. In this case it would be most helpful if the processor could return from a recursive call along with the desired minimum and maximum.[†] The following is the result of extending the notion of a subroutine accordingly, and applying it to the **min&max** problem:

> *subroutine* **find-min&max-of** L:
>
> (1)   if L consists of one element, then set *MIN* and *MAX* to it; if it consists of two elements, then set *MIN* to the smaller of them and *MAX* to the larger;
>
> (2)   otherwise do the following:
>   (2.1)   split L into two halves, L_1 and L_2;
>   (2.2)   call **find-min&max of** L_1, placing returned values in *MIN1* and *MAX1*;
>   (2.3)   call **find-min&max-of** L_2, placing returned values in *MIN2* and *MAX2*;
>   (2.4)   set *MIN* to smaller of *MIN1* and *MIN2*;
>   (2.5)   set *MAX* to larger of *MAX1* and *MAX2*;
>
> (3)   return with *MIN* and *MAX*.

As mentioned, the reason this algorithm is actually a little better than the naive one will become clear in Chapter 6.

The divide-and-conquer paradigm can be used beneficially in *sorting* a list, not only in finding its extremal elements. To sort a list L containing at least two elements, we can similarly split it into its halves L_1 and L_2, and recursively sort them both. The one-element case is treated separately, as in the **min&max** example. To obtain the final sorted version of L, we can proceed by *merging* the sorted halves. To merge two sorted lists, we repeatedly remove and send off to the output the smaller of the two elements currently at the heads of the two lists. The workings of this algorithm, which is called **mergesort**, are illustrated in Figure 4.3, and the reader is urged to write down the algorithm in detail. Mergesort is considerably better than both bubblesort and treesort, a fact we shall have more to say about in Chapter 6.

[†] A subroutine or procedure that returns with values is sometimes called simply a function.

Figure 4.3   The workings of mergesort.

Greedy Algorithms and Railroad Contractors

Many algorithmic problems call for producing some kind of *best* result from an appropriate set of possibilities. Consider a network of cities, and a lazy railroad contractor. The contractor was paid to lay out rails so that it would be possible to reach any city from any other. The contract did not specify any criteria, such as the need for certain nonstop rail connections, or a maximum number of allowed cities on the path connecting any two others. Hence our contractor, being lazy, is interested in laying down the cheapest (that is, the shortest) combination of rail segments. Assume that not all cities can be connected by direct segments of rail to all others, due to objective reasons such as physical obstacles, and that the distances are given only between those pairs of cities that can. We further assume that the cost of directly connecting city A with B is proportional to the distance between them. Also, we do not allow railroad junctions outside cities.

Such a network is called a **labelled graph**, or simply a **graph** for short. Graphs are similar to trees, except that trees cannot 'close on themselves'; that is, they cannot contain **cycles**, or loops, whereas graphs can. Figure 4.4 presents an example of a city graph and its minimal railroad. Notice that the contractor is really after what we call a **minimal spanning tree**. This is a tree that 'spans' the graph, in the sense that it reaches each and every one of its nodes (= cities, in our case), and which is the cheapest such tree, in the sense that the sum of the labels along the edges (= distances between cities, in our case) is the smallest possible. The desired solution must obviously be a tree, since otherwise it would necessarily contain some cycle, and a lazy contractor could have obtained a cheaper railroad, still connecting all cities, by eliminating one of the segments of that cycle.

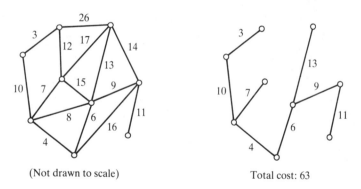

(Not drawn to scale)   Total cost: 63

Figure 4.4   A city network and its minimal spanning railroad.

There is an algorithmic approach to such problems, called the **greedy method**. It recommends constructing the minimal spanning tree edge by edge, choosing as the next edge the best one possible as far as the current situation is concerned. This is really the adoption of a kind of 'eat and drink as tomorrow we die' attitude. One way of doing this for spanning railroads is the following, illustrated in Figure 4.5. Start out with the degenerate tree consisting of the cheapest edge in the graph. At each stage extend the tree constructed so far by adding the cheapest edge not yet considered that results in a new tree (in particular, it should not introduce a cycle; if it does, then go on to the next cheapest edge). It can be shown that this simple strategy actually produces a minimal spanning tree. The reader is encouraged to write down the algorithm in detail.

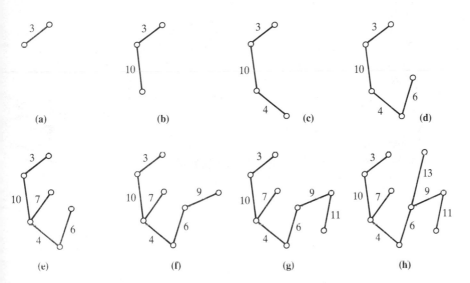

Figure 4.5 The workings of the greedy spanning tree algorithm.

Greedy algorithms exist for a large variety of interesting algorithmic problems. They are usually quite easy to come by, and in some cases they are quite intuitive. The difficult part is usually in showing that a greedy strategy indeed works, and as the next section shows, there are cases in which greed does not pay at all.

Dynamic Planning and Weary Travelers

Here is a problem similar to the minimal spanning tree problem, but one that defies greedy solutions. It too involves a city network, but instead of a lazy railroad contractor we have a weary traveler who is interested in going from one city to another. Though both have a job to do, and both want to minimize the overall cost of getting it done, there is a crucial difference: whereas the contractor has to connect all cities by a subnetwork of rails, the traveler will usually travel only through *some* of the cities. It is clear, therefore, that the traveler is not after a minimal spanning tree. Rather, he is after a **minimal path**; that is, the cheapest trip leading from the start city to the desired destination.

For ease of exposition we assume that all lines in the city graph are **directed**, meaning that if there is a direct connection between two cities it is a one-way connection. Also, we assume that the graph is **connected**, meaning that any city is ultimately reachable from any other. We further assume that the city graph has no cycles, so that a really weary traveler will not be liable to go around in circles, because there will be none to go around in. Such a complex is called a **directed acyclic graph**, or a **DAG** for short.

And so, we are given such a DAG, and the traveler is to travel from A to B. A greedy approach to the problem would construct a path starting at A by continuously adding to the current incomplete path the cheapest edge leading from the city reached so far to some city not yet visited, until the target city B is reached. Figure 4.6 shows an example of applying this natural-looking algorithm to a graph whose minimal path from A to B costs 13 units. The algorithm finds a path of 15 units, which is not as good. Greed does not pay here, as a clever algorithm must be devious enough to take the edge of length 5 to C and then that of length 3 to E, even though these are not the locally best-looking choices.

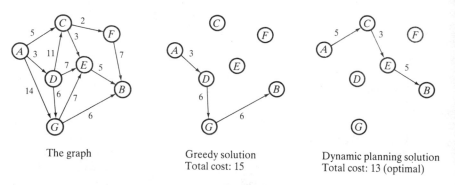

The graph	Greedy solution Total cost: 15	Dynamic planning solution Total cost: 13 (optimal)

Figure 4.6 For weary travelers greed does not pay.

A different, non-greedy algorithmic method, called **dynamic planning**, enables such subtle choices to be made.[†] Dynamic planning is based on a refinement of the rather coarse criterion of immediate greed, and can be described abstractly as follows.

Suppose the solution to some algorithmic problem is to consist of an optimal sequence of choices. As already shown, it is quite possible that

---

[†] Actually, this method is known as dynamic **programming**, not planning, but we have changed terms, both to better reflect the idea behind the method and to avoid a conflict with the algorithmic use of the term 'programming', which refers to the coding of an algorithm for computer execution, as explained in Chapter 3.

simply picking the best-looking choice from among each local set of possibilities will not lead to an optimal sequence. However, it is often the case that an optimal sequence can be obtained by considering all combinations of (a) making a single choice, and (b) finding an optimal subsequence of the choices remaining. For example, in Figure 4.6 the length of the shortest path from A to B is the smallest of the three numbers obtained by first selecting one of the cities C, G and D (those directly reachable from A) and then adding its distance from A to the length of the shortest path leading from it to B. Symbolically, denoting the length of the shortest path from X to B by $L(X)$, we can write:

$$L(A) = \text{minimum of:} \quad 5 + L(C), \quad 14 + L(G), \quad 3 + L(D)$$

(See Figure 4.6.) This means that we can find the optimal path by finding three 'smaller' optimal paths, and then carrying out a few additions and comparisons. This process can then be continued, writing, for example:

$$L(D) = \text{minimum of:} \quad 7 + L(E), \quad 6 + L(G), \quad 11 + L(C)$$

When such derivations yield clauses involving $L(B)$ (i.e., the minimal distance from B to itself) no further development is needed, since even an exhausted traveler knows that $L(B) = 0$, by virtue of the fact that the best way to go from B to B is to just stay where you are.

These observations lead to a dynamic planning algorithm for the general weary traveler problem (sometimes called the **shortest-path problem**).

** If the cities are $C_1, \ldots, C_N$, and the trip is to start at C_1 and end at C_N, the algorithm calls for calculating the optimal partial trip $L(C_I)$, representing the shortest path from C_I to the destination C_N for each 1 between 1 and N. However, $L(C_I)$ is the minimum of all sums of the form:

distance-from-C_I-to-C_K $+ L(C_K)$

where the minimum is taken over all cities C_K to which direct edges lead from C_I. Consequently, since all edges are one way and the graph has no cycles, we can compute all the $L(C_I)$s in this fashion by working *backwards* from B. In Figure 4.6, first calculate $L(F)$ and $L(E)$ directly, yielding 7 and 5; then calculate $L(G)$ as the minimum of 6 and 7 + $L(E)$ (6 in this case); then $L(C)$, $L(D)$, and so on, until finally $L(A)$ is obtained. While doing so, we should also keep track of the backwards path constructed from B to A; it is the optimal path sought for.

As to the actual construction of the algorithm, it is quite tempting to write a *recursive* procedure based on the computation of $L(C_I)$ from the $L(C_K)$s as described above. However, that would be a mistake. The reason is that the same optimal partial path may be needed in more than one 'larger' path, and a naive recursive approach keeps computing it again and again. In Figure 4.6, $L(E)$ is used in the computations of both $L(C)$ and $L(D)$, and the processor carrying out the recursive procedure just outlined will therefore compute it twice. Dynamic planning calls for *iteratively* computing all the $L(C_I)$s in the backwards order, and keeping them stored in a vector, so that once, say, $L(E)$ has been computed for the first time, it can be used repeatedly by simply looking up its value in the vector rather than recomputing it.   * *

Dynamic planning can be thought of as divide-and-conquer taken to the limit: *all* subproblems are solved in an order of increasing magnitude, and the results stored in some data structure to facilitate easy solutions to the larger ones. The method can be applied to many far more elaborate problems, which require data structures more complex than mere vectors to store the partial solutions. The interested reader might want to try to devise a dynamic planning algorithm for the closely related 'traveling salesman' problem described in Chapter 7.

* *

Research on Algorithmic Methods

There are really very few universally accepted paradigms that are general enough to deserve a special name and the title 'algorithmic method', and most of the better-known ones have already been described. Despite this, without particularly aiming at general paradigms, computer scientists are continually searching for better methods to solve increasingly more complex algorithmic problems.

It is somewhat difficult to discuss these attempts further here, since issues of efficiency creep in at a very early stage, and efficiency is not treated until later in the book. Moreover, the notions of concurrency and probabilism, discussed in Chapters 10 and 11, are becoming more and more crucial to recent developments in algorithmic design. We shall therefore have to wait until we have treated these topics before we can discuss other methods for designing good algorithms.

For every matter has its time and method
Ecclesiastes 8: 6

5

The Correctness of Algorithms

OR

Getting It Done Right

behold, I have ... erred exceedingly
I Samuel 26: 21

cause me to understand wherein I have erred
Job 6: 24

- In the early 1960s one of the American spaceships in the Mariner series sent to Venus was lost forever at a cost of millions of dollars, due to a mistake in a flight control computer program.
- In 1981 one of the television stations covering provincial elections in Quebec, Canada, was led by its erroneous computer programs into believing that a small party, originally thought to have no chance at all, was actually leading. This information, and the consequent responses of commentators, were passed on to millions of viewers.

These are just two of numerous tales of software errors, many of which have ended in catastrophes, often with loss of life. The importance of the correctness issue cannot be overestimated. We have been naively assuming throughout that the algorithms and programs we write do precisely what we intend them to do. This has absolutely no justification; in a preliminary manuscript of this book the flowchart of Figure 2.4, which sums salaries of employees earning more than their direct managers, contained an embarrassing error that went undetected for several months. The original version, presented in Figure 5.1, will not always work as desired. More about this example later.

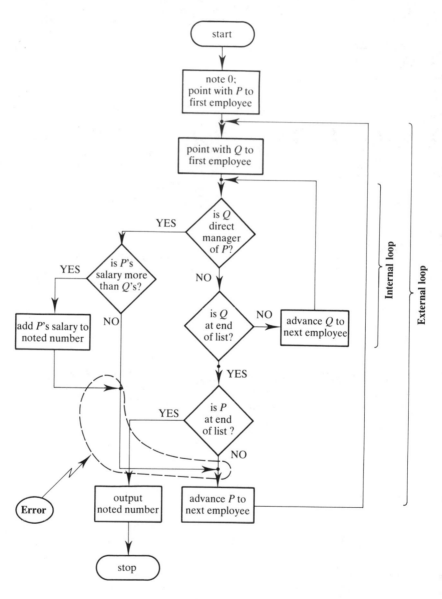

Figure 5.1   Erroneous version of the salary summation flowchart of Figure 2.4.

Language Errors

One of the most frequent kinds of errors occurring in the preparation of computer programs stems from abusing the syntax of the programming language. We met with these in the previous chapter. Writing:

for Y **from** 1 **until** N **do**

instead of:

for Y **from** 1 **to** N **do**

as the language requires, is wrong, but it is not an error in the algorithm. Syntax errors are but a troublesome manifestation of the fact that algorithms carried out by a computer are required to be presented in formal attire.

Compilers and interpreters are made to spot syntax errors, and will notify the programmer, who will typically be able to correct them with little effort. Moreover, and here is where compilers have an edge over interpreters (see Chapter 3), a clever compiler will attempt to *correct* certain kinds of syntax errors on its own, making possible the desired translation into machine language.

A compiler is not limited, as is an interpreter, to looking at one line or one instruction of the program at a time. It is usually also programmed to spot more subtle errors, which, rather than violating local syntactic rules of the language, cause contradictions between possibly distant parts of the program, typically between a definition and an operational instruction. Examples include arithmetical operations applied to non-numerical variables, references to the 150th element of a vector whose indices were defined to range from 1 to 100, and subroutine calls with the wrong number of parameters.

All of these, however, also represent incorrect use of the language. Whether or not a compiler or interpreter catches such an error in advance, an attempt at running the program will fail when the offensive part is reached; the program will be **aborted**, that is, it will be stopped and an appropriate message will be displayed to the user. In contrast to the errors discussed in the next section, and despite the possibly unpleasant nature of program failure, language errors are not considered to be the most serious. Often they are detected automatically, and they can usually be corrected with relative ease.

Logical Errors

Let us recall the 'money'-counting algorithm introduced in Chapter 2. The problem was to count sentences containing occurrences of the word 'money'. The solution consisted of carrying out a search for 'money' followed by a search for the end of the sentence, which, by convention, is always denoted in the input text by the '. ' combination, namely, a period followed by a space. Upon succeeding in both searches, the initially zeroed counter is incremented, and the 'money' search is resumed from the beginning of the next sentence (see Figures 2.5 and 2.6).

What would have happened had the algorithm used '.' (without the space) instead of '. '? Assume for the moment that we are not discussing the algorithm, but its formal version, as a program containing no language errors. It is clear that the new version, which differs from the original only in the absence of the space, contains no language errors either. To an observer, compilers and interpreters included, the new program is perfect. Not only are there no discernible syntax errors, but whenever run on an input text the program dutifully halts and presents a number as the final value of its counter.

Of course, there *is* an error in the new program. It is rooted in the fact that periods can appear *within* sentences. Consider the following:

> The total amount of money in my bank account is $322.56, a truly
> remarkable sum, given my talents for making money. I am a rich man.

When turned loose on this two-sentence text, our modified version will output 2, even though 'money' appears only in the first sentence. The program is fooled by the decimal point appearing in $322.56. The new program is correct as far as the language is concerned, and it actually solves an algorithmic problem, but, unfortunately, not the one we set out to solve. The program contains what we shall be calling a **logical error**, resulting not in a syntactically incorrect or meaningless program, but in a program that does something other than that which it was intended to do.

Logical errors can be notoriously elusive. While it might not be too difficult to notice that a space had been left out of the '. ' combination in the 'money'-counting program, the following mistake is not as easy to find. Let us assume that different pointers to the text are used for the 'money' search and the '. ' search. Clearly, once '. ' has been found and the counter incremented, the first pointer should be forwarded to the position of the second, prior to resuming the search for 'money'. Failing to do so constitutes a logical error that would also yield 2 when run on the previous example, but for a different reason; this time the sentence boundaries are correctly detected, but the counter is incremented twice within the first sentence. (Why?)

Such errors do not indicate that something is wrong with the program *per se*, but that something is wrong with the combination of the program and a particular algorithmic problem; the program, which on its own is fine, does not correctly solve that problem.

Logical errors can be caused by a misunderstanding of the semantics of the programming language ('I thought that $X * Y$ denoted X raised to the power of Y, not X times Y,' or 'I was sure that when a loop of the form **for** Y **from** 1 **to** N is completed the value of Y is N, not $N + 1$'), in which case we might term them **semantic** errors. However, it is far more typical to encounter 'real' logical errors; that is, errors in the logical process used by the designer of the algorithm to solve the algorithmic problem. These have nothing to do with the program written later to implement the algorithm. They represent flaws in the algorithm itself, when considered as a proposed solution to the problem. They are **algorithmic errors**, and are the ones we are interested in here. Failing to forward the 'money' counter to the next sentence is an algorithmic error. So was the erroneous connection, in the early version of Figure 2.4 presented in Figure 5.1, of one of the exits from 'is P's salary more than Q's?' to 'advance P to next employee' instead of to 'is P at end of list?'

Computers Do Not Err

The analogy between algorithms and recipes fails when it comes to issues of correctness. When a cooking or baking endeavor does not succeed there can be two reasons:

(1)   the 'hardware' is to blame, or

(2)   the recipe is imprecise and unclear.

For the most part, the first of these is really the reason, especially after having decided, as we indeed have done, that cooks and bakers are part of the hardware. But if there are problems with a recipe, rather than with the baker, oven, or utensils, they usually have to do with its author's assumptions about the competence of its users. 'Beat egg whites until foamy' requires some knowledge of egg foam on the part of the baker, without which the result of the baking endeavor might not be a chocolate mousse but a chocolate mess!

In contrast to recipes, algorithms written for computer execution end up in a formal unambiguous programming language, which all but eliminates reason (2). Moreover, reason (1) can also be discarded. By and large, computers do *not* make mistakes! A hardware error is such a rarity in modern computers that when our bank statement is in error and the banker mumbles something to the effect that the computer made a mistake, we can be sure that it was not the computer who erred – it was probably one of the bank's employees. Either incorrect data was input to one of the programs, or the program itself, written, of course, by a human, contained an error.

An incorrectly working program is *not* the result of a problem with the computer. If the input data are checked and are found to be correct, the problem is with the program and its underlying algorithm.

Testing and Debugging

Algorithmic errors can go undetected for ages. Sometimes they are never detected. It is quite possible that 'telltale' inputs for which the error produces an incorrect output just do not occur in the life time of the algorithm. Alternatively, such an input might indeed appear, but the incorrect output might never be noticed.

To detect the error in the Figure 5.1 version of Figure 2.4, for example, an input list in which the last employee indeed has a direct manager (and is not, say, the company's president) would be required. (Why?) In a similar vein, the reader should try to figure out why even the better algorithm of Figure 2.4 works correctly only if employees are required to have no more than one direct manager. Since we never imposed this restriction on input lists explicitly when introducing the problem in Chapter 2, the reader has really fallen into the little trap; Figure 2.4, strictly speaking, is also incorrect! Only by either explicitly outlawing employees with multiple managers, or by correcting the algorithm itself (how?) can it be really said to be correct.

Some logical errors show up when the processor cannot carry out an instruction for some unanticipated reason. Attempting to divide X by Y, for example, will fail if Y happens to be 0 at the time. Similarly, failure will result from an attempt to move down a tree from a node that happens to be a leaf (i.e., there is no place to move down to). These are not language errors, and a compiler will, in general, be unable to spot them in advance. They follow from logical flaws in the design of the algorithm. Often the flaw consists simply of forgetting to provide separate treatment for special 'borderline' cases such as zeros (in numbers) and leaves (in trees).

A designer might try out an algorithm on several typical and atypical inputs and not find the error. In fact, a programmer will normally test a program on numerous inputs, sometimes called **test sets**, and will gradually rid it of its language errors and most of its logical errors. He cannot be sure, however, that the program (and its underlying algorithm) is totally error free, simply because most algorithmic problems have infinite sets of legal inputs, and hence infinitely many candidate test sets, each of which has the potential of exposing a new error.

Logical errors, someone once said, are like mermaids. The mere fact that you haven't seen one doesn't mean they don't exist.

The process of repeatedly executing an algorithm, or running a program, with the intention of finding and eliminating errors is called **debugging**. The name has an interesting history. One of the first computers to have been built stopped working one day and was later found to have a large insect jammed in some crucial part of its circuitry. Since then, errors, usually logical errors, are affectionately termed **bugs**.

Debugging a program, especially a complex and lengthy one, can be quite a hefty undertaking. Even if the program is observed to produce the wrong outputs on a certain test case, no indication might be available as to the source of the error. However, there are several techniques for narrowing down the possibilities. A version of the program can be run with artificially inserted instructions for intermediate printouts. These show the debugger's partial results and values during execution. Alternatively, if the program is interpreted, not compiled, its execution can be followed line by line, making it possible to detect suspicious intermediate values, especially when working with an interactive display. We also mentioned programming environments. These support many kinds of testing and simulation tools to aid the algorithm designer and programmer in getting things to work the way they should.

It is necessary to re-emphasize, however, that none of these methods guarantees bug-free algorithms that produce the right outputs on any legal input. As someone once put it, testing and debugging cannot be used to demonstrate the absence of errors in software, only their presence.

⋆   ⋆   ⋆

Infinite Loops

The incorrectness of an algorithm as a solution to an algorithmic problem can thus manifest itself either in an execution that terminates normally but with incorrect outputs, or in an aborted execution.

As if to make things worse, an algorithm set out to run on one of the problem's legal inputs may not terminate at all! Obviously this represents an error too. Infinite computations, or **infinite loops**, as they are sometimes called, can be of oscillating nature, repeating some number of instructions on the same values over and over again, or of non-oscillating, but diverging nature, resulting in ever-larger or ever-smaller values. An example of an oscillating loop is a search routine in which there is no instruction to forward the appropriate pointer; the algorithm keeps searching in the very same area of the data structure. An example of a divergence is a loop that increments X by 1 on each pass and which is instructed to terminate when $X = 100$. If the loop is erroneously reached with an initial value of 17.6 in X, the loop will 'miss' 100 and keep incrementing X for ever (see Figure 5.2). Of course, real computers have limited memories and will generally abort programs of the second kind when the value of X exceeds some ultimate maximum, but the *algorithm* on which the program is based admits the infinite loop nevertheless.

Testing and debugging can also help in detecting potential infinite loops. By printing out intermediate values a debugger may notice suspicious oscillations or abnormal increase or decrease of values, which, if left untouched, might lead to nontermination. As before, there are always more inputs than we can test, hence no such method is guaranteed to find all potential infinite loops.

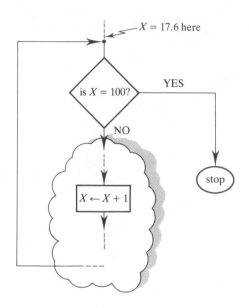

Figure 5.2   An infinitely looping algorithm.

In Chapter 10 we shall discuss algorithms that are not supposed to terminate at all. For these, nontermination is a blessing, and termination indicates the presence of an error. For now, however, a correct algorithm has to terminate normally on all legal inputs and produce the right outputs each time.

Partial and Total Correctness

An algorithmic problem can be concisely characterized as consisting of (1) a set I of legal inputs, and (2) the relationship R between the inputs and the desired outputs. For example, I might contain pairs of the form $\langle N, L \rangle$, where N is a positive integer and L is a list of N words in English, and R might assert that the output L' is a list consisting of the N words in L sorted in ascending lexicographic order. In this way, I and R together serve to completely specify the algorithmic problem that asks for an algorithm A, which, for each input pair $\langle N, L \rangle$ in I, produces an output L' satisfying the relationship to $\langle N, L \rangle$ prescribed by R. In the example, the specified problem is that of sorting the list L.

To facilitate precise treatment of the correctness problem for algorithms, researchers distinguish between two kinds of correctness, depending upon whether termination is or is not included. In one case it is assumed *a priori* that the program terminates and in the other it is not. More precisely, it is said that an algorithm A is **partially correct** with respect to I and R if, for every input set X in I, *if A terminates when run on X then* the relationship R holds between X and the resulting output set. Thus, a partially correct sorting algorithm might not terminate on all legal lists, but whenever it does, a correctly sorted list is the result. We say that A **terminates** on I if A terminates when run on any input in I. Both these notions together yield a **totally correct** algorithm, which correctly solves the algorithmic problem for every legal input: the process of running A on any input X in I indeed terminates and produces outputs satisfying R (see Figure 5.3).

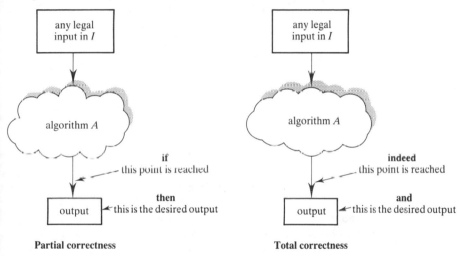

Figure 5.3   Partial and total correctness.

The Need for Proving Correctness

We now know exactly what we would like to establish when confronted with an algorithmic problem and a candidate solution, and we have various testing and debugging techniques to help us in doing so. However, none of these techniques is foolproof, and just like the examples quoted at the beginning of the chapter, computer science folklore is full of stories of catastrophes, some of them fatal, others causing the loss of incredible amounts of money, and all following from algorithmic errors, usually in large and complex software systems.

Claiming that a particular algorithm is correct with respect to an algorithmic problem is perhaps less profound than claiming that mermaids are imaginary, but it can be so crucial as to have many lives depend on it, or many fortunes. It suffices to think of computer systems that control nuclear weapons or multibillion dollar banking systems to appreciate the point.

However, it is not only the many publicized cases of errors that are of concern, nor the many, many more that go unknown. It is commonly believed that more than 70% (!) of the effort and cost of developing a complex software system is devoted, in one way or another, to error correcting. This includes delays caused by misconceived specifications (i.e., unclear and imprecise definitions of the algorithmic problems), extensive testing and debugging of the algorithms themselves, and, worst of all, changes and rewrites of already working systems (generally termed **maintenance**), as a result of newly discovered bugs.

Referring to large commercially used software systems, the situation has been described nicely by saying that software is released for use, not when it is known to be correct, but when the rate of discovering new errors slows down to one that managers consider acceptable.

This situation is clearly bad. We need ways of *proving* that an algorithm is correct. After exhibiting such a proof no more bugs will show up. No one asks whether there might exist some 'undiscovered' equilateral triangle having unequal angles. Someone proved once and for all that *all* equilateral triangles have equal angles, and from then on no doubts remained.

Can anything be done to facilitate such proofs? Can the computer itself help verify the correctness of our algorithms? Actually, what we would like most would be an **automatic verifier**; namely, some sort of super algorithm that would accept as inputs a description of an algorithmic problem P and an algorithm A that is proposed as a solution, and would determine if indeed A solves P. Perhaps it would also point out the errors if the answer was no (see Figure 5.4). In Chapter 8 we shall see that in a very strong sense this is but wishful thinking. No such verifier can be constructed.

For now, however, let us ignore the issue of getting a computer to help. Can we *ourselves* prove our algorithms correct? Is there any way we can use formal, mathematical techniques to become fully convinced of the correctness of our algorithms? Here, fortunately, we have better news.

Invariants and Convergents

There do indeed exist methods for program verification. In fact, in a certain technical sense, any correct algorithm can be rigorously demonstrated to be correct![†] Before illustrating with an example, let us say something about the proof methods themselves.

[†] This fact notwithstanding, in Chapter 8 we shall see that it is impossible to find such proofs algorithmically. All we are saying here is that if the program is correct there is a proof of that fact. At present, we claim nothing about whether such proofs are easy to come by.

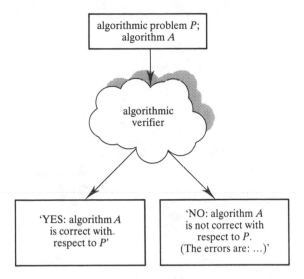

Figure 5.4   A hypothetical algorithmic verifier.

In trying to establish *partial* correctness, we are not interested in showing that certain desirable things *do* happen, but in showing that certain undesirable things *do not*. We do not care whether execution ever reaches the end point, but that if it does we will not be in a situation where the outputs differ from the expected ones. Accordingly, we wish to capture the behavior of the algorithm by making careful statements about what it is doing at certain points. To prove partial correctness we thus attach **intermediate assertions** to various **checkpoints** in the algorithm's text. Attaching an assertion to a checkpoint means that we believe that whenever execution reaches the point in question, in any execution of the algorithm on a legal input, the assertion will be true. This, of course, includes points that are reached many times within a single execution, notably, those within loops. For this reason such assertions are commonly called **invariants**; they remain true no matter how often they are reached.

For example, a sorting algorithm might be such that, at a certain point in its text, exactly half of the input list is sorted, in which case we might attach the assertion 'half the list is sorted' to that point. It is more typical, however, that invariants depend on the values of the variables available at the checkpoint. Thus, to some point we might attach the assertion 'the partial list from the first location to the Xth is sorted', where X is a variable that increases as more of the list gets sorted.

The initial assertion, namely, the one attached to the starting point of the algorithm, is typically formulated to capture the requirements on legal inputs in the set I, and, likewise, the final assertion, the one attached to the ending point, captures the relationship R of outputs to inputs (see Figure 5.5).

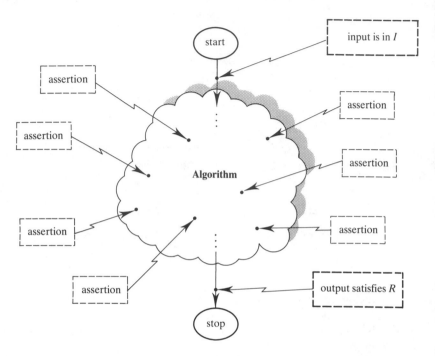

Figure 5.5   Annotating an algorithm with invariants.

Now, suppose we can establish that all the assertions we have attached are indeed invariants, meaning that they are true whenever reached. Then, in particular, the final assertion is also an invariant. But this means that the algorithm is partially correct. (Why?) Hence all we have to do is establish the invariance of our assertions. This is done by establishing certain local properties of our assertions, sometimes called **verification conditions**, to the effect that proceeding locally from checkpoint to checkpoint does not bring about any violations of the invariance properties. This approach to proving correctness is sometimes called the **invariant assertion method**, or **Floyd's method**, after one of its inventors.

How do we go about choosing checkpoints and intermediate assertions, and how do we establish the verification conditions? The example given in the next section should shed some light on these questions.

When considering termination, our main interest is in showing that something good eventually happens (not that bad things do not); namely, that the algorithm indeed reaches its end point and terminates successfully. To prove such a statement we use checkpoints as before, but we now find some quantity depending on the algorithm's variables and data structures, and show it to **converge**. By this we mean that the quantity keeps decreasing as execution proceeds from one checkpoint to another, but it cannot decrease forever – we need to show that there is some bound below which it can never go. Hence there is no way for the algorithm to run forever, since the convergent would then have to decrease forever, contradicting this bound.

In a sorting algorithm, for example, the number of elements not yet in their final positions in the sorted list might be shown to decrease as execution proceeds, but never to be less than 0. When that number reaches 0 the algorithm presumably terminates.

How does one choose such **convergents**, and how are they shown to converge? Again, an example will help to answer these questions.

*   *   *

Reversing a Symbol String: An Example

The input to the following problem is a string S of symbols, say a word or text in English. The goal is to produce the reverse image of S, denoted **reverse**(S), consisting of the symbols of S in reverse order. Thus, for example:

> **reverse**('ajj\$dt8') = '8td\$jja'

Figure 5.6 shows a simple flowchart of an algorithm A that solves the problem. It uses the unique empty string Λ consisting of no symbols at all (which we might denote by the empty quotes ''), and the functions **head**(X) and **tail**(X), which, for any string X, yield, respectively, the first symbol of X and the string X with its head removed. We thus have:

> **head**('ajj\$dt8') = 'a'

and:

> **tail**('ajj\$dt8') = 'jj\$dt8'

Also, we use '·' for string concatenation, or attachment. Thus:

> 'ajj\$dt8' · 'tdd9tr' = 'ajj\$dt8tdd9tr'

We can also verify that for every string X:

> **head**(X) · **tail**(X) = X

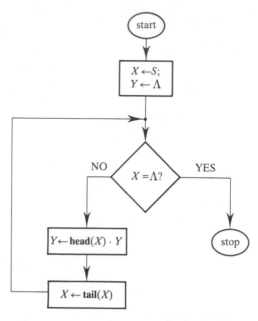

Figure 5.6   A flowchart for reversing a symbol string.

The algorithm works by repeatedly 'peeling off' the symbols of S one by one, attaching each in turn to the *front* of the newly constructed string Y. The new string Y starts out initially as empty. The procedure ends when there is nothing left to peel off S. In order not to destroy S in the process, the peeling off is done in a variable X, which is initialized to the value S.

The claim is that this algorithm correctly produces **reverse**(S) in the variable Y. That is, if the set I of legal inputs contains all the infinitely many (finite) symbol strings S, and the relationship R specifies the connection between any such S and its output Y by the formula:

$$Y = \textbf{reverse}(S)$$

then the algorithm A of Figure 5.6 is totally correct with respect to I and R.

We shall first establish that A is partially correct, using the intermediate assertion method, and then, separately, that it also terminates. We therefore first show that if A happens to terminate on an input string S, then it produces **reverse**(S) in Y.

To this end, consider Figure 5.7, in which three checkpoints have been identified. As already explained, Assertion 1 captures the requirements on the input set I, and Assertion 3 embodies the desired relationship R between the input string S and the output Y.

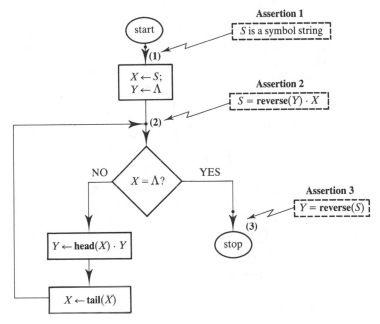

Figure 5.7   An annotated flowchart for reversing a symbol string.

The significance of Figure 5.7, however, is in Assertion 2, which is supposed to capture the situation just prior to either going around the loop once again, or terminating. Assertion 2 states that at checkpoint (2) the current values of X and Y together make up the original string S, in the sense that Y contains some initial portion of S in reverse, and X contains the rest of S unreversed. Hence, concatenating **reverse**(Y) with X yields S.

We want to show that all three assertions are invariants, meaning that in each execution of A on any legal input they are true whenever reached. The trick is to consider all possible direct paths that the processor might take from checkpoint to checkpoint. In this case, given the form of this particular flowchart, there are three possibilities: (1) to (2), (2) to (3), and (2) to (2) (see Figure 5.8). The first of these is traversed exactly once in any execution of A; the second is traversed at most once, since at its end the algorithm terminates; the third can be traversed many times. (How many?) Notice that the algorithmic segments corresponding to these paths are *loop free*. They consist of simple sequences of elementary instructions and tests, and, as we shall see, can be dealt with quite easily.

We now want to show that, for each of these simple segments, if we assume that the assertion attached to its start is true, and that the segment is actually traversed, then the assertion attached to its end will also be true when reached. In this way, the invariance of all three assertions will follow,

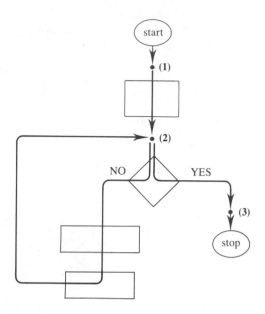

Figure 5.8   The three paths through the **reverse** algorithm.

because any legal execution of A consists of a sequence of segments separated by checkpoints (see Figure 5.9). If the truth of the start assertion of each of these segments implies the truth of the end assertion, and if the first assertion of the entire sequence is the one corresponding to the input being legal, and is hence assumed to be true to begin with, then truth of assertions propagates along the entire sequence, making all assertions true as execution proceeds. In particular, as explained, the final Assertion 3 will be true upon termination, establishing A's partial correctness.

Figure 5.9   A typical execution sequence of the **reverse** algorithm.

To summarize, all we have to show now is the propagation of truth along the simple paths between checkpoints.

**   Consulting Figures 5.7 and 5.8, we find that there are three statements to prove:

$(1 \rightarrow 2)$:   for any string S, after carrying out the two instructions $X \leftarrow S$; $Y \leftarrow \Lambda$, the equality $S = \textbf{reverse}(Y) \cdot X$ will hold.

$(2 \rightarrow 3)$:   if $S = \textbf{reverse}(Y) \cdot X$, and $X = \Lambda$, then $Y = \textbf{reverse}(S)$.

$(2 \rightarrow 2)$: if $S = \textbf{reverse}(Y) \cdot X$, and $X \neq \Lambda$, then after carrying out the instructions $Y \leftarrow \textbf{head}(X) \cdot Y$; $X \leftarrow \textbf{tail}(X)$, the same equality, namely $S = \textbf{reverse}(Y) \cdot X$, will hold for the new values *of* X and Y.

Consider $(1 \rightarrow 2)$. After carrying out $X \leftarrow S$ the variable X has the value S, and after carrying out $Y \leftarrow \Lambda$ too, the variable Y holds the empty string. It is therefore clear that $\textbf{reverse}(Y) = \textbf{reverse}(\Lambda) = \Lambda$, and so $\textbf{reverse}(Y) \cdot X = \Lambda \cdot X = X$. The equality required to hold after carrying out the two instructions is thus simply $S = X$, which indeed does hold as mentioned. It is not too difficult to see that in a similar way statement $(2 \rightarrow 3)$ holds too.

We are left with having to show that $(2 \rightarrow 2)$ is true; namely, that if Assertion 2 holds true and the loop is traversed once then it remains true thereafter. Well, let us assume that $X \neq \Lambda$ so that, in particular, X has a head and a tail – empty strings have neither), and that S is exactly $\textbf{reverse}(Y) \cdot X$. We now carry out the two instructions $Y \leftarrow \textbf{head}(X) \cdot Y$; $X \leftarrow \textbf{tail}(X)$, and want to show that the same equality holds after doing so. But the new value of X after executing these instructions is the tail of its previous value, and the new Y is the head of the previous X concatenated with the previous Y. Hence, what we really have to show is that for any three strings, X, S and Y (where X is nonempty), if $S = \textbf{reverse}(Y) \cdot X$ then $S = \textbf{reverse}(\textbf{head}(X) \cdot Y) \cdot \textbf{tail}(X)$. This amounts to saying that for any Y and nonempty X, $\textbf{reverse}(Y) \cdot X = \textbf{reverse}(\textbf{head}(X) \cdot Y) \cdot \textbf{tail}(X)$. Figure 5.10 shows schematically why this equality indeed holds.   **

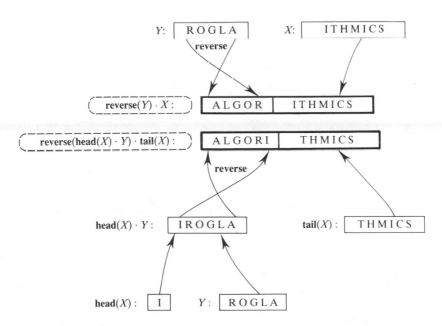

Figure 5.10 $\textbf{reverse}(Y) \cdot X = \textbf{reverse}(\textbf{head}(X) \cdot Y) \cdot \textbf{tail}(X)$.

This concludes the proof that the algorithm is partially correct. We now have to show that it terminates for any input string S. To that end, let us consider checkpoint (2) again. The only way an execution of the algorithm might not terminate is by passing through point (2) infinitely often. That is shown to be impossible by exhibiting a convergent (i.e., a converging function) which, on the one hand, decreases each time checkpoint (2) is revisited, but, on the other hand, cannot become ever smaller.

The convergent that works in our case is simply the length of the string X. Each time the loop is traversed X is made shorter by precisely one symbol, since it becomes the tail of its previous value. However, its length cannot be less than 0 because when X is of length 0 (i.e., it is the empty string) the loop is not traversed further and the algorithm terminates.

This concludes the proof that the algorithm A is totally correct. It might occur to the reader that this proof is not worth the trouble, since the correctness of the program seems obvious enough, and the proof appears to be quite technical and symbol ridden. This is indeed true here, and the example was chosen to illustrate the proof itself, not so much the need for it in the first place. Nevertheless, it is not too difficult to imagine a version of the same algorithm with some subtle bug in one of the extremal cases, or a more complicated version where, say, the even-numbered positions are to be reversed and the odd-numbered ones not. In these cases, verifying the program by just looking at it is dangerously inadequate and formal proofs are a necessity.

As an aside, we need not work with flowcharts when verifying correctness. Although the visual nature of a flowchart is quite helpful in choosing checkpoints and reasoning about the dynamics of the algorithm, there are straightforward ways of attaching intermediate assertions to points in standard textual formats of an algorithm.

What's in a Proof?

The correctness proof given in the last section is one of the simplest of its kind, without being completely trivial. This is rather discouraging, to say the least.

Let us discuss its constituents. Basic to both the partial correctness and termination proofs was the selection of checkpoints in the text of the algorithm. These, in general, consist of the start and stop points, and sufficiently many intermediate locations so that every loop of the algo-rithm's text contains at least one.

Having chosen checkpoints, we must attach intermediate assertions to them, and their invariance has to be established by proving the local verification conditions. These involve only loop-free algorithmic segments because we were careful to 'break open' all of the loops with checkpoints.

We also have to exhibit a convergent and show that it actually converges. But which of these activities can be automated algorithmically? In other words, for which can we expect to get considerable help from a computer?

Finding a set of checkpoints to cover each of the loops, even some kind of minimal set, can be fully automated. Under certain technical conditions, much of the local checking of verification conditions, as well as the local decrease in the value of a convergent, can be automated too. However, the heart of such proofs is to be found elsewhere. It lies in the *choice* of the appropriate invariants and convergents. Here it can be shown that there is *no* algorithm that can automatically find invariants and convergents that 'work', meaning that they satisfy the local conditions needed for producing the proof (this issue is taken up in more detail in Chapter 8). The right choice of an invariant is a delicate and subtle art, and can demand more ingenuity than that involved in designing the algorithm in the first place. Indeed, the algorithm designer can possess the right kind of intuition required to produce a good algorithm, but might be at a loss when asked to formulate precisely 'what is going on' at a certain point therein.

Paradoxically, adequate invariants and convergents always exist, so that, as mentioned earlier, a correct algorithm can, in principle, always be proved correct. This seems to contradict our statements to the effect that the verification process cannot be automated, and that an algorithm designer might not be able to prove correctness. It does not. And the key is the phrase 'in principle'. Although proofs exist, they cannot always be found by a computer – humans are often also at a loss. For large and complex software systems, **after-the-fact** verification is all but impossible, simply because of the unmanageable magnitude and intricacy of the task. When presented with a large piece of software that has been endlessly changed, corrected, patched, and updated, providing formal and precise assertions that completely characterize its behavior at various points is essentially out of the question.

After-the-fact verification is practical only for relatively small, well-structured, coherent algorithms. In other cases an alternative method, called **as-you-go** verification, to be discussed later, has to be adopted.

*   *   *

The Towers of Hanoi: An Example

The foregoing discussion notwithstanding, verification is at times somewhat easier than anticipated. It might appear that the subtle nature of recursion would render the verification of recursive subroutines more difficult than that of mere iterative algorithms. This is not always so.

Recall the Towers of Hanoi problem and the following recursive solution, presented in Chapter 2:

subroutine **move** N **from** X **to** Y **using** Z:

(1) if $N = 1$ then output '$X \rightarrow Y$';

(2) otherwise (i.e., if $N > 1$) do the following:
     (2.1) call **move** $N-1$ **from** X **to** Z **using** Y;
     (2.2) output '$X \rightarrow Y$';
     (2.3) call **move** $N-1$ **from** Z **to** Y **using** X;

(3) return.

That this routine terminates for every N (where the values of X, Y, and Z are A, B, and C in some order) is not too difficult to see: the only kind of infinite computation at all possible is obtained by performing an infinitely deep cascade of recursive calls. However, on observing that the depth of the tree of recursive calls (see Figure 2.8) cannot be greater than N, since the only things that happen to N during execution are a decrease by 1 whenever a lower level recursive call is executed, we find that N must 'hit' the value 1 at some point. But $N = 1$ signifies the **escape clause** of the recursion, causing not another, deeper recursive call, but a simple instruction followed by a *return*, which entails *ascending* the tree. Consequently, the tree of recursive calls is finite and execution must terminate.

Notice that this termination proof does not require any 'understanding' of the workings of the routine; we only used superficial observations about the behavior of N and the presence of an appropriate escape clause.

To prove partial correctness, we use a variant of the intermediate assertion method that befits the non-iterative nature of recursive algorithms. Rather than trying to formulate the local situation at a given point, we try to formulate our expectations of the recursive routine in the most general terms. This, as shown below, is then used in a cyclic-looking, but perfectly sound, fashion to support itself! Here is a possible formulation for the **move** routine.

For any N, the following statement, call it (S), holds true:

> Whenever the ring names A, B, and C are assigned in some order to the variables X, Y, and Z, a terminating execution of the call **move** N **from** X **to** Y **using** Z lists a sequence of ring-moving instructions, which, if started (and followed faithfully) in any legal configuration of the rings and pegs in which at least the N smallest rings are on peg X, correctly moves those N rings from X to Y, possibly using Z as temporary storage, according to the rules of the Towers of Hanoi problem. Moreover, the sequence leaves all other rings untouched.

If we can show that (S) is true for all N, we have established the partial correctness of our solution, since we are interested particularly in a call to **move** N **from** A **to** B **using** C, where A holds N rings and B and C are empty.

In this case, (S) is but a rephrasing of the requirements of the problem, as the reader can verify.

    * *   Statement (S) is established by the classical method of **mathematical induction**. We first show directly that (S) is true for $N = 1$ and then show that under the assumption that it is true for some given $N - 1$ (where $N - 1$ is at least 1, so that N is at least 2), it must also be true for N itself. It follows that (S) must be true for all N, since the separately proven truth for the case $N = 1$ implies truth for $N = 2$ which, in turn, implies truth for $N = 3$ and so on, *ad infinitum*.

    That (S) holds for $N = 1$ is trivial: asserting (S) is simply asserting that a sequence is produced which correctly moves the topmost ring from X to Y. This is immediately seen to be accomplished by the $N = 1$ case of the routine.

    Assume now that (S) holds for some arbitrary $N - 1$. We now have to show that it holds also for N. Accordingly, let us assume that a call to the **move** routine has just been made with the number N, and some assignment of pegs A, B, and C to the variables X, Y, and Z. The three pegs contain a legal arrangement of rings, with peg X containing at least the N smallest rings (see Figure 5.11(a)). Now, since the value of N is 2 or more, the first thing the routine does is to call itself recursively on line (2.1) with parameter $N - 1$. By the **inductive hypothesis**, that is, by our assumption (S) on calls to the routine with $N - 1$, that call, if completed successfully, will correctly and legally move the topmost $N - 1$ rings from X to Z, leaving everything else unchanged (see Figure 5.11(b)). However, since X was guaranteed to contain at least N rings to begin with, there is still at least one ring left on X after the call on line (2.1) is completed, and the instruction on line (2.2) moves that ring directly to Y (see Figure 5.11(c)). The inductive hypothesis applied to the next call, on line (2.3), can now be easily seen to complete the picture by moving the $N - 1$ rings from Z to Y, right on top of the single ring that was moved separately (see Figure 5.11(d)).

    The reader should go through this proof carefully, noticing why the legality of all moves is also guaranteed throughout the process, not only the final outcome. Also, it is easy to see, using the inductive hypothesis for the two calls, that no rings other than the top N ones on peg X are touched by this procedure, so that (S) has been established in full for this call with N, assuming it for calls with $N - 1$. As mentioned, this establishes the truth of (S) for all N.   * *

The partial correctness of the recursive Towers of Hanoi algorithm is thus proven, and since we have already proved termination, the algorithm is totally correct.

More on the Towers of Hanoi: A Simple Iterative Solution

In Chapter 2 we promised to exhibit an extremely simple-to-execute iterative algorithm for the Towers of Hanoi problem. The reason for discussing it here, rather than in Chapter 2, is rooted in the fact that it is not quite clear why it works. In contrast to the recursive solution, there seems to be no natural argument as to its correctness. In particular, there seems to be no obvious invariant for its loop. However, there is an invariant – all correct iterative algorithms have invariants – but in this particular case formulating an invariant is not the best way to go about proving correctness. There is a more direct proof that uses mathematical induction on N to show that the iterative and recursive algorithms are really *equivalent*. In fact, they produce exactly the same sequences of moves. The proof will not be presented here, but the interested reader is invited to try to construct it.

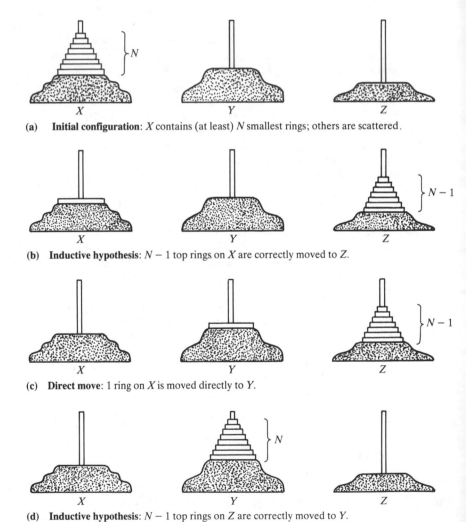

(a)   **Initial configuration**: X contains (at least) N smallest rings; others are scattered.

(b)   **Inductive hypothesis**: $N - 1$ top rings on X are correctly moved to Z.

(c)   **Direct move**: 1 ring on X is moved directly to Y.

(d)   **Inductive hypothesis**: $N - 1$ top rings on Z are correctly moved to Y.

Figure 5.11   Partial correctness of the Towers of Hanoi: proving N from $N-1$.

To describe the algorithm let us assume that the three pegs are arranged in a circle, and that all N rings are piled on one of them (the names of the pegs are unimportant). Here is the algorithm:

(1) do the following repeatedly, until, prior to step (1.2), all rings are correctly piled on some other peg:
   (1.1) move the smallest ring from its current peg to the next peg in clockwise order;
   (1.2) make the only move possible that does not involve the smallest ring.

It should be clear that step (1.2) is well defined and unambiguous, since one of the pegs has to have the smallest ring on top, and of the two remaining pegs one has a smaller ring on top than the other; hence the only move not involving the smallest ring is transferring that smaller ring to the other peg.

This algorithm can be executed easily by a small child, even if many rings are involved. Notice, in passing, that if N is odd the rings will end up on the next peg in clockwise order, and in counterclockwise order if N is even. This fact is crucial to the proof.

* * *

After-the-Fact vs. As-You-Go Verification

The alternative to proving correctness of an already completed algorithm is to develop the algorithm and proof hand in hand. The idea is to match the disciplined, gradual, step-by-step construction of the algorithm or software system with the gradual construction of proof segments, which will ultimately accumulate to form a complete proof of the entire system.

Clearly, this is easier said than done. However, an obvious mechanism that encourages such practice is the subroutine. As explained in Chapter 2, a complex program can be built carefully out of many routines, some nested inside others, resulting in a well-structured and stratified piece of software. Good design practice dictates that each routine be carefully analyzed in terms of its overall purpose, and then verified as a separate entity. In principle, once this has been done, the entire system will also have been verified. The reason is that what has been proved about a given routine can be used to prove things about other routines that call it. If, for example, we verify that the **search-for** routine of Chapter 2 (cf. Figure 2.6) correctly finds X in an input text T and outputs the counter if it reaches the end of T, then that proof could be used to verify the 'money'-finding algorithm.

Here too there are many possible pitfalls. It is far from easy to correctly identify the **interface** of a routine and its intended behavior under all circumstances, but good algorithmic design recommends that we do not construct a subroutine unless we can do so. Of course, a *recursive* routine requires a cyclic-looking verification process, which involves assuming it to be correct for its self-calls, as was done for the Towers of Hanoi. Obviously, this process is not always as straightforward as it sounds.

In short, good stepwise algorithmic design, coupled with informative and precise documentation of design decisions, can form the basis of the construction of verified software, by breaking up the overall proof into pieces that reflect the breakup of the software itself. When *concurrency* is introduced into algorithms, as is done in Chapter 10, things become more difficult, and even a small and innocent-looking algorithm can cause formidable problems when it comes to verification. We shall discuss that bridge, but not quite cross it, when we reach it.

Interactive Verification and Proof Checking

Despite the fact that automatic algorithmic verification is out of the question, there is much that can be done with a computer's aid. We shall only examine a number of issues briefly here since most of them are in rather premature stages of research and development.

A computer can be programmed to help in after-the-fact verification. A possible scenario involves an interactive program that attempts to verify a given algorithm with respect to a formal description of the algorithmic problem. Every now and then it asks the human user to supply it with, say, a candidate invariant (recall that this is the kind of task it cannot, in general, do on its own). It then goes ahead and tries to establish the relevant verification conditions, moving on to additional points in the algorithm if it succeeds, or backtracking to previous decisions if it fails.

Since the whole procedure is interactive, the human user can stop it whenever it seems to be going off in wrong directions, and attempt to put it back on track. The computer is being used here as a fast and meticulous apprentice, checking the details of local logical conditions, keeping track of past invariants, assertions, and comments, and never tiring of trying out another possibility.

This idea can also be used to aid in as-you-go verification efforts. Here, previously established proofs of portions of the algorithm (say subroutines) can be kept track of by the automatic apprentice, and used in an algorithmic attempt to verify larger portions (say calling routines). Such an interactive system can be part of the entire programming environment, which might include the editing, debugging, and testing tools too. A user might be interested in verifying some of the smaller and better identified algorithms in the software system under development, and leave the less manageable parts to be debugged and tested conventionally.

Another possibility for computer-aided verification is in **proof checking**. Here, a human produces what seems to be a proof, invariants, convergents and all, and a computer is programmed to generate and verify the lengthy sequences of logical and symbolic manipulations that constitute the fully fledged proof.

Efforts of the kinds described here are under way, and reasonably good systems exist that can aid in the design of moderately complex algorithms. Many problems, however, remain, and standard use of smooth and widely applicable verification aids is still far off.

*   *   *

Research on Algorithmic Correctness

Considerable research in computer science is devoted to the subject matter of this chapter. Researchers are interested in developing new and useful methods for verification, and the invariant and convergent methods are examples of only the most basic of these. Different language constructs trigger different methods, as will become apparent with the introduction of concurrency and probabilism in Chapters 10 and 11.

One issue we have not treated at all is that of **specification languages**, sometimes called **assertion languages.** How do we specify the algorithmic problem formally? How do we write down the intermediate assertions so that they are unambiguous and lend themselves to algorithmic manipulation? The alternatives reflect not only in pragmatics, but also in the underlying mathematics. For some choices of an assertion language, establishing the local verification conditions of loop-free segments between checkpoints is algorithmically feasible, whereas for others the problem can be shown to be as hard as the global verification problem itself, and hence not solvable algorithmically. In both cases people are interested in developing **theorem-proving** techniques which form the basis of condition checking algorithms.

Many research topics are relevant both to verification and debugging, and to efficient and informative compilation. A good example is **data-flow analysis**, whereby algorithms and methodologies are developed to symbolically follow the flow of data in an algorithm. This means that the possible changes a variable can undergo during execution are analyzed without actually running the algorithm. Such analysis can reveal potential errors, such as out-of-bounds indexes for arrays, possible zero values for divisors in arithmetic operations, etc.

Researchers are also interested in more complex properties of algorithms. At times it may be important to know whether two algorithms are *equivalent*. One reason for this might be the availability of a simple but inefficient algorithm, and a designer's candidate for a more efficient but more intricate algorithm. The desire here is to prove that both algorithms will terminate on the same class of inputs and produce identical results.

One of the approaches to the investigation of such richer classes of algorithmic properties is to formulate **logics of programs**, or algorithmic logics, which are analogous to classical systems of mathematical logic, but which enable us to reason about algorithms and their effects. Whereas classical systems are sometimes called static, algorithmic logics are **dynamic** in nature; the truth of statements made in these formalisms depends not only on the present state of the world (as in the statement 'it is raining'), but on the relationship between the present state and other hypothetical ones.

As an example, consider the basic construct of such **dynamic logics**:

after(A, F)

which is taken to mean that after executing algorithm A the assertion F will necessarily be true. The assertion F might state that the list L is sorted, in which case the statement **after**(A, F) can be used to formalize the partial correctness of A as a sorting routine. The power of such a construct, however, is in the possibility of using it more than once in a statement and combining it with other logical objects. Consider the following, where '$\rightarrow$' stands for 'implies':

if $F1 \rightarrow$ **after**$(A, F2)$ and $F2 \rightarrow$ **after**$(B, F3)$
then $F1 \rightarrow$ **after**$(A;B, F3)$

This statement asserts that if (1) whenever $F1$ is true $F2$ is true after executing A, and if also (2) whenever $F2$ is true $F3$ is true after executing B, then we can conclude (3) whenever $F1$ is true $F3$ is true after executing $A;B$ (that is, A followed immediately by B). This statement might seem obvious, but it is quite subtle. It actually forms the mathematical justification for inserting intermediate assertions into an algorithm. $F2$ can be thought of as an intermediate assertion attached to the point separating A from B, and the statement says that establishing the local conditions on A and B separately amounts to establishing the more global condition on $A;B$.

In such logics, many statements of this kind can be made and proved, thus placing the theory of algorithmic verification on a sound mathematical basis. Moreover, within such frameworks, using methods and results from several branches of classical logic, we can investigate questions concerning the feasibility of automating proof methods for termination, correctness, equivalence, and the like.

Another promising line of research is concerned with automatic or semiautomatic algorithmic **synthesis**. Here the interest is in synthesizing a working algorithm or program from a specification of the algorithmic problem. As with verification, the general synthesis problem is algorithmically unsolvable, but parts of the process can be aided by a computer.

One of the issues relevant to both synthesis and equivalence proofs is that of **program transformations**, in which parts of an algorithm or program are transformed in ways that preserve equivalence. For example, we might be interested in such transformations in order to make an algorithm comply with the rules of some programming language (for example, replacing recursion by iteration when the language does not allow recursion) or for efficiency purposes, as illustrated in the Chapter 6.

Research in the fields of correctness and logics of algorithms blends nicely with research on the semantics of programming languages. It is impossible to prove anything about a program without a rigorous and unambiguous meaning for that program. The more complex the algorithms we use, the more difficult it is to provide them with semantics, and the more difficult it is to devise methods of proof and to investigate them using algorithmic logics.

The Four-Color Theorem

It seems appropriate to close this chapter with a story of some philosophical interest. The **four-color problem** was formulated in 1852, and for about 120 years was considered to be one of the most interesting open problems in all of mathematics. It involves maps, of the kind found in an atlas: diagrams consisting of partitions of a finite portion of the plane by closed regions signifying countries.

Let us assume we want to color such a map, associating a color with each country, but in such a way that no two countries that share part of a border will be colored with the same color. (Figure 5.12 shows a legal coloring of a sample map; notice that two colors sharing only a point may have the same color.) How many colors are necessary to color any map?

Figure 5.12   Coloring a map.

At first sight it seems that we can construct increasingly intricate maps that require ever-larger numbers of colors. When we play with some examples, however, it turns out that four colors always suffice. The four-color problem asks whether this is always true. On the one hand, no one could *prove* that four colors were sufficient to color any map, but, on the other hand, no one was able to exhibit a map requiring five.

Over the years many people worked on the problem, and many deep and beautiful results emerged in the branch of mathematics called **topology**. A couple of 'proofs' that four colors suffice were published, but were later shown to contain subtle errors. Then, in 1976, the problem was finally solved by two mathematicians. They proved what is now known as the **four-color theorem**, which asserts that four colors do indeed suffice.

What has this got to do with us? Well, the 1976 proof was achieved with the aid of a computer. The proof can be viewed as consisting, very roughly, of two parts. In the first, the two researchers used several previously established results, with some additional mathematical reasoning, to prove that the general problem could be reduced to showing that a finite number of special cases, possessing certain properties, could be colored with four colors. Computer programs were then written to meticulously generate all such cases (there turned out to be about 1700 of them) and to go through them all in order to find a four-coloring. The theorem was established when the programs terminated, answering the question positively: all 1700 cases were found to be four-colorable.

Can we put the traditional Q.E.D. (standing for *quod erat demonstrandum*, freely translated as 'that which was to be proved') at the end of the proof? The problem is that no one has ever verified the programs used in the proof. It is quite possible that the algorithms constructed to carry out the subtle case generation were flawed. Not only that, no one has ever verified the correctness of the compiler used to translate the programs into machine-executable code. No one has verified any of the other relevant system programs that could influence the correct running of the programs, and for that matter (though this is not our concern here) no one has verified that the hardware was working the way it should.

In actuality, the mathematics community has accepted the theorem. Possibly relevant to this is the fact that since 1976 a number of additional proofs have appeared, all of which use a computer, but some of which need to check only a smaller and more manageable set of cases, and use shorter and clearer programs. The philosophical question, however, remains: will absolute mathematical truth, as opposed to practical computer applications, be allowed to depend on the somewhat doubtful performance of unverified software?

let thy word be verified
II Chronicles 6: 17

6

The Efficiency of Algorithms

OR

Getting It Done Cheaply

When asked to construct a bridge over a river, it is easy to construct an 'incorrect' one. The bridge might not be wide enough for the required lanes, it might not be strong enough to carry rush-hour traffic, or it might not reach the other side at all! However, even if it is 'correct', in the sense that it fully satisfies the operational requirements, not every candidate design for the bridge will be acceptable. It is possible that the design calls for too much manpower, or too many materials or components. It might also require far too much time to bring to completion. In other words, although it will result in a good bridge, a design might be too *expensive*.

The field of algorithmics is susceptible to similar problems. An algorithm might be too expensive, and hence unacceptable. And so, while Chapter 5 was devoted to proving that *incorrect* algorithms are bad, and that methods are needed for establishing algorithmic correctness, this chapter argues that even a *correct* algorithm might leave much to be desired.

Since manpower and other related costs are not relevant here, we are left with two criteria for measuring economy – materials and time. In computer science these are termed the **complexity measures** of **memory space** (or simply **space**) and **time**. The first of these is measured by the number of variables, and the number and sizes of the data structures used in executing the algorithm. The other is measured by the number of elementary actions carried out by the processor in such an execution.

Both the space and the time required by an algorithm typically differ from input to input, and, accordingly, the performance of an algorithm reflects the way these resources are consumed as the inputs vary. It is clear that the salary summation algorithm takes longer on bigger lists. This does not mean that we cannot formulate its time performance precisely; all it means is that the formulation will have to account for the fact that the algorithm's running time depends on, or *is a function of*, the length of the input list. The same applies to memory space. In the dynamic planning solution to the weary traveler problem of Chapter 4, we calculated many optimal partial trips, and had to store them in a vector since they were used in the calculation of others. Their number, and hence the amount of memory the algorithm uses, depends directly on the number of nodes in the input city graph.

Although we concentrate on the time measure in this chapter, it should be remarked that issues quite analogous to the ones raised here apply to the space measure too.

Improvements Are Needed

It is only proper to start our discussion of time efficiency in algorithmics with a downright rejection of the myth concerning the computer's speed. Some people think that computers are so incredibly fast that there is no real problem of time. Well, this opinion is groundless.

Here are two brief examples, about which we shall have more to say in later chapters. Assume we are interested in finding the shortest route for a traveler who wishes to visit each of, say, 80 cities. As of now, there is no computer that can find the route in less than *millions of years* of computing time! Similarly, no computer is capable of factoring (i.e., finding the prime numbers that divide) large integers, say, 300 digits long, in less than *millions of years*. The status of both of these problems may change, but as of now no one knows of any reasonable solutions for them.

Time is a crucial factor in almost every use of computers. Even in day-to-day applications, such as weather prediction programs, inventory management systems, and library lookup programs, there is vast room for improvement. Time is money, and computer time is no exception. Moreover, where computers are concerned, time can actually be the critical factor. Certain kinds of computerized systems, such as flight control, missile guidance, and navigation programs, are termed **real-time** systems. They have to respond to external stimuli, such as pressing buttons, in 'real' time; that is, almost instantaneously. Failing to do so could prove to be fatal.

After-the-Fact Improvements

There are many standard ways of improving the running time of a given algorithm. Some are incorporated into compilers, turning them into **optimizing** compilers, which actually make amends for certain kinds of poor decisions on the part of the programmer.

Many chores of an optimizing compiler can be thought of as carrying out certain kinds of **program transformations** (see Chapter 5). One of the most widely applicable of these is modifying a program or an algorithm by transferring instructions from the inside to the outside of loops. Sometimes this is straightforward, as in the following example. Assume that a teacher, in the interest of getting a class to register reasonably good results in an exam, wants to normalize the list of grades, by giving the student who scored best in the exam 100 points and upgrading the rest accordingly. A high-level description of the algorithm might look like this:

(1) compute the maximum score in MAX;
(2) for each score Y set $Y \leftarrow Y \times 100/MAX$

(We must assume that there is at least one nonzero grade, for the division to be well defined.) If the list is given in a vector $L(1), \ldots, L(N)$, both parts can be executed by simple loops running through the vector. The first searches for the maximum in the usual way, and the second might be written:

(2) **for** I **from** 1 **to** N **do**:
   (2.1) $L(I) \leftarrow L(I) \times 100/MAX$

Notice that for each grade $L(I)$ the algorithm carries out one multiplication (by 100) and one division (by MAX). However, neither 100 nor the value of MAX changes within the loop. Hence, the time for executing this second loop can be cut almost in two (!) by simply inserting the statement:

$FACTOR \leftarrow 100/MAX$

between steps (1) and (2), and multiplying $L(I)$ by $FACTOR$ within the loop. The resulting algorithm is:

(1) compute the maximum score in MAX;
(2) $FACTOR \leftarrow 100/MAX$;

(3) **for** I **from** 1 **to** N **do**:
         (3.1) $L(I) \leftarrow L(I) \times FACTOR$.

The reason for the near 50% improvement is that the body of the second loop, which originally consisted of two arithmetical operations, now consists of only one. Of course, not in all implementations of such an algorithm will the time be dominated by the arithmetical instructions; it is possible that *updating* the value of $L(I)$ is more time consuming than numerical division. Even so, there is a significant improvement in the running time, and more time is gained for longer lists.

As mentioned, modifications such as this are quite straightforward, and many compilers are able to carry them out automatically. However, even simple instruction removal sometimes requires a sly trick or two. Let us look at another example.

Linear Search: An Example

We are searching for an element X in an unordered list (say for a telephone number in a jumbled telephone book). The standard algorithm calls for a simple loop, within which two tests are carried out: (1) 'have we found X?' and (2) 'have we reached the end of the list?' A positive answer to any one of these questions causes the algorithm to terminate – successfully in the first case and unsuccessfully in the second. Again, we may assume that these tests dominate the time performance of the searching algorithm.

The second test can be taken outside of the loop using the following trick. Prior to commencing the search, the required element X is added fictitiously to the *end* of the list. Then the search loop is carried out, testing only if X has been found, thus improving the time performance of the entire algorithm by a factor of about 50%. Since we have added X to the list, it will *always* be found. However, if the original list did not contain X we will be at the end of the new list when confronting X for the first time, whereas we will end up somewhere *within* it if X does appear in the original list. Consequently, upon reaching X, a test for being at the end of the list is carried out *once*, and the algorithm reports success or failure depending on the outcome. (Incidentally, a common error can occur here if we forget to remove the fictitious X from the end of the list before terminating.)

*   *   *

Order-of-Magnitude Improvements

A 50% decrease in the running time of an algorithm is quite impressive. However, as it happens, we can do much better on many occasions. When we say 'better' we do not mean just fixed decreases of 50%, 60%, or even 90%, but decreases whose *rate* gets increasingly better as the size of the input increases.

One of the best-known examples involves searching for an element in an ordered or sorted list (for example, looking up a telephone number in a normal telephone book). To be more precise, assume that the input consists of a name Y and a list L of the form:

$$\langle X_1, T_1 \rangle, \quad \langle X_2, T_2 \rangle, \quad \langle X_3, T_3 \rangle, \ldots, \langle X_N, T_N \rangle$$

where each X_i is a name and T_i is the corresponding telephone number. The list, which is of length N, is assumed to be sorted into alphabetic order by the names.

A naive algorithm that searches for Y's telephone number is that previously described for an unsorted list: start at X_1, and work through L, checking Y against the current X_i at each step, and either checking for the end of the list at the same time, or applying the trick and checking for it only once, when Y is found. Even if the trick is employed to cut the running time by 50%, there still might be a case in which N comparisons are necessary; namely, when Y does not appear in L at all, or when it appears in the last position. We say that the algorithm, call it A, has a **worst-case** running time which is **on the order of** N. This is described more concisely by saying that A runs in time $O(N)$ in the worst case.

The $O(N)$ notation is quite subtle. Notice that we said 'A runs in time $O(N)$.' We did not particularize the statement to refer only to the number of *comparisons*, although comparisons between Y and the X_i were the only type of instruction we were counting. The reason for this will be explained later. For now, it suffices to say that when using the **big-O notation**, as it is sometimes called, we do not care whether the algorithm takes time N (i.e., executes N elementary instructions), time $3N$, $10N$, or $100N$. Even if it takes a *fraction* of N, say $N/6$, we still say that it runs in time $O(N)$. The only thing that matters is that the running time grows **linearly** with N. This means that there is some constant number K, such that the algorithm runs in time that is no more than $K \times N$ in the worst case. The version that checks for the end of the list each time runs roughly in time $2N$, and the tricky version cuts that down to roughly N. Both, however, have running time directly proportional to N. Thus, they both have a worst-case running time of $O(N)$.

The term 'worst case' means that the algorithm could presumably run for much less on certain inputs, perhaps on *most* inputs. All we are saying is that the constant K works for all inputs of length N, even the worst ones. The algorithm never runs for more than $K \times N$ time, and this is true for any N and for any input of length N. Clearly, if we try to improve the linear search algorithm by starting the comparisons from the *end* of the list, comparing first to X_N, there would be equally bad cases – Y not appearing at all, or Y appearing as the first element, X_1. Actually, if an exhaustive search throughout the list is called for by the algorithm, the order in which elements are compared to X is of no importance. Such an algorithm will still have an $O(N)$ worst-case running time.

Despite this, we *can* do better in searching an ordered list, not only in terms of the constant factor 'hidden inside' the big-O, but in terms of the $O(N)$ estimate itself. This is an **order-of-magnitude improvement**, and we will now see how it can be achieved.

Binary Search: An Example

For concreteness, let us assume that the telephone book has a million entries; that is, $N = 1\ 000\ 000$.

The first comparison carried out by the new algorithm is not between Y and the first or last name in L, but between Y and the *middle* name (or, if the list is of even length, then the first name in the second half of the list), namely $X_{500\,000}$. Assuming that the compared names turn out to be unequal, meaning that we are not done yet, there are two possibilities: (1) $Y < X_{500000}$, and (2) $Y > X_{500000}$. Since the list is sorted, if (1) is the case we know that if Y appears in the list at all it has to be in the first half, and if (2) is the case it must appear in the second half. Hence, we can restrict our successive search to the appropriate half of the list.

Accordingly, the next comparison will be between Y and the middle element of that half: X_{250000} in case (1) and $X_{750\,000}$ in case (2). And again, the result of this comparison will be to narrow the possibilities down to half of the current list; that is, to a list whose length is a *quarter* of the original. This process continues, reducing the length of the list, or in more general terms, the **size of the problem**, by half at each step, until either Y is found, in which case the procedure terminates, reporting success, or the trivial empty list is reached, in which case it terminates, reporting failure (see Figures 6.1 and 6.2).

This procedure is called **binary search**, and it is really an application of the divide-and-conquer paradigm discussed in Chapter 4. The difference between this example and the ones introduced therein (**min&max** search and **mergesort**) is that here after dividing we need only conquer *one* of the parts, not both. Figure 6.1 contains a schematic iterative version of binary search, but it is actually possible to write down a simple recursive version too. The reader is encouraged to do so.

What is the time complexity of binary search? To answer this, let us first count comparisons. It is quite instructive to try to guess how many comparisons the binary search algorithm will require in the worst case on our one-million-name telephone book. Recall that the naive search would require a million comparisons.

Well, in the very worst case (what is an example of one? how many worst cases are there?) the algorithm will require only 20 comparisons!

Moreover, the larger N becomes, the more impressive the improvement. An international telephone book containing, say, a billion names, would require at most 30 comparisons, instead of a billion!

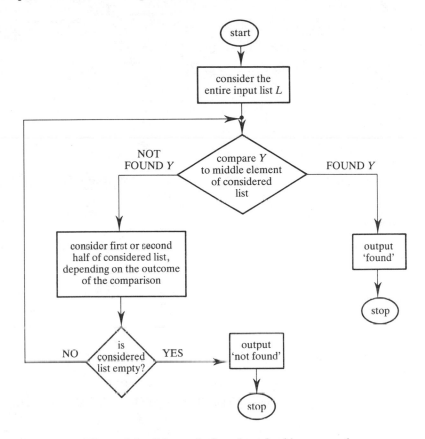

Figure 6.1   Schematic flowchart for binary search.

Recall that each comparison reduces the length of the input list L by half, and that the process terminates when, or before, the list becomes empty. Hence, the worst-case number of comparisons is obtained by figuring out how many times a number N can be repeatedly divided by 2 before it is reduced to 0. (The rules of the game are to ignore fractions.) This number is termed the **base-2 logarithm**[†] of N, and is denoted by $\log_2 N$. Actually, $\log_2 N$ counts the number required to reduce N to 1, not 0, so the number we are really after is $1 + \log_2 N$.[††]

[†] The similarity between the words 'algorithm' and 'logarithm' is purely coincidental.

[††] Actually, we are abusing the term slightly by using the **integer part** of $1 + \log_2 N$. Our 'logarithms' can thus be thought of as always yielding integers.

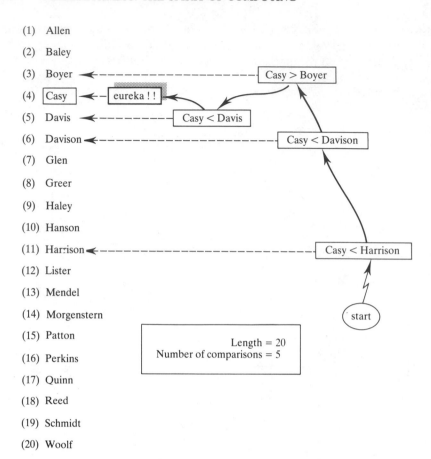

Figure 6.2   Binary search applied to a small telephone book (numbers omitted).

We can get a feel for the kind of improvement binary search offers by studying the following table, which plots several values of N against the number of comparisons required by binary search in the worst case:

N	$1 + \log_2 N$
10	4
100	7
1000	10
a million	20
a billion	30
a billion billions	60

It is noteworthy that we ourselves use a variant of binary search when we search for a number in a telephone book. The difference is that we do not necessarily compare the name at hand with the one occurring precisely at the middle of the book and then with that at the $\frac{1}{4}$ or $\frac{3}{4}$ position, etc. Rather, we make use of additional knowledge we possess, concerning the expected **distribution** of names in the book. If we are searching for 'Mary D. Ramsey', for example, we would open the book roughly at the $\frac{2}{3}$ point. Obviously this is far from being precise, and we work with rough, intuitive rules of thumb, to be discussed under the term **heuristics** in Chapter 12. Nevertheless, there are precise formulations of search algorithms that proceed in a skewed fashion, dictated by the nature and distribution of the elements. In general, while being considerably more economical on the average, these variations also exhibit a similar worst-case behavior of $O(\log_2 N)$ comparisons.

Why Is It Enough to Count Comparisons?

To complete our complexity analysis of binary search, we now show that if we are happy with a big-O estimate, it suffices to count comparisons only. Why? Clearly, in binary search there are considerably more instructions executed than just comparisons. Refocussing on the correct half of the list and preparing it for the next time around the loop would presumably involve some testing and changing of indices. And then there is the test for an empty list, etc.

As it turns out, the checkpoints used in the previous chapter for correctness proofs turn out to be helpful here too. Figure 6.3 shows the schematic flowchart of Figure 6.1 with checkpoints included, and it illustrates the possible local paths between them. Notice that here too the checkpoints cut all loops – there is only one in this case – so that the four local paths are loop free, as in the example given in Chapter 5. Whereas this fact was important for correctness proofs because it gave rise to manageable verification conditions, here it is important because loop-free and subroutine-free segments take at most *fixed* amounts of time. The presence of conditional statements in such a segment might yield several different ways of traversing it. However, the absence of loops (and recursive routines) guarantees that there is a bound on this number, and hence the total number of instructions carried out in any single execution of such a segment is no greater than some constant.

    **   In Figure 6.3 we have associated the constants K_1 through K_4 with the four possible paths. This means, for example, that any execution of the local path from checkpoint (2) back to itself is assumed to involve no more than K_2 instructions. By convention, this is taken to include the comparison made at the beginning of the segment, but not the one made at its end. Now consider a typical execution of binary search (see Figure 6.4). Since checkpoint (2) is the only place in the text of the algorithm involving a comparison, it is reached (in the worst case) precisely $1 + \log_2 N$ times, the total number of comparisons made. All but one of these result in the processor going around the loop again. This means that the total time cost of all traversals of the $(2) \rightarrow (2)$ segment is $K_2 \times \log_2 N$.

Figure 6.3   Binary search with checkpoints and local time bounds.

To complete the analysis, notice that the total number of all instructions carried out, which are not part of $(2) \rightarrow (2)$ segments, is either $K_1 + K_3$ or $K_1 + K_4$ (see Figure 6.4); in both cases it is a constant that does not depend on N. If we denote by K the maximum of these two sums, we can conclude that the total number of instructions carried out by the binary search algorithm on a list of length N is bounded by:

$$K + (K_2 \times \log_2 N)$$

Hence, given that we are using the big-O order-of-magnitude notation, this means simply that binary search runs in time $O(\log_2 N)$ in the worst case.   **

*   *   *

Figure 6.4   A typical worst-case execution of binary search.

The Robustness of the Big-O Notation

As explained earlier, big-Os hide constant factors. Hence, in the worst-case analysis of binary search there was no need for us to be more specific about the details of the particular instructions that make up the algorithm. It was sufficient to analyze the algorithm's loop structure and convince ourselves that between any two comparisons there is only a constant number of instructions in the worst case.

Somehow this does not sound quite right. Surely the time complexity of binary search *does* depend on the elementary instructions allowed. If we were to allow the instruction:

search list L for item Y

the algorithm would consist simply of a single instruction, and hence its time complexity would be $O(1)$; that is, a constant number not depending on N at all. So how can we say that the details of the instructions are unimportant?

Well, the time complexity of an algorithm is indeed a *relative* concept, and it makes sense only in conjunction with an agreed on set of elementary instructions. Nevertheless, standard kinds of problems are usually thought of in the context of standard kinds of elementary instructions. For example, searching and sorting problems usually involve comparisons, index updates, and end-of-list tests, so that complexity analysis is carried out with respect to these. Moreover, if a particular programming language is fixed in advance, then a particular set of elementary instructions has also been fixed, for better or for worse. What makes these observations significant is the fact that for most standard kinds of elementary instructions we can afford to be quite vague when it comes to order-of-magnitude complexity. Writing an algorithm in this or that programming language, or using this or that compiler, can obviously make a difference in the final running time. However, if the algorithm uses conventional kinds of basic instructions, these differences will consist of only a constant factor per basic instruction, and this means that the big-O complexity is *invariant* under such implementational fluctuations.

In other words, as long as the basic set of allowed elementary instructions is agreed on, and as long as any shortcuts taken in high-level descriptions (such as that of Figure 6.1) do not hide unbounded iterations of such instructions, but merely represent finite clusters of them, big-O-time estimates are *robust*.

Actually, for the benefit of those who feel at home with logarithms, it should be added that the logarithmic base is of no importance either. For any fixed K, the number $\log_2 N$ and $\log_K N$ differ only by a constant factor, and hence this difference can also be hidden under the big-O notation. Consequently, we shall refer to logarithmic-time performance simply as $O(\log N)$, not $O(\log_2 N)$.

The robustness of the big-O notation constitutes both its strength and its weakness. When someone exhibits an algorithm that runs in time $O(\log N)$, whereas someone else's algorithm B runs in time $O(N)$, it might very well be found that B runs faster on sample inputs than A! The reason is in the hidden constants. Let us say that we have painstakingly taken into account the constant number of elementary instructions between checkpoints, the programming language in which the algorithm is coded, the compiler which translates it downwards, the basic machine instructions used by the computer running the machine code, and the very speed of that computer. Having done so, we might find that algorithm A performs in time bounded by $C_1 \times \log_2 N$ microseconds, and B performs within $C_2 \times N$ microseconds, but with $C_1 = 1000$ and $C_2 = 10$. This means that for every input of length less than a thousand, algorithm B is superior to A. Only when inputs of size 1000 or more are reached does the difference between N and $\log_2 N$ become apparent, and, as already hinted, when the difference starts paying off, it does so very handsomely: by the time inputs of size a million are reached, algorithm A becomes upwards of 500 times more efficient than algorithm B, and for inputs of size a billion the improvement is over 330 000-fold!

A user who is interested only in inputs of length less than a thousand should definitely adopt algorithm B, despite A's big-O superiority. In most cases, however, the constant factors are not quite as far apart as 10 and 1000, hence order-of-magnitude estimates are usually far more realistic than in this contrived example.

The moral of the story is to first search for a good and efficient algorithm, stressing big-O performance, and then to try improving it by tricks of the kind used earlier to decrease the constant factors involved. In any event, since big-O efficiency can be misleading, candidate algorithms should be run experimentally and their time performances for various typically occurring kinds of inputs should be tabulated.

The robustness of big-O estimates, coupled with the fact that in the majority of cases algorithms that are better in the big-O sense are also better in practice, renders the study of order-of-magnitude time complexity the most interesting to computer scientists. Accordingly, in the name of science and robustness, we shall concentrate in the sequel mainly on big-O estimates and similar notions, although they may hide issues of possible practical importance, such as constant factors.

*   *   *

Time Analysis of Nested Loops

Obviously, complicated algorithms that involve many intertwined control structures and contain possibly recursive subroutines can become quite difficult to analyze. Let us briefly discuss the time complexity of some of the algorithms appearing in previous chapters.

The bubblesort algorithm of Chapter 2 consists of two loops nested as follows:

(1)   do the following $N - 1$ times:
    . . .
    (1.2)   do the following $N - 1$ times:
        . . .

The inner loop is executed $N - 1$ times for each of the $N - 1$ times the outer loop is executed. As before, everything else is constant; hence the total time performance of bubblesort is on the order of $(N - 1) \times (N - 1)$, which is $N^2 - 2N + 1$. In this case, the N^2 is called the **dominant term** of the expression, meaning that the other parts, namely $-2N$ and $+1$, get swallowed by the N^2 when the big-O notation is used. Consequently, bubblesort is an $O(N^2)$ algorithm.

Recall our discussion of the improved bubblesort version, which allowed for traversing smaller and smaller portions of the input list. Here the time analysis results in the sum:

$$(N - 1) + (N - 2) + (N - 3) + \ldots + 3 + 2 + 1$$

which evaluates to $(N^2 - N)/2$. This is less than the $N^2 - 2N + 1$ of the naive version. However, the improved version is also an $O(N^2)$ algorithm, since the dominant factor is $N^2/2$, and the constant factor of $\frac{1}{2}$ gets lost too. We thus have a 50% improvement, but not a big-O one.

The simple salary summation algorithm (Figure 2.3) is $O(N)$, and the one for the more sophisticated version, which entailed a nested loop to search for direct managers (Figure 2.4), is $O(N^2)$. (Why?)

The 'money' -searching algorithm, with or without the use of a routine (Figures 2.5 and 2.6) is $O(N)$, a fact that should be carefully checked. Although there might be two pointers advancing separately, the text is traversed only once, in linear fashion. For such reasons $O(N)$ algorithms are said to be **linear-time** algorithms. In contrast, $O(N^2)$ algorithms are called **quadratic**, and we have already used the term logarithmic for $O(\log N)$ algorithms.

With the knowledge acquired in the present chapter, it should be quite straightforward to figure out the reason we tried to improve the algorithm for maximal polygonal distance in Chapter 4. The naive algorithm, which runs through all pairs of vertices, is quadratic (N is the number of vertices), whereas the improved algorithm cycles around the polygon once, and can be shown to be linear.

Time Analysis of Recursion

Let us now consider the **min&max** problem of Chapter 4, which called for finding the extremal elements in a list L. The naive algorithm runs through the list iteratively, updating two variables that hold the current extremal elements. It is clearly linear. Here is the recursive routine, which was claimed in Chapter 4 to be better:

subroutine **find-min&max-of** L:

(1) if L consists of one element, then set MIN and MAX to it; if it consists of two elements, then set MIN to the smaller of them and MAX to the larger;

(2) otherwise do the following:
    (2.1) split L into two halves, L_1 and L_2;
    (2.2) call **find-min&max-of** L_1, placing returned values in $MIN1$ and $MAX1$;
    (2.3) call **find-min&max-of** L_2, placing returned values in $MIN2$ and $MAX2$;
    (2.4) set MIN to smaller of $MIN1$ and $MIN2$;
    (2.5) set MAX to larger of $MAX1$ and $MAX2$;

(3) return with MIN and MAX.

It will turn out that this recursive routine runs in linear time too. (In fact, as we argue later, no algorithm for the **min&max** problem can possibly be *sublinear*, say, logarithmic.) If this is so, why is the recursive routine better?

To answer this question a more refined complexity analysis is called for. The naive algorithm operates by carrying out two comparisons for each element in the list, one with the current maximum and one with the current minimum. Hence it yields a total comparison count of $2N$. The interesting part is the way one counts time for a *recursive* routine. Since we do not know offhand how many comparisons the routine requires, we use an abstract notation. Specifically, let $C(N)$ denote the (worst case) number of comparisons required by the recursive **min&max** routine on lists of length N.

Although we do not know the explicit value of $C(N)$ as a function of N, we do know two things:

(1) if $N = 1$ or $N = 2$, precisely one comparison is carried out – the one implied by line (1) of the routine;

(2) if $N > 2$, the comparisons carried out are precisely two sets of comparisons for lists of length $N/2$ (since there are two recursive calls), and two additional comparisons, on lines (2.4) and (2.5).

We can therefore write down the following equations, sometimes called **recurrence relations**:

$$C(1) = C(2) = 1$$
$$C(N) = 2 \times C(N/2) + 2$$

Standard methods exist for solving such equations, and in this case, as can be readily checked, the solution turns out to be:

$$C(N) = 3N/2 - 2$$

In other words, recursive routine requires not $2N$ comparisons for lists of length N, but less than $3N/2$. As mentioned, this is still $O(N)$, but it is nevertheless an improvement, especially if comparisons are highly time consuming in the desired application.

The recursive **min&max** routine was presented here to give an example of the time analysis of a recursive algorithm. However, it is noteworthy that a $3N/2$ bound on the number of comparisons for finding the minimum and maximum in a list can be achieved by a simple iterative algorithm as follows. First arrange the N elements into pairs, then compare the two elements within each pair, marking the larger of the two. This costs $N/2$ comparisons. Then go through the $N/2$ larger elements, keeping track of the current maximum, and similarly through the $N/2$ smaller elements, keeping track of the minimum. This costs twice $N/2$ comparisons, yielding a total of $3N/2$.

In Chapters 2 and 4 two additional sorting algorithms were briefly described, treesort and mergesort. We shall not embark on a detailed time analysis here, except to make the following remarks.

Treesort, if implemented naively, is an $O(N^2)$ algorithm. The reason stems from the possibility that certain sequences of elements result in very long and narrow binary search trees, such as the one in Figure 6.5. Although traversing such a tree in left-first traversal is a linear-time procedure, *constructing* the tree from the input sequence can be shown to be quadratic. However, it is possible to employ a *self-adjustment* scheme, of the kind hinted at in Chapter 2, and keep the tree wide and short. Incorporating such a scheme into the construction phase of treesort will result in an order-of-magnitude improvement, yielding an $O(N \times \log N)$ algorithm. The following table should give an idea of the savings this improvement provides, though its effect on the constant factors does not show up.

28	1018	402	396	35	46	354	76	128	112	106	100

first   *last*

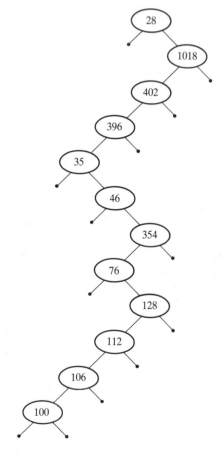

Figure 6.5   A list and its long and thin binary search tree (compare with Figure 2.13).

N	N^2	$N \times \log_2 N$
10	100	33
100	10 000	665
1000	a million	9966
a million	a thousand billions	20 million
a billion	a billion billions	30 billion

Turning to mergesort, the reader is left with the interesting exercise of showing that this algorithm is in itself $O(N \times \log N)$. Mergesort is really one of several time-efficient sorting algorithms, and definitely the easiest to describe from among the $O(N \times \log N)$ ones. It should be remarked, however, that it uses a new list to store partial results. Hence it requires an additional $O(N)$ amount of space, which is a disadvantage when compared to some of the other sorting methods.

Thus, mergesort is one of the most efficient sorting routines and also one of the easiest to describe. We would like to credit recursion with both virtues: it makes the algorithm easy to describe, and it also provides a clean mechanism for splitting the problem into two smaller problems of half the size, which is the root of the algorithm's $O(N \times \log N)$ time performance.

Average-Case Complexity

The worst-case nature of our time analyses can be construed as a disadvantage. It is true that one cannot guarantee, say, linear-time performance of an algorithm unless the time bound applies to *all* legal inputs. However, it might be the case that an algorithm performs very fast for *most* of the standard kinds of inputs, and the ones which cause its worst-case performance to soar are a minority that we are willing to ignore.

Accordingly, there are other useful estimates of an algorithm's time performance, such as its **average-case** behavior. Here we are interested in the time required by the algorithm on the average, taking the entire set of inputs and their probability of occurring into consideration. We shall not go into the technical details here, except to remark that average-case analysis is considerably more difficult to carry out than worst-case analysis. The mathematics required is usually far more sophisticated, and many algorithms exist for which researchers have not been able to obtain average-case estimates at all.

Despite the fundamental difference, many algorithms have the same big-O time bound for both worst-case and average-case behavior. For example, simple salary summation behaves in a fixed fashion, always running to the very end of the list, and is hence $O(N)$ in the worst, best, and average cases. The version that goes looking for direct managers, which is $O(N^2)$ in the worst case, might, on average, have to look through only half of the list for each employee's manager, not through it all. However, this only decreases N^2 to about $N^2/2$, retaining the $O(N^2)$ time bound even in the average case.

However, for some algorithms, average-case analysis can reveal significantly better performance. The classical example of this is yet another sorting algorithm, called **quicksort**, which we shall not describe here. Quicksort, also a naturally recursive algorithm, has a worst-case running time of $O(N^2)$, and hence appears to be inferior to both mergesort and the self-adjusting version of treesort. Nevertheless, its average-case performance can be shown to be $O(N \times \log N)$, matching that of the better sorting algorithms. What makes quicksort particularly interesting is the fact that its average-case performance involves a very small constant. In fact, on only counting comparisons, the time performance of quicksort is a little over $1.4N \times \log_2 N$ on average. Taking into account the fact that it requires only a small fixed amount of additional storage space, and despite its inferior worst-case performance, quicksort is actually one of the best sorting algorithms known, and is definitely the best among the ones mentioned here.

To complete our brief discussion of the sorting methods presented, we should remark that bubblesort is the worst of the lot, having even an average case behavior of $O(N^2)$. (This fact, however, is rather tricky to prove.) Many people are opposed to describing bubblesort in computer science courses, since its elegance is sufficiently misleading, and students might actually be lured into using it in practice . . . .

*   *   *

Upper and Lower Bounds

We showed earlier how the naive $O(N)$ algorithm for searching an ordered list can be improved to $O(\log N)$ by using binary search. More precisely, we showed that there was an algorithm that performed such a search using no more than $\log_2 N$ comparisons in the worst case on a list of length N.

Can we do better? Is it possible to search for an element in a million-entry telephone book in *less* than 20 comparisons in the worst case? Is it possible to find an algorithm for the ordered list search problem that requires only $\sqrt{\log_2 N}$, or maybe only $\log_2(\log_2 N)$, comparisons in the worst case?

To put these questions into perspective, think of any algorithmic problem, say the ordered list search problem, as sitting out there, endowed with an inherent **optimal solution**, which is what we are after. Then, along comes someone with an algorithm, say the naive $O(N)$ one, and thus approaches the desired solution 'from above'. With this algorithm as evidence, we know that the problem cannot be inherently *worse* than $O(N)$, meaning that it cannot require a higher running time. Later on, someone else discovers the better $O(\log N)$ algorithm, thus coming closer to the desired optimal solution, also from above. We are now convinced that the problem cannot be inherently worse than $O(\log N)$, and the previous algorithm becomes obsolete. The question is, how far down can these improvements go?

With the 'approaching-from-above' metaphor in mind (see Figure 6.6), the discovery of an algorithm is said to place an **upper bound** on the algorithmic problem. Better algorithms bring the problem's best-known time bound downwards, closer to the unknown inherent complexity of the problem itself. The questions we have asked are all concerned with the problem's **lower bound**. If we can prove rigorously that algorithmic problem P *cannot* be solved by *any* algorithm that requires less than, say, $O(N^3)$ time in the worst case, then people trying to find efficient algorithms for solving P can essentially give up if and when they find an $O(N^3)$ algorithm, because there is no way they can do better. Such a proof constitutes a lower bound on the algorithmic problem, since it shows that no algorithm can improve on the $O(N^3)$ bound.[†]

In this way, discovering a clever algorithm shows that the problem's inherent time performance is no *worse* than some bound, and discovering a lower bound proof shows that it is no *better* than some bound. In both cases, a property of the *algorithmic problem* has been discovered, not a property of a particular algorithm. This might sound confusing, especially since a lower bound on a problem requires consideration of *all* algorithms for it, while an upper bound is achieved by constructing one particular algorithm and analyzing its time performance (see Figure 6.6).

There is a special notation for lower bounds that is worth knowing about, despite the fact that we do not use it here. On establishing a lower bound of, say, $K \times N^3$ on a problem P, for some constant K, we say that P has an $\Omega(N^3)$ time behavior. We shall stick to the big-O notation, however, and in this case we simply say that P has a lower bound of $O(N^3)$.

Achieving a lower bound seems like an impossibility. How do we prove something about *all* algorithms? How can we be sure that someone will not discover a very subtle but efficient algorithm that we have not anticipated? These are not easy questions to answer, but perhaps contemplation of the following proof will give us some partial answers.

Before doing so, however, we should re-emphasize the fact that any discussion of inherent time complexity, lower bounds included, must be carried out relative to a set of allowed basic instructions. No one can prove

---

[†] All this, of course, is only insofar as order-of-magnitude improvements are concerned. Decreasing the factor hidden within the big-O might still be possible. Chapters 10 and 11 show that using more liberal notions of an algorithm can change things drastically.

that the search problem requires any more than a single time unit if basic instructions like:

search list L for item Y

are allowed. The rules of the game, therefore, must be carefully specified before we make any attempt at proving lower bounds.

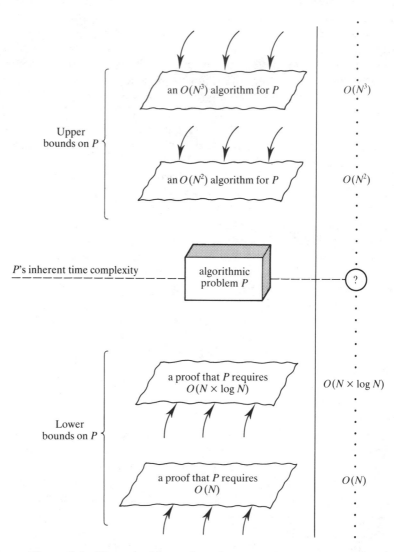

Figure 6.6   Upper and lower bounds on an algorithmic problem.

A Lower Bound for Telephone Book Search

We wish to show that binary search is optimal. In other words, we cannot find a name in a telephone book of length N in less than $\log_2 N$ comparisons in the worst case; 20 comparisons are the minimum for a million names, 30 for a billion, 60 for a billion billions, etc. In more general terms, there is no algorithm for the ordered list searching problem whose worst-case time performance is better than $O(\log N)$.

The rules of the game here are quite straightforward. The only way a proposed algorithm is allowed to extract any kind of information from the inputs is by carrying out two-way comparisons. The algorithm might compare two elements from the input list L among themselves, or an element from L with the input element Y whose position in L is sought for. No other queries can be addressed to the inputs L and Y. However, there are no restrictions on instructions *not* concerning L or Y; any of these can be included, and each will cost only a single time unit.

To show that any algorithm for this problem requires $\log_2 N$ comparisons, we shall argue as follows. Given an algorithm, *any* algorithm we will show that it cannot possibly better the claimed $\log_2 N$ lower bound on the problem. Accordingly, say we have come up with an algorithm A for the ordered list search problem that is based on two-way comparisons. We shall prove that for each N there are input lists of length N upon which algorithm A will *necessarily* perform $\log_2 N$ comparisons.

** To that end, let us observe A's behavior on a typical list L of length N. Since we are merely trying to find bad cases, we can make life easier for ourselves by considering the special case in which L consists precisely of the numbers 1, 2, 3, ..., N in order, and where Y is one of those numbers. We can also safely assume that all comparisons have but two results, '<' or '>', since if a comparison yields '=', Y has been found (unless some useless comparison of an element with itself was carried out, in which case the algorithm can do without it). The algorithm A, working on our special list L, might perform some number of other actions, but eventually it reaches its first comparison. It then presumably branches off in one of two directions, depending on the (two-way) outcome. In each of these, A might work some more before reaching the next comparison, which again splits A's behavior into two further possibilities. A's behavior can be thus described schematically as a binary tree (see Figure 6.7), in which edges correspond to possible sequences of noncomparison actions, and nodes to comparisons and their branching outcomes. Denote this 'comparison tree' by T.

For each N, the tree T captures A's behavior under all circumstances. Now, T is definitely finite, since A has to terminate on all legal inputs, and its leaves correspond to reaching a final decision concerning Y's position in L, or, in other words, concerning Y's value from among 1, 2, ..., N. Clearly, no two different values of Y can be represented by the same leaf, because that would mean that A produces the same output (i.e., position in L) for two different values of Y – obviously an absurdity. Since Y has N possible values, T must have at least N possible leaves. (It might have more, since there may be more than one way of reaching the same conclusion about Y's position.) We now use the following standard fact about binary trees, whose truth the reader should try establishing:

> Any binary tree having at least N leaves has depth at least $\log_2 N$; that is, the tree contains at least one path from the root whose length is $\log_2 N$ or more.

It follows that our comparison tree T contains a path of length at least $\log_2 N$. But a path in T corresponds precisely to the execution of the proposed algorithm A on some input list of length N, with the nodes marking the comparisons made in that very execution (see Figure 6.7). Hence, if there is a path of length at least $\log_2 N$ in T, it follows that there is some input list that requires A to perform at least $\log_2 N$ comparisons. **

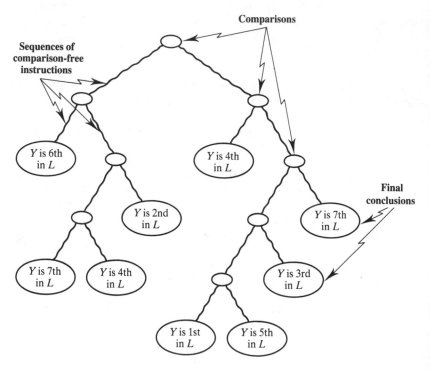

Figure 6.7 A comparison tree for searching in a list.

This completes the $\log_2 N$ lower bound on the number of comparisons, and hence the more general $O(\log N)$ lower bound on execution time, for the algorithmic problem of searching in an ordered list. Notice how the argument was made general enough to apply to *any* proposed algorithm, as long as it used comparisons as the sole means for extracting information from the input list.

Closed Problems and Algorithmic Gaps

Lower bounds can be established for many other algorithmic problems. Searching in an *un*ordered list, for example, is the quintessential linear-time problem, and can be easily shown to require N comparisons in the worst case. It therefore has a lower bound of $O(N)$ for algorithms based on comparisons. The reader might want to work out the argument for this.

Several of the problems we have talked about can be construed as variations of unordered search, and are consequently also bounded from below by $O(N)$. These include the **min&max** problem, simple salary summation, maximum polygonal distance, etc. Notice that for each of these we indeed supplied linear-time algorithms. This means that the upper and lower bounds actually meet (except for the possibly different constant factors). In other words, these algorithmic problems are **closed** as far as big-O time estimates go. We have an $O(N)$ algorithm, and we know that we can do no better.

Searching in an *ordered* list is also a closed problem; it has upper and lower bounds of $O(\log N)$. Sorting is also closed. On the one hand we have algorithms, like mergesort or the self-adjusting version of treesort, that are $O(N \times \log N)$, and on the other we can prove an $O(N \times \log N)$ lower bound for sorting a list of length N. In both these cases the bounds are based on the comparison model, whereby information about inputs is gained only by two-way comparisons.

Many algorithmic problems, however, do not enjoy the property of being closed. Their upper and lower bounds do not meet. In such cases we say that they give rise to **algorithmic gaps**, the best-known upper bound being different from (and therefore higher than) the best known lower bound. In Chapter 4 we presented a quadratic algorithm for finding minimal railroads (the minimal spanning tree problem), but the best-known lower bound is linear. That is, although we can prove that the problem requires $O(N)$ time (here N is the number of edges in the railroad graph, not the number of nodes), no one knows of a linear-time algorithm, and hence the problem is not closed.

In Chapter 7 we shall see several striking examples of algorithmic gaps that are unacceptably large. For now, it suffices to realize that if a problem gives rise to an algorithmic gap, the deficiency is not in the problem but in our knowledge about it. We have failed either in finding the best algorithm for it or in proving that a better one does not exist, or in both.

*   *   *

Barricading Sleeping Tigers: An Example

The following algorithm uses sorting in a rather unexpected way, and inherits its complexity bounds too.

Assume we are confronted with N sleeping tigers, and to avoid being eaten when one or more of them wake up we are interested in constructing a fence around them. Algorithmically, we are given the $\langle X, Y \rangle$ coordinates of the tigers (i.e., their locations, or points), and we want to find the smallest polygon that surrounds them all. Clearly, the problem reduces to finding a minimal sequence of some of the tigers' locations which, when connected by linear pieces of fence (which we shall call **line segments**), will enclose all the others (see Figure 6.8). This enclosure is called the **convex hull** of the set of points.

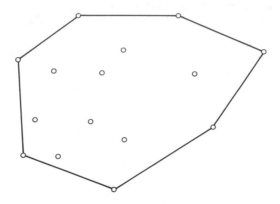

Figure 6.8   Sleeping tigers and their convex hull.

Note that this problem has been presented in a zoological guise only to make it sound a little more entertaining. The convex hull problem is actually one of the basic problems that arise in computer graphics. Finding fast algorithms for this problem and a number of other problems in computational geometry can make a big difference in the speed and applicability of many interactive graphic packages.

The algorithm now presented is based on the following simple observation. Let L be a line segment connecting two points. For L to be part of the convex hull it is necessary and sufficient that all the other points are on the same side of L (or rather, of L's extension to a full line).

This observation gives rise to a straightforward algorithm: consider each potential line segment in turn, and check whether all the $N - 2$ points that are not on it are on one side of it. The test to decide on which side of a line a given point resides can be easily done in constant time using elementary analytic geometry. Since there are N points, there are N^2 segments, and each of them has to be checked against $N-2$ points. This yields an $O(N^3)$ algorithm, as the reader can readily see. However, there is a way of doing far better.

Here are the main steps in the proposed algorithm:

(1)   find the 'lowest' point P_1;

(2)   sort the remaining points by the angle they form with the horizontal when connected with P_1, and let the resulting list be $P_2, \ldots, P_N$;

(3)   start out with P_1 and P_2 in the current hull;

(4)   for I from 3 to N do the following:

    (4.1)   add P_I tentatively to the current hull;

    (4.2)   work backwards through the current hull, eliminating a point P_J if the two points P_1 and P_I are on different sides of the line between P_{J-1} and P_J, and terminating this backwards scan when a J that does not need to be eliminated is encountered.

It may be a little tricky to see what the algorithm is doing, but a glance at Figures 6.9 and 6.10 should help. Figure 6.9 shows the points sorted after step (2) in the order they will be considered in step (4), and Figure 6.10 shows the first few additions and eliminations in step (4). In Figure 6.10 point P_{13} has just been added, and the next step will consider P_{14}. However, since the line between P_{12} and P_{13} goes *between* P_1 and P_{14}, point P_{13} will be eliminated. While proving the correctness of this algorithm is an instructive exercise, we are more interested here in its time analysis. We shall therefore assume that the algorithm is correct.

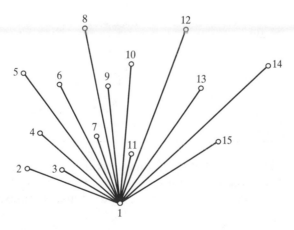

Figure 6.9   The points of Figure 6.8 sorted by angle.

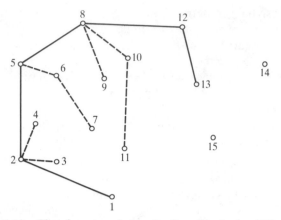

Figure 6.10   First few steps in barricading the tigers of Figure 6.8.

It is easy to see that step (1), which involves a simple search for the minimal vertical coordinate, takes time $O(N)$. Now, step (2) can be carried out by any efficient sorting routine. Therefore, since computing an angle or comparing two angles can be carried out in constant time, step (2) takes total time $O(N \times \log N)$. The interesting part concerns step (4).

It would appear that the nested loop structure of step (4) yields a time performance of $O(N^2)$. However, the right way to analyze this part of the algorithm involves disregarding its structure and accounting for time on a point-by-point basis. Notice that step (4.2) only eliminates points, and it stops when a point that should not be eliminated is encountered. Now, since no point gets eliminated more than once, the total number of times points are considered in the nested loop of step (4.2) cannot be more than $O(N)$. Since the remaining parts of step (4) take no more than $O(N)$ too, step (4) in its entirety takes linear time.

The total time of the algorithm, therefore, is:

step (1)	$O(N)$
step (2)	$O(N \times \log N)$
step (3)	$O(1)$
step (4)	$O(N)$
total	$O(N \times \log N)$

It is a little surprising that sorting has anything at all to do with finding the convex hull. It is more surprising that the sorting part of the algorithm is actually the dominant part as far as computational complexity goes.

*   *   *

Research on the Efficiency of Algorithms

Finding efficient algorithms for pressing algorithmic problems is one of the most common research topics in computer science. Indeed, almost all the issues discussed in this chapter are subjects of considerable research efforts, and are gathered under the general term **concrete complexity theory**.

In this area people are interested in developing and exploiting data structures and algorithmic methods in order to improve existing algorithms or to conceive new ones. Many ingenious ideas find their way into sophisticated algorithms, providing at times surprising cuts in running time. Most often, this is done with the practical goal of solving the problem faster by computer. However, at times the driving force is simply the desire to nail down a problem's inherent order-of-magnitude complexity, even if the results, from a practical point of view, are no better than previously known ones.

A good example of this is the railroad layout (spanning tree) problem of Chapter 4. We presented an $O(N^2)$ algorithm for this, which with some effort can be improved to $O(N \times \log N)$. For all practical purposes, this improved algorithm, or any of a number of other algorithms of similar complexity, works just fine. However, complexity theorists are not happy with this, since the best-known *lower* bound is $O(N)$. They want to know whether or not a linear-time algorithm can actually be found for the problem. Recently, using rather clever and complicated techniques, the upper bound has been brought quite close to $O(N)$. Specifically, there is an algorithm that runs in time bounded by $O(f(N) \times N)$, where $f(N)$ is a function that grows incredibly slowly – much, much slower than, say, $\log_2 N$. The following table shows the smallest Ns for the first few values of this function:

smallest N	such that $f(N)$ is
4	2
16	3
64000	4
far more than the total number of particles in the known universe	5
absolutely unimaginable	6

Clearly, for all practical purposes an $O(f(N) \times N)$ algorithm is really linear; the value of $f(N)$ is 5 or less for any number we shall ever be interested in.

However, we must remember that no matter how slowly growing $f(N)$ is, it would eventually become larger than any constant. Hence, from some point on, that is, for all sufficiently large N, any given $O(N)$ algorithm outperforms the $O(f(N) \times N)$ one, and we say that the former is **asymptotically better** than the latter. Thus, the spanning tree problem is still open, as it still yields an algorithmic gap, and researchers have not given up on it. It is hoped that in the foreseeable future the problem will be closed, one way or another. Either a linear-time algorithm will be discovered, or a nonlinear lower-bound proof, matching the known upper bound, will be found.

As mentioned earlier, lower bounds are very hard to come by, and for many problems no one knows of any nonlinear lower bounds. In other words, despite the fact that the best algorithms for some problems are $O(N^2)$, $O(N^3)$ or worse, no one can prove that there does not exist some $O(N)$ algorithm out there, awaiting discovery. Methods for proving nontrivial lower bounds are extremely scarce, and researchers expend considerable efforts in trying to find them.

Average-case performance yields another difficult research direction, and there are still many known algorithms for which satisfactory average-case analyses have not been performed.

We have not discussed **space complexity** here at all, but it is worth stating that achieving good upper and lower bounds on the space requirements of algorithmic problems is also the subject of considerable research in concrete complexity theory. People are interested not only in separate bounds on time and space, but also in the **joint** time/space complexity of a problem. It might be possible to achieve, say, a linear-space upper bound on a problem P with some algorithm A_1, and, say, a quadratic-time upper bound with A_2, but that does not imply the existence of an algorithm that achieves both simultaneously. It is possible that there is a **time–space tradeoff** inherent in the problem, meaning that we pay for time economy with more space, and for space economy with more time. In such cases researchers try to *prove* that there is such a tradeoff. This usually takes the form of a proof that the performance of any algorithm solving the problem satisfies a certain equation, which holds as either a lower bound or an upper bound (or both). The equation typically relates the (worst case) running time T and space S of the algorithm to the input length N.

** For example, assume that the following equation has been established as both an upper and a lower bound on the time–space complexity of a problem P:

$$S^2 \times T = O(N^3 \times (\log N)^2)$$

This means that if we are willing to spend $O(N^3)$ time we can solve the problem using only $O(\log N)$ space, whereas if we insist on spending no more than $O(N^2)$ time, we would need $O(\sqrt{N} \times \log N)$ space.   **

The next two chapters will focus on the *bad* news complexity theory has for us. They will also discuss notions that are even more robust than the big-*O* notation.

> *how long shall it be then?*
> II Samuel 2: 26

> *In an acceptable time have I answered thee*
> Isaiah 49: 8

PART THREE

LIMITATIONS AND ROBUSTNESS

Thou didst set a bound that they might not pass over

Psalm 104: 9

7

Inefficiency and Intractability

OR

You Can't Always Get It Done Cheaply

In the previous chapter we saw that certain algorithmic problems admit solutions that are far more time efficient than their naive counterparts. We saw, for example, that it is possible to search a sorted list in time $O(\log N)$, not just $O(N)$, a result which, when refined, implies that we can search for a name in a million-entry telephone book with only 20 comparisons in the worst case, not a million. In a similar vein, sorting an unsorted million-entry telephone book can be achieved in only several million comparisons, not many billions, as there exist $O(N \times \log N)$ sorting algorithms that outperform the naive $O(N^2)$ ones.

At this point, the reader may be unimpressed. He may claim to be sufficiently 'rich' to afford a million comparisons for searching a list. He may claim that a few extra seconds of computer time makes no difference, and hence that linear search is just as good as binary search. This argument

151

gains credence on realizing that it is not a human user, but a computer, that carries out the dull and unimaginative chore of leafing through all the names in the book. A similar argument can be made for sorting too, particularly if the application is such that sorting is to be carried out rarely, and the lists to be sorted never contain more than, say, a million items.

Given this attitude, questions of algorithmic gaps become uninteresting too. Once a reasonably good algorithm has been found for a pressing algorithmic problem, we may not be interested in better algorithms or in proofs that they do not exist.

The purpose of this chapter is to show that the 'let's-put-up-with-what-we-have' approach cannot always be adopted. We shall see that in many cases reasonable algorithms, say linear or quadratic ones, do not exist. The best algorithms for many important algorithmic problems will be shown to require formidable amounts of time or memory space, rendering them quite useless.

The Towers of Hanoi Revisited

Recall the Towers of Hanoi problem of Chapter 2, in which we were asked to produce a sequence of one ring moves to transfer N rings from one of three pegs to another according to certain rules (see Figure 2.7). The reader is encouraged to carry out a simple time analysis of the recursive solution **move** described therein, similar to the analysis carried out in Chapter 6 for the **min&max** routine. It will show that $M(N)$, the number of single-ring moves produced by the algorithm for the N-ring case, is precisely $2^N - 1$ that is, one less than $2 \times 2 \times 2 \times \ldots \times 2$, with the 2 appearing N times. Since N appears in the exponent, such a function is called **exponential**. It can be shown that $2^N - 1$ is also a *lower* bound on the required number of moves for solving the problem, so that our solution is really optimal and we cannot do any better.[†]

Is this good or bad? Well, to answer the question in an indirect way, if the Tibetans originally confronted with the 64-ring case were to brush up their act and move a million rings every second, it would still take them more than half a million years to complete the process! If, somewhat more realistically, they were to move one ring every ten seconds, it would take them well over five *trillion* years to get the job done. No wonder they believed the world will end before then!

It seems, therefore, that the Towers of Hanoi problem, at least for 64 rings or more, is hopelessly time consuming. While this statement seems hard to contest, the feeling is that the difficulty stems from the desire to output the entire sequence of moves, and since hopelessly many moves are

---

[†] Incidentally, the iterative solution presented in Chapter 5 and the recursive one of Chapter 2 produce exactly the same sequence of $2^N - 1$ moves.

required, it will obviously take hopelessly long to find them and print them all out. We might be tempted, therefore, to expect such devastating time performance to occur only in problems whose outputs are unreasonably lengthy.

To convince ourselves that this is not so, it is instructive to consider **yes/no problems**; that is, algorithmic problems that do not produce any 'real' outputs except a 'yes' or a 'no'. These problems are sometimes called **decision problems**, as their purpose is merely to decide whether a certain property holds for their inputs. Most of this chapter (and the next) will be devoted to decision problems.

The Monkey Puzzle Problem: An Example

The reader may have encountered one or more versions of the very frustrating **monkey puzzle** (see Figure 7.1). It involves nine square cards whose sides are imprinted with the upper and lower halves of colored monkeys. The objective is to arrange the cards in the form of a 3 × 3 square such that halves match and colors are identical wherever edges meet.

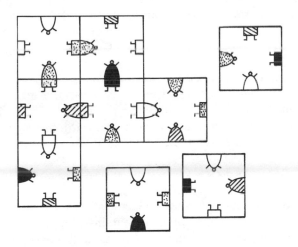

Figure 7.1 A 3 × 3 instance of the monkey puzzle.

In the general algorithmic problem associated with this puzzle, we are given (descriptions of) $N = M^2$ cards, and the problem calls for exhibiting, if possible, an $M \times M$ square arrangement of the N cards, so that colors and halves behave as stated. We shall assume that the cards are **oriented**, meaning that the edges have fixed directions, 'up', 'down', 'right', and 'left', so that they are not to be rotated. We shall concentrate on the seemingly easier yes/no version, that simply asks whether any such $M \times M$ arrangement exists, without asking for one to actually be exhibited.

A naive solution to the problem is not too hard to come by. We need only observe that each input involves finitely many cards, and hence that there are only finitely many different ways of arranging the input cards into a $M \times M$ square. Moreover, a given arrangement can easily be tested for legality (i.e., that all input cards are indeed used, and that halves and colors match) by simply considering each card and each of the meeting edges in turn. Consequently, an algorithm can be designed to work its way through all possible arrangements, stopping and saying 'yes' if the arrangement at hand is legal, and stopping and saying 'no' if all arrangements have been considered, and they have all been found to be illegal. Of course, some bookkeeping is required to make sure that all possible arrangements are indeed considered and that none are considered twice, but we shall not dwell on the details of the algorithm here – we are more interested in its time performance.

Let us assume that N is 25, meaning that the final square is to be of size 5×5. Let us also assume that we have a computer capable of constructing and evaluating a million arrangements every second (i.e., one arrangement every microsecond), including all the bookkeeping involved. This is quite a reasonable assumption, given today's computers. The question is: how long will the algorithm take in the worst case (which is when there *is* no legal arrangement, so that all possible arrangements are checked)?

If we arbitrarily number the locations in a 5×5 grid, there are obviously 25 possibilities for choosing a card to be placed in the first location. Having placed some card in that location, there are 24 cards to choose from for the second location, 23 for the third, and so on. The total number of arrangements can, therefore, reach:

$$25 \times 24 \times 23 \times \ldots \times 3 \times 2 \times 1$$

a number denoted by 25! and called 25 **factorial**. What is astonishing is the *size* of this innocent looking number; it contains 26 digits, a fact that does not seem alarming until we realize that our million-arrangements-per-second computer will take well over 490 *billion years* to work its way through all 25! arrangements. This is much, much longer than the time that has elapsed since the 'Big Bang'.

Obviously, particular monkey card puzzles can be prepared in ways that make life easy; if all cards are either identical to the one in Figure 7.2(a) or identical to that in Figure 7.2(b), the puzzle has trivial solutions. However, we are in the algorithmics business, and *worst*-case analysis is the name of our game. The puzzle designer actually strives for sets of cards that admit many *partial* solutions (in which portions of the square are legally covered with cards), but only very few *complete* solutions – maybe only one. This is what prevents the problem from admitting fast and easy solutions.

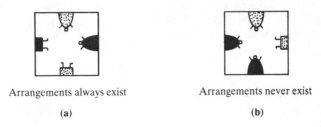

Arrangements always exist   Arrangements never exist

(a)   (b)

Figure 7.2   Trivial monkey puzzles.

The naive solution, therefore, is quite useless, even for a very small 5×5 version. The reader who is expecting a less naive solution to be presented, which would show how to really solve the problem in a useful way, is in for a disappointment. The only known solutions that are better than considering each of the $N!$ arrangements by brute force, are not sufficiently better as to be reasonable; for $N = 25$ they would still require, in the worst case, thousands of years of computation for a single instance.

Is there some hidden solution to the monkey puzzle problem, one that would be practical for a reasonable number of cards, say up to 150? By this we mean that maybe there is some easy way of solving the problem that we have not discovered yet. Perhaps there exists an arrangement precisely when the number of distinct cards is a multiple of 17, for some strange reason. The answer to this question is 'probably not, but we are not quite sure.' We shall discuss this matter further after examining the general behavior of such impractical algorithms as the one just described.

Reasonable vs. Unreasonable Time

The factorial function $N!$ grows at a rate that is orders of magnitude larger than the growth rate of any of the functions mentioned in previous chapters. It grows much, much faster than N, $N \times \log N$ or N^2, and, in fact, easily dwarfs all functions of the form N^K, for any fixed K. It is true that N^{1000}, for example, is larger than $N!$ for many values of N (for all N up to 1165, to be precise). However, for any K, there is some value of N (1165, for $K = 1000$) beyond which the function $N!$ leaves N^K far behind, very, very quickly.

Other functions exhibit similarly unacceptable growth rates. For example, the function N^N, denoting $N \times N \times N \times \ldots \times N$ with N occurrences of N, grows even faster than $N!$. The function 2^N, i.e., $2 \times 2 \times 2 \times \ldots \times 2$, with N 2s, grows slower than $N!$, but is also considered a 'bad' function; it still grows much faster than N^K for any fixed K. Actually, 2^N relates to N·precisely as N does to $\log_2 N$, so that for $N = 20$ the value of 2^N is about a million, and for $N = 30$ it is about a billion. For $N = 150$ the number 2^N is billions of times larger than the number of protons in the entire known universe. Figures 7.3 and 7.4 illustrate the relative growth rates of some of these functions.

N Function	10	50	100	300	1000
$5N$	50	250	500	1500	5000
$N \times \log_2 N$	33	282	665	2469	9966
N^2	100	2500	10 000	90 000	1 million (7 digits)
N^3	1000	125 000	1 million (7 digits)	27 million (8 digits)	1 billion (10 digits)
2^N	1024	a 16-digit number	a 31-digit number	a 91-digit number	a 302-digit number
$N!$	3.6 million (7 digits)	a 65-digit number	a 161-digit number	a 623-digit number	unimaginably large
N^N	10 billion (11 digits)	an 85-digit number	a 201-digit number	a 744-digit number	unimaginably large

For comparison: the number of protons in the known universe has 126 digits.
the number of microseconds since the 'Big Bang' has 24 digits.

Figure 7.3   Some values of some functions.

A more striking illustration of the differences between these functions is in the running times of algorithms. Figure 7.5 gives the actual running times of several hypothetical algorithms for the monkey puzzle problem for various values of N. It is assumed that the algorithms are run on a computer capable of carrying out a million instructions per second. As can be seen, even the smallest of the 'bad' functions, 2^N, might require 400 trillion centuries for a single instance of the 10×10 problem! For functions like $N!$ or N^N, the time is unimaginably worse.

These facts lead to an important classification of functions into 'good' and 'bad' ones. A function $f(N)$ is said to be **bounded from above** by another function $g(N)$ if for all N from a certain point on $f(N)$ is no greater

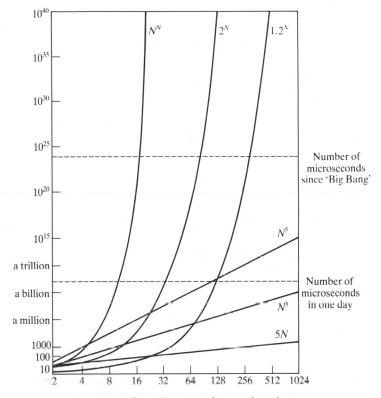

Figure 7.4   Growth rates of some functions.

than $g(N)$. In this way, for example, $\log_2 N$ is bounded by N, $N \times \log_2 N$ is bounded by N^2, 2^N by $N!$ and $N!$ by N^N. The distinction to be made is between **polynomial** and **super-polynomial** functions. For our purposes a polynomial function of N is one which is bounded from above by N^K for some fixed K. All others are super-polynomial. In particular, the exponential functions, that take the form K^N, for fixed $K > 1$, are all super-polynomial. For example, $\log N$, $N \times \log N$, N^6 and $N^7 + N^3 + 67$ are polynomial functions, whereas 2^N, $1.001^N + N^6$, N^N and $N!$ are exponential or worse. Although there are functions, like $N^{\log_2 N}$ for example, that are super-polynomial but not quite exponential, and others, like N^N that are super-exponential, current practice will be followed in abusing the terminology slightly by using 'exponential' as a synonym for 'super-polynomial' in the sequel.

An algorithm whose order-of-magnitude time performance is bounded from above by a polynomial function of N, where N is the size of its inputs, is called a **polynomial-time algorithm**, and will be referred to here as a **reasonable** algorithm. Similarly, an algorithm that, in the worst case, requires super-polynomial, or exponential-time, will be called **unreasonable**.

N Function	10	20	50	100	300
N^2	$1/10\,000$ second	$1/2500$ second	$1/400$ second	$1/100$ second	$9/100$ second
N^5	$1/10$ second	3.2 seconds	5.2 minutes	2.8 hours	28.1 days
2^N	$1/1000$ second	1 second	35.7 years	400 trillion centuries	a 75-digit number of centuries
N^N	2.8 hours	3.3 trillion years	a 70-digit number of centuries	a 185-digit number of centuries	a 728-digit number of centuries

For comparison: the 'Big Bang' was approximately 15 billion years ago.

Figure 7.5   Time consumption of hypothetical solutions to the monkey puzzle problem (assuming one instruction per microsecond).

As far as the algorithmic problem is concerned, a problem that admits a reasonable or polynomial-time solution is said to be **tractable**, whereas a problem that admits only unreasonable or exponential-time solutions is termed **intractable**.

The discussion and examples surrounding Figures 7.3–7.5 are intended to support this distinction. In general, intractable problems require impractically large amounts of time even on relatively small inputs, whereas tractable problems admit algorithms that are practical for reasonably sized inputs. We might be justified in questioning the wisdom of drawing the line between good and bad precisely where we did. As already mentioned, an N^{1000} algorithm, which is reasonable by our definition, is worse than a very unreasonable $N!$ algorithm for inputs under size 1165, and the turning point is much larger if N^{1000} is compared, say, with the exponential function 1.001^N. Nevertheless, in practice, unreasonable algorithms are useless, and most reasonable ones are sufficiently useful to warrant the distinction made. In Chapter 9 evidence will be presented to the effect that the dichotomy introduced here is actually extremely robust, even more so than the ignoring of constants that comes with the use of the big-O notation.

The sphere of all algorithmic problems can therefore be divided into two major classes as illustrated in Figure 7.6. The dividing line embodies one of the most important classifications in the theory of algorithmic complexity. In Chapter 8 another, even more fundamental, line will be drawn.

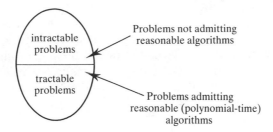

Figure 7.6   The sphere of algorithmic problems: Version I.

*   *   *

More on the Monkey Puzzle Problem

The monkey puzzle problem is really worse than anything we have seen so far. It asks only for a simple yes/no answer, yet even when using the best-known algorithms we could spend our entire life time on a single, very small instance of the problem and never find out what the correct answer is. A problem for which there is no known polynomial-time algorithm is thus not much better than a problem for which there is no known algorithm at all. The crucial question here is whether there really *is* no reasonable solution; in other words, is the monkey puzzle problem *really* intractable?

To sharpen our understanding of the situation, let us focus on several possibly bothersome issues.

(1) Computers are becoming faster by the week. Over the last 10 years or so computer speed has increased roughly by a factor of 10. Perhaps obtaining a practical solution to the problem is just a question of awaiting an additional improvement in computer speed.

(2) Doesn't the fact that we have not found a better algorithm for this problem indicate our incompetence at devising efficient algorithms? Shouldn't computer scientists be working at trying to improve the situation rather than spending their time writing books about it?

(3) Haven't people tried to look for an exponential-time lower bound on the problem, so that we might have a *proof* that no reasonable algorithm exists?

(4) Maybe the whole issue is not worth the effort, as the monkey puzzle problem is just one specific problem. It might be a colorful one, but it certainly doesn't look like a very important one.

These points are well taken, but the following unusual situation provides answers to them all. First of all, let us do away with objection number (1). Figure 7.7 shows that even if the fastest computer were to be made 1000 times faster, then a 2^N algorithm for the monkey puzzle problem would be able, in a given time frame (say, an hour), to cope with only about 10 more cards than it can today. In contrast, if the algorithm were to take time N it could cope with 1000 times the number of cards it can today. Hence, improving the computer's speed will improve things, but only in a very insignificant way.

Function	Maximal number of cards solvable in one hour:		
	with today's computer	with computer 100 times faster	with computer 1000 times faster
N	A	$100 \times A$	$1000 \times A$
N^2	B	$10 \times B$	$31.6 \times B$
2^N	C	$C + 6.64$	$C + 9.97$

Figure 7.7   Algorithmic improvements resulting from improvements in computer speed.

Let us now relate to point (4) – the two other points are treated implicitly later. It so happens that the monkey puzzle problem is not alone. There are other problems in the same boat. Moreover, the boat is large, impressive and manysided. The monkey puzzle problem is just one of close to 1000 diverse algorithmic problems, all of which exhibit precisely the same phenomena. They all admit unreasonable, exponential-time solutions, but none of them are known to admit reasonable ones. Moreover, no one has been able to prove that any of them *require* super-polynomial-time. In fact, the best-known lower bounds on most of the problems in this class are $O(N)$, meaning that it is conceivable (though unlikely) that they admit very efficient *linear-time* algorithms.

For reasons that will be explained later, let us denote this class of problems by NPC. The algorithmic gap associated with the problems in NPC is thus enormous. Their lower bounds are linear, and their upper bounds exponential! The issue is not whether we spend $O(N^2)$ or $O(N^3)$ time in solving them, or whether we need 20 comparisons for a search or a million. It boils down to the ultimate question of whether we can or cannot solve these problems for even very small inputs on even the largest and most powerful computers. It is as simple as that. The location of these algorithmic problems in the sphere of Figure 7.6 is thus unknown, since their upper and lower bounds lie on either side of the dividing line.

There are two additional properties that characterize the special class NPC, and which make it all the more remarkable. However, before discussing them, it should be stressed that the class NPC contains an ever-growing diversity of algorithmic problems, arising in such areas as combinatorics, operations research, economics, graph theory, game theory, and logic. It is worth looking at some of the other problems found there.

Two-Dimensional Arrangement Problems

Some of the most appealing problems in NPC are **arrangement** problems derived from two-dimensional puzzles like the monkey puzzle. Other good examples are those puzzles, sometimes handed out on airlines, which require several irregular shapes to be arranged into a rectangle (see Figure 7.8). The general problem calls for arranging N given shapes into a rectangle, and is in NPC. One reason for the apparent absence of a fast solution is rooted in the existence of many different partial solutions that cannot be extended to complete ones. Sometimes an arrangement puzzle admits only one complete solution.

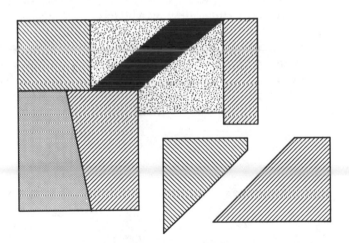

Figure 7.8   An airline puzzle.

Consider ordinary jigsaw puzzles. They admit virtually no partial solutions except as parts of the unique final solution. Adding a piece to a partially solved jigsaw puzzle is usually just a matter of running through all unused pieces and finding the single piece that will fit. This is a consequence of either the unique shapes of the jigs and jags on individual pieces, or the heterogeneous character of the picture to be formed, or of both. Therefore, as we can verify, an ordinary, 'well-behaved' jigsaw puzzle with N pieces can be solved in time $O(N^2)$.

However, anyone who has ever labored on a jigsaw puzzle containing lots of sky, sea or desert knows that not all jigsaw puzzles are that easy. A general jigsaw-based algorithmic problem has to cope with *all* possible input puzzles, including those that involve less heterogeneous pictures and whose pieces contain many identical jigs and jags. The general N-piece jigsaw problem also turns out to be in the class NPC. In essence, it is just the monkey puzzle problem or the irregular shapes problem in disguise.

Path-Finding Problems

In Chapter 4 two problems were described, involving lazy railroad contractors (finding minimal spanning trees) and weary travelers (finding shortest paths). They were both concerned with finding certain structures of minimal cost in city networks. A city network is a graph consisting of N points (the cities), and edges with associated costs (these are the distances between cities). The algorithms presented in Chapter 4 are both quadratic, and therefore both problems are tractable.

Here is another problem, which at first sight looks very similar to the other two. It involves a **traveling salesman** who has to visit each of the cities in a given network before returning to his starting point, whence his trip is complete. The algorithmic problem asks for the cheapest route, namely for a closed **tour** that passes through each of the nodes in the graph and whose total cost (i.e., the sum of the distances labeling the edges) is minimal. Figure 7.9 shows a six-city network, in which such an optimal tour is marked.

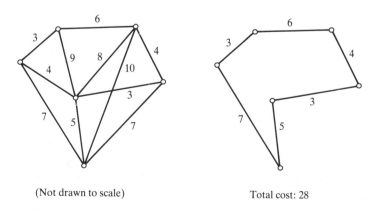

(Not drawn to scale)   Total cost: 28

Figure 7.9   A city network and a minimal round tour.

In the yes/no version the inputs include a number K besides the city graph G, and the decision problem asks whether there is a tour of G with total cost of no more than K. Thus, for the graph of Figure 7.9 the answer would be 'yes' if $K = 30$, but 'no' if $K = 27$.

Despite its somewhat playful description, the traveling salesman problem, like the minimal spanning tree and shortest path problems, is *not* a toy example. Its variants arise in the design of telephone networks and integrated circuits, in planning construction lines, and in the programming of industrial robots, to mention but a few applications. In all of these, the ability to find inexpensive tours of the graphs in question can be quite crucial.

Again, a naive $N!$ solution is easy to come by. Just consider all possible tours, stopping and saying 'yes' if the cost of the tour at hand is no more than K, and 'no' if all tours have been considered, and they have all been found to cost more than K. (Why is this an $O(N!)$ algorithm?) Again, even the $N = 25$ case is simply hopeless, and we must realize that for a traveling salesman with a suitcase full of bits and pieces 25 cities might sound a lot, but it is an almost laughable number for the kind of real-world applications mentioned above. The fact is that the traveling salesman problem is also in NPC, rendering the problem insolvable in practice, as far as we know.

It is worth briefly considering some other path-finding problems. Let us see what happens when we leave out edge lengths altogether. Given a graph consisting of points and edges, we can ask simply whether there exists a path, any path, that passes through all points exactly once. Such paths are termed **Hamiltonian**. Figure 7.10(a) shows a graph that has no Hamiltonian path, and Figure 7.10(b) shows how the addition of a single edge can change the situation. Although seemingly much easier, this problem is also in NPC. There is a simple exponential-time algorithm that checks all $N!$ paths, searching for one that reaches each point once, but no one knows of a polynomial-time solution.

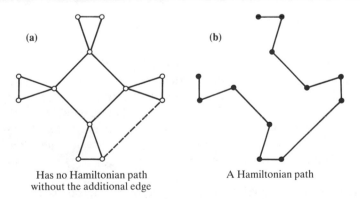

(a)   Has no Hamiltonian path
without the additional edge

A Hamiltonian path

Figure 7.10   Hamiltonian paths.

Curiously enough, if we are after a path that is to pass through all *edges* exactly once, rather than all points, the story is quite different. Such paths are termed **Eulerian**, and Figure 7.11 is an Eulerian analog of Figure 7.10. At first glance it seems that there is no better way to find an Eulerian path than to similarly go through every possible path. (In the worst case there are about $(N^2)!$ of them. Why?) However, a simple but rather clever polynomial-time solution to the Eulerian path problem was found in 1736 by the great mathematician Leonhard Euler. The solution is obtained by showing that a graph contains a precise Eulerian path when it satisfies the following two properties: (1) it is connected (i.e., any point is reachable from any other), and (2) the number of edges emanating from any point (with the possible exception of two points) is even. Accordingly, an algorithm need only check whether an input graph satisfies these properties. The second is trivial, and the first can be easily shown to admit a fast algorithm, one that is actually linear in the number of edges.

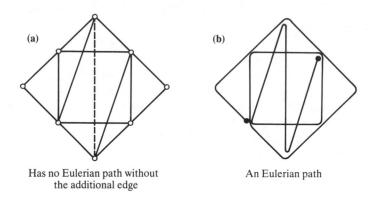

(a) Has no Eulerian path without the additional edge

(b) An Eulerian path

Figure 7.11   Eulerian paths.

Scheduling and Matching Problems

Many NPC problems are concerned, in one way or another, with **scheduling** or **matching**. For example, we are given the particular hours that each of N teachers is available, and the particular hours each of M classes can be scheduled. In addition, we are given the number of hours each of the teachers has to teach each of the classes. The **timetable problem** asks whether it is possible to match teachers, classes and hours so that all the given constraints are met, so that no two teachers teach the same class at the same time, and so that no two classes are taught by the same teacher at the same time.

The timetable problem also belongs to the special class NPC. Other matching problems in NPC involve fitting loads of various sizes into trucks with various capacities, and assigning students to dormitory rooms in a way that satisfies certain constraints.

It must be emphasized that many other scheduling and matching problems are quite tractable, as is the case with arrangements, path finding, etc.

Determining Logical Truth

One of the best-known problems in NPC involves determining the truth or falsity of sentences in a simple logical formalism called the **propositional calculus**. In this language, we are allowed to combine symbols denoting elementary assertions into more complex assertions, using the logical connectives & (denoting 'and'), ∨ (denoting 'or'), ~ ('not') and → ('implies'). Thus, for example, the sentence:

$$\sim (E \to F) \, \& \, (F \vee (D \to \sim E))$$

states that (1) it is not the case that the truth of E implies the truth of F, and (2) either F is true or the truth of D implies the falsity of E.

The algorithmic problem calls for determining the **satisfiability** of such sentences. In other words, given a sentence as an input, we want to know whether it is possible to assign 'true' or 'false' to the basic assertions appearing in it, so that the entire sentence will turn out to be true. An assignment of truth values to the basic assertions is called a **truth assignment**. In the example, we can fix E to be true and D and F to be false. This will cause (1) to be true because E is true but F is not, so that E cannot imply F. Also, (2) is true, despite F's falsity, by virtue of D's falsity.[†] Hence, the sample sentence is satisfiable. The reader might want to verify that the sentence:

$$\sim (((D \, \& \, E) \to F) \, \& \, (F \vee (D \to \sim E))$$

is unsatisfiable; there is no way to assign truth values to D, E and F that will make this sentence true.

It is not too difficult to come up with an exponential-time algorithm for the satisfiability problem, where N is the number of distinct elementary assertions in the input sentence. We simply try out all possible truth assignments. There are precisely 2^N of them, and it is easy to test the truth of the formula with respect to each one of these truth assignments in time that is polynomial in N. Unfortunately, the satisfiability problem for the propositional calculus is also in NPC, so that the naive exponential-time algorithm is, in essence, the best known. It is impossible, as far as is known

---

[†] A false assertion implies anything. The sentence 'if I am an alligator then so are you' is true by virtue of my not being an alligator, regardless of your own standing.

at present, to check algorithmically whether even quite short sentences can be made true.

Coloring Maps and Graphs

In Chapter 5 we described the four-color theorem, which proves that any map of countries can be colored using only four colors in such a way that no two adjacent countries are colored the same (see Figure 5.12). It follows that the algorithmic problem of determining whether a given map can be *four-colored*, as this kind of process is termed, is trivial: on any input map the answer is simply 'yes'. The very same problem, but where only two colors are allowed, is not very hard either. A map can be two-colored exactly when it contains no point that is the junction of an odd number of countries (why?), and this property is easy to check for.

Note that the number of colors is not taken here as part of the input. We are discussing the algorithmic problems obtained by *fixing* the number C of colors allowed, and asking whether an input country map can be C-colored. As we have shown, the cases $C = 2$ and $C = 4$ are trivial. The interesting case is that of three colors. Determining whether a map can be three-colored is in NPC, meaning that we know of only unreasonable solutions, thus making the problem unsolvable in practice except for extremely small numbers of countries.

A related problem involves coloring graphs. The coloring rule here is similar to that of map coloring, except that nodes (points in the graph) play the role of countries. No two neighboring nodes (i.e., nodes connected by an edge) may be monochromatic. In contrast to country maps, whose flatness restricts the possible configurations of bordering countries, any node in a graph can be connected by edges to any other. It is easy to construct graphs that require large numbers of colors. A graph containing C nodes, each connected to all others, clearly requires C colors. Such a graph is called a **clique**. The algorithmic problem asks for the minimal number of colors required to color a given graph G. The yes/no version, which asks if G can be colored with C colors, C being part of the input, is in NPC, and hence is not known to have a reasonable solution. Since the original version is at least as hard as the yes/no version (why?), it too is not known to be solvable in reasonable time.

* * *

Short Certificates and Magic Coins

All these NPC problems seem to require, as part of their inherent nature, that we try out *partial* matchings, *partial* truth assignments, *partial* arrangements, or *partial* colorings, and continuously extend them in the hope of reaching a final complete solution. When a partial solution cannot be extended, we apparently have to *backtrack*; that is, to undo things already done, in preparation for trying an alternative. If this process is carried out carefully no possible solution is missed but an exponential amount of time is required in the worst case.

Thus, given an input to an NPC problem, it appears to be extremely hard to tell whether the answer to the question embodied in the problem is a 'yes' or a 'no'. However, it is interesting that in all these problems if the answer happens to be 'yes' there is an easy way to convince someone of it. There is a so-called **certificate**, which contains conclusive evidence to the effect that the answer is indeed 'yes'. Moreover, this certificate can always be made to be reasonably short. Its size can always be bounded by a polynomial in N. (In fact, most often it is *linear* in N.)

For example, we know that it is notoriously difficult to tell whether a graph contains a Hamiltonian path, or whether it contains one whose length is no greater than K. On the other hand, if such a path indeed exists, it can be exhibited (as in Figures 7.9 and 7.10) and easily checked to be of the desired kind, thus serving as an excellent proof that the answer is 'yes'. Similarly, although it is difficult to *find* a truth assignment that satisfies a sentence in the propositional calculus, it is easy to *certify* that the sentence is satisfiable, by simply exhibiting an assignment that satisfies it. Moreover, it is easy to verify in polynomial-time that this particular truth assignment does the job. In a similar vein, exhibiting a legal $M \times M$ arrangement of the M^2 monkey puzzle cards serves as conclusive evidence that the corresponding algorithmic problem says 'yes' when applied to the puzzle as an input. Here, too, the legality of the arrangement (colors and halves match) can be verified easily in polynomial-time.

Figuring out whether an NPC problem says 'yes' to an input is thus hard, but certifying that it indeed does, *when* it does, is easy.

There is another way of describing this phenomenon. Assume we have a very special magic coin, to be used in the backtracking procedure just described. Whenever it is possible to extend a partial solution in two ways (e.g., two monkey cards can be legally placed at a currently empty location, or the next assertion symbol can be assigned 'true' or 'false'), the coin is flipped and the choice is made according to the outcome. However, the coin does not fall at random; it possesses magical insight, always indicating the best possibility. If only one of the two possibilities can be extended to a complete solution the coin will select that very one, without the need for explicit lookahead. (If both can be so extended, or if neither can, the coin acts like a normal random coin.)

Technically, we say that such algorithms are **nondeterministic**, in that they always 'guess' which of the available options is better, rather than having to employ some deterministic procedure to go through them all. Somehow, they always manage to make the right choice. Clearly, if algorithms were allowed to exploit such magical nondeterminism we might have been able to improve the solutions to certain algorithmic problems, since the work associated with trying out possibilities is avoided. For the NPC problems this improvement is not at all marginal: every NPC problem has a *polynomial-time* nondeterministic algorithm. This fact can be proved by showing that the 'short' certificates discussed above correspond directly to the polynomial-time 'magical' executions, so that all we have to do is follow the instructions of the magic coin and when we have a complete candidate solution simply check whether it is legal. Since the coin always indicates the best possibility, we can safely say 'no' if the candidate solution is in violation of the rules; a legal solution would have been found by the coin if one existed.

Thus, NPC problems are apparently intractable, but become 'tractable' by using magical nondeterminism. This explains part of the acronym NPC ('Nondeterministic Polynomial-time'), with NP standing for problems that admit short certificates. We now turn to the C, which stands for 'Complete'.

NP-Completeness: Standing or Falling Together

Besides admitting deterministic solutions that take unreasonable time, and 'magical', nondeterministic ones that take reasonable time, NPC problems have an additional, most remarkable, property. Each one's fate is tightly bound to that of all the others. Either *all* NPC problems are tractable, or *none* of them are! The term 'complete' is used to signify this additional property, so that the problems in NPC are known as the **NP-complete** problems.

Let us sharpen this statement. If someone were to find a polynomial-time algorithm for *any* single NP-complete problem, there would immediately be polynomial-time algorithms for *all* of them. This implies the following dual fact: if someone were to prove an exponential-time lower bound for *any* NP-complete problem, establishing that it cannot be solved in polynomial-time, it would follow immediately that *no* such problem can be solved in polynomial-time. In terms of Figure 7.6, it is not known on which side of the line the NP-complete problems belong, but it *is* known that they all belong on the same side. How do we prove such a sweeping claim? Recall that close to 1000 different problems in diverse areas are known to be NP-complete!

The concept that is used to establish this stand-or-fall-together phenomenon is that of a **polynomial-time reduction**. Given two NP-complete problems P_1 and P_2, a polynomial-time reduction is an algorithm that runs in polynomial-time, and *reduces* one problem to the other, in the following sense. If someone comes along with a P_1-input X and wants the 'yes' or 'no' answer, we use the algorithm to transform X into a P_2-input Y such that P_2's answer to Y is precisely P_1's answer to X.

For example, it is quite easy to reduce the Hamiltonian path problem to the traveling salesman problem.[†] Given a graph G with N nodes, construct a traveling salesman network G' as follows. The nodes of G' are the N nodes of G, and edges are drawn between every two nodes, assigning cost 1 to an edge if it was present in G, and 2 if it was not. Figure 7.12 illustrates the transformation. It is not too difficult to see that G' has a traveling salesman tour of length no greater than $N + 1$ (passing once through each point) precisely if G contains a Hamiltonian path. Thus, to answer questions about the existence of Hamiltonian paths, take the input graph G and carry out the transformation to G'. Then ask whether G' has a traveling salesman tour that is no longer than $N + 1$, where N is the number of nodes in G. The answer to the first question on G is 'yes' precisely when the answer to the second on G' is 'yes'. Notice too that the transformation takes only a polynomial amount of time.

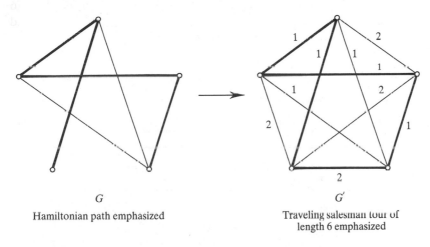

G

Hamiltonian path emphasized

G'

Traveling salesman tour of
length 6 emphasized

Figure 7.12   Reducing Hamiltonian paths to traveling salesmen.

Why is this fact of interest? Because it shows that, in terms of tractability, the Hamiltonian path problem is no worse than the traveling salesman problem; if the latter has a reasonable solution then so does the former. Figure 7.13 illustrates how the reduction is used to obtain a reasonable Hamiltonian path algorithm from a (hypothetical) reasonable traveling salesman algorithm.

Now comes the fact that establishes the common fate phenomenon of the NP-complete problems: every NP-complete problem is polynomially reducible to every other! Consequently, tractability of one implies tractability of all, and intractability of one implies intractability of all.

[†] Here we take the version of the traveling salesman problem that forbids tours to pass through points more than once.

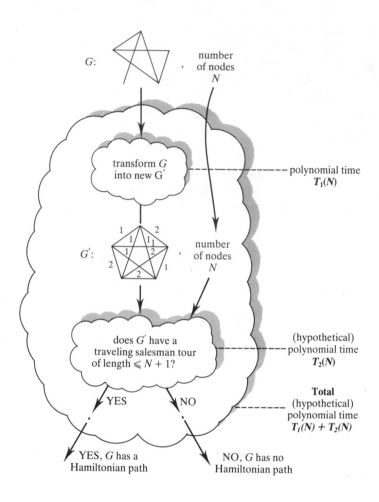

Figure 7.13 Using the reduction of Figure 7.12.

To show that a newly considered problem P is indeed NP-complete we need not construct reductions from P to all other NP-complete problems and from them to P. It suffices, in fact, to prove that P reduces (in polynomial-time) to at least one problem Q, already known to be NP-complete, and that at least one problem R, already known to be NP-complete, reduces to P. The first of these facts shows that, in terms of tractability, P cannot be any *worse* than Q, and the second shows that it cannot be any *better* than R. Thus, if Q is tractable so is P, and if P is tractable so is R. But since Q and R are both NP-complete, they stand and fall together, hence P stands and falls with them too, implying its own NP-completeness.[†]

It follows that once we know of one NP-complete problem we can show that others are NP-complete too by using the reduction mechanism. Now, clearly all this had to start somewhere. There had to be a *first* NP-complete problem. In 1971 the satisfiability problem for the propositional calculus was shown to be NP-complete, thus providing the anchor for NP-completeness proofs. The result, known as **Cook's theorem**, is considered to be one of the most important results in the theory of algorithmic complexity. Its proof relies on concepts we shall discuss in Chapter 9.

Reducing Oranges to Apples

Polynomial-time reductions between NP-complete problems can be far subtler than the one just given. While it is not at all clear what timetables and monkey puzzles have to do with each other, we know that there *must* be a reduction between them, for they are both NP-complete. Since a new problem requires only one reduction in each direction, often the best-known reduction between two problems consists of a chain of reductions leading through several other NP-complete problems.

It would be fruitless to tire the reader with one of the really difficult cases, so here is an example of a reduction that is not too difficult but not quite trivial either. We show how to reduce the problem of three-coloring a map to that of satisfiability in the propositional calculus. This establishes that the former cannot be any worse, in terms of tractability, than the latter. Specifically, we have to describe an algorithm that inputs the description of some arbitrary map M, and outputs a propositional sentence F, such that M can be three-colored if, and only if, F is satisfiable. Furthermore, the algorithm must run in polynomial-time, which, among other things, implies that the number of symbols in the formula F is allowed to be at most polynomially more than the number of countries in M.

Let M be a given map, assumed to involve the countries $C_1, \ldots, C_N$. We shall describe the sentence F, and argue that its size is polynomial in N. The reader will be able to see quite easily how this can be turned into a general polynomial-time algorithm that works for every M.

** Assuming the three colors are R, B and Y (red, blue and yellow), the sentence F involves $3N$ elementary assertions, one for each combination of color and country. The assertion 'C_I-is-Y', for example, is

---

[†] Actually, in practice, only the second of these reductions is carried out. To establish the fact that P cannot be any worse than the NP-complete problems, it is usually easier to exhibit a short certificate or a reasonable magical nondeterministic algorithm than to explicitly reduce to P some known NP-complete problem.

intended to mean that country C_I is colored yellow. We construct F by 'and'-ing together two parts.

The first part asserts that each country is colored with exactly one of the three colors, no more and no less. It consists of 'and'-ing together the following subsentences for each country C_I:

$$((C_I\text{-is-}R \ \& \sim C_I\text{-is-}B \ \& \sim C_I\text{-is-}Y)$$
$$\vee (C_I\text{-is-}B \ \& \sim C_I\text{-is-}R \ \& \sim C_I\text{-is-}Y)$$
$$\vee (C_I\text{-is-}Y \ \& \sim C_I\text{-is-}B \ \& \sim C_I\text{-is-}R))$$

meaning that C_I is colored red and not blue or yellow, *or* blue and not red or yellow, *or* yellow and not blue or red. The second part is obtained by identifying all pairs of countries C_I and C_J that are adjacent in the map M, and 'and'-ing together the following subsentences for each such pair, asserting that the two countries are not colored with the same color:

$$\sim((C_I\text{-is-}R \ \& \ C_J\text{-is-}R)$$
$$\vee (C_I\text{-is-}B \ \& \ C_J\text{-is-}B)$$
$$\vee (C_I\text{-is-}Y \ \& \ C_J\text{-is-}Y))$$

meaning that it is *not* the case that both C_I and C_J are colored red, or both are colored blue, or both are colored yellow.

How long is the sentence F? The first part is linear in N, since it contains one subsentence of fixed length for each country C_I. The second is no worse than quadratic in N, since it contains one fixed-length subsentence for each pair of adjacent countries I and J, and there can be no more than N^2 pairs. Hence, clearly F is polynomial in N.

It remains to show that F is satisfiable if, and only if, M is three-colorable. To prove this, we proceed in both directions. If M is three-colorable by some coloring scheme S (which, it can be assumed, involves the colors red, blue and yellow), we can satisfy F simply by assigning 'true' to the elementary assertion $C_I\text{-is-}X$ if the scheme S calls for coloring country C_I with color X, and 'false' otherwise. It is easy to see that all parts of F are thus satisfied. Conversely, if F is satisfied by some truth assignment S, then M can be colored with three colors by assigning color X to country C_I precisely when the assignment S assigns 'true' to the assertion $C_I\text{-is-}X$. The construction of F guarantees that each country is colored with exactly one color, and that there are no conflicts. This concludes the reduction.   **

Is P Equal to NP?

Just as NP stands for the class of problems that admit nondeterministic polynomial-time algorithms, P stands for what we have been calling tractable problems; namely, those that admit polynomial-time algorithms. The large class of problems we have been extensively discussing, the NP-complete problems, are the 'hardest' problems in NP. If one of them turns out to be easy, i.e., in P, then *all* problems in NP are also in P. Now, since obviously P is part of NP (why?), the question really boils down to whether P is equal to NP or not.

The P = NP? problem, as it is called, has been open since it was posed in 1971, and is one of the most difficult unresolved problems in computer science. It is definitely the most intriguing. Either all of these interesting and important problems can be solved reasonably by computer, or none of them can. Many of the most talented theoretical computer scientists have worked on the problem, but to no avail. Most of them believe that P ≠ NP, meaning that the NP-complete problems are inherently *in*tractable, but no one knows for sure. In any case, showing that an algorithmic problem is NP-complete is regarded as weighty evidence of its probable intractability.

Some problems that have been shown to be *in* NP are not known to be either NP-complete or in P. A well-known example involves testing a number for **primality**; that is, asking whether it has any factors (numbers that divide it exactly) other than 1 and itself. If the problem is phrased in a form that asks whether the number is *not* a prime, there is a short certificate in case the answer is 'yes' (i.e., the number is not prime). The certificate is simply a factor that is neither 1 nor the number itself. We check that it is indeed a factor by a simple division. Thus, the *non*primality problem is in NP. On the other hand, if the problem asks whether the number *is* a prime, it is far from obvious that there is a short certificate. Nevertheless, it has been shown that the primality problem is also in NP. Neither of these dual problems is known to be NP-complete, which means that finding a polynomial-time algorithm for one or both of them does not necessarily imply that P = NP, as it does for problems that are NP-complete.[†]

Imperfect Solutions to NP-complete Problems

Many NP-complete decision problems are yes/no versions of what are sometimes called **combinatorial optimization** problems. The traveling salesman problem is a good example. Clearly, the problem of actually *finding* an optimal tour cannot be tractable without the yes/no version being tractable too, since once we have found an optimal tour we can easily check whether its overall length is no greater than a given K. For this reason the original problem is also said to be NP-complete, and thus, as far as current knowledge goes, it is intractable.

[†] It should be noted that in number-theoretic problems the size N of the input is usually not the number itself but its length in digits, which is on the order of the *logarithm* of the number. Therefore, while we can check for primality of a number by simply trying to divide it by all numbers between 2 and its square root, there are exponentially many of them to be tested if N is the number's length. The algorithm, therefore, is exponential. We shall return to primality testing in Chapter 11.

In some cases, however, we can solve optimization problems in ways that are less than perfect, yet of considerable practical value. The algorithms designed for this purpose are generically called **approximation algorithms**, and are based on the assumption that in many cases a less than optimal tour is better than no tour at all, and a timetable with a few constraint violations is better than no timetable at all.

One type of approximation algorithm produces results guaranteed to be 'close' to the optimal solution. For example, there is a rather clever algorithm for a certain version of the traveling salesman problem (where the graph is assumed to represent a realistic two-dimensional map) that runs in time $O(N^3)$ and produces a tour that is guaranteed to be no longer than 1.5 times the (unknown) optimal tour. The guarantee, of course, is based on a rigorous mathematical proof. Actually, there is a much less sophisticated algorithm that guarantees a tour of no longer than *twice* the optimal tour, and which the reader might want to try constructing. It is based on finding the minimal spanning tree (see Chapters 4 and 6) and traversing each edge in it twice. (Why is the tour no longer than twice the optimum?)

Another approach to approximation yields algorithms that are not guaranteed to be *always* within some fixed range of the optimum, but to be very close to the optimum *almost* always. Here the analysis required is similar to that carried out for the average-case performance of algorithms, and usually involves somewhat sophisticated probability theory. For example, there is a fast algorithm for the traveling salesman problem that for some input graphs might yield tours much longer than the optimum. However, in the vast majority of cases (the number of them has been proved to approach the total number of graphs with N nodes as N becomes larger) the algorithm yields almost optimal tours. This particular algorithm is based upon a **heuristic**, i.e., rule of thumb, whereby the graph is first partitioned into many local clusters containing very few points each. One then finds the optimal tours within each of these, and then combines them into a global tour using an algorithm similar to the greedy algorithm for the spanning tree problem.

Some problems can be shown to be resistant to certain approaches to approximation. Consider, for example, the problem that asks for the minimal number of colors required to color an arbitrary graph. It has recently been shown that if there is some polynomial-time algorithm that is guaranteed to yield a coloring with no more than twice the minimal number of colors, then there is a polynomial-time algorithm for the problem itself. Since the problem is NP-complete, this means that finding a good approximation algorithm for it is just as difficult as showing that $P = NP$.

*   *   *

Provably Intractable Problems

Despite our inability to find reasonable solutions to the numerous NP-complete problems, we do not know for sure that such solutions do not exist. It should be realized, however, that there are many problems that have been *proved* to be intractable, and these are not restricted only to ones (like the Towers of Hanoi) whose outputs are unreasonably lengthy. Here are some examples.

Towards the end of Chapter 1 we discussed the problem of deciding whether, given a board configuration of chess, White has a guaranteed winning strategy. As the reader will have realized, the **game tree** for chess grows exponentially. In other words, if we fix some initial configuration at the root of the tree and each node is extended downwards by descendants corresponding to all possible next configurations, the size of the tree, in general, becomes exponential in its depth. If we want to look N moves ahead we might have to consider K^N configurations, for some $K > 1$.

This fact does not mean that chess, as a game, is intractable. In fact, since there are only finitely many configurations in the entire game (albeit a very large number of them) the lookahead problem is not really an algorithmic problem for which we can talk about order-of-magnitude performance. The algorithmic problem commonly associated with chess involves a **generalized** version, where the game is played on an $N \times N$ board, the set of pieces and allowed moves being extended appropriately. Generalized chess, as well as generalized checkers, has indeed been shown to have an exponential-time lower bound. It is thus **provably intractable.**

In addition to these somewhat contrived generalizations of fixed-size games, several very simple games whose initial configurations vary in size have also been shown to have exponential-time lower bounds. One of them is called **roadblock**, and is played by two players, A and B, on a network of intersecting roads, each colored with one of three colors. (Roads may pass under others.) Certain intersections are marked 'A wins' or 'B wins', and each player has a fleet of cars that occupy certain intersections. In his turn, a player moves one of his cars along a stretch of road, all of whose segments must be of the same color, to a new intersection, as long as no cars are met along the way. The winner is the first player to reach one of his 'win' intersections.

The algorithmic problem inputs the description of a network, with cars placed at certain intersections, and asks whether player A (whose turn it is) has a winning strategy. Figure 7.14 shows a roadblock configuration that A can win, no matter what B does. (How?)

The roadblock problem has an exponential-time lower bound, meaning that there is a constant $K > 1$ such that any algorithm solving it takes time that grows at least as fast as K^N, where N is the number of intersections in the network. In other words, while certain configurations might be easy to analyze, there is no practical algorithmic method, and *there never will be*, for determining whether A has a guaranteed strategy for winning a roadblock game. For the best algorithm we might design there will always be configurations, even relatively small ones, that will cause it to run for an unreasonable amount of time.

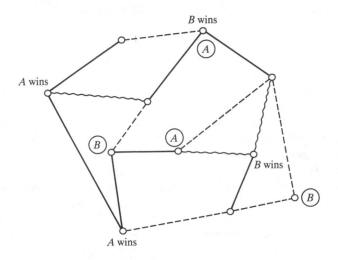

Figure 7.14   A roadblock configuration that A can win.

We should remark that these inherently exponential-time problems do not admit the kind of short certificates that NP-complete problems do. Not only is it provably difficult to tell whether there is a winning strategy for a roadblock player from a given configuration, it is also impossibly time consuming to convince someone that there is one, *if* there is.

A Provably Intractable Satisfiability Problem

Another example of a provably intractable problem involves logical satisfiability. Earlier, we met with the propositional calculus, a formalism that enables us to write sentences consisting of logical combinations of basic assertions. A set of truth values for the basic assertions determines a truth value for the sentence itself. A sentence in the propositional calculus is thus 'static' in nature – its truth depends only on the present truth values of its constituents. In Chapter 5 we briefly discussed *dynamic* logics, in which we are allowed to use the construct:

after(A, F)

where A is an algorithm and F is an assertion, or statement. It asserts that F is true after A is executed. Here, of course, the truth of a sentence no longer depends only on the state of affairs at present, but also on the state of affairs after the algorithm is executed.

One version of dynamic logic, called **propositional dynamic logic** (or **PDL** for short), restricts the algorithms, or programs, allowed inside the **after** construct to be combinations of unspecified elementary programs. Just as we can build up complex assertions from basic assertion symbols, using &, ∨, ~ and →, we can now build up complex programs from basic program symbols, using programming constructs such as sequencing, conditional branching and iteration. Programs and assertions are then combined using the **after** construct. The following is a sentence of PDL, which states that E is false after the two programs inside the **after** are executed in order:

after(**while** E **do** A **end**; **if** E **then do** B **end**, $\sim E$)

This sentence is always true, no matter what assertion E stands for, and no matter what programs A and B stand for, even if B might have the ability to change E's truth value. The reader is encouraged to convince himself of this fact.

The satisfiability problem for the propositional calculus is interesting because it concerns the feasibility of reasoning about logical sentences of *static* nature. In the same vein, the satisfiability problem for PDL is interesting because it concerns the feasibility of reasoning about logical sentences of *dynamic* nature, involving programs and some of their most elementary properties. The satisfiability problem for the propositional calculus is NP-complete, and is hence *suspected* to be intractable. The satisfiability problem for PDL, on the other hand, has an exponential-time lower bound, and is hence *known* to be intractable. There is no algorithmic method, and there never will be, which can be used in practice to decide whether PDL sentences can be made true. Any such algorithm will necessarily run for formidable amounts of time on certain sentences of very reasonable size. As a matter of fact, the problem also happens to admit an exponential-time algorithm, so that we know its precise algorithmic status; it is an inherently exponential-time problem.

Proving Exponential-Time Lower Bounds

In Chapter 6 we saw that proving lower bounds is far from easy. Here the difficulty is as acute as ever. How do we show that there is no algorithm, and there never will be, that will solve the algorithmic problem P in less than an exponential amount of time?

Such a statement can be proved in two steps. First, using a rather abstract and general kind of argument, we show that there exists at least *one* problem, call it Q, that has both upper and lower bounds of exponential-time. The argument, however, says nothing of the particular problem of interest, P. Next, we use another general argument to show the existence of a polynomial-time reduction from *any* problem solvable in exponential-time, to the problem P. Now, since Q is actually solvable in exponential-time, it too is polynomially reducible to P, and it follows that P cannot be solved in less than an exponential amount of time, otherwise Q would be also. Therefore, P is inherently exponential too.

In Chapter 9, after learning more about the robustness of the tractable/intractable dichotomy, we shall be able to say more about these two general arguments.

Problems that Are Even Harder!

This chapter has been based on the assumption that algorithmic problems whose best algorithms are exponential in time are intractable. However, there are problems that are even worse. Among these, some of the most interesting ones involve satisfiability and truth determination in various rich logical formalisms.

We have already met with the propositional calculus and PDL, in which basic assertions were simply symbols like E and F that could take on truth values. However, when statements are made about real mathematical objects, such as numbers, we want the basic assertions to be more expressive. We would like to be able to write $X = 15$, or $Y + 8 > Z$; we would like to be able to consider *sets* of objects, and talk about all elements in a set; we would like to talk about the *existence* of elements with certain properties, and so on. There are numerous logical formalisms that cater for such desires, and most interesting mathematical theorems, conjectures, and statements can be written in one or more of them.

It is, therefore, natural that computer scientists seek efficient methods for proving that sentences in such formalisms are true, since such methods can be used to establish absolute mathematical truth. We know that truth in the propositional calculus *most probably* cannot be determined in less than exponential time, since the problem is NP-complete, and that truth in PDL *definitely* cannot, since this problem is provably exponential. Several of the more elaborate formalisms are much worse.

Consider the function 2^{2^N} which is $2 \times 2 \times \ldots \times 2$, with 2 appearing 2^N times. For $N = 5$ the value is well over a billion, while for $N = 8$ the value is much larger than our friend, the number of protons in the known universe. The function 2^{2^N} of course, relates to the unreasonable 2^N just as 2^N relates to the very reasonable function N. It is therefore *doubly* unreasonable, and in fact is referred to as a **double-exponential**. The **triple-exponential** function $2^{2^{2^N}}$ is defined similarly, as are all the K-fold exponential-time functions $2^{2^{\cdot^{\cdot^{2^N}}}}$ with K appearances of 2.

Several formalisms have been shown to have lower bounds of double-exponential-time. Among these is a logic known as **Presburger arithmetic**, which allows us to talk about positive integers, and variables whose values are positive integers. It also allows the '+' operation, and the '=' symbol. We combine assertions using the logical operations of propositional calculus, as well as the **quantifiers** $\exists X$ and $\forall X$, standing for 'there exists X' and 'for all X', respectively. For example, the following formula states that there are infinitely many even numbers, by stating that for every X there is an even Y that is at least as large as X:

$$\forall X \; \exists Y \; \exists Z \; (X + Z = Y \,\&\, \exists W(W + W = Y))$$

While truth in Presburger arithmetic is provably double-exponential, another formalism, called WS1S, is far worse.

In WS1S we can talk not only about (positive) integers, but also about *sets* of integers. We can assert that a set S contains an element X by writing $X \in S$.

** The following is a true formula of WS1S, stating that every even number is obtained by adding 2 to 0 some number of times.

$$\forall B \; [(0 \in B \,\&\, \forall X(X \in B \to X + 2 \in B)) \to \forall Y \; (\exists W(Y = W + W)$$
$$\to Y \in B)]$$

It accomplishes this by asserting that any set B, which (1) contains 0, and (2) contains $X + 2$ whenever it contains X, must contain all even numbers. **

WS1S is unimaginably difficult to analyze. It has been actually shown to admit no K-fold exponential algorithm, for any K! (Exclamation mark here, not factorial... .) This means that for any algorithm A that determines truth of WS1S formulas (and there are such algorithms), and for any fixed K, there will be formulas of length N, for larger and larger N, that will require A to run for longer than $2^{2^{\cdots^{2^N}}}$ time units, with K appearances of 2. In such devastating cases we say that the decision problem is provably **nonelementary**. Not only is it intractable, it is not even doubly or triply intractable. Its time performance is worse than any K-fold exponential, and we might justifiably say that it is of unlimited intractability.

Unreasonable Amounts of Memory Space

Although we have committed ourselves to concentrate on time performance, we must spend a moment contemplating unreasonable memory-space requirements. There are algorithmic problems that have been proven to have lower bounds of exponential-space. This means that any algorithm A solving them will require, say, 2^N memory cells on certain inputs of ever-growing sizes N. In fact, it can be shown that a consequence of a double-exponential-time lower bound (like that of the truth problem for Presburger arithmetic) is an exponential-space lower bound. Similarly, a nonelementary lower bound on time (like that of truth in WS1S) implies a nonelementary lower bound on space too.

These facts have striking consequences. If a problem has a 2^N lower bound on memory space, then for any algorithm there will be inputs of quite reasonable size (considerably less than 150) that would require so much space for intermediate data that even if each bit were to be the size of a *proton*, the whole known universe would not suffice to write it all down! The situation is clearly unimaginably worse for nonelementary space bounds.

Research on Complexity Classes and Intractability

In the mid 1960s people began to realize the importance of obtaining polynomial-time algorithms for algorithmic problems, and the significance of the dividing line of Figure 7.6 became apparent. Ever since, the issues and concepts discussed in this chapter have been the subject matter of intense and widespread research by many of the most talented computer scientists.

Every now and then, a polynomial-time algorithm or an exponential-time lower bound is found for a problem whose tractable/intractable status was unknown. A rather striking example is linear planning, better known as **linear programming**. Linear planning is a general framework within which we can phrase many kinds of planning problems arising in organizations where time, resources and personnel constraints have to be met in a cost-efficient way. The linear planning problem, it must be emphasized, is not NP-complete, but the best algorithm that anyone was able to find for it was an exponential-time procedure known as the **simplex method**. Despite the fact that certain inputs forced the simplex method to run for an exponential amount of time, they were rather contrived, and tended not to arise in practice; when the method was used for real problems, even of nontrivial size, it usually performed very well. Nevertheless, the problem was not known to be in P, nor was there a lower bound to show that it wasn't.

In 1979, an ingenious polynomial-time algorithm was found for the problem, but it was something of a disappointment. The exponential-time simplex method outperformed it in many of the cases arising in practice. Nevertheless, it did show that linear programming is in P. Moreover, recent work based on this algorithm has produced more efficient versions, and people currently believe that before long there will be a fast polynomial-time algorithm for linear planning, that will be useful in practice for all inputs of reasonable size.

This kind of work is aimed at improving our knowledge about specific problems, and is analogous to the search for efficient algorithms within P itself, as discussed in Chapter 6.

Work of more general nature involves **complexity classes** such as P and NP themselves. Here we are interested in identifying large and significant classes of problems, all of which share inherent performance characteristics. Using the prefix LOG for logarithmic, P for polynomial, EXP for exponential, and 2EXP for double exponential, we can write LOGTIME for the class of problems solvable in logarithmic time, PTIME for the class called P above, PSPACE for the problems solvable with a polynomial amount of memory space, etc. We can then establish the following inclusion relations (where $\subseteq$ means 'is a subset of') (see Figure 7.15):

$$\text{LOGTIME} \subseteq \text{LOGSPACE} \subseteq \text{PTIME} \subseteq \text{PSPACE}$$
$$\subseteq \text{EXPTIME} \subseteq \text{EXPSPACE} \subseteq \text{2EXPTIME} \ldots$$

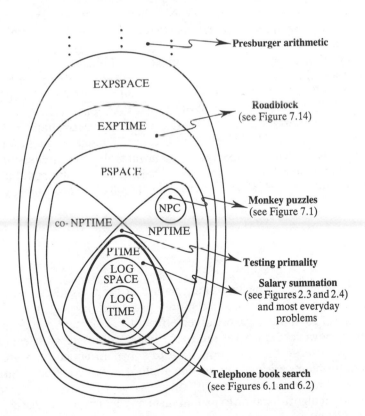

Figure 7.15 Some complexity classes with sample problems.

If we add the prefix N for 'nondeterministic', writing, for example, NPTIME for NP, we obtain many more classes, and many interesting questions of the interrelationships arise. For example, it is known that NP falls between PTIME and PSPACE, but in many cases no one knows whether the $\subseteq$ symbols represent *strict* inclusions or not. Is there a problem in PSPACE that is not in PTIME? If there is, is it the first or the second $\subseteq$ in the sequence:

$$\text{PTIME} \subseteq \text{NPTIME} \subseteq \text{PSPACE}$$

that is strict? The strictness of the first, of course, is just the P vs. NP problem.

What happens when we consider **dual** complexity classes? The class **co-NP**, for example, is the class of problems whose complement, or dual version (in which the 'yes' and 'no' answers are interchanged) is in NP. We have already seen that the primality and nonprimality problems are both in NP, a fact which, stated differently, asserts that primality is both in NP and in co-NP. It is not known, for example, whether NP = co-NP. On the other hand, it *is* known that if NP ≠ co-NP, then also P ≠ NP. The converse, however, is not true; it might be the case that NP and co-NP are equal, while P and NP are not.

Many other questions arise, for some of which the answers are known, and for others they are not. If P ≠ NP, are there any problems in NP that are neither in P nor in the intersection of NP and co-NP? Are NEXPTIME and co-NEXPTIME equal? How about LOGSPACE and NLOGSPACE?

Another important area of research concerns approximate solutions, and solutions guaranteed to be good on average. These are sought for even if a problem is known or suspected to be intractable. Researchers are still trying to understand the connections between a problem's inherent worst-case time complexity, and the availability of fast approximate solutions.

*   *   *

Despite the rather disheartening nature of the facts discussed in this chapter, it appears that most common problems arising in everyday applications of computers *can* be solved efficiently. This statement is slightly misleading, however, since we tend to equate 'common' and 'everyday' problems with those that we know how to solve. In actuality, a growing number of problems arising in nontrivial applications of computers turn out to be NP-complete or worse. In such cases, we have to resort to approximation algorithms, or to probabilism and heuristics, as discussed in Chapters 11 and 12.

Before we return to more cheerful material, however, there is worse news to come. Some algorithmic problems admit no solutions at all, not even unreasonable ones.

Multitudes, multitudes in the valley of decision
Joel 4: 14

8

Noncomputability and Undecidability

OR

Sometimes You Can't Get It Done At All!

this thing is too heavy for thee
Exodus 18: 18

though a man labour to seek it out, yet he shall not find it
Ecclesiastes 8: 17

In April 1984, *TIME* magazine ran a cover story on computer software. In the otherwise excellent article, there was a paragraph that quoted the editor of a software magazine as saying:

> *"Put the right kind of software into a computer, and it will do whatever you want it to. There may be limits on what you can do with the machines themselves, but there are no limits on what you can do with software."*

In a way, the results of Chapter 7 already contradict this claim, by showing certain problems to be provably intractable. We might argue, however, that intractability is really a consequence of insufficient resources. Given enough time and memory space (albeit, unreasonably large amounts), perhaps *any* algorithmic problem can, in principle, be solved by the right software. Indeed, the reasons that people often fail in getting their computers to do what they want seem to fall roughly into three categories: insufficient money, insufficient time, and insufficient brains. With more money one could buy a larger and more sophisticated computer, supported by better software, and perhaps then get the job done. With more time one could wait longer for time-consuming algorithms to terminate, and with more brains one could perhaps invent algorithms for problems that seem to defy solution.

The algorithmic problems we wish to discuss in this chapter are such that no amount of money, time or brains will suffice to yield solutions. We still require, of course, that algorithms terminate for each legal input within some finite amount of time, but we now allow that time to be unlimited. The algorithm can take as long as it wishes on each input, but it must eventually stop and produce the desired output. Similarly, while working on an input, the algorithm will be given any amount of memory it asks for. Even so, we shall see problems, both interesting and important, for which there simply are no algorithms, and it doesn't matter how clever we are or become, or how sophisticated and powerful our computers are or become.

Such facts have deep philosophical implications, not only on the limits of man-made machines, but also on our own limits as mortals with finite mass. Even if we were given unlimited pencil and paper, and an unlimited life span, there would be precisely defined problems we could not solve. There are people who are opposed to drawing such extended conclusions from mere algorithmic results, and for various reasons. In consideration of the fact that the issue in this extended form definitely deserves a much broader treatment, we shall stick to pure algorithmics here, and leave the deeper implications to philosophers and neurobiologists. However, the reader should keep the existence of such implications in mind.

The Rules of the Game

Just to reclarify things, it should be emphasized that questions regarding the computer's ability to run companies, make good decisions, or love, are not relevant to our present discussions, since they do not involve precisely defined algorithmic problems.

Another fact worth recalling is the requirement that an algorithmic problem be associated with a set of legal inputs, and that a proposed solution apply to all inputs in the set. As a consequence, if the set of inputs is *finite*, the problem always admits a solution. For a decision problem whose sole legal inputs are the K items $I_1, I_2, \ldots, I_K$, there is an algorithm that 'contains' a table with the K answers. The algorithm might read:

(1) if the input is I_1 then output 'yes' and stop;
(2) if the input is I_2 then output 'yes' and stop;

(3)   if the input is I_3 then output 'no' and stop;

. . .

(K)   if the input is I_K then output 'yes' and stop.

This works, of course, because the finiteness of the set of inputs makes it possible to tabulate all input/output pairs and 'hardwire' them into the algorithm. It might be difficult to *carry out* the tabulation (i.e., to *construct* such a table-driven algorithm), but we are not interested in this 'meta-difficulty' here. For our present purposes it suffices that finite problems always have solutions. It is the problems with infinitely many inputs that are really interesting. With them, a finite algorithm must be able to cope with infinitely many cases, prompting one to question the very existence of such algorithms for all problems.

To be able to state our claims as precisely, yet as generally, as possible, the reader will have to put up with a certain kind of terminological looseness in this chapter, to be fully justified in the next. Specifically, an arbitrary, but fixed, high-level programming language L is hereby implicitly assumed to be the medium for expressing algorithms, and the word 'algorithm' will be used as a synonym for 'program in L'. In particular, when we say 'no algorithm exists', we really mean that no program can be written in the language L. This convention might look a little pretentious here, apparently weakening our claims considerably. Not so. In the next chapter we shall see that, under the unlimited resources assumption, all programming languages are equivalent. Thus, if no program can be written in L, no program can be written in *any* effectively implementable language, running on any computer of any size or shape, now or at any time in the future.

* * *

The Tiling Problem: An Example

The following example is reminiscent of the monkey puzzle problem of Chapter 7. The problem involves covering large areas using square cards with colored edges, such that adjacent edges are monochromatic. A card is a 1×1 square, divided into four by the two diagonals, each quarter colored with some color (see Figure 8.1). As with monkey cards, we assume that the cards have fixed orientation and cannot be rotated. (In this case the assumption is, in fact, necessary. Can you see why?)

The algorithmic problem inputs some finite set T of card descriptions, and asks whether any finite area, of any size, can be covered using only cards of the kinds described in T, such that the colors on any two touching edges are the same. It is assumed that an unlimited number of cards of each type is available.

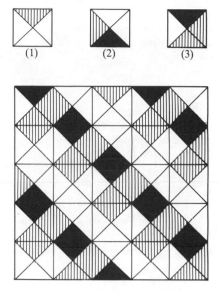

Figure 8.1   Tile types that can tile any area.

Think of tiling a house. The input T is a description of the various types of tiles available, and the color-matching restriction reflects a rule enforced by an interior designer for aesthetic reasons. The question we would like to ask ahead of time is this: can a room of any size be tiled using only the available tile types, while adhering to the restriction?

This algorithmic problem and its variants are commonly known as **tiling problems**, but are sometimes called **domino problems**, the reason being the domino-like restriction on touching edges.

Figure 8.1 shows three tile types and a 5 × 5 tiling, and the reader will have no difficulty verifying that the pattern can be repeated to yield a tiling of any area at all. In contrast, if we exchange the bottom colors of tiles (2) and (3) it can be shown quite easily that even very small rooms cannot be tiled at all. Figure 8.2 is meant as an illustration of this fact. An algorithm for the tiling problem, then, should answer 'yes' on the inputs of Figure 8.1 and 'no' on those of Figure 8.2.

The problem is to somehow mechanize or 'algorithmicize' the reasoning employed in generating these answers. And here comes the interesting fact: this reasoning is impossible to mechanize. There is no algorithm, and there never will be, for solving the tiling problem! More specifically, for any algorithm we might design for the problem, there will always be input sets T (there will actually be infinitely many such sets) upon which the algorithm will either run forever and never terminate, or terminate with the wrong answer.

Figure 8.2   Tile types that cannot tile even small areas.

How can we make such a general claim, without restricting the basic operations allowed in our algorithms? Surely, if *anything* is allowed, then the following two-step procedure solves the problem:

(1)   if the types in T can tile any area, output 'yes' and stop;

(2)   otherwise, output 'no' and stop.

The answer lies in our use of 'algorithm' here to stand for a program in a conventional programming language L. No program in any effectively executable language can correctly implement the test in line (1) of the procedure, and hence, for our purposes, such a procedure will not be considered an algorithm at all.

An algorithmic problem that admits no algorithm is termed **noncomputable**; if it is a decision problem, as is the case here and with most of the examples that follow, it is termed **undecidable**. The tiling, or domino, problem is therefore undecidable. There is no way we can construct an algorithm, to be run on a computer, any computer, regardless of the amount of required time and memory space, that will have the ability to decide whether arbitrary finite sets of tile types can tile areas of any size.

We can now refine the sphere of algorithmic problems appearing in Chapter 7 (see Figure 7.6), taking noncomputable problems into account. Figure 8.3 is the current version.

It is interesting to observe that the following, slightly different-looking problem, is actually equivalent to the one just described. In this version, instead of requiring that T be able to tile finite areas of any size, we require that T be able to tile the entire integer grid; that is, the entire infinite plane consisting of the points $\langle I, J \rangle$ for all integers I and J. One direction of the equivalence (if we can tile the entire plane then we can tile any finite area) is trivial, but the argument that establishes the other direction is quite delicate, and the reader is encouraged to try to find it for himself.

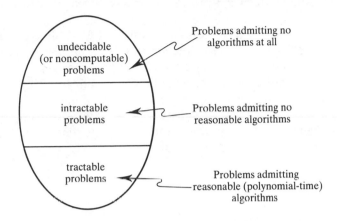

Figure 8.3   The sphere of algorithmic problems: Version II.

Interestingly, the undecidability of this version means that there must be tile sets T which can tile the entire grid, but not periodically. That is, while such a T admits a complete tiling of the grid, the tiling, unlike that of Figure 8.1, does *not* consist of a finite portion that repeats indefinitely in all directions. The reason for this is that otherwise we could decide the problem by an algorithm that would proceed to check all finite areas exhaustively, searching either for a finite area that cannot be tiled at all or for one that admits a repeat in all directions. The reader might want to try devising such an algorithm.

Unboundedness Can Be Misleading

Some people react to results like this by saying: 'Well, obviously the problem is undecidable, because a single input can give rise to a potentially infinite number of cases to check, and there is no way you can get such a job done by an algorithm that must terminate after finitely many steps.' And indeed, here a single input T apparently requires all areas of all sizes to be checked, and there seems to be no way to *bound* the number of cases to be checked.

This unboundedness-implies-undecidability principle is quite wrong, and can be very misleading. It is just like saying that any problem that seems to require exponentially many checks is necessarily intractable. In Chapter 7 we saw the two similar problems of Hamiltonian paths and Eulerian paths, both of which seemed to require a search through all of the exponentially many paths in the input graph. The second problem, however, was shown to admit an easy polynomial-time algorithm. With undecidability it is also possible to exhibit two very similar variants of a problem, both of seemingly unbounded nature, which contrast in a rather surprising way to violate the principle.

The inputs in both cases contain a finite set T of tile types and two locations V and W on the infinite integer grid. Both problems ask whether it is possible to connect V to W by a 'domino snake' consisting of tiles from T, with every two adjacent tiles having monochromatic touching edges (see Figure 8.4). Notice that a snake originating from V might twist and turn erratically, reaching unboundedly distant points before converging on W. Hence, on the face of it, the problem requires a potentially infinite search, prompting us to conjecture that it is undecidable.

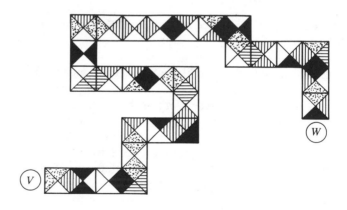

Figure 8.4   A domino snake connecting V to W.

It is interesting, therefore, that the decidability of the domino snake problem depends on the portion R of the plane available for laying down the connecting tiles. Clearly, if R is finite the problem is trivially decidable, as there are only finitely many possible snakes that can be positioned in a finite area. The distinction we wish to make is between two *infinite* portions, and is quite counter-intuitive. If snakes are allowed to go anywhere (i.e., if R is the entire plane), the problem is decidable, but if the allowed area is only a half of the plane (say, the upper half), the problem becomes undecidable! The latter case seems to be 'more bounded' than the former, and therefore perhaps 'more decidable'. The facts, however, are quite different.

Word Correspondence and Syntactical Equivalence

Here are two additional undecidable problems. The first, the **word correspondence problem**, involves forming a word in two different ways. Its inputs are two sequences, $\langle X_1, X_2, \ldots, X_N \rangle$ and $\langle Y_1, Y_2, \ldots, Y_N \rangle$, consisting of words over some finite alphabet. The problem asks whether it is possible to choose some sequence of Xs whose concatenation forms a new word, so that the same sequence of choices, but from the Ys, form the same word. For example, Figure 8.5(a) shows an $N = 5$ example where the answer is 'yes', since choosing the words according to the sequence 2, 1, 1, 4, 1, 5 from either the Xs or the Ys yields the same word, '*aabbabbbabaabbaba*'. On the other hand, the input described in Figure 8.5(b), which is obtained from Figure 8.5(a) by omitting the first letters of X_1 and Y_1, does not admit any such choice, as the reader can verify. Its answer is therefore 'no'.

	1	2	3	4	5
X	abb	a	bab	baba	aba
Y	bbab	aa	ab	aa	a

(a) Admits a correspondence: 2, 1, 1, 4, 1, 5

	1	2	3	4	5
X	bb	a	bab	baba	aba
Y	bab	aa	ab	aa	a

(b) Admits no correspondence

Figure 8.5   An instance of the word correspondence problem.

The word correspondence problem is undecidable. There is no algorithm that can distinguish, in general, between the likes of Figures 8.5(a) and 8.5(b). The unbounded nature of the problem stems from the fact that the length of the sequence of indices that might yield the common word is not bounded by any computable function of N. However, here too, we can point to a seemingly 'more unbounded' variant, in which it seems that there are more cases to check for, but which nevertheless is decidable. In it, the inputs are as before, but the sequences of indices yielding the common word are not required to be the same for the Xs and Ys. In Figure 8.5(b), which gave rise to a 'no' for the standard version of the problem, the word '*babaa*', for example, can be obtained from the Xs by the sequence 3, 2, 2, and from the Ys by 1, 2, and hence is a 'yes' in the new version. This more liberal problem actually admits a fast polynomial-time algorithm!

The second problem concerns the syntax of programming languages. Suppose someone provides us with the syntax rules of some language, say in the diagrammatic form of Figure 4.1. If someone else comes along with a different set of rules, we might be interested in knowing whether the two definitions are equivalent, in the sense that they define the same language; i.e., the same class of statements (or programs). This problem is of relevance to the construction of compilers, since compilers, among their other chores, are also responsible for recognizing the syntactic validity of their input programs. In order to do so they have a set of syntactic rules built in. It is quite conceivable that in the interest of making a compiler more efficient its designer would want to replace the set of rules with a more compact set. Clearly, it is important that the two sets define the same language.

This problem is also undecidable. No algorithm exists that, upon reading from the input two sets of syntax rules, will be able to decide in finite time whether they define precisely the same language.

Problems with Outputs Are No Better

We should perhaps restress the fact that technical convenience is the only reason that we limit ourselves here to decision problems. Each of the undecidable problems we describe has variants that ask for outputs, and which are also noncomputable. Trivial variants are those that are basically decision problems in (rather transparent) disguise. An example is the problem that asks, for a given set of colored tile types T, to output the size of the smallest area not tileable by T, and 0 if every finite area is tileable. It is clear that this problem cannot be computable, since the distinction in the output between 0 and all the other numbers is precisely the distinction between 'yes' and 'no' in the original problem.

    **   More sophisticated problems hide the ability to make an undecidable decision far better. The following problem is noncomputable too. In order to define it, let us say that a finite portion of the grid is a **limited area** for a set T of tiles, if it can be tiled legally by T, but cannot be extended in any way by more tiles without violating the tiling rules. Now, the problem involves finding particular sets T that have large limited areas. Specifically, the algorithmic problem is given a number N (which should be at least 2), and is asked to output the size of the largest limited area, for *any* set of tiles, that involves no more than N colors. The reader should convince himself that for any $N > 1$ this number is well defined.

It is far from obvious that in order to solve the limited area problem we need the ability to decide the likes of the tiling problem. And so, although the problem gives rise to a well-defined, non-yes/no function of N, this function simply cannot be computed algorithmically.   **

Algorithmic Program Verification

In Chapter 5 we asked whether computers can verify our programs for us. That is, we were after an **automatic verifier** (see Figure 5.4). Specifically, we are interested in the decision problem whose inputs are the description of an algorithmic problem P, and the text of an algorithm, or program, A, that is believed to solve P. The **verification problem** calls for determining whether indeed A solves P or not. In other words, we want a 'yes' if for each of the legal inputs specified by the problem P, the algorithm A will terminate and its outputs will be precisely as specified by P, and we want a 'no' if there is even one input for which A either fails to terminate or terminates with the wrong results. Note that the problem calls for an algorithm that works for *every* pair $\langle P, A \rangle$.

Clearly, the verification problem cannot be discussed without being more specific about the allowed inputs. Which programming language is to be used for coding the input algorithms? Which specification language is to be used for describing the input algorithmic problems?

As it happens, even very humble choices of these languages render the verification problem undecidable. Even if the allowed programs can manipulate only integers or strings of symbols, and can employ only the basic operations of addition or attachment of symbols to strings, they cannot be verified algorithmically. Candidate algorithmic verifiers might work nicely for many sample inputs, but the general problem is undecidable, meaning that a verifier will always fail in infinitely many cases; there will always be algorithms that the verifier will not be able to verify.

As discussed in Chapter 5, this implies the futility of hoping for a software system that would be capable of automatic program verification. It also reduces the hope for optimizing compilers capable of transforming programs into optimally efficient ones. Such a compiler might not even be able to tell, in general, whether a new candidate version even solves the same problem as the original program, let alone whether it is more efficient.

But not only full verification is undecidable. We cannot even decide whether a given algorithm merely *terminates* on all its legal inputs. Moreover, it is not even decidable whether the algorithm terminates on *one* given input! These problems of termination deserve special attention.

The Halting Problem

Consider the following algorithm A_1:

    (1)   while $X \neq 1$ do the following: $X \leftarrow X - 2$;
    (2)   stop.

Assuming that its legal inputs consist of the positive integers $\langle 1, 2, 3, \ldots \rangle$, it is quite obvious that A_1 halts precisely for *odd* inputs. An even number will be decreased repeatedly by 2 until it reaches 2, and will then 'miss' the 1, running forever through 0, -2, -4, -6, etc. Hence, for this particular algorithm, deciding whether a legal input will cause it to terminate is trivial: just check whether the input is odd or even and answer accordingly.

Here is another, similar looking, algorithm A_2:

    (1)   while $X \neq 1$ do the following:
         (1.1)   if X is even do $X \leftarrow X/2$;
         (1.2)   otherwise (X is odd) do $X \leftarrow 3X + 1$;
    (2)   stop.

The algorithm A_2 repeatedly halves X if it is even, but *increases* it more than threefold if it is odd. For example, if A_2 is run on 7, the sequence of values is: 7, 22, 11, 34, 17, 52, 26, 13, 40, 20, 10, 5, 16, 8, 4, 2, 1, eventually resulting in termination. Actually, if the algorithm is run on *any* positive integer, we will find that it always terminates. The sequence of values is often quite unusual, reaching surprisingly high values, and fluctuating unpredictably before it reaches 1. Indeed, over the years A_2 has been tested on numerous inputs and has always terminated. Nevertheless, no one has been able to prove that it terminates for *all* positive integers, although most people believe that it does. The question of whether or not this is the case is actually a difficult open problem in the branch of mathematics known as **number theory**. Now, if indeed A_2 (or any other program) terminates for all its inputs, there *is* a proof of this fact, as discussed in Chapter 5, but for A_2 no one has found such a proof yet. These examples illustrate just how difficult it is to analyze the termination properties of even very simple algorithms.

    Let us now define a specific version of the problem of algorithmic termination, called the **halting problem**. We define it here in terms of our agreed on high-level programming language L.

    The problem has two inputs, the text of a legal program R in the language L and a potential input X to R.[†] The halting problem asks whether R would have terminated had we run it on the input X, a fact we denote

---

[†] We can assume that R expects just one input, since a number of inputs can be encoded into a single string of symbols, with the various parts separated by some special symbol like '#'. This point is treated in more detail in Chapter 9.

by $R(X) \downarrow$. The case of R not terminating, or *diverging*, on X is denoted $R(X) \uparrow$ (see Figure 8.6).

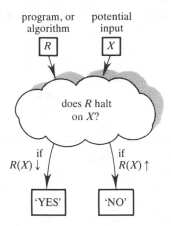

Figure 8.6   The halting problem.

As already stated, the halting problem is undecidable, meaning that there is no way to tell, in a finite amount of time, whether a given R will terminate on a given X. In the interest of solving the problem, it is tempting to propose an algorithm that will simply run R on X and see what happens. Well, if and when execution terminates, we can justly conclude that the answer is 'yes'. The difficulty is in deciding when to stop waiting and say 'no'. We cannot simply give up at some point and conclude that since R has not terminated until now it never will. Perhaps if we had left R just a little longer it *would* have terminated. Running R on X, therefore, does not do the job, and, as stated, *nothing* can do the job, since the problem is undecidable.

*   *   *

Proving Undecidability

How do we prove that a problem P is undecidable? How do we establish the fact that no algorithm exists for solving P, no matter how clever the algorithm designer is?

This situation is similar to that described in Chapter 7 for the NP-complete problems. First there has to be one initial problem, whose undecidability is established using some direct method. Once such a 'first' problem exists, the undecidability of other problems is established by exhibiting **reductions** from problems known to be undecidable to the problems in question. The difference is that here a reduction from problem P to problem Q need not necessarily be bounded; it can take any amount of time or memory space. All that is required is that there is an algorithmic way of transforming a P-input X into a Q-input Y, in such a way that P's yes/no answer to X is precisely Q's answer to Y. In this way, if P is already known to be undecidable Q must be undecidable too, since otherwise we could have solved P by an algorithm that would take an input X, transform it into an input Y for Q and ask the Q algorithm for the answer. Such a hypothetical algorithm for Q is called an **oracle**, and the reduction can be thought of as showing that P is decidable given an oracle for deciding Q. In terms of decidability, this shows that P cannot be any worse than Q.

> **   As a simple example of a reduction, assume that the halting problem is undecidable (we will actually prove this directly in the next section). To show that the verification problem is undecidable too we have to reduce halting to verification, so that a verification oracle would enable us to decide the halting problem too. Well, given an algorithm R and one of its potential inputs X, we transform the pair $\langle R, X \rangle$, which is an input to the halting problem, into the pair $\langle P, R \rangle$ which is an input to the verification problem (see Figure 8.7). The algorithm R remains the same, and the algorithmic problem P is described by specifying that X is the sole legal input to R, and that the output for this one input is unimportant. Now, to say that R is (totally) correct with respect to this rather simplistic problem P is just to say that R terminates on all legal inputs (i.e., on X) and produces some output, which is really just to say that R terminates on X. In other words, the verification problem says 'yes' to $\langle P, R \rangle$ if, and only if, the halting problem says 'yes' to $\langle R, X \rangle$. Consequently, the verification problem is undecidable, since otherwise we could have solved the halting problem by constructing an algorithm that would first transform any $\langle R, X \rangle$ into the corresponding $\langle P, R \rangle$, and then use the verification oracle for deciding the correctness of $\langle P, R \rangle$.   **

Other reductions are far more subtle. What on earth have tiling problems got to do with algorithmic termination? How do we reduce domino snakes to two-way word formations? Despite the apparent differences, these problems are all intimately related, by being inter-reducible, and in Chapter 9 we shall be able to provide some hints as to the reductions themselves.

Proving the Undecidability of the Halting Problem

Our task now is to prove that the halting problem, as described in Figure 8.6, is undecidable. Faithful to our terminological convention, however, what we really have to show is that there is no program in the agreed on high-level programming language L that solves the halting problem for programs in L. (As mentioned earlier, this language-dependent fact will

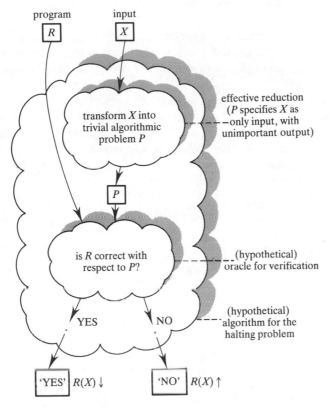

program   input

transform X into
trivial algorithmic
problem P

effective reduction
(P specifies X as
only input, with
unimportant output)

P

is R correct with
respect to P?

(hypothetical)
oracle for verification

YES   NO

(hypothetical)
algorithm for the
halting problem

'YES' $R(X) \downarrow$ 'NO' $R(X) \uparrow$

Figure 8.7   If verification is decidable, halting is too.

be extended into a far more general statement in Chapter 9.) More precisely, we want to prove the following claim:

> There is no program Q in L which, upon accepting any pair $\langle R, X \rangle$, consisting of the text of a legal program R in L and a string of symbols X, terminates after some finite amount of time, and outputs 'yes' if $R(X) \downarrow$ (i.e., if R halts on input X) and outputs 'no' if $R(X) \uparrow$ (i.e., if R does not halt on input X).

Such a Q, if it exists, is just some legal program in L; it can use as much memory space and as much time as it requests, but it must work, as described, for *every* pair $\langle R, X \rangle$.

We shall prove that a program Q satisfying the requirements is nonexistent, *by contradiction*. In other words, we shall assume that Q does exist, and derive a downright contradiction from that assumption. Throughout, the reader should be wary, making sure that anything we do is legal and according to the rules, so that when the contradiction becomes apparent we shall be justified in pointing to the assumption about Q's existence as the culprit.

Let us now construct a new program S in L, as illustrated schematically in Figure 8.8. The program S has a single input, a legal program W in L. Upon reading its input, S makes another copy of it, so that it is now holding on to the pair $\langle W, W \rangle$. This copying is obviously possible in any high-level programming language, given sufficient memory. The next thing that happens is that S activates the (assumed-to-exist) program Q on the input pair $\langle W, W \rangle$. This can be done by calling Q as a subroutine with parameters $\langle W, W \rangle$, or by inserting the (assumed-to-exist) text of Q into the right place, and assigning the values W and W to its expected input variables R and X, respectively.

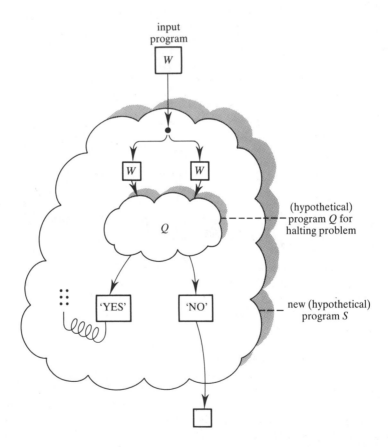

Figure 8.8 Proving undecidability of the halting problem: The program S.

The program S now waits for Q to terminate, or, in the metaphorical terms used earlier in the book, S's processor Runaround$_S$ waits for Q's processor Runaround$_Q$ to report back to headquarters. The point is that by our assumption Q *must* terminate, since its first input, W, is a legal program in L, and its second, although admittedly a program too, is really only a string of symbols, and is therefore a perfectly acceptable potential input to W.[†] And so, by our hypothesis, Q must eventually terminate, saying 'yes' or 'no'. We now instruct the new program S to react to Q's termination as follows. If Q says 'yes', S is to promptly enter an infinite loop, and if it says 'no', S is to promptly terminate (the output being unimportant). This can also be achieved in any high-level language, by the likes of:

. . .

(17)   if $OUT =$ 'yes' then goto (17), otherwise stop;

where OUT is the variable containing Q's output. This completes the construction of the (strange-looking) program S, which, it should be emphasized, is a legal program in L, assuming, of course, that Q is.

We now want to show that there is something quite wrong with S. There is a logical impossibility in the very assumption that S can be constructed. In exposing this impossibility we shall rely on the obvious fact that, for every choice of a legal input program W, the new program S must either terminate or not. We shall show, however, that there is a certain input program for which S cannot terminate, but it also cannot *not* terminate! This is clearly a logical contradiction, and we shall use it to conclude that our assumption about Q's existence is faulty, thus proving that the halting problem is indeed undecidable.

**   The input program W that causes this impossibility in S is S itself. To see why S as an input to S causes a contradiction, assume for the moment that S, when given its own text as an input, terminates. In other words, we are assuming that $S(S) \downarrow$. But what *really* happens to S when given its own text as an input? Well, first, two copies are made of the input S (see Figure 8.9). Then they are fed into the assumed-to-exist program Q. Now, by our hypothesis, Q must terminate after some finite time, and in fact, since we assumed $S(S) \downarrow$ and since Q is presently working on the pair $\langle S, S \rangle$, it must say 'yes'. However, once it has terminated and said 'yes', execution enters an infinite loop and never terminates. But this means that on the assumption that S applied to S terminates (an assumption that caused Q to say 'yes'), we have discovered that S applied to S does *not* terminate; in other words, $S(S) \downarrow$ implies $S(S) \uparrow$! We thus conclude that $S(S) \downarrow$ is impossible, since it implies its own negation. This means that S

[†] The fact that the very string W itself is considered an input to the program W should not bother the reader too much; it is perhaps a little strange, but not impossible. Any compiler written in the language it compiles can compile itself!

applied to S does not terminate. However, as can be easily verified with the help of Figure 8.9, the assumption $S(S)\uparrow$ leads in a very similar way to the conclusion that $S(S)\downarrow$, since when Q says 'no' (and it *will* say 'no', because we have assumed $S(S)\uparrow$), the execution of S applied to S promptly terminates. Thus, $S(S)\uparrow$ is also impossible.

In other words, neither one of $S(S)\downarrow$ nor $S(S)\uparrow$ is possible, although one of them must be the case. Consequently, something is very wrong with S itself. However, since all other parts of S were constructed quite legally, the only part that can be held responsible is the program Q, whose assumed existence enabled us to construct S. The conclusion is that a program Q, solving the halting problem as required, simply cannot exist.   **

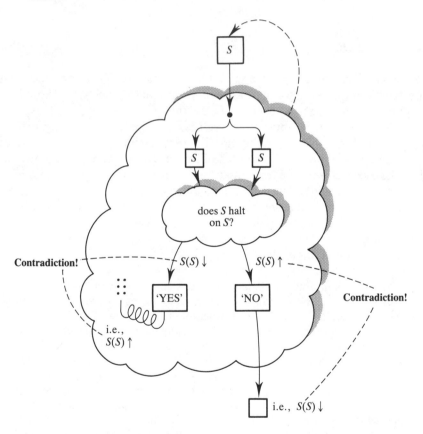

Figure 8.9   Proving undecidability of the halting problem: S swallowing S.

Some people feel a little uneasy with this circular-looking proof. It is a rigorous mathematical proof nonetheless. We might propose that the strange self-referential programs, whose behavior is exploited in the proof, be somehow outlawed. In this way, perhaps for 'well-behaved' programs, decidability will follow. Well, all that can be said is that the proof holds up very nicely against any such attempts, and, in fact, the self-referential character of the argument can be completely hidden from an observer. The best evidence of this is in the fact that other undecidable problems are but disguised versions of the halting problem, although they do not seem to have anything at all to do with programs that refer to themselves. The tiling problem, for example, can be shown to encode the halting problem quite directly, as is illustrated in Chapter 9.

*   *   *

Finite Certificates for Undecidable Problems

In Chapter 7 we saw that certain problems that have no known polynomial-time solutions give rise, nevertheless, to polynomially sized *certificates* for inputs that yield a 'yes' answer. Finding such a certificate might take an exponential amount of time, but, once found, it can be checked easily to be a valid proof of the fact that the answer is indeed 'yes'. If the answer is 'no', nothing can be said about the existence of short certificates.

In the context of the present chapter, the dichotomy is not that of reasonable vs. unreasonable (i.e., polynomial vs. exponential), but that of finite vs. infinite. Intractable problems have no algorithms that are guaranteed to terminate in a reasonable amount of time, while undecidable problems have no algorithms that are guaranteed to terminate at all. The certificate phenomenon is similarly analogous. Some problems of the previous chapter (namely, those in NP) have reasonably sized certificates, checkable in a reasonable amount of time, despite the fact that they are not known to admit reasonable algorithms; analogously, some problems have *finite* certificates, checkable in *finite* time, despite the fact they have no finitely terminating algorithms. In fact, most of the undecidable problems described so far indeed admit finite certificates.

For example, to convince someone that some input yields a 'yes' answer to the word correspondence problem, we can simply exhibit the finite sequence of indices that gives rise to the same word when formed from either the Xs or the Ys. Moreover, we can easily check the validity of this (possibly very long, but finite) certificate by concatenating the Xs prescribed by the indices, and then the Ys in the same way, and verifying that both of them result in one and the same word.

As to the halting problem, to convince someone that P halts on X, we can simply exhibit the sequence of values of all variables and data structures that constitute a complete *trace* of a legal, finite, terminating execution of P on X. We can then check the validity of the certificate by simulating the action of P on X, comparing the values reached at each step to those in the given sequence, and making sure that the program indeed terminates at the end of the sequence.

Similarly, it is easy to see that a domino snake leading from point V to point W is a perfectly good and checkable finite certificate of the fact that the appropriate inputs to the domino snake problem yield a 'yes'. As to the ordinary tiling problem, here certificates exist for the 'no' inputs, rather than for the 'yes' ones. If a set T of tile types *cannot* tile all finite areas of all sizes, there must be some area R that cannot be tiled by T in any way. The certificate showing that T yields a 'no' will simply be R itself. To check that R is indeed a certificate, we have to verify that T cannot tile R. Since both T and R are finite, there are only finitely many (albeit an unreasonable number of) possible tilings to try out, and hence the checking can be carried out algorithmically in finite time. In this sense it is the *non-tiling* problem that is comparable to the others; namely, the problem that asks whether it is *not* the case that T can tile all areas.

Problems with Two-Way Certificates Are Decidable

Notice that each of these problems has certificates for only one of the directions, either for 'yes'-ness or for 'no'-ness. This does not contradict the undecidability of the problems, since without knowing ahead of time whether an input is a 'yes' or a 'no', we cannot exploit the existence of a certificate for one of the directions to help find an algorithm for the problem. The reason is that any attempt at running through all candidate certificates and checking each for validity will not terminate if the input is of the wrong kind, as it has no certificate at all, and the search for one will never end. This point was implicitly present when it was explained earlier why simulating a program R on an input X cannot serve to decide the halting problem.

The interesting question is whether an undecidable problem can have certificates for both 'yes'-ness *and* 'no'-ness. Well, it cannot, since if certificates exist for both directions, they *can* be exploited to yield an algorithm for the problem, rendering it decidable. To see how, assume that we have a decision problem P, for which each legal input has a finite certificate. The 'yes' inputs have certificates of one kind (call them yes certificates), and the 'no' inputs have certificates of another kind (no certificates). One kind might consist of finite sequences of numbers, another of certain finite areas of the integer grid, etc. Furthermore, certificates of both kinds are verifiable as such in finite time. To decide for a given input X whether P answers 'yes' or 'no', we can proceed by cycling systematically through all candidate certificates, alternating between those of the two kinds. We thus consider first a yes certificate, then a no certificate, then another yes certificate, and so on, without missing a single one (see Figure 8.10). We are actually trying, simultaneously, to find either a yes certificate or a no certificate, anything that will serve to convince us of the status of the input X. The crucial fact is that this process is guaranteed to terminate, since X definitely has either a yes certificate or a no certificate, and whichever it is, we will find it sooner or later. Once found, the whole process can be made to terminate, producing 'yes' or 'no', according to the kind of certificate discovered.

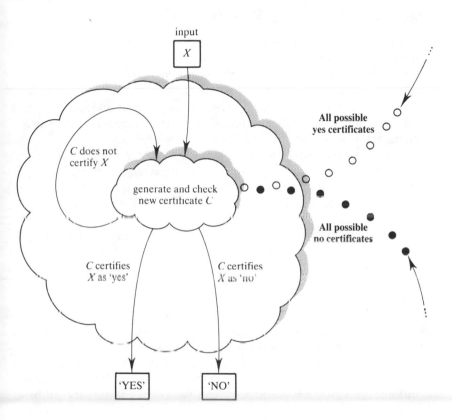

Figure 8.10   Deciding a problem P by searching for certificates of either kind.

Thus, undecidable problems cannot have two-way certificates without contradicting their own undecidability.

Undecidable problems that have one-way certificates, like those we have described, are sometimes termed **partially decidable**, since they admit algorithms that, in a manner of speaking, come about halfway towards a solution. When applied to an input X, such an algorithm is guaranteed to terminate and say 'yes', if 'yes' is indeed the answer, but will not terminate at all if the answer is 'no'. This is the case for those having yes certificates; the algorithm runs through them all trying to find a certificate for X's 'yes'-ness. For problems having no certificates, like the tiling problem, the 'yes' and 'no' switch roles.[†]

* * *

Problems that Are Even Less Decidable!

As it turns out, all partially decidable problems, including the halting problem, the domino snake problem, the word correspondence problem, and the tiling problem (actually, the non-tiling problem) are **computationally equivalent**, meaning that each of them is effectively reducible to each of the others. Consequently, although they are all undecidable, each one of them can be decided with the aid of an imaginary oracle for any one of the others: if we could decide whether a given program halts on a given input, we could also decide whether a given tile set T can tile the integer grid, and whether given X-segments and Y-segments can form a common word by concatenation, and vice versa.

Again, the situation is similar to that of the NP-complete problems, except that here we *do* know the precise status of the problems in the class, whereas there we do not. Thus, all NP-complete problems are **polynomially equivalent**, since there are polynomial-time reductions from each of them to all the others. Partially decidable problems, on the other hand, are just algorithmically equivalent, with no constraints on the time that reductions can take.

Now, just as there are decidable problems that are even worse than the NP-complete ones, so are there undecidable problems that are even worse than the partially decidable ones. We saw earlier that halting reduces to verification. The converse is not true. It is possible to prove that even if we have a hypothetical algorithm for the halting problem, we cannot algorithmically verify programs, nor can we solve the **totality problem**, which asks whether a program halts on *all* its legal inputs. It follows that the verification and totality problems are even worse than the halting problem; they are, so to speak, 'less decidable'.

Among other things, this means that the totality problem, for example, has no certificates of any kind. This is actually quite intuitive, as there seems to be no finitely checkable way to prove either that a program halts on all of its infinitely many inputs, or that it does not halt (i.e., it entails an infinite computation) on at least one of them. The first of these assertions might seem contradictory to the statement made in Chapter 5 to the effect that any correct program indeed has a (finite) proof, proving, in particular,

---

[†]The technical term used for problems with yes certificates is **recursively enumerable**, or **r.e.** for short. Thus, the halting and word correspondence problems are r.e., whereas the tiling problem is **co-r.e.**, meaning that its dual problem (with 'yes' and 'no' interchanged) is r.e.

that the program halts on all its inputs. However, while a finite proof of termination for all inputs is guaranteed to *exist*, it cannot qualify as a certificate since it is not necessarily checkable algorithmically. In fact, the logical statements whose truth we need to establish in order to verify the validity of the proof are formulas in a logical formalism which itself is undecidable!

Here is another example. Recall the formalism of Presburger arithmetic, which enables us to talk about the positive integers with '+' and '='. The problem of determining truth of formulas in Presburger arithmetic is decidable, but, as stated in Chapter 7, it has a double-exponential lower bound. Surprisingly, if we add the multiplication operator '×' to the formalism, obtaining a logic called **first-order arithmetic**, the problem becomes undecidable. Moreover, it is not even partially decidable, so that its status is more akin to that of verification and totality than to that of halting, word correspondence, domino snakes, or tiling. Actually, it is even worse than those.

Highly Undecidable Problems

Just as decidable problems can be grouped into various complexity classes, so can *un*decidable problems be grouped into levels, or **degrees**, of undecidability. There are those that are partially decidable, or, we might say, *almost* decidable, and they are all computationally equivalent, and then there are those that are worse. The many worse problems, however, are far from being computationally equivalent among themselves. In fact, there are infinite **hierarchies** of undecidable problems, each level of which contains problems that are worse than all those residing on lower levels.

Besides the low level of undecidability, that of partial decidability, there is another, particularly natural and significant level, that turns out to be much higher. Without getting into too many technical details, we shall call it simply the level of **high undecidability**, and shall illustrate it here with two examples.[†] It is noteworthy, however, that between these two levels, as well as both below and beyond them, there are many additional levels of undecidability. There is actually an infinite hierarchy of problems, all of which are increasingly 'less decidable' than the ones already described but 'more 'decidable' than the highly undecidable problems we now describe. Among these intermediate problems are the problems of totality, verification and truth in first-order arithmetic. Likewise, there are infinite hierarchies of problems that are all even worse than those we now describe!

Both examples are somewhat surprising, as they seem to be but insignificant variants of problems we have already seen. Consider the

---

[†] In technical terms it is called the **inductive–coinductive** level of undecidability. Symbolically, it is called the Σ_1^1 / Π_1^1 level.

satisfiability problem for propositional dynamic logic (PDL). In Chapter 7 the problem was described as (decidable, and) having both upper and lower bounds of exponential-time. The programs that can appear in PDL formulas are constructed from unspecified elementary programs using sequencing, conditionals, and iteration. If we leave all other aspects of the formalism as they are, but allow these schematic programs to be constructed using recursion too, the satisfiability problem becomes not only undecidable, but *highly* undecidable! It is thus not decidable even if we are given free solutions to all the partially decidable problems we have described, or to the many undecidable problems residing on intermediate levels.

The other example is a variant of that version of the regular tiling, or domino problem, that asks whether the infinite integer grid can be tiled using only tile types appearing in the finite input set T. (This version is preferred here, rather than the equivalent one involving areas of all finite sizes.) Suppose we add a small requirement: we would like the tiling, whose existence we are asking about, to contain infinitely many copies of one particular tile, say the first tile listed in T. We want a 'yes' if a tiling containing an infinite **recurrence** of this special tile exists, and a 'no' if it does not, even if other tilings of the entire grid do exist.

It would appear that the extra requirement should make no real difference since, if T can indeed tile the entire infinite grid, *some* of the types in T *must* occur in the tiling infinitely often. The crucial difference, however, is that here we are pointing to a *specific* tile whose recurrence we are interested in. Despite the apparent similarity, this **recurring dominoes** problem is highly undecidable. (In fact, it is computationally equivalent to the PDL+recursion problem just described.) It too is not decidable even with free solutions to the many other problems on lower levels.

Proving high undecidability is again a question of finding a 'first' problem and then carrying out reductions. As far as our two examples go, it is possible to exhibit a rather direct reduction from recurring dominoes to PDL+recursion, so that once the former has been shown (by other means) to be highly undecidable, the latter will have been shown to be no better.

The Four Fundamental Levels of Algorithmic Behavior

An interesting multi-sided story concerning tiling, or domino, problems emerges. First there are the **bounded** problems, such as whether T can tile an $N \times N$ square for a given N. Then there are the **unbounded** problems, such as whether T can tile the infinite integer grid. Finally, there are the **recurring** problems, such as whether T can tile the infinite grid such that a particular given tile recurs indefinitely. The bounded problems can be shown to be NP-complete, the unbounded ones are undecidable (but partially decidable), and the recurring ones are highly undecidable!

To complete the picture, there is also a **fixed-width** version of the bounded problem. It asks whether, given the set T and a number N, a rectangle of size $C \times N$ can be formed from T, where the width C is fixed and is not part of the input to the problem. (Note that in the special case of $C = 1$ we are asking about the existence of a *line* of tiles, adhering to the coloring restriction.) For each fixed C this problem admits a polynomial-time algorithm, which the reader might enjoy finding for himself.

And so, on the (believable) assumption that $P \neq NP$ (i.e., that the NP-complete problems are actually intractable), we have four versions of the tiling problem, which nicely represent the four fundamental classes of algorithmic behavior illustrated in Figure 8.11:

Type of problem	Algorithmic status
fixed-width bounded	tractable
bounded	intractable
unbounded	undecidable
recurring	highly undecidable

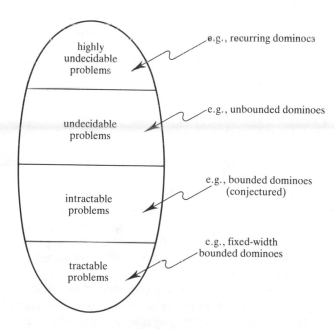

Figure 8.11 The sphere of algorithmic problems: Version III.

It must be emphasized that it is the property appearing in the left column of this table that is responsible for the fundamental difference in the status of the problems, and not some petty technicalities in the problem's definition. Two arguments can be offered to support this point. First, other problems can be similarly generalized to yield the same four-level behavior. The word correspondence problem, for example, becomes NP-complete if the length of the required sequence of indices is bounded by N, tractable if the X-sequence is to be of fixed length and the Y-sequence of length N, and highly undecidable if we are interested in an infinite sequence producing the same infinite word, but where one particular index is required to occur in the sequence infinitely often.

The other justification can be found in the insensitiveness of these four levels to technical variations in the definition of the problems. Numerous variants of these tiling problems can be defined, and as long as the fundamental left-hand characteristic is retained their algorithmic status usually does not change. For example, we can work with hexagonal or triangular tiles instead of squares, and with matching shapes and/or notches instead of colors (so that monkey puzzles or jigsaw puzzles can be the basis for the four-way phenomenon, rather than colored tiles). We can require zigzags or spirals of length N in the fixed-width case, rectangles or triangles of given (input) dimensions in the bounded case, half-grids or a given start tile in the unbounded case, and a recurring color, rather than a tile, or the recurrence restricted to a single row, in the recurring case. In all of these variants, and in many others, the right-hand status remains the same.

It is, therefore, fair to say that the four-level classification depicted in Figure 8.11 is extremely robust, and Chapter 9 will, in fact, provide further weighty evidence to support it.

*   *   *

Research on Undecidability

Besides being of obvious relevance to computer science, the undecidability of algorithmic problems is also of interest to mathematicians. It actually forms the basis of a branch of mathematical logic known as **recursive function theory**. (The term is somewhat unfortunately reminiscent of that used to describe self-calling subroutines.) Perhaps surprisingly, many of the basic results, such as the undecidability of the halting problem, were obtained by mathematicians in the mid 1930s, long before working computers were built!

The detailed classification of undecidable problems into the various levels of undecidability is still an active research direction. Much work is devoted to refining and understanding the various hierarchies of undecidability and their interrelationships. Also, scientists are interested in

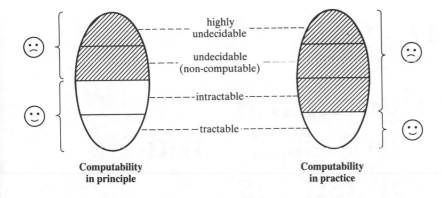

Figure 8.12   Computability: The good and bad news.

finding simple problems that can serve as the basis for reductions that exhibit the undecidability or high undecidability of other problems. For many problems of interest, such as the satisfiability problem for PDL, or the problem of syntactical equivalence of languages, the line separating the decidable versions from the undecidable ones is not sufficiently clear, and a deeper understanding of the fundamental issues involved is required.

*   *   *

Problems that are not solvable by any kind of effectively executable algorithms actually form the end of the pessimistic part of the story, and it is time to return to happier, brighter issues. It must be remembered, however, that when trying to solve an algorithmic problem there is always the chance that it might not be solvable at all, or might not admit any practically acceptable solution. Figure 8.12 is an attempt at summarizing the situation.

they shall never see light
Psalm 49: 20

9

Algorithmic Universality and Its Robustness

OR

The Simplest Machines that Get It Done

In this chapter we shall examine algorithmic devices of the simplest imaginable kind, strikingly primitive in contrast with today's computers and programming languages. Nevertheless, they are powerful enough to execute even the most complex algorithms.

Given the current trend, whereby computers are becoming more intricate and more sophisticated by the year, this goal might appear to be a mere thought experiment, and probably quite useless. However, our purposes are three-fold. To begin with, it is intellectually satisfying to discover objects that are as simple as possible yet as powerful as anything of their kind. Secondly, the reader deserves a justification as to the sweeping nature of the negative claims made in the last two chapters, concerning the nonexistence, now or hereafter, of any reasonable solutions, or any solutions whatsoever, to certain problems. The facts described herein will carry weighty evidence to support these statements. Finally, on purely technical grounds, these primitive devices will be shown to give rise to rigorous proofs of many of the intractability and undecidability results stated earlier.

Let us first see how far we can go in a direct attempt at simplifying things.

An Exercise in Simplifying Data

The first thing to notice is that any data item used by an algorithm, whether as an input, output or intermediate value, can be thought of as a string of symbols. An integer is but a string of digits, and a fractional number can be defined to be a string of digits optionally containing a period. A word in English is a string of letters, and an entire text is nothing more than a string of symbols consisting of letters and punctuation marks, spaces included. Some other items we have had occasion to meet earlier in the book are colors, nodes in a graph, lines, monkey halves, rings, pegs, sides of squares, road segments, chess pieces, logical operators, and, of course, the very texts of programs. In all these cases, we could have easily encoded such objects as numbers, words or texts, and treated them symbolically throughout.

The number of different symbols used in all such encodings is actually finite, and can always be fixed ahead of time. This is the ingenuity of a standard numbering system, such as the decimal system. We do not need infinitely many symbols, one for each number – ten symbols suffice to encode them all. (The binary system uses just two, 0 and 1.) The same obviously applies to words, texts, etc.

Consequently, we can write any data item of interest along a one-dimensional tape, perhaps a long one, which consists of a sequence of squares, each containing a single symbol that is a member of some finite **alphabet**.

This idea can be taken much further. It is not too difficult to see that even the most complicated data *structures* can also be 'linearized' in this fashion. A vector, for example, is just a list of data items and can be depicted as a sequence of the linearized versions of each of the items, separated by a special symbol, such as '*'. A two-dimensional array can be spread out row by row along the tape, using '*' to separate items within each row and, say, '**' to separate rows (see Figure 9.1).

Linearizing trees requires more care. If we attempt to naively list the tree's items level by level, the precise structure of the tree may be lost, since the number of items on a given level is not fixed. In the level-by-level encoding in Figure 9.2, for example, there is no way of knowing whether

$$\begin{bmatrix} 15 & -4 & 6 & 104 \\ 6.5 & 0 & -61 & 3 \\ 586 & 1 & 7 & 102 \end{bmatrix}$$

$\downarrow$

$15*-4*6*104**6.5*0*-61*3**586*1*7*102$

Figure 9.1 Linearizing a two-dimensional array.

S is an offspring of V or of G. One way of avoiding the problem is to adopt a variant of the nested lists approach of LISP, as illustrated in Figure 4.4. (The parentheses are considered as special symbols, like '*' and '**'.) This is especially beneficial when the trees have information only in the leaves. Alternatively, we can refine the method of Figure 9.2 by marking off clusters of immediate offspring, level by level, always starting at the left. Here is the resulting linearization for the tree of Figure 9.2:

$(T)(V,\ G)(Q,\ R,\ S)(W,\ L)(\ )(M,\ N)(\ )(P)(\ )$

The reader is encouraged to devise algorithms both for representing trees by such lists, and for reconstructing the trees from the lists.

Similar transformations can be carried out for any kind of data structure, however complex. A multitude of variables or data structures can be described in linear fashion using some new symbol to separate their linearized versions from each other. In fact, entire databases, consisting of

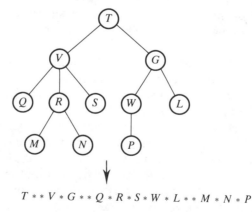

$T**V*G**Q*R*S*W*L**M*N*P$

Figure 9.2 'Steam rolling' a tree with information loss.

scores of tables, records and files, can be encoded as long lists of symbols, with appropriate special-symbol codes signifying breakpoints between the various parts. Of course, it might be very *inefficient* to work with a linear version of a highly structured collection of data. Even the simple clustered-tree representation just given requires quite an unpleasant amount of running around in order to carry out standard tree-oriented chores, such as traversing paths or isolating subtrees rooted at given nodes. However, efficiency is not one of our concerns right now; conceptual simplification is.

Algorithms do not deal only with *fixed* amounts of data. They may ask for more as they go along. Data structures may grow in size, and variables may be assigned ever-larger data items; information may be stored, to be used later in the algorithm, and so on. However, given that any such additional data can also be linearized, all we need is to allow our tape, with its marked-off squares, to be of unlimited length.

The conclusion is this. When it comes to the *data* manipulated by an algorithm, *any* effectively executable algorithm, it suffices to have a one-dimensional tape of potentially unbounded length, divided into squares, each of which contains a symbol taken from a finite alphabet. This alphabet includes the 'real' symbols that make up the data items themselves, as well as special symbols for marking breakpoints. It is also assumed to include a special blank symbol for indicating the absence of information, which we shall denote by #, and which is understood to be distinct from the space symbol separating words in a text. Since at any given point in time an algorithm deals with only a finite amount of data, our tapes will always contain a finite **significant portion** of data, surrounded on either side by infinite sequences of blanks. This portion may be very long, and may grow longer as execution proceeds.

An Exercise in Simplifying Control

How can we simplify the *control* part of an algorithm? Various languages, we have seen, support various control structures, such as sequencing, conditional branching, subroutines, and recursion. Our question is really about simplifying the work of the processor Runaround, who runs around carrying out basic instructions. For now we shall ignore the basic instructions themselves and concentrate on simplifying the very chore of running around.

One of the things crucial to simplifying control is the finiteness of an algorithm's text. The processor can be in one of only finitely many locations in that text, and hence we can make do with a rather primitive mechanism, containing some kind of **gearbox** that can be in one of finitely many positions, or **states**. If we think of the states of the gearbox as encoding locations in the algorithm, then moving around in the algorithm can be modeled simply by changing states.

At any point during the execution of an algorithm the location to be visited next depends on the current location, so that the next state of our mechanism's gearbox must depend on its current state. However, the new location may also depend on the values of certain data items; many control structures test the values of variables in order to channel control to particular places in the text (e.g., to the **then** or **else** clauses of an **if** statement, or to the beginning or end of a **while** loop). This means that a change in the state of our mechanism must be allowed to depend on parts of the data as well as on the current state. But since we have encoded all of our data along a single lengthy tape, we shall have to allow our primitive mechanism to inspect the tape before deciding on a new state.

In the interest of minimalism and simplicity, this inspection will be allowed to be carried out only one square at a time. At any given moment, only a single symbol will ever be 'read'. Our mechanism can thus be viewed as having an 'eye' of very limited power, which can contemplate one square of the tape at a time, seeing and recognizing the symbol residing there. Depending upon that symbol and its current state, the mechanism 'changes gear', entering a new state (see Figure 9.3).

Figure 9.3 A primitive mechanism: tape, gearbox, and narrow eye.

As a consequence of the finiteness of the alphabet, we shall see later that the mechanism can actually 'remember' the symbol it has seen by going into an appropriately meaningful new state. This enables it to act according to combined information gathered from several tape squares. However, in order to inspect different parts of the data, we have to allow our mechanism to **move** along the tape. Again, we shall be very ungenerous, allowing movement to take place only one tape square at a time. The direction of movement (right or left) will also depend both on the current state of the gearbox and on the symbol the eye has just seen.

These observations simplify the control component of an algorithm considerably. What we have is a simple mechanism, capable of being in one of a finite number of gears, or states, chugging along the tape one square at a time. In the process, it changes states and switches directions as a function of the current state and the single symbol it happens to see in front of it.

Simplifying the Basic Operations

Having thus simplified the data and control parts of algorithms, we are left with the basic operations that actually get things done. If processors were just to run around reading parts of the data and changing gears, algorithms could not do very much. We need the ability to **manipulate** the data, to apply transformations to it, to erase, write or rewrite parts of it, to apply arithmetical or textual operations to it, and so on.

Without offering any kind of justification right now, we shall endow our mechanism with only the most trivial manipulation capabilities. Other than to change states and move one square to the right or left, all it will be allowed to do, when in a particular state and looking at a particular symbol on the tape, is to transform that symbol into one of the finitely many symbols available. That's all.

The mechanism resulting from this long sequence of simplifications is called a **Turing machine**, after the British mathematician Alan M. Turing, who invented it in 1936.

*   *   *

The Turing Machine

Let us be a little more precise. A Turing machine M involves:

(1)   a finite **alphabet** of symbols,
(2)   a finite set of **states**,

(3)   an infinite **tape** marked off with squares, each of which is capable of carrying a single symbol,

(4)   a mobile sensing-and-writing **head** that can travel along the tape one square at a time, and

(5)   a **state-transition diagram**, sometimes called simply a **transition diagram**, containing the instructions that cause changes to take place at each step.

A transition diagram is simply a directed graph whose nodes represent the states. We use rounded rectangles (**rountangles** in the sequel) for states (see Figure 9.4). An edge leading from state *s* to state *t* is called a **transition**, and is labeled with a code of the form ⟨*a*/*b*, *direction*⟩, where *a* and *b* are symbols and *direction* is either 'left' or 'right'. The *a* part of the label is the transition's **trigger** and the ⟨*b*, *direction*⟩ part is its **action**. The meaning of a transition from *s* to *t* labeled with ⟨*a*/*b*, *direction*⟩ is as follows:

> During its operation, whenever the Turing machine is in state *s* and *a* is the symbol sensed at that moment by the head, the machine will erase the symbol *a*, writing *b* in its place, will move one square in the *direction* direction, and will enter state *t*.

To prevent ambiguity as to the machine's next move (i.e., in order that its behavior be **deterministic**), we require that no two transitions with the same trigger emanate from a single state. One of the states in the

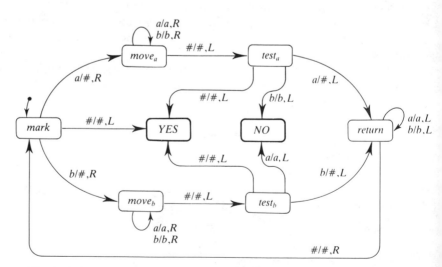

Figure 9.4   The state-transition diagram of a simple Turing machine.

diagram is marked with a special small entering arrow (*mark* in Figure 9.4) and is called the **start state**. Also, states that have no outgoing transitions are called **halting states**, and are emphasized by double rountangles. For convenience, several labels may be attached to a single transition (as in the self-cycling arrows of Figure 9.4).

The machine is assumed to start in its start state on the leftmost nonblank square of the tape, and to proceed step by step as prescribed by the diagram. It halts if and when a halting state is entered.

Detecting Palindromes: An Example

Let us take a closer look at the Turing machine whose transition diagram is shown in Figure 9.4. In particular, let us simulate its actions on a tape consisting of the word '*a b b a*' (surrounded, as explained above, by infinitely many blanks on either side). The machine's head is positioned at the leftmost *a*, and *mark* is the initial state. Figure 9.5 shows the entire simulation, step by step, with the current state indicated by a solid rountangle within the miniature version of the transition diagram.

Intuitively, the machine 'remembers' the first symbol it has seen (by entering *move$_a$* or *move$_b$*), erases it by replacing it with a blank, and then runs all the way to the right until it reaches a blank (frame 5). It then moves one symbol to the left, so that it is stationed at the rightmost symbol in state *test$_a$* or *test$_b$*, depending on the leftmost symbol (frame 6). If it were now to sense a symbol different from the one it remembered it would enter the special state *NO*. In our case, however, it remembered an *a* and now also sees an *a*, so it erases this rightmost *a*, and enters *return*, which brings it leftwards all the way to the first blank, in state *mark* (frame 9). As before, the machine now moves one square to the right and remembers the symbol it sees. This symbol, however, is the second one of the string, since the first was erased earlier, and its rightward run will now compare this second symbol with the string's penultimate symbol (frame 13). This comparison is also successful, and the machine erases the *b* and moves off to the left in search of further symbols. Finding none, and not having reached the *NO* state by virtue of a mismatch, it enters *YES*, indicating that all pairs matched.

In essence, this Turing machine checks for **palindromes**; that is, for words that read the same from either end. Whenever started at the leftmost symbol of a finite word consisting of *a*'s and *b*'s, it halts in the *YES* state if the word is a palindrome and in *NO* if it isn't. The reader should simulate the machine also on '*a b a b a*' and '*a b a a b b a*' to get a better feel for its behavior. Observe that this particular machine uses four fixed states and an additional two for each of the letters in the alphabet. The reader may want to extend Figure 9.4 to deal with the case of a three-letter alphabet.

Figure 9.5   A sample run of the Turing machine of Figure 9.4.

Turing Machines as Algorithms

A careful look reveals that we can really view any Turing machine as a computer with one single fixed program. The software is the transition diagram, and the hardware consists of the tape and head, as well as the (implicit) mechanism that actually moves through the transition diagram changing states and controlling the head's reading, writing, erasing, and moving activities. The computer is thus the same for all Turing machines; it is the programs that are different. As a consequence, people sometimes talk about **programming** a Turing machine, rather than constructing one.

The palindrome example actually shows how a Turing machine can be programmed to solve a decision problem. For a problem P whose legal set of inputs has been encoded as a set of linearized strings, we try to devise a Turing machine M with a start state s and two special states YES and NO, that does the following:

> For any legal input string X, if M is started in state s at the leftmost symbol of X on an otherwise blank tape containing one copy of X, it eventually enters YES or NO, depending upon whether P's answer to X is 'yes' or 'no'.

Detecting palindromes with a Turing machine may seem easy, but other problems are not. How do we detect strings with the following property. The only appearances of a's in the string are in blocks whose lengths form some initial portion of the sequence of prime numbers 2, 3, 5, 7, 11, ... Within X, the blocks are not required to appear in any particular order. Here we cannot simply run back and forth, erasing symbols; we need the ability to **count** and to compute, and a finite number of states is not sufficient to 'remember' arbitrarily large numbers. (The input word, of course, can be arbitrarily long.)

> ** The trick is to compute the next prime number on the blank part of the tape, say to the right of the input word X, and then to go searching for a block of a's with precisely the required length. Assuming the current prime has been computed and appears as a string of 1's to the right of X on the tape,[†] the search for the appropriate block of a's can be carried out as follows. The machine repeatedly runs through every block of a's, checking off each a against one of the 1's, by running back and forth and changing both temporarily into some new symbol. If a perfect match is found, the entire block is erased, and the next prime is computed. If not, the block is restored to its original form and the next block is tried. If no matching block is found in the entire string, the machine enters NO. If the block matches and the tape contains no more a's, the machine enters YES.
>
> Notice how we are using the potentially infinite blank portion of the tape as scrap paper, both to compute and to jot down our current count of the a's. **

[†] The primality problem itself is discussed in Chapter 11.

Turing machines can also be programmed to solve non-yes/no algorithmic problems. The only difference is in the need to produce outputs. By convention, we may agree that when a Turing machine halts (by virtue of its entering any halting state) the output is the string contained between two '!'s on the tape. If there are not precisely two '!'s on the tape at the time of halting we agree that it is as if the machine had entered an infinite loop, and will thus never halt. In other words, if M wants to produce an output, it had better see to it that the output is enclosed between two '!'s, and that it does not use '!'s for any other purpose. (Obviously, it is possible to use this convention for decision problems also, writing '!yes!' or '!no!' on the tape and entering some halting state, rather than entering the special *YES* or *NO* states.)

>   **   With this definition in mind, it is an instructive exercise to program
> a Turing machine to add two decimal numbers X and Y. One way of
> proceeding is as follows. The machine runs to the rightmost digit of X (by
> reaching the separating symbol '*' and moving one square to its left) and
> erases it, while 'remembering' it in its state; it will need 10 different states
> to do so, say $digit_0$ through $digit_9$. It then runs to the rightmost digit of Y
> and erases it too, while entering a state that remembers the *sum* digit of
> the two numbers and whether or not there is a carry. (These, of course,
> depend only on the current digit and the memorized one, and can be
> encoded into, say, states sum_0 through sum_9 and sum_0^c through
> sum_9^c.) The machine then moves to the left of what remains of X and
> writes the sum digit down, having prepared a '!' as a delimiter. The next
> step is similar, but it involves the currently rightmost digits and takes the
> carry into account (if there is one). The new sum digit is written down to
> the left of the previous one, and the process continues. Of course, we have
> to remember that each of the numbers might run out of digits before the
> other, in which case after adding the carry (if there is one) to the remaining
> portion of the larger number, that portion is just copied down on the left.
> Finally, a second '!' is written down on the extreme left and the machine
> halts.
>
>   Here are the main configurations of the tape for the numbers 736
> and 63 519:
>
> ```
> ...# # # # # # # # # 7 3 6 * 6 3 5 1 9 # #...
> ...# # # # # # # # 5 ! 7 3 # * 6 3 5 1 # # #...
> ...# # # # # # # 5 5 ! 7 # # * 6 3 5 # # # #...
> ...# # # # # # 2 5 5 ! # # # * 6 3 # # # # #...
> ...# # # # # 4 2 5 5 ! # # # * 6 # # # # # #...
> ...# # # # 6 4 2 5 5 ! # # # * # # # # # # #...
> ...# # ! 6 4 2 5 5 ! # # # * # # # # # # #...
> ```
>
>   Again, the (masochistic) reader might be interested in constructing the
> entire transition diagram of a Turing machine for decimal addition.   **

*   *   *

The Church/Turing Thesis

These examples are perhaps a little surprising. A Turing machine has only finitely many states, and can only rewrite symbols on a linear tape one at a time. Nevertheless, we can program it to add numbers. It might be tedious to do the programming (try to construct a Turing machine to *multiply* numbers), and it is no easier to take over the controls and actually carry out a simulation of the machine's actions. Nevertheless, it gets the job done.

With this in mind, let us forget about tedium and efficiency for the time being, and ask ourselves what indeed *can* be done with Turing machines, for whatever cost? Which algorithmic problems can be solved by an appropriately programmed Turing machine?

The answer is not a little surprising, but *very* surprising indeed. Turing machines are capable of solving any effectively solvable algorithmic problem! Put differently, any algorithmic problem for which we can find an algorithm that can be programmed in some programming language, *any* language, running on some computer, *any* computer, even one that has not been built yet but *can* be built, and even one that will require unbounded amounts of time and memory space for ever-larger inputs, is also solvable by a Turing machine. This statement is one version of the so-called **Church/Turing thesis**, after Alonzo Church and Turing, who arrived at it independently in the mid 1930s.

It is important to realize that the CT thesis, as we shall sometimes call it (both for Church/Turing and for Computability Theory), is a *thesis*, not a theorem, and hence cannot be proved in the mathematical sense of the word. The reason for this is that among the concepts it involves there is one that is informal and imprecise, namely that of 'effective computability'. The thesis equates the mathematically precise notion of 'solvable by a Turing machine' with the informal, intuitive notion of 'solvable effectively', which alludes to all real computers and all programming languages, those that we know about at present as well as those that we do not. It thus sounds more like a wild speculation than what it really is: a deep and far-reaching statement, put forward by two of the most respected pioneers of theoretical computer science.

It is instructive to draw an analogy between Turing machines and typewriters. A typewriter is also a very primitive kind of machine, enabling us only to type sequences of symbols on a piece of paper that is potentially infinite in size and initially blank. (A typewriter also has finitely many 'states' or modes of operation – upper or lower case, red or black ribbon, etc.) Yet despite this, any typewriter can be used to type *Hamlet* or *War and Peace*, or any other highly sophisticated string of symbols. Of course, it might take a Shakespeare or a Tolstoy to 'instruct' the machine to do so, but it can be done. In analogy, it might take very talented people to program Turing machines to solve difficult algorithmic problems, but the basic model, so the CT thesis tells us, suffices for all problems that can be solved at all.

Our exercises in simplification have thus turned out to have profound consequences. Simplifying data down to sequences over a finite alphabet, simplifying control down to a finite number of states that prescribe square-by-square moves along a tape, and adopting symbol rewriting as the only primitive operation, yields a mechanism that is as powerful as any algorithmic device whatsoever.

Evidence for the Church/Turing Thesis

Why should we believe this thesis, especially when it cannot be proved? What evidence is there for it, and how does that evidence fare in an age of day-to-day advances in both hardware and software?

Ever since the early 1930s researchers have suggested models for the all-powerful absolute, or **universal**, computer. The intention was to try to capture that slippery and elusive notion of 'effective computability', namely the ability to compute mechanically. Long before the first digital computers were invented, Turing suggested his primitive machines and Church devised a mathematical formalism of functions called the **lambda calculus** (mentioned in Chapter 3 as the basis for the programming language LISP). At about the same time Emil Post defined a certain kind of symbol-manipulating **production system**, and Stephen Kleene defined a class of objects called **recursive functions**. (As mentioned in the research section of Chapter 8, this 'recursive' has a meaning that is somewhat different from the one used throughout this book.) All these people tried, and succeeded, in using their models to solve many algorithmic problems for which there were known 'effectively executable' algorithms. Other people have since proposed numerous different models for the absolute, universal algorithmic device. Some of these models are more akin to real computers, having the abstract equivalent of storage and arithmetical units, and the ability to manipulate data using control structures such as loops and subroutines, and some are purely mathematical in nature, defining classes of functions that are realizable in a step-by-step fashion.

The crucial fact about these models is that they have *all* been proven equivalent in terms of the class of algorithmic problems they can solve! And this fact is still true today, even for the most powerful models conceived of.

That so many people, working with such a diversity of tools and concepts, have essentially captured the very same notion is evidence for the profundity of that notion. That they were all after the same intuitive concept, and ended up with different-looking, but equivalent, definitions is justification for equating that intuitive notion with the results of those precise definitions. Hence the CT thesis.

Computability Is Robust

The CT thesis implies that the most powerful super-computer, with the most sophisticated array of programming languages, interpreters, compilers, assemblers, and what have you, is no more powerful than a home computer with its simplistic programming language! Given an unlimited amount of time and memory space, both can solve precisely the same algorithmic problems. The noncomputable (or undecidable) problems of Chapter 8 are solvable on neither, and the computable (or decidable) problems mentioned throughout are solvable on both.

As a result of the CT thesis the class of computable, effectively solvable, or decidable algorithmic problems becomes extremely *robust*. It is *invariant* under changes in the computer model or programming language, a fact alluded to in Chapter 8. Proponents of this or that computer architecture or programming discipline must find reasons other than raw solving power to justify their recommendations, since problems solvable with one are also solvable with the other, and all are equivalent to the primitive machines of Turing or the various formalisms of Church, Post, Kleene, and others.

The line drawn between the decidable and the undecidable in Chapter 8 (see Figures 8.3, 8.11 and 8.12) is thus fully justified, as is our reliance on an unspecified language *L* for discussing undecidability therein. Moreover, it is intellectually satisfying to be able to point to a most simple model that is as powerful as anything of its kind.

*   *   *

Variants of the Turing Machine Model

The robustness afforded by the CT thesis starts with variants of the Turing machines themselves. As it turns out, it is possible to limit the machines in a number of ways without reducing the class of problems they can solve. For example, we can require that (unlike the erasing effect of the palindrome machine) inputs are kept intact, and that the 'work areas' of the tape are cleared up, so that upon halting, the tape is to contain only the input and output, surrounded by blanks. We can define Turing machines with a tape that is infinite to the right only, the input appearing justified to the left, and the machine being constrained never to attempt to move 'off' the leftmost square. Both variants can solve precisely the same problems as the basic model, and therefore they are really no weaker.

In a similar vein, adding any powerful (but 'effectively executable') feature to the machines also yields precisely the same class of solvable problems, so that in the context of computability this extra power is merely an illusion. For example, we can allow *many* tapes, each with its own read/write head, in such a way that the transitions are based on the entire set of symbols seen simultaneously by the heads; the actions specify a new symbol to be written on each tape and a direction for each head to move in. Similarly, we can define machines involving **two-dimensional** tapes, giving rise to four, not two, possible moving directions, and so on. None of these extensions can solve problems that the basic model cannot.

One of the most interesting extensions involves **nondeterministic** Turing machines. The idea is to allow many transitions with the same trigger to emanate from a state. The machine then has a choice of which transition to take. The way a nondeterministic machine is said to solve a decision problem is very similar to the way 'magical nondeterminism' was defined in Chapter 7: whenever there *is* a choice to be made, the machine can be thought of as making the best one – i.e., the one that will eventually lead to a 'yes' answer, if that is at all possible. In this way, the nondeterministic Turing machine says 'yes' to input X precisely if there exists some sequence of choices that leads to the *YES* state, even if there are others that don't (e.g., they lead to *NO* states or into infinite loops). Here too, perhaps somewhat surprisingly, no solving power is gained. Even this 'magical' notion of computation does not enable us to solve any algorithmic problems that could not have been solved without it.

Folding Over an Infinite Tape: An Example

The Church/Turing thesis thus claims that no effective model of computation is more powerful than the basic Turing machine model, extensions of that model included. As explained, scores of distinct models, often of radically different nature, have been suggested over the years and have all been proven equivalent, thus providing weighty evidence of the truth of the thesis.

How do we establish such equivalences? How do we show that even two similar variants of the Turing machine model (let alone two completely different models) give rise to the very same class of solvable problems. The answer lies in the notion of **simulation**, whereby we show that for each machine of one type there is an *equivalent* machine of the other. In other words, we show how to *simulate* one type of machine with another.

For example, suppose we wish to show that machines with a two-way infinite tape are no more powerful than those with a tape that is infinite only to the right. Assume we are given a machine M that employs a two-way infinite tape. We can construct an *equivalent* new machine M_1, whose one-way tape is 'viewed' as a two-way tape folded over into two merged halves. Figure 9.6 shows the correspondence. (The '$'s are used to prevent the machine from 'falling off', as is explained following.)

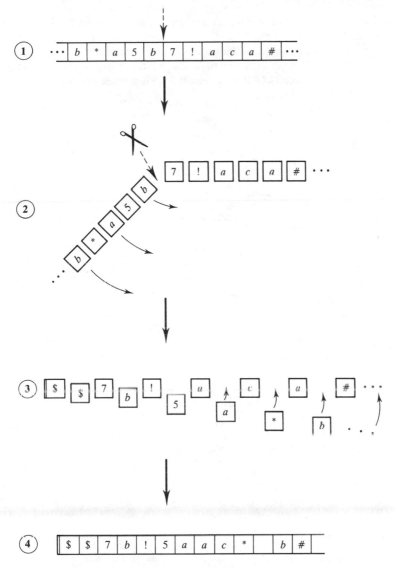

Figure 9.6 'Folding over' a two-way infinite tape.

**   For simplicity, assume that M solves a decision problem, so that it does not provide any real output other than entering the *YES* or *NO* states. Here is how the new machine M_1 behaves when started on an input X of length K, positioned along the leftmost portion of its tape (i.e., in squares 1, 2, 3, ..., K). As a first step, M_1 spreads X out to occupy squares 3, 5, 7, ..., $2K + 1$, inserting '$'s in squares 1 and 2 and blanks in the rest (see Figure 9.7). This can be achieved by looping through the symbols one at a time, starting from the right. Each time around, the symbol in question is first shifted one square to the right, with a blank being placed in its original position, and then the symbols already dealt with are shifted, one at a time, one square to the right. When this process ends the entire resulting sequence (which is of length $2K$) is shifted one more time and the two '$'s are inserted.

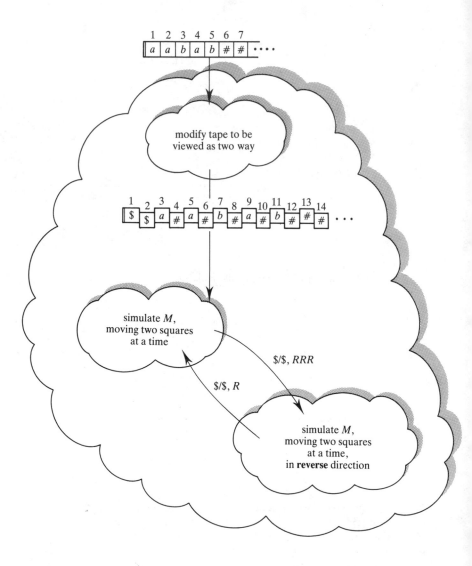

Figure 9.7   Scheme for simulating a two-way infinite tape with a one-way infinite tape.

Having thus prepared its tape, M_1 then moves to square 3 and starts simulating M, but taking *two* steps in each direction, not one, so that 'R' is interpreted as a two-square shift to the right, and similarly for 'L'. This can easily be achieved by modifying the transition diagram of M using transformations such as the one in Figure 9.8(a). The result is that M_1 works on the odd-numbered squares just as M would have worked on the right-hand portion of its own tape. Whenever, during this simulation, M_1 hits a '$\$$', it moves three squares to the right (thus reaching the first blank) and continues to simulate M two steps at a time, but *in reverse* – that is with right and left moves interchanged. This can be achieved by having another, separate copy of M's diagram, modified as hinted in Figure 9.8(b). The two diagrams are connected, state to corresponding state, by appropriate '$\$$'-sensing transitions (see Figure 9.7). In this way, M_1 is now working on the *even*-numbered squares just as M would have worked on the *left*-hand portion of its tape, but with the directions reversed. Again, whenever a '$\$$' is hit, it is time to shift modes, and the machine moves one square to the right (reaching square number 3, which corresponds to the leftmost input symbol) and resumes the first kind of simulation on the *odd*-numbered squares. The '$\$$'s, of course, mark the leftmost part of the tape, and so prevent M_1 from 'falling off' its end.

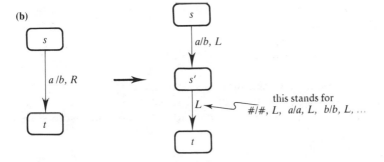

Figure 9.8   Modifications of M as used in Figure 9.7.

The claim is that M_1 performs exactly as M does, in the sense that on any input X one of the following is the case: (1) both M and M_1 terminate in a *YES* state, (2) both terminate in a *NO* state, or (3) both enter an infinite loop. Thus, if M solves the decision problem P, then so does M_1, and since this translation can be carried out for *any* machine M, we have shown that Turing machines with one-way infinite tapes are as powerful as ones with two-way tapes.   **

This particular simulation is conceptually quite simple, although technically somewhat tedious. Others can be quite intricate, even conceptually. In all cases, however, simulation techniques exist, hence there are Turing machines for solving any problem that can be solved on even the most sophisticated modern computers.

Counter Programs: Another Very Primitive Model

On the face of it, there is little reason to choose the Turing machine model above all others to be the one the CT thesis mentions explicitly. The thesis might have talked about the model underlying a large IBM or Cray computer. In fact, one of the most striking formulations of the thesis does not mention any particular model at all, but rather states simply that all computers and all programming languages are equivalent in computational power, given unlimited time and memory space.

However, as we shall see later, there are technical reasons for investigating extremely primitive models. Accordingly, we now describe the **counter program** model, which is another one of the truly simple, yet universal, models of computation.

Instead of arriving at them by starting out with general algorithms and simplifying things, we shall first define the counter programs themselves and then try to see how they relate to Turing machines. A counter program can manipulate non-negative integers stored in variables. The model, or language, allows just three types of elementary operations on variables, interpreted in the standard way (where, by convention, $Y - 1$ is defined to be 0 if Y is already 0):

$$X \leftarrow 0, \quad X \leftarrow Y + 1, \quad \text{and} \quad X \leftarrow Y - 1$$

(The variables are called counters because the limited operations enable them, in essence, only to count.) The control structures of a counter program include simple sequencing and the conditional **goto** statement:

if $X = 0$ **goto** L

where X is a variable and L is a label that is possibly attached to a statement. A counter program is just a finite sequence of optionally labeled statements.

Execution proceeds in order, one statement at a time, branching off to the specified statement when a **goto** is encountered and the appropriate variable is indeed zero. A counter program halts if and when it attempts to execute a nonexistent statement, by reaching the end of the sequence or by trying to go to a nonexistent label.

Here is a counter program that computes $X \times Y$, the product residing in Z upon termination:

$$U \leftarrow 0$$
$$Z \leftarrow 0$$
A: **if** $X = 0$ **goto** L
$$X \leftarrow X - 1$$
$$V \leftarrow Y + 1$$
$$V \leftarrow V - 1$$
B: **if** $V = 0$ **goto** A
$$V \leftarrow V - 1$$
$$Z \leftarrow Z + 1$$
if $U = 0$ **goto** B

The reader might want to ponder this program for a while. First, there is a **goto** L but no statement labeled L. This is in accordance with our convention, and the program halts in a normal fashion when it attempts to carry out that **goto**. We have also used two small tricks, achieving, respectively, the effect of the statement $V \leftarrow Y$ and the unconditional instruction **goto** B, both of which are not really allowed by the formal syntax. The product $X \times Y$ is computed by two nested loops. The outer loop repeatedly adds Y to an initially zeroed Z, X times, and the inner one carries out the addition by repeatedly adding 1 to Z, V times, where V is initialized to Y each time around.

How powerful are counter programs? Can they solve really complicated problems? The answer: they are precisely as powerful as Turing machines, and hence as powerful as any computer whatsoever.

Turing Machines vs. Counter Programs

Since counter programs manipulate numbers only, this last statement requires clarification. It might make sense to claim that counter programs can solve the *numerical* problems that are solvable by Turing machines (especially having seen how tediously Turing machines add numbers). But how, for example, does a counter program find shortest paths in a graph, or occurrences of 'money' in a text? Turing machines are capable of these feats because, as shown earlier, every kind of data structure, graphs and texts included can be encoded as a sequence of symbols on a tape. But can such objects be encoded also as numbers, to be manipulated by mere one-step increments and decrements?

The answer is yes. If the alphabet used in these sequences were to contain precisely ten symbols we could easily associate them with the ten decimal digits, and we would then have no problem viewing any (finite) sequence as a number. Using standard methods, the same can be done for an alphabet of *any* (finite) size, since non-negative integers can be represented in a uniform and unambiguous way using any fixed number of digits. Binary numbers involve only two digits, and those involving sixteen are called **hexadecimal** numbers.[†] Thus, using an easily programmable encoding mechanism, any finite sequence of symbols over a finite alphabet can be viewed as a number.

Now, at any point during a Turing machine's execution (assuming it starts on a finite input) only a finite portion of the tape contains nonblank information. Consequently, the tape itself, together with the head's position, can be represented by two numbers, encoding the portions of the tape on either side of the head. To make things easier, it is useful to represent the right-hand portion in reverse, so that the least significant digits of both numbers are close to the head. Figure 9.9 shows the numerical representation of a tape assuming, for simplicity, an alphabet of ten symbols. On this basis it is possible to carry out a simulation of any Turing machine with a counter program.

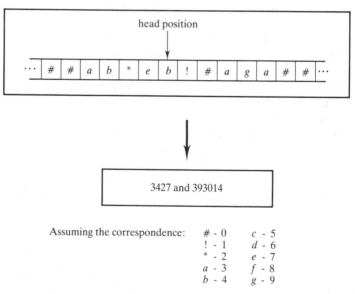

Figure 9.9   Encoding a Turing machine's tape and position as two numbers.

[†]The binary representation is particularly useful when real digital computers are involved, because of the 0/1 nature of bits, and the hexadecimal notation likewise, since one hexadecimal digit is represented precisely by four binary digits, or bits.

** How? Well, two variables are used to carry the two crucial values encoding the nonblank portions of the tape on either side of the head and (implicitly) the head position itself; another variable is used for the state. The subtlety of the simulation is in the fact that the effect of one step of the Turing machine is quite 'local'. One side of the tape gets 'longer' because the head moves away from it, adding a new symbol to its 'end', and the other gets shorter, losing its last symbol (unless the machine moves off the nonblank portion into the all-blank area, in which case the side which was to become empty gets a new blank symbol for nothing, in effect making the entire relevant part of the tape one symbol longer). All these changes can be simulated in the counter program by relatively straightforward arithmetical manipulation of the two main variables. As a consequence, the entire transition diagram of the Turing machine can be 'worked' into the counter program by 'chunks', each of which simulates one transition of the diagram. To actually simulate the workings of the machine, the program repeatedly inspects the state-carrying variable and the symbol seen by the head (i.e., the least significant digit of the right-hand number), executes the relevant chunk, and changes the value of the state variable. **

And so programs that can merely increment and decrement integers by 1 and test their value against 0 can be used to do anything any computer can do. Not only can they calculate numerically, but, in principle, they can also represent, traverse, and manipulate any kind of data structure, including lists, graphs, trees, and even entire databases.

As to the other direction, Turing machines can be shown to simulate counter programs, with the values of the various counters spread out on the tape, separated by '*'s. The simulating machine uses special states to represent the different statements in the program. Entering each such state triggers a sequence of transitions that carries out the statement itself.

Turing machines and counter programs both achieve universality by making use of a potentially infinite amount of memory, but in different ways. With Turing machines, the *number* of objects containing information (the tape's squares) is potentially unbounded, but the *amount* of information in each is finite and bounded. With counter programs it is the other way around. There are only finitely many variables in any given program, but each can contain an arbitrarily large value, thus, in effect, encoding a potentially unbounded amount of information.

It is perhaps of interest to the minimalists among us that we can always do with only *two* counters. It is possible to simulate any counter program with one that uses only two variables, though the details of this simulation are more complicated.

*   *   *

Universal Algorithms

The CT thesis talks about universal models, or languages. One of its most interesting consequences is the existence of **universal algorithms**. A universal algorithm has the ability to act like any algorithm whatsoever. It accepts as inputs the description of *any* algorithm A and *any* legal input X, and simply runs, or **simulates**, A on X, halting if and when A halts, and producing the outputs that would have been produced if A had indeed been run on X. Thus, fixing the input algorithm A and letting X vary has the effect of making the universal algorithm behave precisely like A.

In a sense, a computer, or an interpreter (see Chapter 3), is very much like a universal algorithm: we present it with a program and an input and it runs the former on the latter. However, the term 'universal' suggests independence, meaning that a universal algorithm should be *insensitive* to the choice of a language or machine – computers and interpreters are not. It would thus appear that no universal algorithm could ever be implemented, since both the universal algorithm itself and its input algorithms must be written in some language, intended for some machine.

To our help comes the CT thesis, with its simulations between models, and its claim that all programming languages and computation models are equivalent. To obtain a universal algorithm we have only to use some language L_1 to write an effectively executable program U, which accepts as inputs any program written in some fixed universal language or model L_2, and any input, and simulates the running of that program on that input. Once written, U can be thought of as being language- and machine-independent because, by the thesis, (1) it could have been written in *any* universal language, running on *any* machine, and (2) it can simulate *any* effectively executable algorithm, written in *any* language. That is, given an algorithm A and input X, rewrite A in the language L_2 (this is possible by the thesis), and submit the new program with X to U (see Figure 9.10).

Turing machines are a perfect candidate for both L_1 and L_2, and indeed it is not too difficult to construct a so-called **universal Turing machine** – namely, one that can simulate the effect of arbitrary Turing machines on arbitrary inputs. But to do so we must first find a way to describe any Turing machine as a linear sequence of symbols, suitable for input on a tape. This can be done easily, since we only have to linearize the machine's transition diagram, each transition of which can be given by its source and target states, followed by the $\langle a/b, direction \rangle$ label. By convention, the list of transitions is preceded by the name of the start state. Here, for example, is the initial part of an encoding of the Turing machine of Figure 9.4:

mark $**$ *mark YES* $\langle \#/\#, L \rangle$ $*$ *mark move$_a$* $\langle a/\#, R \rangle$ $*$ *move$_a$ move$_a$* $\langle a/a, R \rangle$ $*$ . . .

The universal Turing machine U accepts as inputs a description of any Turing machine M, followed by a finite sequence X, viewed as a potential input to M (the description of M and the input X are separated, say, by '$'). It then proceeds to simulate M's action on a tape that contains the input X surrounded by blanks, with the very same consequences: if T would not have halted on such a tape, then neither does U, and if it would, then so does U. Furthermore, if and when U halts, the tape looks precisely as it would have looked upon M's termination, including the output enclosed between '!'s.

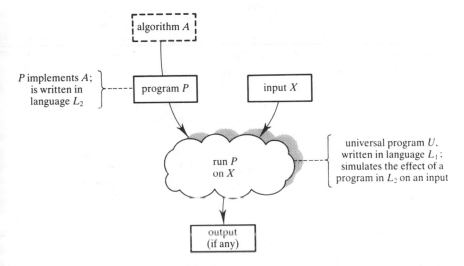

Figure 9.10   A universal program written in language L_1 for programs in L_2.

To really construct a universal Turing machine is an interesting exercise, not unlike the task of writing an interpreter for a simple programming language L in the language L itself. There exist, in fact, extremely concise universal Turing machines with only very few states. In a similar vein, of course, it is also possible to construct a **universal counter program**, which accepts as inputs two numbers, the first encoding an input counter program, and the other its potential input, and simulates the one on the other. In fact, being just another counter program itself, the universal counter program can therefore be constructed with only two counters, as already mentioned.

More important than the number of states or counters, however, is the profound nature of a universal algorithm or machine U. Once constructed, U is a *single* object of *maximal* algorithmic power, and its significance cannot be overestimated. If a universal algorithm were written for use on a personal desk computer it would literally be able to simulate even the largest and most sophisticated mainframe computer, provided that it was given enough time, that a description of the simulated machine were given as its first input, and that sufficiently many memory units were available.

Simulations as Reductions

The concept of a universal algorithm can also be used to enhance the significance of the simulations between models of computation. When we say that one model can simulate another we are really saying that we have a *reduction* (in the sense of Chapter 8) between two universal algorithm problems. For example, the simulation of Turing machines by counter programs, described informally earlier, can be formalized as a *single* algorithm that constitutes a reduction of the universal Turing machine problem to the universal counter program problem. Given an input to the first problem (i.e., a sequence containing a description of a Turing machine M followed by an input X), the reduction transforms it into an input to the second problem (i.e., into two numbers encoding, respectively, the counter program C equivalent to M and the input X). The reduction then runs a universal counter program on C and the number Y encoding X, thus precisely simulating what M would have done on input X. If the reduction algorithm itself is given in the form of a Turing machine, the result is a universal Turing machine (see Figure 9.11).

This point of view provides a firm mathematical basis for certain discussions in earlier chapters. Whenever we talked about programs that accept other programs as inputs we were not being restrictive at all. Since effective simulations exist between any two sufficiently powerful models of computation, we can always start with a program or algorithm in any language or model and translate it into the language we happen to be working with.

Consider, for example, the undecidability of the halting problem, as proved in Chapter 8. Proper use of the reductions associated with the CT thesis enables us to show that this result is extremely general. It can first be proved rigorously for Turing machines by (1) assuming that the input program W in Figure 8.8 is the description of some Turing machine, and (2) constructing the hypothetical program S also as a Turing machine (quite an easy adaptation of the construction given therein). The contradictory nature of this construction is then established, resulting in the seemingly humble conclusion that no Turing machine exists that solves the halting problem for Turing machines. This result, however, is not humble at all. Using the appropriate reductions to transform the input Turing machines into a language or model L_2, and then rewriting the program S in L_1, we conclude that the halting problem is undecidable in a very strong sense: in no effective language or model L_1 is it possible to solve the halting problem for programs in an arbitrary universal language or model L_2. (A special case is when $L_1 = L_2$.)

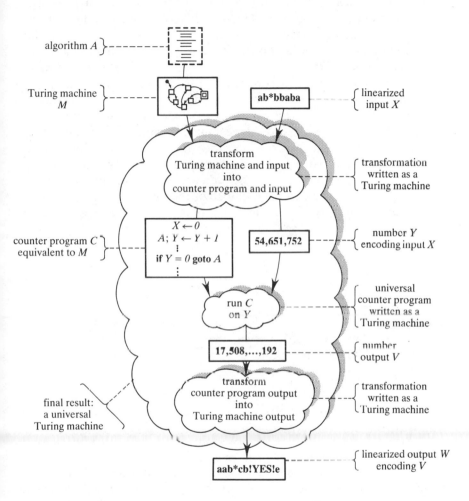

Figure 9.11   Constructing a universal Turing machine from a universal counter program.

It is these language- and model-independent facts, coupled with the confidence we have in the Church/Turing thesis, that justify our use in previous chapters of phrases concerning the nonexistence, for certain problems, of *any* algorithms, now or in the future.

*   *   *

A Slight Modification of Counter Programs

We will now make a slight change in the primitive instructions of counter programs. As defined earlier, counter programs can only add or subtract 1 to a counter. Thus, if they are to work on the numbers that represent Turing machine tapes, they would have to do so one *unit* at a time, whereas the Turing machines work on their tapes one *symbol* at a time. And since the Turing machine tape is thought of as representing numbers in, say, decimal notation, Turing machine numbers are manipulated one *digit* at a time, which is exponentially more efficient than working on them one *unit* at a time. And so, while counter programs based on +1 and −1 instructions alone are indeed as powerful as Turing machines, they are exponentially slower. This is not because of some inherent limitation of the counter program model itself, but because the primitive instructions are exponentially weaker. To remove this discrepancy, counter programs must be allowed to add and subtract whole digits, be they binary, decimal, or otherwise. (Why is the particular choice of the number base unimportant here?) In essence, the programs are allowed to work on **non-unary** numbers. Accordingly, let us add the two instructions:

$$X \leftarrow X \times 10 \quad \text{and} \quad X \leftarrow X/10$$

to the repertoire of basic operations of counter programs. (By convention, the division operator ignores fractions.) The new operations clearly add no computational power to the model, as they could have been simulated by the +1 and −1 operations. However, they do enable us to compare Turing machines and counter programs in a more realistic way, as will now be shown.

Tractability Is also Robust

By providing reductions between all sufficiently powerful models of computation we convince ourselves that the class of problems solvable by these models is insensitive to the differences between them. By labeling the problems in the class **effectively computable** (or **effectively decidable**, if we are interested in the yes/no case), we express our opinion that the notion we have captured is important and profound. This is the crux of the Church/Turing thesis.

With a small effort, however, we can do even better. Careful inspection shows that if both models involved in such a reduction deal with numbers in a non-unary fashion, then all these reductions are polynomial time; that is, reasonable in the sense of Chapter 7. For example, the transformation from a Turing machine M and its input X into an equivalent counter program C and the corresponding input Y (see Figure 9.11) takes time that is only polynomial in the length of the descriptions of M and X. Moreover – and this fact is not true without allowing the $X \times 10$ and $X/10$ operations – the time taken by the resulting counter program C to *run* on input Y (assuming it halts) is at most only polynomially longer than the time M would have taken to run on X.[†]

It follows, of course, that if the Turing machine M solves some algorithmic problem in polynomial-time, then, not only does the counter program C also solve the problem, it does so in polynomial-time too. The converse reduction, from counter programs to Turing machines, is also polynomial-time, so that the dual fact holds too: if a counter program solves some problem in polynomial-time then so does the resulting equivalent Turing machine.

The conclusion is that Turing machines and counter programs (with the $X \times 10$ and $X/10$ instructions) are **polynomially equivalent**. The class of problems having reasonable solutions ($=$ polynomial-time ones) is the same for both models. The really surprising fact is that this polynomial-time equivalence holds not only for the reductions among the very primitive models, but also for those between them and even the most sophisticated ones. Turing machines and counter programs are obviously very inefficient even for quite trivial tasks, having to either shuttle back and forth on a tape, or repeatedly increase and decrease counters. However, they are only *polynomially* less efficient than even the fastest and most intricate computers, which support the most advanced programming languages with the most sophisticated compilers! In solving some algorithmic problem, the Turing machine or counter program resulting from the appropriate reduction might take *twice* as much time as it takes a fast computer, or a *thousand* times as much, or even that amount of time *squared*, *cubed*, or raised to the power 1000, but not *exponentially* as much.

** More concisely, if a fast computer solves a certain problem in time $O(f(N))$, for some function f of the input length N, then there is an equivalent Turing machine that will take no more than time $O(p(f(N)))$, for some fixed polynomial function p. In particular, if f itself is a polynomial, meaning that the fast computer solves the problem *reasonably*, then some very primitive-looking Turing machine also solves it reasonably – in polynomial-time $p(f(N))$, to be precise. Thus, the time might grow from, say, $O(N^2)$ to $O(N^5)$ or $O(N^{85})$, but not to $O(2^N)$. In fact, most known reductions involve *lower-order* polynomials of no more than about N^4 or N^5, so that 'good' polynomial-time algorithms on one model will not become unacceptably worse on another. **

The conclusion is this: not only is the class of *computable* problems robust (i.e., insensitive to model or language), but so is the class of *tractable* problems. This is really a refinement of the CT thesis that takes running

---

[†] For counter programs time is measured by the number of instructions executed, and for Turing machines by the number of steps taken.

time into consideration too. The refined thesis does not hold for certain models that incorporate unlimited amounts of *concurrency*, as explained in Chapter 10. For this reason it is sometimes called the **sequential computation thesis**. The term 'sequential' is meant to capture algorithmic executions that proceed in a sequential, stepwise manner, rather than by carrying out lots of things simultaneously.

The refined CT thesis thus claims that all sequential universal models of computation, including those that have not yet been invented, have polynomially related time behaviors, so that the class of problems solvable in reasonable time is precisely the same for all models. Thus, the refined thesis justifies another of the lines appearing in our sphere of algorithmic problems, the one separating the tractable from the intractable (see Figures 7.6, 8.3, 8.11 and 8.12).

Many other complexity classes, such as NP, PSPACE and EXPTIME (see Figure 7.15) are also robust in the same sense, justifying much of the language- and model-independent research in complexity theory. However, some classes, like the problems solvable in *linear* time, are not, and can be highly sensitive to changes in the model. A Turing machine with an additional counter, for example, can compare the number of a's and b's appearing in a sequence in linear-time, but bare Turing machines require $O(N \times \log N)$ if a rather clever method is used, and take $O(N^2)$ if they naively run back and forth. (Can you find the $O(N \times \log N)$ method?)

Incidentally, the polynomial-time version of the CT thesis could not have been formulated as early as the 1930s because complexity theory did not exist then. The significance of the class P was only recognized in the late 1960s, and gained credence a few years later with the realization of the importance of the P vs. NP problem.

(Although we have not defined it precisely, it happens that the line separating the undecidable from the *highly* undecidable in Figures 8.11 and 8.12 is also robust in the sense of the present discussion. Thus, all universal models of computation give rise to the same division, and the recurring domino problem, for example, is highly undecidable in them all.)

Turing Machines and the P vs. NP Problem

The NP-complete problems of Chapter 7 deserve special mention here. Both P and NP are usually defined in terms of the rigorous notion of Turing machine computations; NP is defined to contain precisely those decision problems solvable by *nondeterministic* Turing machines running in polynomial-time, while P is defined to contain those solvable by *ordinary* Turing machines in polynomial-time. Once such formal definitions are given, we can state the refined CT thesis as claiming that all reasonable sequential computation models are polynomially equivalent to ordinary Turing machines, and continue to discuss the ramifications of this fact from there.

The notions of P and NP have been introduced here without a precise model, stating the CT thesis first, and only later introducing formal models such as Turing machines. The reasons for this are pedagogic in nature; the consequences remain the same.

Now, had nondeterministic Turing machines satisfied the criterion of sequentiality, the refined thesis would have implied a positive solution to the P vs. NP problem, since it would have equated the classes of problems solvable in polynomial-time on both versions of Turing machines. As it happens, nondeterministic machines are *not* considered sequential, since they employ 'magic' to make the best choices, and without magic they would have had to try out many possibilities *simultaneously* to find the best one. (Trying them out sequentially would take exponential-time.) Therefore, the thesis does not apply to such machines, and it thus cannot help much with regards to P vs. NP.

Formulating the P vs. NP problem in this formal fashion is interesting because it implies that to solve the problem in the negative (i.e., to show that $P \neq NP$) we need only show that *Turing machines* cannot solve some NP-complete problem in less than exponential-time. For example, if someone were to show that the monkey puzzle problem cannot be solved on any Turing machine in polynomial-time, it would follow from the refined thesis that it cannot be solved in polynomial-time on *any* sequential model, and hence that it is truly intractable. And, as we know, if the monkey puzzle problem is intractable, then so are *all* the NP-complete problems, yielding $P \neq NP$.

Using Turing Machines for Lower Bound Proofs

To prove an *upper* bound on an algorithmic problem – that is, to find a good algorithm – the richest and most powerful formalism available should be used. In fact, researchers typically employ very high-level programming constructs and intricate data structures to devise nontrivial algorithms. They then rely on the robustness afforded by the variants of the Church/Turing thesis to make claims about the implications of those algorithms to *all* models. Thus, if someone ever manages to prove that P = NP, the chances are that it will be done using a very high-level model to describe a complex polynomial-time algorithm for some NP-complete problem. However, when proving *lower* bounds, primitive models are much better suited, since they employ only a few extremely simple constructs and there is less to worry about, so to speak. Thus, if someone ever proves that $P \neq NP$, the chances are that it will be done using a very primitive model, like Turing machines or counter programs.

Turing machines are, in fact, used widely in lower bound proofs of all kinds. As an example, here is how Turing machines can be used to show the undecidability of a certain tiling problem. (Undecidability, of course, is a kind of lower bound – it brings bad news about the status of the problem.) For reasons of exposition, the problem we shall discuss is slightly less general than the simple unbounded domino problem of Chapter 8. The inputs are a finite set T of tile types and one particular type t, and the problem asks whether the T can be used to tile the upper half of the infinite integer grid, with a tile of type t placed somewhere along the bottom row. In Chapter 8 the precise connection between the seemingly unrelated notions of tiling with colored dominoes and algorithmic termination was deferred. Now is the time to explain: to show that this tiling problem is undecidable we reduce to it the halting problem for Turing machines (actually, the *non*-halting problem, as explained below).

Assume we are given a Turing machine M and an input sequence of symbols X. We will show how to construct a set of tile types T and a particular tile t such that M does not halt on X precisely if T can tile the upper half-grid with t appearing somewhere along the bottom line. The transformation from $\langle M, X \rangle$ to $\langle T, t \rangle$ will be described informally, but the reader should have no trouble seeing that it could have been turned into an algorithm that works for any M and X (see Figure 9.12).

Figure 9.12   Reducing halting Turing machines to tiling half-grids. (Notice how 'yes' and 'no' switch roles.)

The underlying idea is very simple. The tile set T is constructed in such a way that tiling the half-grid in the upward direction corresponds to making progress in the computation of the Turing machine M on X. The effect is achieved by making each row of tiles encode, using appropriate colors, the current contents of M's infinite tape, together with the current state and the location of the head within the tape. Moreover, the tiles are constructed to guarantee that progressing upward from tiled row to tiled row is possible only in precise accordance with the instructions given in M's transition diagram. Thus, a tiled portion of the grid necessarily corresponds to a legal computation of the machine, the horizontal dimension corresponding to memory space (the tape) and the vertical dimension to time. As a consequence, tiling the *entire* half-grid using T necessarily corresponds to an *infinite* computation of M.

** How do we get colored tiles to encode tapes, states and transitions? To make life easier, we shall use symbols instead of colors. Thus if we associate some side of a tile with 'color' s^+, we really mean that we are using a unique color represented by the symbols s^+, and that that color is different from any color represented by a different combination of symbols.

First, we shall force the bottom row of the tiling to encode an otherwise completely blank tape containing the input X, with the indication that M's head is pointing to the leftmost symbol of X and that the state is M's start state. Figure 9.13 shows how this is done for the palindrome machine of Figure 9.4 with input '*a b b a*'. Notice that the special tile t is taken to be the one encoding the start state attached to the leftmost symbol of the input. The idea can be easily applied to any finite input, over any alphabet of symbols. (For conciseness, we have abbreviated the names of states as follows: *mark* becomes mk, *move* becomes mv_a, *test* becomes ts_a and *return* becomes rt.)

Besides those that encode the input, we need several other tile types to enable upwards tiling. Figure 9.14 shows all the additional ones needed. The first type, t_1, enables symbols to be passed up to the next configuration, untouched. Next, t_2 and t_3 deal with the case where the state is 'approaching' the symbol in question, from the right or left, respectively; the resulting color on the top encodes the state and the symbol it is looking at (as in the *mk, a* case of Figure 9.13). Finally, t_4 and t_5 cover the change of symbol and state. Tile type t_5, for example, captures the case where the machine M is in state r looking at symbol v, and it moves to the left after changing v to w and entering state s. This can match up on the left only with a tile of type t_2, because of the state name appearing as its left-hand color. (Why do we need the '+' symbol?)

This completes the construction of the set T of tile types and the special type t, from the given Turing machine M and its input X. Notice, of course, that T contains only finitely many tile types, the precise number depending on both the machine M and the length of X.   **

(1)   **If** input tape is:

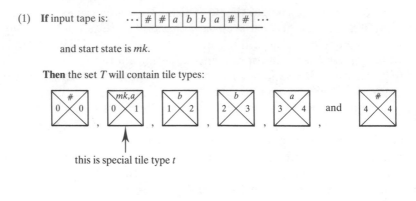

and start state is mk.

Then the set T will contain tile types:

this is special tile type t

(2)   **Consequently**, since t is required to appear in bottom row, bottom row is forced to be precisely:

this tile is required to appear

(it encodes input tape – head position – start state in top colors.)

Figure 9.13   Forcing the bottom row of tiles to encode the initial configuration of a Turing machine.

The general claim about the construction is as just stated: any possible tiling of the upper half-grid with the tile types of T, in which t appears in the bottom row, corresponds directly to a computation of M on X. Consequently, if the half-grid tiling problem were decidable the halting problem for Turing machines would be decidable too, and since the halting problem is not, neither is the tiling problem.

Figure 9.15 shows the tiling that results from constructing the tile set for the palindrome machine of Figure 9.4. Notice how the rows correspond perfectly to the frames of Figure 9.5, and how the tiling cannot be continued because the machine halts. Tiling with colored tiles and computing with algorithms are thus almost the same thing. Had we drawn Figure 9.15 with colored or shaded tiles, the connection would not have been as clear, even if we had meticulously used quite different colors for the different symbol codes appearing therein.

*   *   *

(1)   For every symbol x, the set T contains:

(t_1)

(2)   For every symbol x and state s the set T contains:

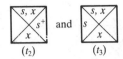

(t_2) (t_3)

(3)   Whenever $\boxed{r} \xrightarrow{v/w,\ R} \boxed{s}$ appears in M's transition diagram, the set T contains:

(t_4)

(4)   Whenever $\boxed{r} \xrightarrow{v/w,\ L} \boxed{s}$ appears in M's transition diagram, the set T contains:

(t_5)

Figure 9.14   The other tile types needed in the reduction of Figure 9.12.

Proving Lower Bounds by Diagonalization

One of the most important techniques for establishing lower bounds, using primitive models such as Turing machines, is the method of **diagonalization**. The idea goes back to Georg Cantor, a prominent 19th century mathematician, who used it in a non-algorithmic context. Actually, we have already used diagonalization, albeit in disguise, when proving the undecidability of the halting problem in Chapter 8. After seeing the example now presented, the reader should try to rephrase that proof in terms of this technique.

In Chapter 7 it was stated that to prove that problem P cannot be solved in less than exponential-time we first construct a possibly contrived problem Q, having both upper and lower bounds of exponential-time, and then exhibit a general polynomial-time reduction from *all* exponential-time problems to P. For reasons explained there, this establishes P's intractability.

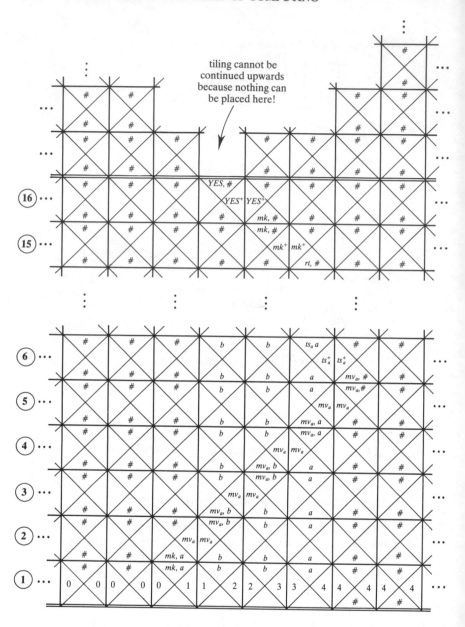

Figure 9.15 The tiling corresponding to the computation of Figure 9.5.

As far as the second task is concerned, little will be said here, except to note that the refined CT thesis allows us to consider only a single model, say Turing machines: to show that the roadblock problem, or the satisfiability problem for PDL (see Chapter 7), is intractable, assuming that the problem Q has already been defined, it suffices to establish a reduction from Turing machines that run in no more than exponential-time to the problem in question. This, though rarely trivial, is much easier than considering exponential-time solutions in *all* languages and models.

Let us concentrate on the first task. We wish to construct an algorithmic problem Q that is solvable in exponential-time; it need not necessarily be a natural or practical problem in any sense, but it has to be *un*solvable in *less* than exponential-time.

** As we know, it is possible to describe any Turing machine as a string of symbols. Using this fact, we can imagine an effective (infinite) list that contains, in some definite order, precisely *all* descriptions of decision-making Turing machines; no more and no less. The way to become convinced of this is to first imagine a list containing all sequences of symbols, in order, starting with one symbol sequences, then two symbol ones, then those with three, etc. Some sequences correctly encode yes/no Turing machines as per the conventions agreed on earlier, and this fact can easily be checked algorithmically. The description must start with some *-free sequence constituting the name of the start state, followed by '**', followed by zero or more blocks separated by '*'s, each of which contains two state names, and a label of the form $\langle a/b, direction \rangle$, where *direction* is L or R. It is now possible to check that such an encoding contains the two special states *YES* and *NO*.

Consequently, there is an algorithm which, given a number I, will eventually halt and produce the description of M_I, the Ith decision-making Turing machine on the list. The algorithm simply starts generating all finite sequences in order, missing none, and checks each one as to whether it constitutes a correct encoding of a Turing machine with the two states mentioned. While doing so, it maintains a count of how many such machines it has already found, halting when the Ith one is reached, and delivering it as an output.

We can now add something to this algorithm, so that the Turing machines it produces are *time bounded* in a certain way. When the algorithm (call it A) encounters the description of the Turing machine M_I, it modifies that description before releasing it to the output, yielding a new machine (call it EM_I). The modification forces EM_I to first compute the length N of its input (by counting how many squares it sees before reaching a blank) and then to act just as the original machine M_I, but, in addition, to count the number of steps M_I takes, halting prematurely and entering its *NO* state if that number exceeds 2^N. The step counting has to be done carefully, by pausing after carrying out each step of the original M_I, running all the way to one side, where the current count is incremented by 1 and is compared to 2^N. The new machine thus simulates M_I for 2^N steps, and halts and says 'no' if by that time M_I has not yet halted on its own. The behavior of this grand algorithm A is illustrated in Figure 9.16.

The algorithm A can really be thought of as producing, or listing, *decision problems*, not Turing machines, since each of the machines it outputs is a pure yes/no machine, and hence solves *some* decision problem.

Moreover, each problem it produces is Turing-machine solvable within time 2^N. Not only that, in a strong sense A produces *all* such 2^N-bounded decision problems, because if M is *any* Turing machine that solves a decision problem in time 2^N or less, then for some number I the machine EM_I is equivalent to M – i.e., it solves precisely the same problem. Let us denote by DP_I the decision problem solved by the machine EM_I, the Ith modified machine on the list.

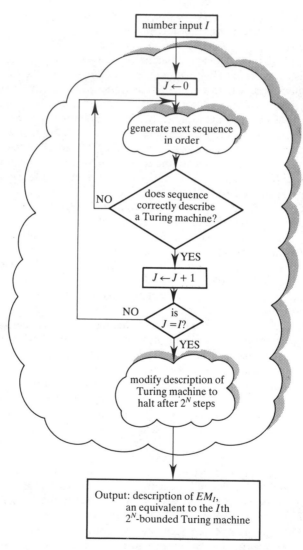

Figure 9.16   Super-algorithm A for listing 2^N-bounded Turing machines.

Now, consider Figure 9.17, in which the *EM* machines and their decision problems have been plotted against all possible inputs. (Listing all inputs effectively poses no problem; every finite sequence of symbols from the alphabet in question is a legal input to a Turing machine, so the list of inputs $X_1, X_2, \ldots$ is just the list of all finite sequences in order.) At the junction of the *I*th row and *J*th column the answer given by the *I*th machine on the *J*th input has been written, and since the *EM* machines were constructed to halt on every input they will always produce well-defined answers. In this way the *I*th row in Figure 9.17 is a complete, albeit infinite, description of the decision problem DP_I, the one solved by the machine EM_I .

A special decision problem R, called the **diagonal problem**, is now constructed. It corresponds to the *diagonal* row of Figure 9.17. On the *I*th input X_I, the answer offered by R is the same as that offered by the problem residing on the *I*th row, DP_I. Now define Q to be the 'negative' of the diagonal problem R; whenever R says 'yes' Q says 'no', and vice versa. Using the super-algorithm A described above, and some universal Turing machine, it is easy to see that Q is decidable. Given any input Y, first run through the list of all inputs in order to figure out Y's position. Having found that Y is really some X_I, apply A to the number I, yielding the Turing machine EM_I. Then, using the universal machine, run EM_I on Y (i.e., on X_I), reversing the answer when execution terminates. A closer look shows that the entire procedure can be carried out in exponential-time, the dominant time being that taken by the simulation of EM_I on X_I. So the decision problem Q is solvable in exponential-time.

It is now claimed that Q is an *inherently* exponential-time problem; in particular, no Turing machine can solve it within time 2^N; the base of its exponent must, in fact, be greater than 2. The reason is simple. If it were solvable by any Turing machine in time 2^N or less, then already one of the *EM* machines would solve it, since these machines faithfully represent *all* Turing machines that halt within time 2^N. But Q cannot be solved by any one of the *EM* machines, because its list of answers differs from that of any machine on the list in at least one position – that falling on the diagonal. If Q were solved, say, by the fifth machine on the list, EM_5, that would mean that Q was really the decision problem DP_5, and its answer on the fifth input X_5 would have to be 'no' by Figure 9.16. However, by the very construction of the problem Q, the answer is the opposite, namely, 'yes', and this is a contradiction.   **

Thus, Q is solvable in exponential-time, but it also has an exponential-time lower bound, as desired. Both bounds are insensitive to model or language, despite the fact that they were proved using the Turing machine model, because of the robustness afforded by the refined version of the CT thesis. The proof that roadblock, or PDL, or any other problem of interest, is intractable can then proceed using Q, as explained in Chapter 7.

*   *   *

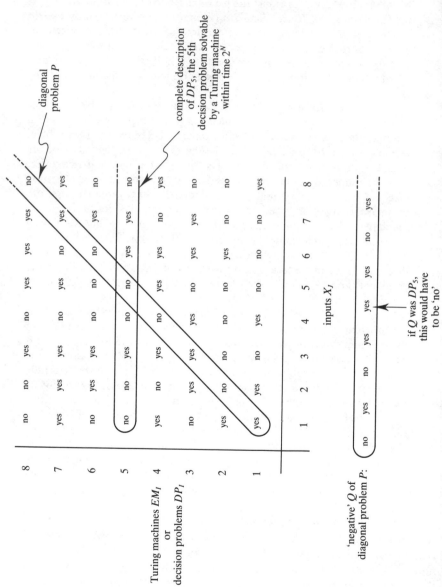

One-Way Turing Machines, or Finite-State Automata

We have seen that certain restrictions on Turing machines (such as using a tape that is infinite only to the right) do not detract from the universality of the model; the class of solvable problems remains the same even when the model is so restricted. Clearly, not all restrictions have this property. Machines that are required to halt immediately upon starting cannot do very much, and the same goes for those that are not allowed to halt at all. These examples, however, are not very interesting. In the interim many kinds of limitations can be imposed on universal models of computation, and on Turing machines in particular, which result in weaker classes of problems that are nevertheless of great interest.

One obvious approach is to restrict the machine's use of resources. We already know that the class P is obtained by allowing only Turing machines that halt within a polynomial amount of time. PSPACE is the class obtained by allowing Turing machines access to only a polynomial amount of tape (any attempt to go beyond the limit is punished, say, by halting in state *NO*). Other complexity classes can be similarly defined as consisting of the problems solvable by appropriately resource-bounded Turing machines.

There is, however, another approach to restricting the Turing machine model. It involves limiting the machine's very mechanism. One of the most interesting of these downgrades is obtained by allowing Turing machines to travel along the tape in only one fixed direction – say to the right. The result is a device called a **finite-state automaton**, or simply a **finite automaton** for short.

Let us think about this for a moment. If the machine is not allowed to move left it cannot inspect any square more than once. In particular, it cannot make any use of anything it writes down itself, save to produce output, since it cannot go back to read its own notes, so to speak. Therefore, if the discussion is restricted to *decision* problems, we can assume that finite automata do not write at all; saying 'yes' or 'no' can be achieved via two special halting states, and the new symbols it writes down as it moves along are worthless, having no effect whatsoever on the automaton's final verdict. Moreover, beyond the input sequence the tape contains only blanks; hence, the automaton might as well stop when it reaches the end of the input sequence, since it is not going to see anything new that will make a difference.

In conclusion, a finite automaton solving a decision problem acts as follows. It simply runs through the input sequence of symbols, one by one, changing states as a result of the current state and the new symbol it sees. When it reaches the end of the input sequence it stops, the answer depending upon whether it stopped in state *YES* or *NO*. (By convention, we shall consider stopping in any other state to be like saying 'no', so that a finite automaton need only have one state or more called *YES*; if it is in

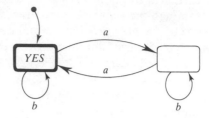

Figure 9.18   A finite automaton that detects words with an even number of *a*'s.

that state when it reaches the end of the input the answer is 'yes', and otherwise it is 'no'.) We can depict a finite automaton as a state transition diagram, just as we did for Turing machines, but now we have no need for the ⟨*b*, *direction*⟩ part of the labels; a transition is labeled only with the symbol that triggers it.

On the Power of Finite Automata

What are finite automata capable of? Figure 9.18 shows a finite automaton defined over the alphabet {*a*, *b*}, which decides whether or not its input sequence contains an even number of *a*'s. (What does the automaton of Figure 9.19 do?) Answering questions of *parity* (i.e., evenness and oddness) might appear at first to require the ability to count. It does not. The automaton of Figure 9.18 does the job not by counting how many *a*'s it has seen, but by alternating between two states that indicate the current parity status of that number.

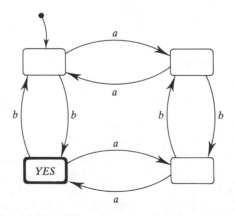

Figure 9.19   What does this automaton detect?

In fact, it is quite easy to show that finite automata *cannot* count. As an illustration, let us prove that no finite automaton can decide whether its input sequence contains precisely the same number of a's and b's.

** The proof will be by way of contradiction. Assume that some automaton F *can* indeed solve this decision problem, meaning that for any sequence of a's and b's, F says 'yes' if the number of occurrences of both is equal. Denote by N the number of states in F. Consider the sequence X that consists of precisely $N + 1$ a's followed by $N + 1$ b's. Our automaton must obviously say 'yes' when handed X as an input.

The argument now uses the so-called **pigeon hole principle**: if all the pigeons have to enter pigeon holes, but there are more pigeons than holes, then at least one hole will have to accommodate more than one pigeon. In our case the pigeons are the $N + 1$ a's appearing as the first half of the input sequence X, and the holes are the N states of the automaton F. As F moves along X there must be at least two different squares within the initial sequence of a's where F will be in the same state. For definiteness, assume that $N = 9$, that the two squares are the third and the seventh, and that the state entered in the two cases is s (see Figure 9.20). Now, F cannot move backwards, cannot jot any information down, and acts solely on the basis of the one symbol it sees and its current state. It is therefore obvious that when it reaches the seventh square its behavior on the rest of the input will not depend on anything it has seen earlier except by way of the fact that it is now in state s. Consequently, if we were to *remove* squares 3 through 6, resulting in a sequence of 6 a's, not 10, followed by the 10 b's, the automaton F would still reach the third a in state s and would proceed just as if it had reached the seventh a in the original sequence. In particular, since it said 'yes' on the original sequence, it will say 'yes' on the new one. But this contradicts our assumption that F says 'yes' only on sequences with the same number of a's and b's.   **

The reader might enjoy constructing a similar proof, also using the pigeon hole principle, to show that finite automata cannot detect palindromes.

Finite automata are indeed very limited, but they do capture the way many everyday systems work. For example, Figure 9.21 shows a finite-state automaton describing part of the behavior of a simple digital watch, with four control buttons, a, b, c, and d. The names of the states are self-explanatory, and we can associate with each state detailed descriptions of the actions that are carried out therein. Notice that the input symbols are really the **signals**, or **events**, that enter the system from its outside environment – in this case, the user pressing buttons. An input word is thus just a sequence of incoming signals. In Chapter 10 we shall further discuss this correspondence.

*   *   *

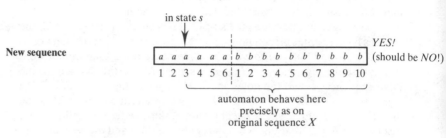

Figure 9.20   Applying the pigeon hole principle to a finite automaton.

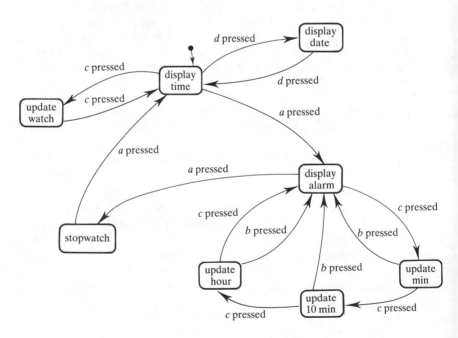

Figure 9.21   An automaton describing a simple digital watch.

Research on Abstract Models of Computation

In a sense, the material of this chapter forms the underpinnings of nearly all the topics mentioned in the book so far. Primitive models of computation, whether they are universal, like Turing machines and counter programs, or less powerful, like finite automata or resource-bounded devices, are extremely important objects for research in computer science. They focus attention on the essential properties of algorithmic devices, such as computers and programming languages, and give rise to fundamental and robust notions that are insensitive to the particular device used.

In Chapters 7 and 8 we touched upon the research areas of computational complexity and undecidability, both of which use the likes of Turing machines and counter programs in an essential way. Finite automata are the basis of a very large body of research, of both theoretical and practical nature, which has fundamental implications to such diverse areas as the design of power stations and the understanding of the brain.

Other restrictions of Turing machines have been, and are still being, heavily studied, in the research areas of **automata** and **formal language theory**. Notable among these are **pushdown automata**, which can be viewed as finite automata endowed with a stack, upon which symbols can be pushed, read off the top, and popped. Pushdown automata are of importance in a variety of endeavors, including compiler design and structural linguistics, as they can be used to represent recursively defined syntactical structures, such as computer programs or legal sentences in English. It turns out, for example, that in terms of the classes of problems they can solve, *non*deterministic pushdown automata are more powerful than deterministic ones, a fact that is not true either for the weaker finite automata or for the stronger Turing machines. A nondeterministic pushdown automaton can detect palindromes, for example, by pushing the symbols it sees on to the stack one by one, 'guessing' nondeterministically when it has reached the middle of the input, and henceforth repeatedly comparing the next input symbol with the symbol currently at the top of the stack and popping that top symbol off. It says 'yes' if (1) all comparisons result in equality, and (2) the stack becomes empty when the end of the input is reached. It is possible to prove that no deterministic pushdown automaton can detect palindromes.

Researchers are interested in decision problems involving the models themselves. For example, we know that algorithmic equivalence is undecidable, so that, in particular, it is undecidable whether two given Turing machines solve the same algorithmic problem. However, if we go all the way down to finite automata, equivalence becomes decidable. For *non*deterministic pushdown automata, on the other hand, equivalence is still undecidable, whereas for deterministic pushdown automata we do not know. In fact, this is one of the most difficult unresolved questions in formal language theory, and it is of significance in the design of programming languages and compilers. Whenever such decision problems are found to be decidable, research turns to the task of determining their computational complexity, and, here too, many interesting and applicable results have emerged.

Scientists are also interested in finding the right 'CT thesis' for certain variants of the standard notions of computability and tractability. One case that has been addressed is that of databases, where the following questions are of interest. What is the basic universal notion of a 'computable' query on a database or knowledge base? What are the 'Turing machines' of databases? The difficulty is in trying to naively encode databases on Turing machine tapes. While this can be done, of course, the resulting linearization may, by its very nature, enforce an order on sets of data items that are not intended to be ordered in any particular way (say a list of equally important employees). The only allowed queries should take all possible orderings of such items into account, and any proposed universal model or language should reflect that fact.

The research areas of computability theory, automata and formal language theory, recursive function theory and complexity theory, are thus closely interrelated. Ever since the pioneering work of the 1930s, abstract models of computation have played a crucial role in obtaining fundamental results in these areas, thus forming the basis for many of the most important developments in algorithmics.

All things come alike to all
Ecclesiastes 9: 2

PART FOUR

RELAXING THE RULES

so shall it be easier for thyself

Exodus 18: 22

10

Parallelism and Concurrency

OR

Getting It Done by Cooperating

> *many shall run to and fro,*
> *and knowledge shall be increased*
>
> Daniel 12: 4

A while ago, people say, there was a contest in the Los Angeles area for the world title in fast house building. Several companies were involved, and parts of the activity were televised. Certain rigid rules had to be adhered to, such as minimal overall living area, number of rooms, utilities required, materials allowed, etc. No prefabrication was permitted, but the foundations were to be prepared ahead of time. Houses were deemed finished when people could literally start living in them; all plumbing and electricity had to be in place and functioning perfectly, appliances had to be plugged in, trees and grass had to adorn the front, and so on. However, no limit was placed on the number of people allowed to be working on the project at any one time. The winner used about 200 workers, and had the house ready in a little over *four hours*!

This is a striking example of the benefits offered by **simultaneity**, or **concurrency**; one person working alone would need rather more than a few hours to complete the house, and quite possibly would never be able to do so at all. It was only by working together, amid quite incredible feats of cooperation, coordination and mutual effort, that the task could be accomplished in so short a time.

In this chapter it is time to relax one of the main conventions imposed throughout – that algorithms are carried out by the little processor Runaround, working all on its own. We shall be interested in the consequences of having many processors achieve algorithmic goals jointly, by working together. This relaxation is motivated in part by the desire to exploit **parallelism** in hardware, namely, the availability of so-called **parallel computers,** which consist of many separate processing elements, cooperating and working in parallel. Later we shall also generalize the rigid input/output notion of an algorithmic problem to cases involving **perpetuity,** or **ongoing behavior**, that need not lead to termination at all. Such problems stem from **distributed** environments of inherently parallel nature, such as flight reservation systems or telephone networks.

Parallelism Helps

The house-building story makes it obvious that doing things in parallel can work wonders. Let us see what these wonders boil down to in terms of algorithmic efficiency.

If an algorithm calls for the sequence of instructions:

$$X \leftarrow 3; \; Y \leftarrow 4,$$

then we could obviously save time by carrying them out simultaneously, in parallel. We must be very careful, however, not to 'parallelize' just anything; if the instructions were:

$$X \leftarrow 3; \; Y \leftarrow X$$

the story would be quite different, since following a parallel execution Y's new value might be X's *old* value, rather than its new one, 3. Here the effect of the second instruction depends on the results of the first, and hence the two cannot be parallelized. Of course, they can be modified in ways that will circumvent the problem, but in their original form they must be carried out in order.

To further illustrate the point, consider the problem of digging a ditch, one foot deep, one foot wide, and ten feet long. If a single person can dig a one-by-one-by-one foot ditch in, say, an hour, ten people could dig the desired ditch in one hour in the obvious way. Parallelism is at its best here. However, if the desired ditch is to be one foot wide, one foot long, and ten feet *deep*, parallelism will achieve nothing, and even a hundred people would need ten hours to get the job done.[†]

[†] A similar example involves the futility of an attempt to have a child in one month with nine women, rather than in nine months with one woman . . . .

Some algorithmic problems have very little **inherent sequentiality**, despite the fact that the first solutions that come to mind are heavily sequential. Indeed, many problems can be solved far more efficiently by parallel processing. Consider the salary summation problem of Chapter 1. It would perhaps appear necessary to run through the list of employees in order, yielding the $O(N)$ algorithm described therein. Not so. A parallel algorithm can be devised that will run in time $O(\log N)$ – a momentous improvement indeed, as shown in Chapter 6. The method is to first consider the entire list of N employees in pairs, $\langle first, second \rangle$, $\langle third, fourth \rangle$, and so on, and to sum the two salaries in all pairs *simultaneously*, thus yielding a list of $N/2$ new numbers. This takes the time of only one addition, namely, a single time unit. The new list is then also considered in pairs, and the two numbers in each are again added simultaneously, yielding a new list of $N/4$ numbers. This continues until there is only one number left; it is the sum of the salaries in the entire list. Figure 10.1 illustrates this simple idea. As explained in Chapter 6, the number of times N can be divided by 2 until it reaches 1 is about $\log_2 N$, and hence the time bound. With the numbers of Chapter 6 in mind, it follows that a 1000 salaries can be summed in the time it takes to carry out just ten additions, and a million salaries can be summed in the time of only 20 additions.

Figure 10.1   Summing salaries in logarithmic time.

Fixed vs. Expanding Parallelism

Notice that to simultaneously carry out the 500 additions required in the first step of summing 1000 salaries, we need 500 processors. The *same* ones can then be used to carry out the 250 additions of the second stage in parallel (half of them, of course, would be idle), then the 125 additions of the third stage, etc. Of course, a large number of processors alone is not enough; we also have to arrange the data in such a way that the right numbers are quickly accessible to the right processors when they need them. This is why good data structures and communication methods are crucial to fast algorithms. However, concentrating on the number of processors at the moment, we see that to achieve the reduction from $O(N)$ to $O(\log N)$ we need $N/2$ processors, a number that depends on N, the length of the input. This is necessarily the case. If we only had a *fixed* number of processors we could not improve things beyond the constant hidden under the big-O: we might be able to do things twice as fast, or 100 times as fast, but there would not be an order-of-magnitude improvement.

The reader might claim that a growing number of processors is just not feasible. But then neither is a growing amount of time or memory. The purpose of complexity measures is to provide means for estimating the *inherent* difficulty of solving algorithmic problems as inputs become larger, the estimate being given as a function of the size of the input. As we shall see, certain complexity measures also enable us to estimate the amount of help we can expect to get by employing parallelism. One way to view such estimates is to try to bound the size of inputs we will ever want to deal with. If we are going to be summing lists of no more than a million salaries, and if we have half a million processors at hand, we will need very little time (roughly that of 20 additions). If we have fewer processors we can parallelize up to a point; that is, up to a certain depth in the tree of Figure 10.1. From that point on, a mixture of parallelism and sequentiality will have to be used. Clearly, the result will not be as good.

To achieve an order-of-magnitude improvement, therefore, requires *expanding* parallelism – i.e., a number of processors that grows as N grows. However, that number need not necessarily be $N/2$. For example, it is possible to add the salaries in a list of length N in time $O(\sqrt{N})$ if $\sqrt{N}$ processors are available – e.g., a million salaries in the time of about 1000 additions with 1000 processors. (How?) Of course, the time of 1000 additions is not as good as that of 20, but then 1000 processors are less than half a million, so that we get what we pay for, so to speak.

Sorting in Parallel

Sorting a list of length N (for example, putting a jumbled telephone book into order) is an excellent problem for discussing the benefits of parallel processing. Consider the mergesort algorithm of Chapter 4 (see Figure 4.3). It called for splitting the input list into halves, sorting them both recursively, and then merging the sorted halves. The merge is achieved by repeatedly comparing the currently smallest (first) elements in the halves, resulting in one of them being sent off to the output. The algorithm can be described schematically as follows:

subroutine **sort-L**:

(1)   if L consists of one element then it is sorted;

(2)   otherwise do the following:
    (2.1)   split L into two halves, L_1 and L_2;
    (2.2)   call **sort-L_1**;
    (2.3)   call **sort-L_2**;
    (2.4)   merge resulting lists into a single sorted list.

In Chapter 6 it was claimed that the time complexity of this algorithm is $O(N \times \log N)$. (You, dear reader, were asked to prove it as an exercise; did you?) Now, obviously, the two activities of sorting the halves do not interfere with each other, since they involve disjoint sets of elements. Therefore, they can be carried out in parallel. Even doing so only once, on the *top* level of the algorithm, resulting in the need for just *two* processors, would improve things, but only within the big-O constant, as already explained. However, we can carry out the two sorts in parallel on *all* levels of the recursion, yielding:

subroutine **parallel-sort-L**:

(1)   if L consists of one element then it is sorted;

(2)   otherwise do the following:
    (2.1)   split L into two halves, L_1 and L_2;
    (2.2)   call **parallel-sort-L_1** and **parallel-sort-L_2**, simultaneously;
    (2.3)   merge resulting lists into a single sorted list.

If followed meticulously, this algorithm can be seen to work very much like the tree-based parallel summation algorithm of Figure 10.1. First, at the bottom level of the recursion, it simultaneously compares the two elements in each of the $N/2$ pairs, arranging each pair in the right order. It then, again simultaneously, merges each pair of pairs into a sorted four-tuple, then each pair of four-tuples into an eight-tuple, and so on. The first step takes the time of only one comparison, the second takes three (why?), the third seven, the fourth fifteen, etc. Assuming for simplicity that N is a power of 2, the total number of comparisons is:

$$1 + 3 + 7 + 15 + \ldots (N-1)$$

which is less than $2N$. Hence the total time is $O(N)$. The price paid for improving $O(N \times \log N)$ to $O(N)$ is the need for $N/2$ processors. Here too there is a tradeoff; we can sort N elements in time $O(N \times \log N)$ with one processor, or in linear-time with a linear number of processors. Actually, as we shall see later, we can do even better.

The Product Complexity: Time × Size

The number of processors required by a parallel algorithm as a function of its input is one way of measuring the complexity of the hardware required to run the algorithm. By abusing terminology slightly, we can call this measure simply the **size complexity** of the algorithm, with the understanding that we do not mean either the length of the algorithm or the amount of memory it requires, but, rather, the size of the required army of processors.

Since not only the time measure plays a role in the analysis of parallel algorithms, but also the size, it is not obvious how we should determine the relative superiority of such algorithms. One approach to estimating the quality of a parallel algorithm is to combine both measures, by multiplying time by size (see Figure 10.2). The algorithm with a better **product complexity** is considered better. It is noteworthy that the best product measure cannot be any less than the lower bound on the problem's sequential-time complexity. The reason is that it is possible to *sequentialize* any parallel algorithm. This is done by simulating the actions of the various processors on a *single* processor, in an order that is consistent with the order prescribed by the parallel algorithm. (For example, if we were sequentializing the parallel mergesort algorithm, we would be allowed to sort the two halves in any order, but both sorts would have to be completed before the merging could be carried out.) The overall time this simulation takes is roughly the total of all the time taken by all the processors; that is, the product time × size of the original parallel algorithm. Thus, if we could find a parallel sorting algorithm that took time $O(\log N)$ and used only $O(N/\log N)$ processors, a sequentialized version could be derived that would run in time that was in the order of the product, namely, $O(N)$. But this would contradict the $O(N \times \log N)$ lower bound on sequential sorting.

The best we can hope for, then, is a parallel sorting algorithm that exhibits the *optimal* product performance of $O(N \times \log N)$. In this sense, the sequential mergesort algorithm, for example, is optimal. But then, it is not a parallel algorithm. Particularly intriguing is the question of whether or not there exists a parallel, comparison-based, sorting algorithm that runs in *logarithmic*-time but requires only a *linear* number of processors. This, in a way, would represent the ideal parallel sorting routine – extremely fast, but of reasonable size. As we shall see, this problem was recently solved in the affirmative.

*   *   *

	Name	Size (no. of processors)	Time (worst case)	Product (time × size)
SEQUENTIAL	Bubblesort	1	$O(N^2)$	$O(N^2)$
	Mergesort	1	$O(N \times \log N)$	$O(N \times \log N)$
PARALLEL	Parallelized mergesort	$O(N)$	$O(N)$	$O(N^2)$
	Odd-even sorting network	$O(N \times (\log N)^2)$	$O((\log N)^2)$	$O(N \times (\log N)^4)$
	'Optimal' sorting network	$O(N)$	$O(\log N)$	$O(N \times \log N)$

Figure 10.2   The performance of some sorting algorithms.

Networks: Fixed-Connection Parallelism

So far, we have said nothing about the way different processors cooperate. Obviously, they do not work in total seclusion, since they have to pass intermediate results to each other. Even the simple parallel summation algorithm of Figure 10.1 requires some kind of cooperation, between the processors that produce intermediate sums and those that use them next. The performance of a parallel algorithm can vary greatly under different cooperation methods.

One approach advocates **shared memory**, which means, roughly, that certain variables or data structures are shared by many processors. Within this approach, it is important to specify whether the sharing is only in **reading** the values from the relevant memory, or also in **writing** them. If the latter approach is chosen, we have to decide how to resolve writing conflicts (for example, two processors attempting to write simultaneously into the very same variable or memory location), and the particular method chosen can make quite a difference in the resulting algorithmic power.

Unrestricted shared memory is considered unrealistic, mainly because when it comes to building real parallel computers the pattern of interconnection becomes impossibly complicated. Either each processor has to be connected to essentially every memory location, or (if the memory is physically distributed between the processors) every processor has to be connected to every other one. In both cases this is usually a hopeless situation: if the required number of processors grows with N, as is the case with all nontrivial parallel algorithms, the interconnections quickly become unreasonably intricate.

A more realistic approach is to use **fixed-connection networks**, or just **networks** for short, and to design parallel algorithms specifically for them. The word 'fixed' implies that each processor is connected to at most some *fixed* number of **neighboring processors**. In many cases it also means that the entire network is constructed as a special-purpose machine, solving one particular algorithmic problem very efficiently. The processors in a special-purpose network typically have very limited computational capabilities.

One well-known kind of network is the **Boolean network**, or **Boolean circuit**, named after the 19th century logician George Boole, who invented the rules for manipulating the logical values *true* and *false* (and hence also the rules for manipulating the corresponding bit values, 1 and 0). In a Boolean network the processors are called **gates**, and they compute simple logical functions of one or two bit values. An AND gate produces a 1 precisely when both of its inputs are 1s, an OR gate produces a 1 precisely when at least one of its two inputs is 1, and a NOT gate inverts the value of its single input.

** In a certain sense, every effectively solvable algorithmic problem P can be solved by an effectively computable **uniform collection** of Boolean networks. To be able to state this fact more precisely, think of the inputs of P as being encoded using just 0s and 1s. The claim is that, for every such problem P, there is an algorithm (say a Turing machine) that accepts a number input N and outputs the description of a Boolean network that solves the problem P for inputs consisting of N bits (see Figure 10.3). However, this somewhat strange kind of universality is not our reason for introducing networks. We are more interested in networks that are especially designed to yield efficient solutions to specific problems. **

The Odd–Even Sorting Network

Special-purpose networks have been found for many problems, but most notably for sorting and merging. A **sorting network** can be viewed as a special-purpose computer architecture, providing a fixed interconnection pattern of extremely simple processors, cooperating to sort N elements in parallel. Most sorting networks employ only one very simple kind of processor, called a **comparator**, which inputs two elements and outputs them in order, as shown in Figure 10.4.

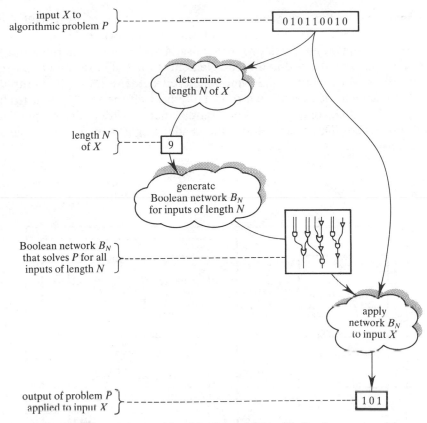

$\left.\begin{array}{c}\text{input } X \text{ to}\\ \text{algorithmic problem } P\end{array}\right\}$ ----------------------- 0 1 0 1 1 0 0 1 0

determine
length N of X

$\left.\begin{array}{c}\text{length } N\\ \text{of } X\end{array}\right\}$ ------ 9

generate
Boolean network B_N
for inputs of length N

$\left.\begin{array}{c}\text{Boolean network } B_N\\ \text{that solves } P \text{ for all}\\ \text{inputs of length } N\end{array}\right\}$ ---------------------------------

apply
network B_N
to input X

$\left.\begin{array}{c}\text{output of problem } P\\ \text{applied to input } X\end{array}\right\}$ --------------------------------------- 1 0 1

Figure 10.3   Solving an algorithmic problem with Boolean networks.

Let us illustrate the approach with the so-called **odd–even** sorting
network. Figure 10.5 shows the (recursive) rule for constructing this
network for N elements, given the networks for $N/2$ elements. (For
simplicity, we assume that N is a power of 2, but the idea can be quite easily
adapted to work for any N.) Figure 10.6 shows the resulting network for
the case $N = 8$, with an example written-in along the lines. As can be seen
from studying Figure 10.5, the network sorts N elements by first sorting the
two halves recursively (i.e., by odd–even networks for each half) and then

$X \longrightarrow$ ▨ $\longrightarrow$ smaller of X and Y
$Y \longrightarrow$ ▨ $\longrightarrow$ larger of X and Y

Figure 10.4   A comparator used in sorting networks.

merging the sorted halves using a rather clever subnetwork called the
odd–even merger. The functioning of this subnetwork is based on the
following observation. Take two sorted lists A and B, form a third (sorted)
list C by merging the odd-numbered elements from both lists, and a fourth
(sorted) list D by merging the even-numbered elements. Now, first output
the top element of C, and then repeatedly peel off the top element from
each of C and D, compare them and output them in order. The output list
will be sorted! This is something the reader might want to try proving
rigorously.

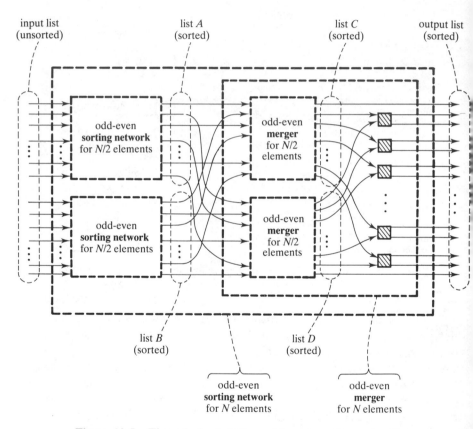

Figure 10.5   The rule for building odd–even sorting networks.

The time taken by the odd–even sorting network is $O((\log N)^2)$, and
its size (number of processors) is $O(N \times (\log N)^2)$, hence it is not optimal.
A breakthrough of sorts was achieved in 1983 with the advent of an
ingenious sorting network that uses $O(N \times \log N)$ processors and takes only
logarithmic-time. Recently, this solution has been combined with a variation of the odd–even network, to finally yield an optimal logarithmic-time

network of linear size. This, then, is the optimal parallel sorting algorithm mentioned earlier. Unfortunately, besides being extremely complicated, the big-O constants in both of these logarithmic time networks are huge, rendering them quite useless in practice for reasonably sized N. In contrast, the constants for many of the theoretically worse networks are very small; those of the odd–even network, for example, are less than 1 (about $\frac{1}{2}$ for the time measure and $\frac{1}{4}$ for size). Specifically, we can construct an odd–even sorting network with a little more than 1000 comparators, which will sort 100 elements in the time it takes to carry out just 25 comparisons. For 1000 elements it would take just the time of about 55 comparisons, but we would need about 23000 comparators. If time is a crucial factor, and the lists to be sorted will all be of roughly the same length, a sorting network such as this one becomes quite practical.

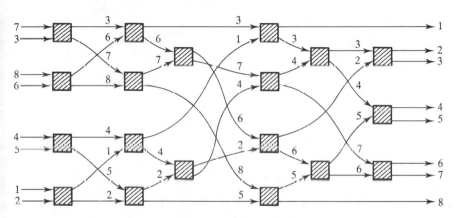

Figure 10.6   The odd–even sorting network for eight elements.

More About Networks: Computing Weighted Averages

In the odd–even network each comparator is used only once in sorting a given list. The input list arrives all together, and the entire life cycle of each comparator consists of waiting for its own two inputs, comparing them, sending the maximum and minimum along the appropriate output lines, and shutting itself off.

Other kinds of networks are characterized by processors that are activated repeatedly within a single run, in a regular kind of pattern. Such networks are sometimes termed **systolic**, the word deriving from the physiological term 'systole', which refers to the repeated contractions responsible for pumping blood through our bodies.

As an example, consider a teacher who is interested in computing the final grades of N students in a course in which there are M examinations.

Each examination has a different *weight* associated with it, and the final grade is to be the weighted average of those M examinations. The input grades are arranged in an $N \times M$ array, and the weights are given by a list of M fractions, totalling 1. For each student it is required to multiply each grade by the appropriate weight and then to sum the M results. The final output is to be a list of the N final grades. A sequential algorithm would obviously take time $O(N \times M)$, since one multiplication has to be performed for each grade.

Figure 10.7   A systolic network for computing weighted averages.

Figure 10.8 Simulating the behavior of the network of Figure 10.7.

Figure 10.7 shows a systolic network for solving this problem (which, in mathematical terminology is called the **matrix-by-vector multiplication problem**). The network consists of a linear arrangement of M interconnected processors. The array of grades, the **matrix**, in technical terms, is fed into the network from the top in the fashion shown, a diagonal row at a time. Thus, the network first accepts the grade of student 1 in exam 1, then, simultaneously, student 2's grade in exam 1 and student 1's grade in exam 2, then, simultaneously, student 3's grade in exam 1, 2's grade in exam 2 and 1's grade in exam 3, and so on. The final step is to accept student N's grade in exam M. The vector of weights, on the other hand, is constantly available along the bottom lines. Zeros are fed in from the left, and the output vector is produced at the right, an element at a time. (This linear configuration is sometimes called a **pipeline** arrangement.) Each processor is extremely simple: whenever it receives a set of new inputs it just multiplies its top and bottom ones, adds the product to the left-hand input and sends the result off to the right. The algorithm induced by this network is clearly linear in $N + M$. Figure 10.8 shows a simple simulation of the network for $N = 4$ and $M = 3$.

Systolic networks have been constructed to solve many problems. The arrangement of processors is typically linear, rectangular, or diamond shaped, and the processors are either square, resulting in a so-called **mesh-connected array**, or hexagonal, resulting in a **beehive**, as in Figure 10.9.

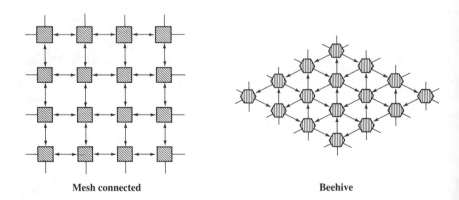

Mesh connected   Beehive

Figure 10.9   Two typical arrangements of processors for systolic networks.

*   *   *

Can Parallelism Be Used to Solve the Unsolvable?

The facts we have discussed so far leave no doubt that parallelism can be used to improve the time behavior of sequential algorithms. Problems that require a certain amount of time for sequential solution can be solved faster, even in order-of-magnitude terms, if (expanding) parallelism is allowed. It is natural to ask whether parallelism can be used to solve problems that could not have been solved at all without it. Can we devise a parallel algorithm for an undecidable problem? The answer is no, since, as explained earlier, every parallel algorithm can be simulated sequentially by a single processor, running around and doing everyone's work in an appropriate order. In this sense, the Church/Turing thesis applies to parallel models of computation too: the class of solvable problems is insensitive even to the addition of parallelism.

The next question to ask is whether parallelism can turn *in*tractable problems into tractable ones. Is there a problem requiring an unreasonable (say, an exponential) amount of time for sequential solution that can be solved concurrently in a reasonable (i.e., polynomial) amount of time?

To be able to better appreciate the subtlety of this question, let us first consider the NP problems of Chapter 7. As the reader may recall, all problems in NP have reasonable solutions that are nondeterministic; they employ a magic coin which, if tossed when confronted with a choice, will use its wizardry to point to the direction that leads to a positive solution. Now, if we have an unlimited number of processors, we do not need the magic coin: whenever a 'crossroad' is reached we can simply send new processors off to follow both possibilities simultaneously. If one of the processors sent off in this way ever comes back and says 'yes', the entire process halts and says 'yes' too; if the predetermined polynomial amount of time has elapsed and none has said 'yes', the process halts and says 'no'. Since the NP-ness of the problem guarantees that if the answer is 'yes' it will be found by the magic coin in a polynomial amount of time, our exhaustive, multiple processor traversal of all possibilities will find the 'yes' in the same amount of time too. If it does not, then the answer must be 'no'.

The consequence is clear. The problems in NP, including the NP-complete ones, such as monkey puzzles, traveling salesmen and timetables, all have polynomial-time parallel solutions. However, three comments should be made, before the reader rushes off to tell everyone that intractability is but a slightly bothersome consequence of conventional one-processor models of computation, and can be removed by using parallel computation. The first is that the number of processors required to solve an NP-complete problem in a reasonable amount of time is itself exponential. If we want to find out, in less than billions of years of computer time, whether our local high school can come up with a class schedule to satisfy all of its constraints, we would need a wholly unreasonable computer containing trillions of intricately connected processors. This is something we shall return to later.

The second comment is rooted in the fact that the NP-complete problems are not *known* to be intractable – they are merely conjectured to be so. Thus, the possibility of simulating NP-complete problems in parallel in polynomial-time does not imply that parallelism can rid a problem of its inherent intractability, since we do not know whether or not the NP-complete problems are actually intractable.

Finally, even if we have a parallel algorithm that uses only a polynomial number of instructions but requires an exponential number of processors, it is far from clear that we can really run the algorithm in polynomial-time on a real parallel computer. In fact, there are results that show that under quite liberal assumptions about the width of communication lines and the speed of communication, a super-polynomial number of processors would require a super-polynomial amount of real time to carry out even a polynomial number of steps, no matter how the processors are packed together. These results are based on the inherent limitations of three-dimensional space. Thus, the complexity analysis of parallel computation with unreasonable size seems to require more than merely estimating the number of processing steps; the amount of communication is also crucial.

The question thus remains: can we use parallelism, even with unreasonably many processors, to solve in a reasonable amount of time a problem that we can *prove* to be unsolvable sequentially in reasonable time? And this question is still open, as will now be shown.

The Parallel Computation Thesis

In Chapter 9 we saw that the Church/Turing thesis holds also in a refined sense, whereby, under very natural assumptions, all sequential models of computation are equivalent to within a polynomial amount of time. As a consequence, tractability is insensitive to the choice of such a model. The thesis claims that this situation will not change as new models are proposed.

A similar claim holds for *parallel* models of computation. Under natural assumptions, all universal models of expanding parallelism that have been suggested so far, including numerous variants of shared-memory models, communication-based models, uniform classes of networks, etc., can be shown to be polynomial-time equivalent. Each model can be simulated by the other with at most a polynomial loss of time. This means that, as in the sequential case, the class of problems solvable in *parallel* in polynomial-time is also robust, in its own way; it does not depend on the particular kind of parallel computer model chosen, nor on the programming language used to program it.

As in the sequential case, we have to be careful here. Models that allow *concurrent* reading and writing may be exponentially more efficient than ones which allow only reading and writing by one processor at a time. Without getting into the details, it should be said that in order for this claim to be true the basic instructions related to the simultaneous manipulation of low-level elements must be of similar nature (just as the basic instructions for manipulating numbers have to be comparable in order for the polynomial-time equivalence of sequential models to hold).

This fact leads to one part of the so-called **parallel computation thesis**. It claims that this situation too will not change as new models are suggested. In other words, up to polynomial differences, the important complexity classes for parallel computation are also robust, and will remain so even as science and technology makes progress. This half-thesis, however, is not quite enough, as it talks about parallelism only. We also want to know whether there is any inherent relationship *between* sequentiality and parallelism, as far as efficiency is concerned. All we know is that parallelism does not help in solving totally *un*solvable problems; but just how much better can it make things for problems that *are* solvable?

To our help comes the second part of the parallel computation thesis. It claims that (again, up to polynomial differences) parallel time is the same as sequential memory space. If we can solve a problem sequentially using a certain amount of space, say $f(N)$ for inputs of length N, then we can solve it concurrently in time that is no worse than, say, $(f(N))^2$, or $(f(N))^{10}$, or some other amount that is polynomially related to $f(N)$. The converse holds too: if we can solve a problem concurrently in $f(N)$ time, we can also solve it sequentially using memory space that is bounded by a polynomial in $f(N)$. Of particular interest is the consequence of this fact to the case where f is itself a polynomial: any problem solvable sequentially using only a polynomial amount of memory space is solvable in parallel in a polynomial amount of time, and vice versa. Symbolically:

Sequential-PSPACE = *Parallel*-PTIME

Thus, the question of whether there are intractable problems that become tractable with the introduction of parallelism boils down to whether the sequential complexity class PSPACE contains intractable problems; that is, ones that can be proved to admit no polynomial-time sequential solutions. This question, phrased purely in sequential terms, is still open, and, like the P vs. NP problem, is probably very difficult too.

Nick's Class: Towards Reasonable Parallelism

In general, polynomial-time parallel algorithms cannot be claimed to be reasonable, since they may require a totally unreasonable (viz. exponential) number of processors. Moreover, one of the purposes of introducing parallelism is to drastically *reduce* running time. In fact, one of the objectives here is to find *sub*linear algorithms; that is, algorithms that are parallel to such an extent that they do not even read the entire input sequentially (otherwise they would require at least linear time). Hence, it would appear that *Parallel*-PTIME is not the best choice for the class of problems that are tractable in the presence of parallelism. What then is the 'right' definition of parallel tractability?

One of the most interesting proposals regarding this question is a class of problems called NC (Nick's Class, after one of its first investigators). A problem is in NC if it admits a very fast parallel solution, which requires only polynomially many processors. 'Very fast' is taken to mean that it runs in *polylogarithmic* time; that is, in time $O(\log N)$, $O((\log N)^2)$, $O((\log N)^3)$, or any other fixed power of $\log N$. Salary summation, sorting, weighted average computation, and a host of other problems are all in NC (the first two by the algorithms described earlier, and the third by an algorithm not described here). The NP-complete problems, for example, may or may not be in NC – we do not know. All we were able to show was that they admit polynomial-time parallel solutions; being in NC is a stronger requirement.

The class NC is robust in the same sense that classes like P, NP and PSPACE are. It remains insensitive to differences between the various models of parallel computation, and hence can be used in the investigation of the inherent power of parallelism. It can be shown, for example, that all problems in NC are also in P (i.e., in *Sequential*-PTIME), but the converse is not known to be true: is there a problem that is tractable in the sequential sense (i.e., in P) but not in this parallel sense? Here too, as in the P vs. NP question, most researchers believe that the two classes are distinct, so that P is different from NC. In particular, the problem of finding the greatest common divisor of two integers (its gcd) is in P – Euclid found a polynomial-time algorithm for it as early as 2300 years ago, as mentioned in Chapter 1. However, the gcd problem is suspected not to be in NC. No one knows how to exploit parallelism to significantly speed up the computation of this most important quantity, the way we can speed up sorting and salary summation.

Thus, we have

$$NC \subseteq P \subseteq NP \subseteq PSPACE$$

and many computer scientists believe that all three inclusions are actually strict. Recalling the aforementioned connection between PSPACE and *Parallel*-PTIME, this set of conjectured inequalities can be described (from right to left) by saying:

(1) There are problems that can be solved in reasonable sequential space – that is, in reasonable parallel time (but unreasonable hardware size) – that cannot be solved in reasonable sequential time even with magical nondeterminism.

(2)   There are problems solvable in reasonable sequential time with magical nondeterminism that cannot be solved in such time without it.

(3)   There are problems solvable in reasonable sequential time that are not solvable in very little parallel time with reasonable hardware size.

However, none of these inequalities is actually known to be strict, and hence it is just possible (though very unlikely) that these classes of problems are actually all equal. It should be mentioned that, as with NP vs. P, the P vs. NC question also gives rise to a natural notion of completeness. Thus, although we do not know whether P = NC, it is very helpful to show that a problem is P-*complete*, implying that if it *is* in NC then all the problems in P are in NC too.

$$* \quad * \quad *$$

Distributed and Ongoing Concurrency

It would be nice to be able to end this chapter here. And why not? We have discussed parallel algorithms and their complexity, and have seen how they can improve things, and to what extent. We have even admitted that we do not know nearly as much about parallelism as we should. What, then, is missing?

Well, introducing parallelism in order to solve conventional algorithmic problems more efficiently is only one of its facets. The other has to do with situations in which parallelism is not something we introduce in order to improve things, but something we have to live with because it's just there.[†] Also, it has to do with a different kind of algorithmic problem, which does not always involve transforming inputs that are given at the start into desired outputs that are produced at the end. Rather, it involves desired *behavior* over time, with various properties required of that behavior. Moreover, in many cases the process that has to be described as a solution to these problems is not required to terminate at all. It merely has to sit there, doing things in accordance with those requirements.

Let us consider an example. Suppose a certain hotel has only one bathroom on each floor. (Many inexpensive hotels are of this kind.) Also, suppose there is heating only in the rooms – the corridor is unpleasantly chilly. (Many inexpensive hotels satisfy this assumption too.) Every now and then guests have to take showers. (Most guests in such hotels indeed do.) How should they go about satisfying these needs? They cannot line up in front of the bathroom door, because of the shivering factor involved.

[†] To keep the distinction clear we shall use the term **concurrency**, rather than parallelism, for this case.

If a guest simply tries the bathroom door once in a while he might stay unclean forever, since quite possibly it will be occupied whenever he happens to try. This is true despite the fact that showers take only a finite amount of time; someone else might always manage to get in first. We assume that the guests come from a variety of countries and all speak different languages, so that direct communication is out of the question.

One apparent solution calls for attaching a small blackboard to the exterior of the bathroom door. Whenever a guest leaves the bathroom, he erases the room number written on the blackboard (it will be his own) and writes down the number of the next room in some fixed order. (Think of the rooms on the floor as being arranged in a cyclic order, so that each room has a unique predecessor and successor.) An unclean guest simply walks up to the bathroom door every now and then, entering if his own room number is written on the blackboard, and returning to his room if it is not. Clearly, every guest will eventually get a turn to shower.

However, this solution still has severe problems. First, it is possible that room number 16 is never occupied, that its occupant never wants to take a shower, or that he has just been kidnapped, never to be seen again. The blackboard will then have a 16 written on it forever, and none of the other guests will ever become clean. Secondly, even if all rooms are inhabited by live, available people, this solution imposes an impossible one-shower-per-cycle discipline on all guests, forcing the more fastidious ones to shower as rarely as those who could not care less.

This problem illustrates some of the main issues arising in the design of systems that are inherently **distributed**. Distributivity is a special kind of concurrency, where the concurrent components are physically remote. Accordingly, people concern themselves not only with figuring out what each component should do, but also with minimizing the amount of communication that takes place between the components. Communication, whether explicit or implicit (say in the form of shared memory), can become extremely expensive in a distributed system. As before, we shall use the term 'processors' for the separate entities, or components.

The processors in an inherently concurrent or distributed system are not required to achieve a mere input/output relationship, but rather to exhibit a certain desired behavior over time. In fact, the system might not be required to terminate at all, just as in the shower problem. Parts of the desired behavior can be stated as **global constraints**. The shower, for example, can accommodate at most one person at a time, and everyone needs it from time to time. Thus, it is really a **crucial resource**, of the kind everyone needs for some finite amount of time, after which it can be given up for the benefit of someone else. An important constraint in the shower problem is that we must prevent **deadlock** situations, in which no progress can be made by any processor (e.g., when guest 16 never shows up), and **starvation** situations – sometimes called **lockouts** – in which one or more of the processors, but not every one of them, is prevented from making progress (e.g., when guests are instructed to simply try the bathroom door once in a while).

These notions are typical of many real-world systems. Most standard computers, for example, have several crucial resources, such as tape and disk drives, printers and plotters, communication channels, etc. In a way, a computer's memory can also be viewed as a crucial resource, since we would not like two jobs that run together to simultaneously write on to the same location. A flight reservation system, to give another example, is highly distributed. It might consist of a world-wide network containing one computer in New York, another in Los Angeles, and 2000 terminals. It would be embarrassing if two of the terminals assigned seat 25D on the same flight to two different passengers. A flight reservation system is also not required to terminate. It has to keep working, making its resources available to any processors who request them, while preventing deadlock and starvation.

These are really not algorithmic problems in the usual sense of the word. They involve different kinds of requirements, and are not solved by ordinary algorithms. A solution has to dictate **algorithmic protocols** for the behavior of each of the processors, which guarantee fulfilment of all the requirements and constraints specified in the problem, for the entire (potentially infinite) life time of the system.

Solving Hotel Shower Problems

The blackboard suggested for the problem of showering in inexpensive hotels can be thought of as shared memory, and the shower as a crucial resource. Notice that we have skirted the problem of writing conflicts by allowing at most one guest to be writing on the blackboard at any one time.

Let us now describe a satisfactory solution to this problem. Actually, we shall solve a more difficult problem, in which there *are* bathrooms in every room, yet no more than one guest is allowed to take a shower at any given time. (The reason might have to do with the pressure or temperature of the water, another reasonable assumption for inexpensive hotels.) This situation is clearly more delicate, since there is no direct way of knowing if anyone is indeed taking a shower. Nevertheless, the solution must ensure that everyone showers, but that two guests never shower simultaneously.

A more general description of the problem is as follows. There are N processors, each of which has to repeatedly carry out certain 'private' activities, followed by a **critical section**:

life cycle of the Ith processor:
(1) do the following again and again forever:
    (1.1) carry out *private activities* (e.g., eat, read, sleep);
    (1.2) carry out *critical section* (e.g., take a shower).

The private activities are processor P's own business – they have nothing to do with anyone else. The critical section, on the other hand, is *everyone's* business, as no two processors may be in their critical section simultaneously. The problem is to find a way to enable the N processors to live their life forever, without deadlock or starvation, while respecting the critical nature of the critical sections. We must instruct the processors to carry out certain actions, like inspecting blackboards and writing on them, before and/or after they enter their critical sections, so that these requirements are met. When presented in this form, the problem is sometimes called the **mutual exclusion problem**, as processors have to be guaranteed exclusivity in entering the critical sections.

Let us first present a solution for $N = 2$; that is, for the case of just two guests, or processors, P_1 and P_2. We shall be using three variables, X_1, X_2 and Z, which, in the shower example, are represented by three small areas on a blackboard that hangs in the corridor. Z can be either 1 or 2, and both processors can change its value. In such cases we say that Z is a **shared variable**. The Xs can be either *yes* or *no*, and they can be read by both processors but changed only by the processor with the corresponding index. In such cases we say that the Xs are **distributed variables**. The initial value of both the Xs is *no*, and that of Z is either 1 or 2, it does not matter. Here are the protocols for the two processors:

protocol for P_1:
(1)   do the following again and again forever:
    (1.1)   carry out *private activities* until entrance to critical section is desired;
    (1.2) $X_1 \leftarrow yes$;
    (1.3) $Z \leftarrow 1$;
    (1.4)   wait until either $X_2 = no$ or $Z = 2$ (or both);
    (1.5)   carry out *critical section*;
    (1.6) $X_1 \leftarrow no$.

protocol for P_2:
(1)   do the following again and again forever:
    (1.1)   carry out *private activities* until entrance to critical section is desired;
    (1.2) $X_2 \leftarrow yes$;
    (1.3) $Z \leftarrow 2$;
    (1.4)   wait until either $X_1 = no$ or $Z = 1$ (or both);
    (1.5)   carry out *critical section*;
    (1.6) $X_2 \leftarrow no$.

What is happening here? Well, think of X_1 as being an indication of P_1's desire to enter its critical section: $X_1 = yes$ means that it would like to enter, and $X_1 = no$ means that it has finished and would like to go back to its private activities. X_2 plays the same role for P_2. The third variable, Z, is a **courtesy indicator** of sorts: after P_1 has made it clear that it wants to enter its critical section it immediately sets Z to 1, indicating that, as far as it is concerned, P_2 can enter if it wants to. It then waits until either P_2 has indicated that it has left its own critical section and is back to its private activities (i.e., $X_2 = no$), or P_2 has set the courtesy variable Z to 2, giving P_1 the right of way. P_2 acts in a similar way. (We can think of Z as representing the processors' signatures in a logbook. The last to sign in is the one who, most recently, has given the other the right of way.) The waiting in clause (1.4) is sometimes called **busy waiting**, as the processor cannot simply idle until it is prodded by someone else. Rather, it has to keep checking the values of Z and the other processor's X variable itself, while doing nothing else in the meantime.

** Let us now prove that this solution is correct. Well, first of all, we claim that P_1 and P_2 cannot possibly be in their critical sections simultaneously. Assume that they can. Obviously, during the time they are in their critical sections together, both X_1 and X_2 have the value *yes*, so that the last processor to enter must have entered by virtue of the Z part of its waiting test in clause (1.4), since the other's X value was *yes*. (The two could not have passed their tests at the very same time, since Z cannot be both 1 and 2 together; one of them must have passed its test before the other.) Assume that P_1 passed the test first. Then Z must have been 1 when P_2, later, passed *its* test. This means that between the moment P_2 set Z to 2 in its clause (1.3) and the moment it passed its test in clause (1.4), P_1 must have set Z to 1, and from that point on P_2 did nothing else until it entered its critical section by virtue of $Z = 1$. But then how did P_1 manage to enter *its* critical section earlier? It could not have entered by $Z = 2$ because, as we have just said, it set Z to 1 after P_2 set it to 2. Also, it could not have entered by $X_2 = no$ because X_2 was set to *yes* by P_2 before it set Z to 2. And so there is no way for P_2 to enter its critical section as long as P_1 is in its own critical section. A similar argument holds for the dual possibility, where P_1 enters while P_2 is already in. The conclusion is that mutual exclusion indeed holds.

Let us see why starvation and deadlock are impossible. (Here starvation occurs when one of the processors wants to enter its critical section but is forever prevented from doing so, and deadlock occurs when neither processor can make progress.) The first thing to note is that it is impossible for both processors to be stuck in their (1.4) clauses together, because Z is always either 1 or 2, and one of them can therefore always free itself from the wait. Now, assume that P_1 is forced to stay in its (1.4) clause, while P_2 does not. If P_2 never wants to enter its critical section, i.e., it stays in clause (1.1), the value of X_2 will be *no* and P_1 will be free to enter whenever it wants to. The only other possibility is that P_2 continues to cycle around its protocol forever. In such a case it will sooner or later set Z to 2, and since it can never change it back to 1 (only P_1 can), P_1 will eventually be able to pass its test and enter (1.5). Thus, starvation and deadlock are prevented, and the solution satisfies all the requirements.   **

Things Are Trickier than They Seem

This two-processor solution appears at first sight to be quite elementary, and the correctness argument, while slightly involved, does not look overly complicated either. However, this kind of simplicity can be quite deceptive. As an illustration of just how delicate things really are, let us study a minor variation of the foregoing solution.

What would happen if we switched the order of clauses (1.2) and (1.3) in the protocols? In other words, when P_1, for example, wants to enter its critical section, it first does P_2 the courtesy of setting Z to 1, letting it through if it wants, and only then sets X_1 to yes to indicate its own desire to enter. On the face of it, there seems to be no difference: P_1 can still enter its critical section only if P_2 is either disinterested (i.e., if $X_2 = no$), or is explicitly giving P_1 the right of way (i.e., if $Z = 2$). What can go wrong?

At this point the reader should try to work through the informal proof of correctness given, but for the amended version, to see where it fails. It does fail, and here is a scenario that leads to both processors being in their critical sections simultaneously. Initially, as agreed on, $X_1 = no$ and $X_2 = no$, and both processors are busy with their private activities. Now comes the following sequence of actions:

- P_2 sets Z to 2;
- P_1 sets Z to 1;
- P_1 sets X_1 to yes;
- P_1 enters its critical section, by virtue of X_2 being no;
- P_2 sets X_2 to yes;
- P_2 enters its critical section, by virtue of Z being 1.

The problem, of course, is that now P_2 can take a shower (i.e., enter its critical section) even though P_1 is taking one himself, because P_1 was the last to be courteous, and hence Z's value is 1 when P_2 indicates its desire to enter. In the original protocol this was impossible, since the last thing P_2 was required to do before entering was to set Z to the unfavorable value 2 .

Thus, even this apparently simple two-processor solution hides a certain amount of subtlety. Let us now take a look at the general solution for N processors.

A Solution to the *N*-Processor Mutual Exclusion Problem

When there are more than two guests it is not enough just to say 'I would like to take a shower' and then to be courteous to one of the others. Neither will it do any good to be courteous to *all* the others together and hope that everything will work out nicely. We have to make our processors more sophisticated.

** Processors will be instructed to increase their insistence on entering the critical section as they keep waiting. Each processor will thus run through a loop, each execution of which will correspond to being at a higher level of insistence. The number of levels is precisely N, the total number of processors, and the first level (actually the zeroth) indicates disinterest in entering the critical section. Each of the insistence levels has its own courtesy variable, and at each level a processor is courteous to everyone else by writing its own number in that variable. Once a processor has indicated its desire to increase its level of insistence, and has been courteous to all the others, it waits to increase the level until either all the others are less insistent than itself or it has been given the courtesy of proceeding to the next level by someone else. The critical section is finally entered when the green light for proceeding beyond the highest level appears. Upon leaving the critical section a processor starts the whole procedure anew at the zeroth level.

Here is the protocol for the *I*th processor. In it, the vector Z is indexed by the insistence levels, not by the processors. Thus, processor I sets $Z(J)$ to I (not $Z(I)$ to J as with the X vector) to indicate that on level J it gives the right of way to everyone else. It is worth noting that if $N = 2$ these protocols are precisely the ones just presented, so that this is indeed a direct extension of the two-processor solution.

protocol for the *I*th processor, P_I:

(1) do the following again and again forever:
    (1.1) carry out *private activities* until entrance to critical section is desired;
    (1.2) for each J from 1 to $N - 1$ do the following:
        (1.2.1) $X(I) \leftarrow J$;
        (1.2.2) $Z(J) \leftarrow I$;
        (1.2.3) wait until either $X(K) < J$ for all $K \neq I$, or $Z(J) \neq I$;
    (1.3) carry out *critical section*;
    (1.4) $X(I) \leftarrow 0$.

It is possible to provide an informal proof of correctness for this general case, along the lines of the proof for the two-processor case. Here we show that at each level the processors proceed only one at a time, so that, as a special case, there is at most one processor in the critical section at any given time. Freedom from deadlock and starvation is established similarly. ******

*   *   *

Safety and Liveness Properties

Distributed concurrent systems are in many senses more demanding than normal sequential systems. The difficulties start with the very task of specifying the problem and the properties desired of a solution. The 'algorithmic problems' associated with such systems can no longer be defined naively by specifying a set of legal inputs together with a function describing the desired outputs. Correctness no longer consists simply of termination plus the generation of correct outputs, and efficiency can no longer be measured naively as the number of steps taken before termination or the size of memory used. Consequently, techniques developed for proving the correctness or estimating the efficiency of conventional algorithms are insufficient when it comes to protocols that solve problems of concurrent and distributed nature.

It turns out that most correctness requirements of protocols for ongoing concurrent systems fall into two main categories, **safety** and **liveness** properties. Safety properties state that certain 'bad' things must not happen, or, equivalently, that the corresponding 'good' things will *always* be the case, and liveness properties state that certain 'good' things will *eventually* happen. Mutual exclusion – preventing two processors from being in their critical sections simultaneously – is a safety property, whereas preventing starvation is a liveness property, since it asks for a guarantee that any processor wanting to enter its critical section will eventually be able to do so.

Interestingly, the partial correctness and termination properties of conventional algorithms are special cases of safety and liveness. Partial correctness means that the program must never terminate with the wrong outputs – clearly a safety property – and termination means that the algorithm must eventually reach its logical end and terminate – clearly a liveness property.

To show that a given protocol violates a safety property, it suffices to exhibit a finite, legal sequence of actions that lead to the forbidden situation. This was done for the erroneous version of the two-processor solution, and is just like showing that an algorithm violates partial correctness by exhibiting a terminating execution sequence that produces the wrong results. Showing that a *liveness* property is violated is quite a different matter. We must somehow prove the existence of an *infinite* sequence of actions that *never* leads to the promised situation. This difference is actually one way of characterizing the two classes of properties.

When it comes to ongoing concurrency, testing techniques are usually of little help. We can become reasonably convinced of the correctness of an ordinary sorting algorithm by trying it out on a number of standard lists of elements, and on some 'borderline' cases, such as lists with one element or none, or lists with all elements equal. On the other hand, many of the errors that turn up in the realm of concurrent systems have nothing to do with unexpected inputs. They stem from unexpected interactions between processors, and the unpredictable order in which actions are carried out. Proving the correctness of such systems, therefore, is more slippery and error prone than that of conventional, sequential algorithms. A number of published 'solutions' to concurrent programming problems were later found to contain subtle errors that eluded referees and readers alike, despite the presence of seemingly valid arguments of correctness.

The need for formal verification is thus more acute here than in the sequential case, and several approaches have indeed been proposed. Typically, those that deal with safety properties are extensions of the intermediate-assertion method for verifying partial correctness, and those tailored for liveness properties expand upon the method of convergents for proving termination (see Chapter 5).

Showing that the parallel mergesort algorithm, for example, is partially correct requires, among other things, a formal proof that the two processors assigned to sorting the two halves of a list in parallel, on any level of the recursion, do not interfere with each other. In this particular case, the processors working in parallel on some level do not interact at all, and such a proof is relatively easy to come by. When processors *do* interact, as in the solution to the shower problem, things become much trickier. We have to somehow verify the behavior of each individual processor in isolation, taking into account all possible interactions with others, and then combine the proofs into one whole.

Intermediate assertions cannot be used here in the usual way. A claim that assertion F is true whenever a certain point in the protocol of processor P is reached no longer depends on P's actions alone. Moreover, even if F is indeed true at that point, it might become false before P's next action, because another processor was quick enough to change the value of some variable in the interim. Certain formal proof methods overcome this problem by requiring the separate proofs to satisfy some kind of **interference freedom** property, which has to be proved separately.

All this sounds quite complicated. In fact, it is. One of our reasons for presenting only an informal proof for the two-processor solution, and even less than that for the N-processor case, was the rather technical nature of the formal proofs. In principle, however, there *are* adequate proof methods, and, as in the sequential case, formal proofs *do* always exist if the solutions are indeed correct.

Temporal Logic

In Chapter 5 dynamic logics were mentioned. These are formal frameworks that can be used to specify and prove various properties of algorithms. It would be nice if we were able to use such logics for specifying and proving the safety and liveness properties of concurrent systems. The central logical construct used in dynamic logics is **after**(A, F), which means that F is true after A terminates. Such logics are thus based on the input/output paradigm, relating the situation before executing part of an algorithm to the situation after the execution. This paradigm has been found to be inadequate for dealing with concurrency. It seems essential to be able to talk directly about what is happening *during* execution.

A formalism that has proved to be more fitting here is **temporal logic**, or TL. It is a variant of a classical logic known to mathematicians as **tense logic**, especially tailored for algorithmic purposes. Its formulas make statements about the truth of assertions as time goes by, and can also refer explicitly to the current location of control in the protocols. Two of the central constructs here are **henceforth**(F) and **eventually**(F). The first states that F is true from now on – until termination if the protocol terminates, and forever if it does not – and the second states that F will eventually become true, i.e., at some point in the future. Thus, the first can be used to state safety properties, by writing **henceforth**$(\sim F)$(that is, F will never become true), and the second to state liveness properties.

As an example, consider the solution of the two-processor shower problem, and the following formulas of TL:[†]

P_1-**at**(1.4) $\rightarrow$ **eventually** $(P_1$-**at**$(1.5))$
P_2-**at**(1.4) $\rightarrow$ **eventually** $(P_2$-**at**$(1.5))$
$\sim(P_1$-**at**(1.5) & P_2-**at**$(1.5))$

The first two formulas state that if a processor is waiting to enter the critical section then it eventually will enter, and the third states that both processors will never be in their critical section simultaneously. Taken together, and stated to be true at all points of the computation, these formulas assert that the solution is correct. More precisely, if we denote by C the conjunction of these three formulas, proving correctness would mean proving that the formula:

henceforth(C)

is true for these protocols. A formal proof of this formula involves logical manipulation that adheres to the strict axiomatic rules of temporal logic, which we shall not dwell upon here. However, to make a comparison with the proof methods of Chapter 5, it turns out that pure safety properties (like that in the third part of C) can be proved in a manner similar to that of the invariant assertion method for partial correctness. Eventualities (like those

---

[†] The fact that processor P is at location L in the protocol is described by the construct P-**at**(L).

in the first two parts of C) can be proved by first analyzing each possible single step of the protocols, and then using mathematical induction to deduce eventualities that become true within some number of steps from those that become true in less.

As mentioned, if the protocols are indeed correct, a proof of correctness exists, and once found, parts of it can be checked algorithmically. Actually, in many applications of temporal logic each variable has only a finite number of possible values (the mutual exclusion protocol given employs three variables, each with only two possible values). These **finite-state protocols**, as they are sometimes called, *can* be verified algorithmically. That is, there are algorithms that accept as inputs certain kinds of protocols and the temporal logic formula stating correctness, and verify the former against the latter. Thus, while finding proofs of correctness for the transformational, or computational, parts of concurrent systems is, in general, not effectively solvable, it *is* possible to effectively find proofs of the **control** parts, such as the mechanisms for scheduling processors and preventing starvation and deadlock, as these usually involve variables with a finite range only. However, these automatic verifiers are not always as efficient as we would hope, since, among other things, the number of combinations of values grows exponentially with the number of processors. Thus, even short and innocent-looking protocols may be quite difficult to prove automatically, and in hand-produced proofs, of course, subtle errors are the rule, not the exception.

Fairness and Real-Time Systems

There are two additional issues that deserve mention here, although neither of them will be treated in any detail. The first concerns a global assumption that is usually made when dealing with ongoing concurrency. We typically make no assumptions about the relative speed of the processors involved in solving problems of concurrency, but we do assume that they all respond and make progress within some finite, though possibly lengthy, amount of time. In our solutions to the mutual exclusion problem we used this assumption, of course, since otherwise P_1 could reach clause (1.3) and never get round to setting Z to 1 and proceeding.

This assumption is sometimes called **fairness**, since if you think of concurrency as being implemented by a central processor, sometimes called a **scheduler**, who gives each of the concurrent processors a turn in carrying out a few instructions, then to say that each processor eventually makes progress is just like saying that the simulating processor is being fair to all, eventually giving each one its turn.

Consider the following protocols for two processors P and Q.

protocol for P:

(1) $X \leftarrow 0$;

(2) do the following again and again forever:
     (2.1) if $Z = 0$ then stop;
     (2.2) $X \leftarrow X + 1$.

protocol for Q:

(1) $Z \leftarrow 0$;

(2) stop.

Let Z's initial value be 1. If we do not assume fairness, P may be continuously given the right to proceed, with poor Q being forever left out of the game. This, of course, leads to an infinite loop. The only way of ensuring that the protocols terminate is to let Q make progress. On the other hand, under the fairness assumption this concurrent algorithm terminates, setting Z to some unknown, possibly very large, non-negative integer. The way it does so is as follows. The scheduler is free to schedule P and Q to take turns any way it wants, and, in particular, it can let P execute many times before it lets Q in for the first time. However, it must let Q take a turn at some point in time, by the fairness assumption. Thus, P will increment X from 0 some unknown number of times, but once Q gets the green light execution will terminate. Obviously, the final value of X can be any number from 0 up, but the process will eventually terminate, as a result of the fairness.

Of course, that these protocols might produce very large numbers is based on the assumption that some processors can be arbitrarily slower than others. Stronger notions of fairness are sometimes useful, especially those that bound the **delay** that can occur between actions. We might want to say that Q has a slower response than P, but that it is no worse than twice as slow. Such fairness assertions are quantitative in nature, and introduce **timing** issues into the game.

In many kinds of systems timing constraints are crucial, particularly in **real-time** systems. These are required to respond to certain events immediately, or at least within unnoticeable and negligible amounts of time. Examples include flight control, missile guidance and fast communication systems. Here too temporal logic can help, using the **nextstep** operator. It is possible, for example, to write a TL formula that states that whenever F holds G will become true no later than, say, 10 steps later. This still does not solve the problems of programming such systems, which are usually not only time critical but also large and complex. More will be said about methods for describing their behavior later.

*   *   *

The Dining Philosophers Problem

One of the most popular examples of ongoing concurrency, which illustrates many issues of synchronization and cooperation, is the following. We have a table, around which are seated N philosophers. In the center there is a large plate containing an unlimited amount of spaghetti. Half-way between each pair of adjacent philosophers there is a single fork (see Figure 10.10). Now, since no one, not even a philosopher, can eat spaghetti with one fork, there is a problem. The desired life cycle of a philosopher consists of carrying out his private activities (e.g., thinking, and then writing up the results for publication), becoming hungry and trying to eat, eating, and then back to the private activities, *ad infinitum*. (A related problem involves Chinese philosophers, with rice and chopsticks replacing spaghetti and forks.)

Figure 10.10   The dining philosophers.

How should the philosophers go about their rituals without starving? We can instruct them to simply lift up the forks on either side when hungry, and eat, laying them down again when finished. This solution will not work, since one or both of the forks may be taken by neighboring philosophers at the time. Also, two adjacent philosophers may try to pick up the same fork at the same time. Using forks that are beyond a philosopher's reach is forbidden. Here, eating can be considered a critical section of sorts, as two adjacent philosophers cannot eat simultaneously, and the forks are crucial resources of sorts, as they cannot be used by two philosophers simultaneously.

This problem typifies many real-world situations, such as computer operating systems, for example, in which many processors compete for certain shared resources. The interconnection pattern of such systems is usually quite sparse (not all resources are accessible to each processor) and the number of resources is too small for everyone to be happy together.

To solve the problem, we introduce a new player into the game, the dining room doorman. Philosophers are instructed to leave the room when they are not interested in eating, and to try to re-enter when they are. The doorman is required to keep count of the number of philosophers currently in the room, limiting it to $N - 1$. That is, if the room contains all but one philosopher, the last one will be kept waiting at the door until someone leaves. Now, if at most $N - 1$ philosophers are at the table at any one time, then there are at least two philosophers who have at least one neighbor absent, and thus at least one philosopher can eat. (Why?) When properly formalized, this solution can be shown to be satisfactory. However, it uses an additional person (whose monthly salary will probably be more than the sum needed for buying an additional set of forks, at least for reasonably small N).

Can the dining philosophers problem be solved without a doorman, and without resorting to shared memory or its equivalents? In other words, is there a fully distributed, fully symmetric solution to the problem that does not employ any additional processors? Here 'fully distributed' means that there is no central shared memory and the protocols may use only distributed variables (shared, say, only by two neighboring philosophers). 'Fully symmetric' means that the protocols for all the philosophers are essentially identical – we do not allow different philosophers to act differently, and we do not allow them to start off with different values in their variables. This might sound a little too restrictive. However, if the philosophers have different programs or different initial values, it is like saying that they use their own personal knowledge and talents in the mundane quest for food. We would like to save all that for thinking and publishing; eating should be a procedure that is standard and common to all.

The answer to these questions is no. To solve the problem we need something more, such as shared memory, direct communication between processors, special centralized controlling processors, or the use of different information for different philosophers.

** Why? The argument is really quite simple. Think of a correct solution as one that guarantees all the desired properties, even against the most malicious scheduler (i.e., even against a scheduler that tries as hard as it can to cause deadlock or starvation). In other words, to show that there is no fully distributed, fully symmetric solution, it suffices to exhibit one particular order in which the philosophers carry out the actions in a candidate solution, and to show that something must go wrong. Assume, therefore, that we have some such candidate. Also, assume we have numbered the philosophers 1, 2, ..., N, in some order. (The philosophers themselves are not aware even of their own numbers; they are not allowed to have any private information that might turn out to be useful.)

The schedule we adopt is the following. At each stage, every philosopher in the order 1, 2, ..., N is allowed to carry out one of his basic actions. An action might be a *busy wait* test, in which case testing and deciding whether to wait or to proceed are taken together as one indivisible basic action. It is possible to show that at each stage precisely the same action is carried out by each processor. This follows from the fact that both the initial situation and the protocols are fully symmetric, there are no processors other than the philosophers themselves, and the table and its contents are symmetrically cyclic. Consequently, the situation at the end of each stage will still be fully symmetric; the values of the variables will be the same for all philosophers, as will their locations within the protocols. Could any philosopher have eaten within one or more of the stages? No, because stages involve basic actions only, and at the end of a stage the fact that a philosopher is eating or has eaten will be detectable. But it is impossible for all the philosophers to be eating at once, and the process of two philosophers eating, one after the other, cannot be carried out within one stage. It thus follows from the necessary symmetry that at the end of every stage no processor will have eaten. Hence, none ever will.   **

In Chapter 11 we shall see that the dining philosophers problem *can* be solved in a fully distributed and fully symmetric fashion, but with a more liberal notion of correctness.

*   *   *

Concurrent Programming Languages

There are several programming languages that support concurrency one way or another. These include SIMULA 67, Concurrent PASCAL, ADA, OCCAM, MODULA-2, and a number of concurrent variants of PROLOG. Rather than describe the languages themselves, we shall look at some of the features that have been considered in their design.

First, there has to be a way of saying 'carry out A and B concurrently'. Two common notations for this are:

$(A \parallel B)$ and   **cobegin** A ; B **coend**

Alternatively, instead of explicitly enclosing concurrent portions of the program in such 'concurrency brackets', some languages allow the definition of subroutine-like constructs called **tasks** or **processes**. These are activated by an **initiate** instruction, and hence:

> **initiate** P, Q

will have the effect of starting P and Q together.

The interesting part of implementing concurrency in a programming language is the method used for describing the *cooperation* that is to take place between concurrently executing processes. We already know that shared memory and direct communication represent the two main approaches. If the former is used, there must be a mechanism for solving the writing conflicts that shared memory raises. One of the most popular of these is the **semaphore**.

Semaphores and Monitors

A semaphore is a special kind of object that employs two operations to control the use of critical sections (such as those that entail writing into a portion of shared memory). An attempt to enter is represented by the **request** operation, and **release** indicates an exit. A semaphore S can actually be viewed as an integer-valued variable. Executing **request**(S) is an atomic action that tries to decrease S by 1, doing so without interruption if its value is positive and waiting for it to become positive otherwise. The effect of **release**(S) is simply to increment S by 1. The important point is that, by its very definition, a semaphore S yields only one **request** or **release** operation at a time. In a typical use of semaphores to achieve mutual exclusion, S is given an initial value of 1, and each processor's critical section is enclosed as follows:

> . . .
> **request**(S);
>   carry out critical section;
> **release**(S);
> . . .

The effect of this is to allow only one processor into its critical section at a time. The first one that tries to enter succeeds in decreasing S to 0 and enters. The others must wait until the first one exits and increments S to 1 in the process. A semaphore that starts with 1, and hence takes on only the values 1 and 0, is termed a **binary semaphore**. A simple way of using semaphores for critical sections that can handle up to K processors at a time is to use a non-binary semaphore with initial value K. It is easy to see that this has the desired effect. In the dining philosophers problem, for example, the doorman can be modeled by a semaphore with an initial value of $N - 1$, controlling a critical section that includes the activities involved in trying to eat, eating and leaving the room. The use of each fork can be modeled by a binary semaphore.

It is noteworthy that this simple definition of semaphores does not assume that all processors waiting at blocked **request** operations are eventually given the right to enter when S becomes nonzero. It is quite possible that a malicious implementation of semaphores always gives the right of way to the most-recently-arrived processor, locking others out forever. This is one of the cases in which some kind of fairness assumption appears to be necessary.

Semaphores can thus be described as a very simple data type, whose operations (increment, test-and-decrement) are guarded against writing conflicts by a built-in mechanism of mutual exclusion. Mutual exclusion for more complicated data types that employ many operations can be achieved by surrounding each occurrence of a writing operation with the appropriate semaphore operations. However, in a sense, semaphores are like **goto** statements; too many **request** and **release** operations sprinkled all over a lengthy program may become unclear and susceptible to errors. Semaphores can be used to solve the standard kinds of problems in programming concurrency, but they do constitute an *un*structured programming construct.

Another useful construct, that is also nicely structured, is the **monitor**. A monitor can be thought of as a tool for defining, at one and the same time, a data type with its allowed operations and the mechanism for achieving mutual exclusion when the data is to be manipulated concurrently. On the face of it, a monitor is similar to a subroutine. It has variables of its own, and when initiated it executes a certain program segment consisting of statements. After executing this initial segment, however, the monitor itself remains passive. Its subsequent use is through a number of additional procedures that it contains, each of which corresponds to an operation on the data type that the monitor defines. These procedures can be called from outside the monitor. The main characteristic of a monitor is that no two internal procedures may execute simultaneously. If simultaneous calls are made (to different procedures or to the same one) all but one of the calling processors are put on a waiting queue until the one that was let in exits, and the monitor becomes available for the next in line.

Here is a schematic definition of a monitor that models a file system with a delete instruction, a write instruction, and two different kinds of updates:

```
monitor file;
    ... definition of relevant variables ...
    begin
        ... body of monitor (carried out when monitor is initiated) ...;
    end;
```

```
        procedure delete;
        ... instructions for carrying out delete ...
        end;
        procedure write;
        ... instructions for carrying out write ...
        end;
        procedure update1;
        ... instructions for carrying out first kind of update ...
        end;
        procedure update2;
        ... instructions for carrying out second kind of update ...
        end;
    end-monitor file.
```

To define a new file F of the type described by this monitor, we write:

```
    instance F: file;
```

and henceforth refer to the various procedures by $F.$ *update1*, $F.$ *update2*, $F.$ *delete* and $F.$ *write*. Since mutual exclusion is guaranteed, these can be used safely.

At times, monitors are augmented with the special instructions **wait**(G) and **signal**(G), appearing within the monitors themselves. Here G is a special object, sometimes called a **signal**. When the former instruction is reached by some processor P it waits until the latter is reached by some other processor Q, at which time Q can be thought of as signaling G, and P as sensing the signal and proceeding. This is an elegant way of achieving a certain kind of **synchronization** between two processors; P waits for Q to reach some point before proceeding.

It is noteworthy that with the use of **wait** and **signal** semaphores and monitors are interchangeable. A simple monitor can be defined that simulates a semaphore (can the reader construct one?), and, conversely, it is possible to simulate any monitor with semaphores.

Direct Communication Rendezvous

A simple and effective method for describing direct communication between processors is the following. When processor P wants to send the value of X to Q, it tries to execute the statement:

$Q!X$

The statement will not be executed unless, and until Q has reached an instruction of the form:

$P?Y$

If and when P and Q find themselves at the same time about to execute these statements, both are carried out, with the effect that in one step Q's variable Y is set to the current value of P's X. This is called a **communication rendezvous**. Actually, instead of sending a variable, P may also send an expression, as in:

$Q!(X^2 + 6)$

which is evaluated at the moment of rendezvous and the value sent to Y.

Often there is more than one target processor Q, and P might want to send a message to several of them. A variation that caters for such cases calls for using **channels**, rather than processors. A channel can be viewed as a pipe, or a communication line, connecting two or more processors, through which a signal or item of data can be transmitted. In this way, P and Q, and other processors too, may contain instructions of the form:

$C!X$ and $C?Y$

where C is defined as a channel name. A rendezvous occurs when, at one and the same time, some processor is at a send instruction $C!X$ and at least one processor reaches a receive instruction $C?Y$ with the same channel name C.

Notice that the rendezvous mechanism achieves not only the communication itself, but also a strong form of synchronization. For example, to ensure that P and Q wait for each other before proceeding to carry out some work that has to be started by both simultaneously, things can be set up so that P contains:

```
...
C!0;
P's important work;
...
```

and Q contains:

```
...
C?Y;
Q's important work;
...
```

where C is a new channel name and Y a new variable, and neither is used elsewhere.

This send/receive communication mechanism, like **goto** statements and semaphores, is somewhat unstructured in nature, and could possibly lead to errors when used in abundance. On the other hand, the better structured monitor construct has the disadvantage of being somewhat asymmetric; the calling procedure is active, whereas the monitor itself remains passive, its main role being to control the other processors' use of its procedures. It would be nice to combine the power of an explicit communication mechanism with the flexibility afforded by a set of structured procedures.

An attempt to do just that constitutes one of the interesting features of the ADA programming language. There, processes, or tasks, can contain **accept** statements, which look just like subroutines, with parameters and bodies of instructions. If a process P reaches the statement:

accept $R(X$:in, Y :out) **do** . . . all-kinds-of-things . . . **end**

it is left waiting until some other process Q reaches a calling statement of the form:

$R(Z, W)$

Similarly, if Q reaches *its* calling statement first, it is left waiting until some P reaches a corresponding **accept** statement. If and when both are at the appropriate points, a rendezvous occurs. First, Q delivers its value Z to P's variable X, just like parameters in a subroutine. Then P proceeds to carry out its body *all-kinds-of-things*, which should eventually set Y to some value. Finally, P delivers the final value of its Y to Q, who, in turn, receives it in W, much as some subroutines return values. The rendezvous then ends and both processes continue their normal execution.

*   *   *

Specifying Large and Complex Reactive Systems

Some systems of ongoing concurrent nature are **data driven** in nature. This means that they owe their complexity mainly to the fact that various kinds of data are transmitted between components, and it is the flow of data that controls the system's behavior. A typical activity within such a system waits for its input data to arrive, processes it, sends off its output data to some other activities, and goes back to sleep until prompted by new input data. Such systems can be described in a satisfactory manner by **data-flow**

diagrams, which identify the various activities and the data that flows between them.

Most of the cloud-like figures in this book are data-flow diagrams of sorts. Typically, they describe activities in clouds and data in rectangles, with arrows prescribing the data flow itself. The meaning of these diagrams is usually quite obvious, although no rigorous conventions are imposed regarding when and why the data indeed flows. For example, despite the fact that activities may generate more than one output simultaneously (see Figure 9.12), we should have no problem in understanding that if the two outputs are *yes* and *no*, then at most one of them is produced at any given time. Our cloud-like diagrams are also **hierarchical**, containing low-level activities clustered into higher level ones. Hierarchical and modular descriptions are important both for the designer of a system and for someone who is to understand it later. This fact is a manifestation of the widely held belief that large programs should be developed gradually, using subroutines and other means to provide them with structure and levels of detail.

There are several methods based on data-flow descriptions that are satisfactory for the specification and design of large systems. They allow the identification of the activities of the system and its flow of data in a hierarchical and modular fashion. A number of such methods are supported by computerized graphical systems that can automatically check the descriptions for loose ends, inconsistencies, and mismatches. These tools, sometimes referred to as tools for **functional decomposition**, are clearly invaluable for the designer of data-driven systems.

Unfortunately, data-driven systems constitute the easier case. Far more problematic are large and complex systems that are heavily **control driven**, or **event driven**. Such systems may be termed **reactive**. Their role in life is not just to manipulate data in ways that can be described by the flow to and from activities, but predominantly to react to many different kinds of events, signals, and conditions in intricate ways. Reactive systems need not necessarily be concurrent, although they usually are. In fact, the vast majority of complex systems are, to a large extent, reactive in nature. Examples include chemical plants, avionics systems, integrated circuits, telephone and communication controllers, industrial robots, and even standard interactive software packages such as word processors and program editors. These systems have to maintain some required relationship with their environment, reacting to buttons being depressed, levers being pulled, binary signals being flipped, temperatures rising above critical levels, receivers being hung up, cursors being moved on a screen, etc.

While the data-flow and functional decomposition of such systems are important facets of their specification, they do not provide an adequate dynamic description of their behavior. A precise behavioral description is a crucial requisite for all stages of the design of a complex reactive system, and for its usage and maintenance stages too. All too often, this aspect of a system's specification is provided by imprecise and verbose descriptions in natural language that tend to fill enormous volumes.

It would appear that finite-state automata and their associated diagrams are a possible answer. We identify the system's **states**, or modes of operation, and proceed to specify the **events** and **conditions** that cause transitions between states, and the **actions** (e.g., the sending and receiving of data, the starting or stopping of activities, etc.) that are carried out within them. Chapter 9 contained a simple example of a finite-state diagram describing part of the behavior of a digital watch (see Figure 9.21).

However, there are several problems with this naive use of state diagrams. First, the diagrams are 'flat', whereas complex systems cannot be adequately dealt with without providing designers and observers with some kind of hierarchy, so that the system can be specified and contemplated at the appropriate levels of detail. Given that *control* is what makes reactive systems complex, this need clearly applies not only to the data-flow and functional decomposition but also to the dynamic behavior. Consider the watch of Figure 9.21. Its description is not yet complete; we would like to continue it by describing the behavior of the stopwatch feature (e.g., what it shows and how and when it is started and stopped), and the various possibilities of updating. All we have for updating is a state named *update-watch*, which presumably denotes, or contains, a number of **substates** that deal with updating the seconds, minutes, hours, and months, much as there are three states for updating the alarm. We would like to be able to send someone off to *refine* the updating or stopwatch states separately, and, when completed, to be able to see these lower level descriptions, either separately or integrated into the whole description. We need a useful notion of *depth* in a state-based behavioral description.

Secondly, conventional state diagrams are sequential and do not cater for concurrency. As an example, suppose our watch has a light for illumination, which can be turned on or off independently of other things that are happening elsewhere. If the light is a totally separate entity controlled, say, by a separate button, then all we need is a new two-state diagram describing it as a separate system. In truth, however, lights in digital watches are more subtle than that. They are usually controlled by one of the standard buttons that play other roles in the watch's behavior. Also, the light feature may not always be applicable – perhaps it does not work in the stopwatch state.

Of course, it is possible to combine the light information with the rest of the description, yielding two states for each of the old ones; one for the case where the light is on, and one for when it is off. This, however, results in an **exponential blow-up** in the number of states that must be explicitly described. Adding a new two-state feature doubles the number of states, and thus making the system larger by an additive factor can make the number of states larger by a multiplicative one, resulting in exponential growth of the state space as the system grows linearly. In a system with a million states, a new on/off component results in *two million* states, and when less trivial components are added things get much, much worse.

Obviously, these problems, which arise even in such small systems as digital watches, are far more acute in large and complex reactive systems, which typically have huge numbers of states.

Statecharts: Visualizing Reactive Behavior

In an attempt to address both the depth and modularity problem and the concurrency problem, state diagrams have been extended, yielding a formalism called **statecharts**. Figure 10.11 shows a statechart for a more detailed version of the watch of Figure 9.21, which includes a light component, refinements of the stopwatch and update states, and the beeping phenomenon. (For brevity, we have omitted the word 'pressed' from the button-pressing events.)

The rountangles of regular state diagrams can now appear clustered within others, with inner ones constituting lower level refinements of outer ones. The state *update-watch* of Figure 10.11, for example, has no real existence in its own right, except for the fact that it consists of the six enclosed substates, related among themselves by an exclusive 'or': being in *update-watch* actually means being in precisely one of its six substates.

Why would we want to cluster these six states into a single state on a higher level? There are several reasons. First of all, for clarity. Somehow, it helps to see the six grouped together logically, with a common name. Secondly, for purposes of gradual development. We might have first decided that there will be a state for updating (as indeed we did; see Figure 9.21) and only later we, or someone else, went ahead and carried out the refinement itself. Thirdly, the six updating states *do* have at least one real property in common: they all respond to the pressing of *b* by stopping the process of updating and returning to *display-time*. If 'flat' diagrams were used this would require six separate arrows, one coming out of each state. If we are in *update-watch* and *b* is pressed, we leave and enter *display-time*, but, since being in *update-watch* is being in any one of the substates, the desired effect follows. Similarly, if the battery is removed or if it dies, a transition to the *dead* state is caused, no matter what state we were in. These are sometimes called **interrupts**. In Figure 9.21 we also used three *b*-arrows leaving the three alarm updating states, whereas in Figure 10.11 the three states were clustered into one, resulting in a single arrow.

Notice that we have not given the six updating states any inner description, and the particular method by which the updating is carried out is left unspecified. Later, a designer can fill in this lower level information, or delegate the job to someone else. Of course, in larger systems such separation of concerns will turn out to be far more significant.

Figure 10.11   Statechart for a more detailed version of the digital watch of Figure 9.21.

The other extension statecharts offer is the possibility of specifying **orthogonal** state components. With this feature, which is depicted by dashed lines, concurrency and independence can be described, and some of the problems arising from the exponential blow-up in the number of states can be avoided. The relationship between orthogonal components is not 'or' but 'and'. For example, if we are in the *stopwatch* state of Figure 10.11, but not in *zero*, then we must be simultaneously both in *displays* and in *running-status*. Within each of these there are two possibilities, related by 'or', and resulting in a total of four possible state configurations. To contrast with these four, consider the *light* component, where we have added two states instead of 12, and the *beeping-status*, where two are added instead of 29. (Where did the 12 and 29 come from?)

There is some subtlety even in this relatively simple example. The light is easily seen not to be applicable to the stopwatch states, since it is orthogonal to the *watch-and-alarm* state, and exclusive to *stopwatch*. But this relationship has other implications. In particular, suppose we are in the configuration ⟨*hour, light-off, beeping*⟩, meaning that we are in the midst of updating the hour, the light is off, and the beeper is beeping because the alarm time has arrived. Now we press *b*. What happens? Well, whether we like it or not, three things will happen simultaneously. The beeping will stop (by virtue of the *b or c* transition to *quiet*), the light will turn on until *b* is released, and the updating will end, with the watch returning to *display-time*.

Thus, external events such as pressing buttons are sensed throughout the statechart, as are internal events such as transitions. This is sometimes referred to as **broadcast communication**. For example, the *displays* component of Figure 10.11 'knows' which internal state *running-status* is in even without receiving a direct message, and uses that information to decide which state to enter when *d* is pressed in state *regular*. (An event written along a transition arrow can have a guarding condition attached; the transition is taken only if the condition is true when the triggering event occurs.)

The small arrows denoting start states in ordinary state diagrams can appear on any level in a statechart. Here they are called **defaults**. Within the high-level state *main-component*, for example, the combined state consisting of the orthogonal states *watch-and-alarm* and *light* is the default, so that if a battery is inserted when in the *dead* state, we enter this combination, and not *stopwatch*. (Of course, we also enter *quiet* in state *beeping-status*.) Now, within each of these orthogonal components there is also a default arrow – there must be one, otherwise we would not know which of their substates to enter – so that we really end up in the configuration ⟨*display-time, light-off, quiet*⟩.

Statecharts have a number of additional features, such as the ability to specify timing constraints on any level, and the possibility of deciding which substate of a high-level state to enter on the basis of the last one visited, rather than by the default. They also allow states to overlap, which makes it possible to specify a variety of synchronization mechanisms for concurrently active processors.

We should remember, however, that formalisms like statecharts are capable of describing only the control part of a reactive system, and not its data flow or physical structure. Such a behavioral specification, therefore, must be combined with some kind of functional and physical decomposition. If the system under description consists solely of software, the physical, functional, and state-based behavioral decompositions may turn out to be very similar. If this is the case, a single combined description may suffice, and a concurrent programming language can possibly be used throughout. Otherwise, there seems to be no alternative but to have a three-way, interrelated specification, describing the system from its three different angles.

There is no magic solution to the problem of designing large and complex systems, except to use carefully fashioned methods, languages, and formalisms that enable the work to be carried out gradually, module by module and level by level. The resulting descriptions ought to be both coherent and precise, sufficiently so to be both useful to an observer and amenable to computer simulation, enabling as much computerized support in formal verification and analysis as possible.

*   *   *

Research on Parallelism and Concurrency

Many people believe that computer science really starts here. If we have claimed in previous chapters that intensive research is being carried out on many of the topics discussed, then in the realm of parallelism and concurrency this is truer than ever. Researchers are trying to come to terms with virtually all aspects of algorithmic cooperation, and it would not be too much of an exaggeration to say that the research of most computer scientists has some connection to the topics discussed in this chapter.

Intensive research is being carried out in finding fast parallel algorithms for a variety of algorithmic problems. The solutions employ a wide spectrum of data structures and mechanisms for achieving parallelism, and at times involve very clever ideas. Many problems (such as gcd computation) have resisted attempts to usefully exploit any kind of parallelism. Boolean circuits and systolic networks are also the subject of much current research, and interesting connections have been discovered between these approaches and conventional sequential algorithmics.

The abstract complexity theory of parallelism poses a number of important, and apparently very difficult, unresolved questions, concerning classes like NC and PSPACE, some of which were described earlier. While, as we have seen, sequentiality already poses many unresolved problems, parallelism undoubtedly raises many more. In fact, it seems clear that we understand the fundamentals of sequential algorithms far better than those of parallel algorithms, and there is a long and difficult way ahead.

Other subjects of current research include parallel computer design, proof and analysis techniques for reasoning about concurrent processes, the creation of useful and powerful concurrent programming languages, and the search for clear yet precise methods for the reliable development of complex systems.

As illustrated by the house building story at the beginning of this chapter, concurrency is a fact of life, and the better we understand it the more we can use it to our advantage. In a way, recent scientific and technological advances in concurrency are ahead of each other. Many of the best parallel algorithms known cannot be implemented because existing parallel computers are inadequate in some way. On the other hand, we still do not know enough about designing concurrent programs and systems to take full advantage of the features those same computers do offer. The work continues, however, and many people hope that the next few years will produce developments that will put algorithmic and computerized concurrency on a par with the more manageable notion of sequentiality.

> *Two are better than one;*
> *because they have a good reward for their labour*
> Ecclesiastes 4: 9

11

Probabilistic Algorithms

OR

Getting It Done by Tossing Coins

I offer thee three things: choose one of them
I Chronicles 21: 10

Come, and let us cast lots
Jonah 1: 7

In the previous chapter we took steps that landed us outside the standard framework of algorithmic problems and their solutions. We allowed algorithms that employ a number of little Runarounds, not just one, and we also considered ongoing or perpetual problems that are not necessarily based on the usual input/output paradigm. These departures required little justification: the first can be easily seen to improve performance, and the second reflects the nature of a growing number of computerized systems.

In this chapter we shall take a more radical step, renouncing one of the most sacred requisites in all of algorithmics, namely, that a solution to an algorithmic problem must solve that problem correctly, for all possible inputs. We cannot completely abandon the need for correctness, since, if we do, any algorithm would 'solve' any problem. Nor can we afford to recommend that people solve algorithmic problems with algorithms that they *hope* will work, but whose performance they can only observe, not analyze. What we are interested in are algorithms that might not always be correct, but whose possible incorrectness is something that can be safely

302

ignored. Moreover, we insist that this fact be justifiable on rigorous mathematical grounds.

If we assume that spinning a revolver's barrel is a truly random way of selecting one of its six bullet positions, then some people might consider the chances of getting killed in a single attempt at Russian roulette to be safely ignorable. Most people would not. Let us now suppose that the revolver has 2^{200} bullet positions, or (equivalently) that the trigger in an ordinary six-bullet revolver is actually pulled only if the single bullet always ended up in the shooting position in 77 consecutive spins. In such a case the chances of getting killed in a single (77-round) play are many orders of magnitude smaller than the chances of achieving the same effect by drinking a glass of water, driving to work, or taking a deep breath of air. Clearly, in such a case the chances *can* be safely ignored; the probability of a catastrophe is unimaginably minute.

This chapter is concerned with one way of exploiting **probability theory** in algorithmic design. We shall consider algorithms that in the course of their action can toss fair coins, yielding truly random outcomes. The consequences of adding this facility turn out to be quite surprising. Rather than constituting a step backwards, leading to algorithms that produce unpredictable results, the new ability will be shown to be extremely useful, yielding fast probabilistic solutions to problems that have only very inefficient conventional ones. The price paid for this is the possibility of error, but, as in the 77-round version of Russian roulette, this possibility can be safely ignored. Curiously, we shall see that probabilism in algorithmics is most advantageous when used together with negative results, concerning problems for which no good solutions are known, not even probabilistic ones.

More on the Dining Philosophers

In Chapter 10 we became acquainted with the dining philosophers. It was shown that the problem admits no deadlock-free solutions if we insist on total symmetry and use no centralized variables. The rules prescribed that a candidate solution must work correctly even against the most malicious scheduler; for example, even for the case in which everyone becomes hungry and tries to lift up the forks at precisely the same time.

It is now shown that the problem *is* solvable if we let the philosophers toss coins. The basic idea is to use coin tossing to break the symmetry in the long run. Specifically, consider the following candidate solution:

protocol for each philosopher:
(1)   do the following again and again forever:
    (1.1)   carry out *private activities* until hungry;
    (1.2)   toss coin to choose a direction, *left* or *right*, at random;

(1.3)   wait until fork lying in chosen direction is available, and then lift it;

(1.4)   if other fork is not available do the following:

(1.4.1)   put down fork that was lifted;

(1.4.2)   go to (1.2);

(1.5)   otherwise (i.e., other fork is available) lift other fork;

(1.6)   *critical section*: eat to your heart's content;

(1.7)   put down both forks (and back to (1.1)).

This solution can be shown to be deadlock free **with probability** 1. What does this mean? Well, it means that in the course of an infinite time period, the chances of a deadlock occurring are zero. Not just small, or negligible, but zero!

This statement requires further clarification. It is possible that the system of philosophers *will* deadlock, but the chances that deadlock will occur, relative to the chances that it will not, are nil. Let us consider a scheduler that causes all philosophers to become hungry simultaneously. Say the philosophers are all positioned at clause (1.2) together. One way for the system to deadlock is that all philosophers, simultaneously, choose the *same* direction in (1.2), say *right*, lift up their right-hand fork, discover that the other fork is not available (in (1.4)), put down the right-hand fork (in (1.4.1)), go back to (1.2) and again, all choose the same direction, perhaps *left* this time, again lift up the appropriate fork, then put it down, then choose the same direction again, and so on, *ad infinitum*. This is clearly a deadlock situation, as no philosopher can eat.

That the philosophers are all perfectly synchronized, all reaching the same instruction at the same time, is the devious work of this special scheduler, and scheduling is not something that is chosen at random. As explained in Chapter 10, our solutions must work even against the worst of schedulers. Coin tossing may only be used within the protocols to influence the behavior of individual processors, but not to influence the order or timing in which they are told to carry out their instructions. Chance is thus not to be used as part of the scheduling but only as part of the operation of the processors themselves. Thus, malicious scheduling cannot be the reason that a particular scenario such as this one has zero chance of happening; the scheduler might just behave in precisely this way. The real reason has to do with the probability that certain outcomes of the coin-tossing activities occur. To achieve deadlock under this scheduler, all N coins have to indicate the same direction, each and every time they are tossed. This can be shown to be a **zero-probability event**, to use the terminology of probability theory. There is no real chance that this will indeed happen in the process of tossing N coins, simultaneously, infinitely many times. (Is this true for all N? What happens when $N = 1$?) In other words, in an infinite execution of these protocols for N philosophers the apparent symmetry will be broken with probability 1; that is, for sure, by some unequal set of outcomes in one of the coin-tossing stages. Such a break in symmetry is easily seen to result in at least one eating philosopher, so that deadlock is avoided.

It is important to realize that the preceding argument does not constitute a *proof* that the protocol is deadlock free with probability 1. We have only discussed one particular scheduler, and one particular set of coin tosses that results in deadlock, and have shown it to be of zero probability. What if the coin indicates *left* for even-numbered philosophers and *right* for odd-numbered ones, and the scheduler repeatedly gives the former philosophers one turn and then the latter ones one turn? What if there are seven philosophers and they are given turns in a cyclic fashion, skipping two each time? Generalizing the argument to hold for all schedulers is not straightforward, but it can be done. The protocol presented then is indeed deadlock free under *any* scheduling.

However, although it avoids deadlock, this solution is not satisfactory, as it admits lockouts, or starvation.

** Here is a scheduler that, with certainty, will cause all but one philosopher to be locked out; in other words, they will all be deprived of food with probability 1.

The scheduler first arranges a situation in which all philosophers are at (1.2). It will now work things in such a way as to guarantee that, with probability 1, one of the philosophers, say Plato, will eat infinitely often, while each of the others will eventually eat a last supper and thereafter starve forever. The idea is based on the fact that if a philosopher is given the opportunity of eating repeatedly until his coin toss in (1.2) happens to yield some particular desired direction, then with probability 1 the desired direction will indeed eventually appear. Utilizing this fact, the scheduler will now ignore everyone but Plato, letting him find his forks and eat repeatedly as long as he draws *right* in the coin toss of (1.2). Plato will be stopped when he draws *left* for the first time, and, as mentioned, with probability 1 this will indeed happen. Plato is now left in limbo after this last execution of (1.2) but before the check-and-lift instruction of (1.3), and his right-hand neighbor is given the green light. He too is allowed to eat repeatedly until he draws *left*, at which time he is also left lingering after the completion of (1.2) and the execution of (1.3). This goes on around the table in cyclic counter-clockwise order, giving each philosopher the floor (and the spaghetti) until he draws *left*. When this is over, all philosophers are ready to carry out clause (1.3), with *left* being their chosen direction. Since the probability is 1 that each philosopher's eating spree will eventually terminate with the coin showing *left*, the probability of reaching this common situation is also 1. Now, all the philosophers are allowed by the scheduler to materialize their most recent choice of *left*, and to pick up their left-hand fork. None yet have started (1.4).

From this point on, our scheduler will only allow Plato to eat; all others will starve forever. The way to achieve this is as follows. Plato's right-hand neighbor is allowed to proceed. He looks to his right, sees that the fork is unavailable (*his* right-hand neighbor has it), puts down his left-hand fork and tosses the coin again. This goes on without him eating until he draws *right*. He is then left in limbo by the scheduler, before (1.3), so that he has not even determined that his right-hand fork is unavailable, and control goes to *his* right-hand neighbor (the second from Plato). This philosopher is similarly given the opportunity to proceed (similarly without succeeding to eat) until he also draws *right*, and is stopped at the same point, just before (1.3). This procedure is carried out for all philosophers, in counterclockwise order around the table, up to, but excluding, Plato himself. The situation now is that all forks are on the table, except Plato's left-hand one, which Plato is holding, and all the other philosophers are ready to look to their right in (1.3). Now Plato is allowed to proceed, which he does by lifting his right-hand fork and eating. In fact, he is allowed to go through his entire protocol repeatedly as long as he chooses *left* in (1.2), eating well each time, and is stopped by the scheduler when he draws *right* for the first time. Now the situation is exactly as it was after Plato's initial eating spree, but with *right* being his latest choice, not *left*. The scheduler now continues precisely as before, but with the directions reversed throughout, going around from neighbor to left-hand neighbor in clockwise order, waiting for them all to draw *left*, until Plato is reached. Again, he eats repeatedly until he draws *left*, and the whole procedure repeats itself.

Except for Plato, all philosophers clearly starve after the initial round of eating is over. Plato, on the other hand, eats infinitely often. Furthermore, all the eventualities that were invoked in describing this most malicious scheduler actually occur with probability 1. Consequently, all philosophers except for Plato will be starved with probability 1. Thus, as we said, the protocol presented earlier avoids deadlock but, unfortunately, it admits starvation.   **

The protocol can be extended and refined to yield a satisfactory solution to the problem, with zero probability of starvation too. This version will not be presented here, except to remark that it uses the same coin-tossing mechanism for choosing directions, as well as variables that are somewhat similar to those used in the solution to the shower problem. Among these are two variables for each philosopher – used to notify his two neighbors that he desires to eat – and two that he shares with his two neighbors – to indicate which of them ate last. None of the variables are centralized, as each is shared by at most two locally adjacent philosophers.

This, then, is a fully symmetric, fully distributed solution, and it is quite satisfactory, in spite of the proof given in Chapter 10 that such a solution does not exist. It exists only in the presence of the more liberal notion of correctness used here: not absolute correctness, but, rather, correctness with probability 1.

*   *   *

Probabilistic Algorithms for Conventional Algorithmic Problems

The dining philosophers problem, with the requirements of symmetry and distributivity, is thus not solvable without probabilism, or randomization, but *is* solvable with it. However, there is something a little disconcerting about the probabilistic solutions just discussed. They seem to rely, for their success, on the infinite, perpetual nature of the protocols, since what causes certain events to occur with probability 1 therein is the fact that we are reasoning about an infinite time span, and things can happen arbitrarily late in time. However, we get the feeling that, if presented with some version of the problem that involves finite time spans only, the entire probabilistic building constructed above would collapse, and there would not be much that we could say. Somehow, it appears that the really interesting problem is this: can probabilism, or randomization, improve things when it comes to ordinary, conventional algorithmic problems, those that accept inputs and have to halt with the desired outputs? And the answer to this is also a resounding yes.

Before giving concrete examples, let us imagine the following situation, which is not unlike the Russian roulette story, except that we prefer to talk about people's money, not their lives. Let us assume that, for some unexplained reason, all our money was tied up to the monkey puzzle problem of Chapter 7 in the following way. We are given a single large instance of the problem (say 100 monkey cards), and are told that our money will be doubled if we give the right yes/no answer to the question of whether the cards can be arranged in a legal 10×10 square, but that we lose the lot if we give the wrong answer. Moreover, the money is unavailable until we give *some* answer. Since the monkey puzzle problem is NP-complete, we have a problem of our own. What shall we do?

We could run our favorite exponential-time algorithm on the input cards, hoping that this particular set is an easy one, so that the algorithm will be able to deal with it reasonably fast, or we could position ourself on the floor and start trying things out on our own. Given the discussions in Chapter 7, these possibilities have certain obvious drawbacks. Alternatively, realizing the hopelessness of the situation, we might simply toss a coin, say yes or no at random, and hope for the best. Is there any better way?

Remaining in an imaginary mode of thought, suppose we were offered an algorithm that solved the monkey puzzle problem, but with a slight chance of error. Say we were guaranteed that, randomly, once in every 2^{200} executions it gave the wrong answer. This would appear immediately to be an excellent way of resolving the dilemma. We would undoubtedly just run the algorithm on the input cards and present our tormentor with the answer. The chances of losing the money would be, as in the 77-round Russian roulette game, far less than the chances of getting run over in crossing the road to the computer center, and far, far less than the chances that, during execution, a hardware error will occur in the computer on which the algorithm is implemented.

The fact is that for many algorithmic problems, including some that appear to be intractable, there *are* such algorithms (not, as far as we know, for the monkey puzzle problem, but for many similar ones). These algorithms are probabilistic in nature, as they employ random coin tossing, and are thus sometimes called **probabilistic**, or **randomized**, **algorithms**. For all practical purposes that come to mind such algorithms are perfectly satisfactory, whether it is an individual's money or life, a company's financial future, or an entire country's security or welfare that is at stake.

Let us now look at an important example of a useful probabilistic solution to an otherwise extremely hard problem.

Generating Large Primes

Chapter 7 mentioned **prime numbers**, or just **primes** for short. A prime is a positive integer whose only **factors** (i.e., numbers that divide it exactly, with no remainder) are 1 and the number itself. Other numbers are termed **composite**; they are just the multiples of the primes. The first few primes are 2, 3, 5, 7, 11, 13, 17, 19, 23, 29, 31, ... There are infinitely many prime numbers, and they are spread out over the entire spectrum of positive integers in the following way. The number of primes less than a given number N is on the order of $N/\log N$. As specific examples, there are 168 primes less than 1000, about 78500 primes less than a million, and about 51 million primes less than a billion. Among all 100-digit numbers, roughly one in every 300 is prime, and for 200-digit numbers it is about one in every 600.

The primes undoubtedly constitute the most interesting class of numbers ever to have caught mathematicians' attention. They play a central role in the branch of mathematics known as **number theory**, and have many remarkable properties. Their investigation has led to some of the most beautiful results in all of mathematics. Moreover, as we shall see later, prime numbers are fast becoming indispensable in several exciting applications of algorithmics, where it is important to be able to generate large primes reasonably fast.

Suppose we are interested in generating a new large prime number, say 150 digits long. If only we had a good way of *testing* the primality of large numbers, we would be able to take advantage of the way the primes are distributed among all positive integers to find a 150-digit prime in a moderate amount of time. To do so, we simply generate, at random, odd 150-digit numbers repeatedly (by tossing coins to choose the digits), and test each one for primality until we hit one that is prime. There is a very high likelihood (more than 90%) that we will find one within the first 1000 attempts, and a good chance that we will find one after far less. In any event, if we are careful not to choose the same number twice we are sure to find one before long. The problem of *generating* large primes efficiently is therefore reduced to that of *testing* the primality of large numbers.

How do we test a number for primality? Here is one straightforward way. Given a number N, divide it by all numbers from 2 all the way to $N - 1$. If any of these are found to divide N evenly, stop and say no, since you have just found a factor of N other than 1 and N itself. If all the $N - 2$ divisions are found to leave remainders, stop and say yes – N is a prime. This algorithm is fine, except that it is unreasonably inefficient. In fact, it runs in exponential-time, where the size of the input is taken to be the number of digits in N. Testing numbers of 10 or 15 digits in this way is feasible, but testing 150-digit numbers is not, as it would take many billions of years on the fastest computers (see Chapter 7). Of course, this algorithm can be improved by dividing the candidate number N only by 2 and by the odd numbers from 3 to $\sqrt{N}$, or, more significantly, by carefully leaving out all multiples of divisors already considered. However, none of these improvements eliminates the super-polynomial-time that the solution takes, and hence this brute force approach is quite useless.

In fact, as claimed in Chapter 7, while primality testing is both in NP and in co-NP, it is not known to be in P. No one knows of a polynomial-time algorithm for testing primality, and there is a possibility that the problem is indeed intractable. However, in contrast to many other problems, most notably the NP-complete ones, there is little evidence to suggest that primality testing is intractable. In fact, there *is* a polynomial-time algorithm for primality testing, but it relies for its correctness on a deep, but unproven, conjecture in mathematics, called the **extended Riemann hypothesis**. If this conjecture is ever proved to be true we shall have a fast algorithm for testing primality. Moreover, without relying on the Riemann hypothesis there are 'almost' polynomial-time algorithms for primality testing. The one that is best in terms of order-of-magnitude performance runs in time $O(N^{O(\log\log N)})$, which can be considered very close to polynomial time, since $\log\log N$ grows ever so slowly: if the base of the logarithm is 2, the first N for which $\log\log N$ reaches 5 is more than four billion.

In apparent contrast with this discussion, there *are*, in fact, extremely fast polynomial-time algorithms for testing primality – probabilistic ones.

Probabilistic Algorithms for Testing Primality

In the mid 1970s two very elegant probabilistic algorithms for testing primality were discovered. These were among the first probabilistic solutions to be found for hard algorithmic problems, and they have triggered extensive research that has led to randomized solutions to many other problems. Both algorithms run in time that is a (low-order) polynomial in the number of digits in the input number N, and both can test the primality of a 150-digit number with a negligible probability of error in a few seconds on a medium-sized computer!

The algorithms are based on searching at random for certain kinds of certificates, or **witnesses**, to N's compositeness. If such a witness is found, the algorithm can safely stop and say 'no, N is not prime,' since it has acquired indisputable evidence that N is composite. However, the search must be constructed in such a way that at some reasonably early point in time the algorithm will be able to stop searching and declare that N is prime, with a very small chance of being wrong. The idea is to find a rapidly testable definition of a witness, with the property that, if N is indeed composite, more than half of the numbers between 1 and $N-1$ are witnesses to N's compositeness. In this way, if we choose at random a number K in the range $[1, \ldots, N-1]$, and N is indeed composite, the probability that K will serve to convince us of that fact is greater than $\frac{1}{2}$. Notice, of course, that we cannot define K to be a witness simply if it divides N exactly, although obviously if $K \neq 1$ such a fact constitutes undisputed evidence that N is composite. The reason is that, in general, far less than half of the numbers between 1 and $N-1$ divide N exactly. The definition of a witness has to be more subtle.

Before seeing a satisfactory approach to witness definition it is worth understanding the significance of this 'more-than-half-are-witnesses' property. If we choose just one K at random, and say 'yes, N is prime' if K is found *not* to be a witness to N's compositeness, we have a chance of less than $\frac{1}{2}$ of being wrong. If we choose *two* such Ks at random, and say yes if *neither* of them is found to be a witness, the probability that we are wrong is reduced to $\frac{1}{4}$. If we choose *three* Ks the probability of error becomes $\frac{1}{8}$, and so on. This fact translates immediately into an algorithm. Choose, say, 200 random numbers between 1 and $N-1$ and test each for being a witness to N's compositeness. Stop and say no if (and when) any one of them is found to be a witness, and stop and say yes if they all pass the witness-testing procedure in the negative. Since the choices of the Ks are mutually independent, the following statement holds (see Figure 11.1):

> Whenever this algorithm is run on a prime number, the answer is sure to be *yes*. When it is run on a composite number, the answer will almost certainly be *no*, and the probability that it will be *yes* (when it should not) is less than 1 in 2^{200}.

It seems unnecessary to repeat the Russian roulette story here, or the breathing, drinking or crossing-the-road facts, but the reader will undoubtedly agree that this performance is perfectly satisfactory for any practical purpose, including cases where a person's money or life depend on giving a correct answer. If a user is not satisfied with the $1 - 1/2^{200}$ success probability of this algorithm, he can run it on 201 *K*s instead of 200, and thus halve the chance of error, or on, say, 500 *K*s, making it an incredibly small $1 - 1/2^{500}$. In practice, we might add, running such algorithms on as little as 50 *K*s has proved to be quite adequate.

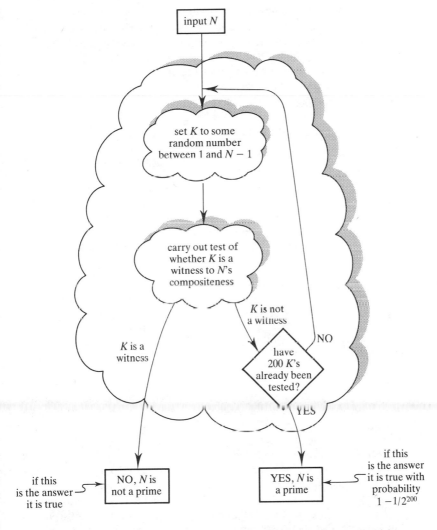

Figure 11.1   The scheme of a probabilistic primality-testing algorithm.

We are left with having to exhibit a workable definition of a witness to *N*'s compositionality, and it is here that the two algorithms differ. Here is a brief description of one of them.

** We shall need a few notions from elementary number theory. For two positive integers K and N, we say that K is a **quadratic residue modulo** N if there is some X such that X^2 and K yield the same remainder when divided by N. This is denoted by:

$$X^2 \equiv K(\text{mod } N)$$

If K and N have no common factors and N is odd, we associate a special number (that is always either 1 or -1) with the pair $\langle K, N \rangle$. This number is known as the **Jacobi symbol** of K and N, and we shall denote it here by $Js(K, N)$. If N is a prime, then define $Js(K, N)$ to be 1 if K is a quadratic residue modulo N, and -1 otherwise. If N is not a prime, then $Js(K, N)$ is defined to be the grand product of the Jacobi symbols of K and each of the prime factors of N, where each factor appears in the product as many times as it appears in N's unique decomposition into prime factors. For example, since $261 = 3 \times 3 \times 29$, we have:

$$Js(35, 261) = Js(35, 3) \times Js(35, 3) \times Js(35, 29)$$

Now, $Js(35, 3)$ and $Js(35, 29)$ can be shown, respectively, to be -1 and 1 (the latter because $8^2 = 64$, and 64 and 35 yield the same remainder modulo 29). Hence, the final value for $Js(35, 261)$ is:

$$-1 \times -1 \times 1 = 1$$

If K is the number chosen at random from among $1, 2, \ldots, N-1$, first determine if K and N, the number whose primality we are trying to test, have any factors in common other than 1. If they do, then obviously N is not a prime and the test is over. Assume, therefore, that they do not. Now compute:

$$X \leftarrow K^{(N-1)/2} \ (\text{mod } N)$$

that is, set X to the remainder obtained when $K^{(N-1)/2}$ is divided by N. Also, compute:

$$Y \leftarrow Js(K, N)$$

If $X \neq Y$ we say that K is a witness to N's compositeness, and the entire procedure stops and says 'no, N is not a prime.' If, on the other hand, $X = Y$, K is not a witness.

It is possible to show, using number-theoretic arguments, that for every *prime* N the resulting X and Y are equal, so that if indeed the K chosen gives rise to $X \neq Y$ we are fully justified in concluding that N is not prime. On the other hand, $X = Y$ does not guarantee that N *is* a prime. However, it so happens (though this is by no means easy to prove) that if N is really not prime, then the equality $X = Y$ holds for at most *half* of the $N-2$ numbers between 1 and $N-1$. Thus, as required, the probability of erring in giving the indicated yes/no answers for a randomly chosen K is no more than $\frac{1}{2}$, so that reiterating the procedure for, say, 200 such Ks yields the desired algorithm.

To complete the story, we must be able to tell efficiently whether K and N have any common factors, and to compute X and Y rapidly. The former can be achieved by applying Euclid's fast gcd algorithm, and for the latter there are also fast algorithms that we shall not dwell upon here.**

This completes the brief description of a fast probabilistic algorithm for testing primality. It is noteworthy that the other solution yields smaller error probabilities, in the sense that the fraction of witnesses to N's compositeness among the numbers from 1 to $N - 1$ is at least $\frac{3}{4}$, not $\frac{1}{2}$. Thus, as more Ks are chosen at random, the probability of error diminishes twice as fast. A 1-in-2^{200} effect can thus be achieved with 100 random Ks, not 200.

In contrast to primality testing, the problem of finding the *factors* of a number, even a number known ahead of time to be composite, does not seem to admit a polynomial-time probabilistic solution. Thus, while primality testing has become tractable for all practical purposes, factoring has not. As promised, we shall see some surprising applications of fast primality testing later, and interestingly, they hinge on precisely this difference between primality testing and factoring.

Fast Probabilistic Pattern Matching

Testing for primality is a striking example of a difficult, possibly intractable problem that becomes quite tractable when coin tossing is allowed. In a more humble vein, there are many examples of problems that *do* have reasonable solutions, but for which randomization can nevertheless improve things significantly. Let us consider an example.

Suppose we wish to determine whether a given pattern of symbols occurs in a lengthy text. Assume that the pattern is of length M and the text of length N (see Figure 11.2). Clearly, any algorithm that solves the problem must, in the worst case, consider every position in the entire text, so that $O(N)$ is clearly a lower bound on the time complexity of the problem. A naive algorithm calls for running through the text, and at each position checking whether the next M symbols of the text match the M symbols of the pattern perfectly. This may give rise to a worst-case time behavior of $O(N \times M)$, which is inadequate unless the pattern is very short. If we are looking for a short word in the *Encyclopaedia Britannica*, for example, this procedure may be feasible, even though N is approximately a billion. However, if the *Britannica* is to be searched for a symbol string of length 1000, or a million, the naive algorithm is hopelessly slow. While there are a number of rather clever linear-time algorithms for this problem, they are somewhat intricate, and their constants are too high to be of much help when M is also large. Most of them also require a considerable amount of memory space. Enter coin tossing.

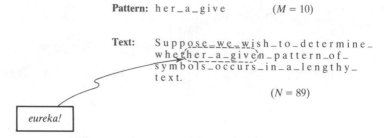

Pattern: h e r _ a _ g i v e $(M = 10)$

Text: S u p p o s e _ w e _ w i s h _ t o _ d e t e r m i n e _
w h e t h e r _ a _ g i v e n _ p a t t e r n _ o f _
s y m b o l s _ o c c u r s _ i n _ a _ l e n g t h y _
t e x t.

$(N = 89)$

eureka!

Figure 11.2   The pattern-matching problem.

The following algorithm uses an idea called **fingerprinting**. Instead of comparing the pattern symbol by symbol with every possible block of M contiguous symbols of text, we use a fingerprinting function that associates a number with each symbol string of length M. Then, as the algorithm runs through the text, considering each M-symbol block in turn, it is these representative numbers, rather than the strings themselves, that are compared. This sounds quite straightforward, but for it to improve the $O(M \times N)$ upper bound two requirements must be met: (1) the fingerprint number has to be much shorter than M, ideally of length $\log M$, and (2) the fingerprint of an M-symbol block must be computable in time less than $O(M)$, ideally in constant time. These requirements imply that a simple translation of an M-block of symbols into digits (as was done in Chapter 9 in the reductions between Turing machines and counter programs) will not work.

Instead, a prime number K of about $\log N$ binary digits is chosen at random, and the fingerprint of an M-symbol block B is taken to be the remainder of the digitized version of B modulo K. Thus, for the *Britannica* we would need a prime of about 30 binary digits, or about 10 decimal ones.

** Requirement (1) is satisfied by this definition, because remainders of divisions by K are between 0 and $K - 1$, and are hence no longer than $\log N$, which is on the order of the length of K itself. Requirement (2) is also satisfied. To see how, suppose (as in Chapter 9) that the text is constructed from an alphabet of 10 symbols, so that it can be considered simply as a lengthy decimal number. In this way, M-symbol blocks become simply M-digit numbers, which, to make things a little easier, are considered in reverse, the least significant digit being the leftmost one. In general, computing the fingerprint of an M-digit number (i.e., its remainder modulo K) takes a *non*-constant amount of time, depending on M. However, here we are traveling along a lengthy string of digits, and we can use the fingerprint of one M-digit number to rapidly compute that of the next. For example, consider the text

9 8 3 3 4 1 1 5 8 6 4 4 9 3 2 2 9 1 6 1 5 . . .

Let $M = 6$, and assume, as illustrated, that we have reached the ninth position (i.e., the second 8 from the left), having already computed the fingerprint J to be the remainder of the number 394 468 modulo the chosen prime K. The new fingerprint, call it J', is the remainder of 239 446 modulo K. Using the fact that the second of these six-digit numbers is obtained from the first by subtracting 8, dividing by 10 (leaving 39 446) and then adding 200 000, J' can be obtained from J with three simple arithmetical operations, carried out modulo K, i.e., with remainders modulo K in mind. Each of these operations takes only constant time, since, for example, there are only 10 possibilities for the number that has to be added, 200 000 in this example, and the remainders of these modulo K can be computed in advance and kept in a table. Consequently, the entire algorithm (which runs through the whole text, comparing every M symbols with the pattern until it finds matching fingerprints) can be easily seen to run in low-order linear time. More precisely, it takes time $O(N + M)$, with a very small constant and negligible memory space.   **

This is the good news. The bad news is that the algorithm, as it stands, may err. Obviously, if the fingerprints turn out to be *un*equal, the real strings (the pattern and the M symbol block against which it is being checked) must be unequal too. However, the converse is not necessarily true. Two different M-symbol blocks might have the very same fingerprint, since they are only required to yield the same remainder when divided by K. The algorithm might thus find incorrect 'matches'. However, like any good story, this one has a happy ending too.

It can be shown that if K is a random prime of length log N (and, as we know, primes are easy to find) the probability that one of the M-symbol blocks in the text will have the same remainder modulo K as the M-symbol pattern, although they are *un*equal as symbol strings, is about 1 in N. In other words, even if a malicious adversary tries to set up a text and pattern that will generate many different blocks with the same fingerprint, the fact that K is chosen at random *after* the text and pattern are given, guarantees that, probabilistically speaking, a mismatch will be erroneously declared to be a match only once during an entire run of the algorithm. To make sure that even this remote event will not lead to the wrong answer, we can modify the algorithm so that when a fingerprint match is found the algorithm will actually check the supposedly matching blocks symbol for symbol before stopping and declaring a match. If it so happens that this is the one case in which the fingerprint comparison errs, the algorithm will continue to search for other matches. As mentioned, there is only a very small chance that many of these expensive double checks will be necessary. Usually there will be only one in each run of the algorithm, and this will not change its $O(M + N)$ performance.

There is thus a choice of two versions of this algorithm. The first is guaranteed to run in linear-time but (with low probability) it might err, and the second is guaranteed not to err but (with low probability) it might run for longer than linear-time. There are names for these different kinds of probabilistic algorithms. Those that are always fast and probably correct are dubbed **Monte Carlo**, and those that are always correct and probably fast are termed **Las Vegas**. The probabilistic primality-testing algorithms are thus of the Monte Carlo variety, and for pattern matching we have one of each.

*   *   *

Probabilistic Complexity Classes

Probabilistic algorithms can be formalized using **probabilistic Turing machines**. These are nondeterministic Turing machines, in which the choices are made by tossing unbiased coins. One possible definition of the function computed by such a machine M is as follows. Given an input X, we say that M's output on X is Y if, with probability greater than $\frac{1}{2}$, M produces Y when run on X. If no Y is produced with such probability, then it is as if M does not halt on X at all. (Why does this result in a well-defined function?)

Actually, this definition is primarily of theoretical interest, and a slightly stronger one is more appropriate for capturing probabilistic algorithms such as those just presented for testing primality. The class RP (standing for Random Polynomial-time) is defined as the class of decision problems for which there is a polynomial-time probabilistic Turing machine with the following property. If the correct answer for an input X is *no*, the machine says *no* with probability 1, and if the correct answer is *yes*, the machine says *yes* with probability greater than $\frac{1}{2}$. Of course, the interest in RP problems stems from the fact that for any given X these possibly erroneous algorithms can be reiterated many times, achieving a diminishing probability of error, as explained earlier. Thus, the probabilistic primality-testing algorithms show that the compositeness problem (showing that a number is not prime) is in RP. (Why?) Equivalently, the primality problem is in co-RP, the class of problems whose complements are in RP. A co-RP problem thus admits a probabilistic polynomial-time Turing machine that with probability 1 says *yes* for yes inputs, and with probability greater than $\frac{1}{2}$ says *no* for no inputs.

The class RP lies between P and NP. Every tractable problem, i.e., one that is solvable in conventional polynomial-time, is in RP (why?), and every RP problem is in NP, and is thus solvable by magical nondeterminism in polynomial-time. (Why?) The co-RP problems are similarly between P and co-NP (see Figure 11.3, and compare with Figure 7.15). Here too, some researchers believe that the inclusions in the sequence:

$$P \subseteq RP \subseteq NP$$

are strict, but no one knows for sure. Primality, for example, might very well turn out to be in P; indeed all the NP problems might. It is thus interesting that in the realm of reasonable time we do not know whether coin tossing provides any real additional power, or whether magical coin tossing provides even more.

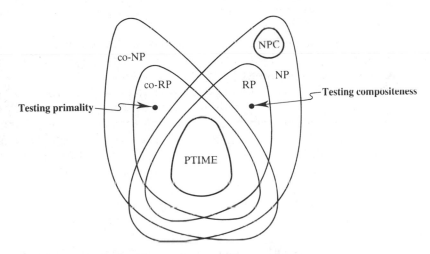

Figure 11.3 Random polynomial-time complexity classes.

As far as universal algorithmic power goes, the Church/Turing thesis extends to probabilistic algorithms too. Probabilism, like concurrency, cannot be used to solve the noncomputable, or the undecidable, at least not under these definitions: it is possible to simulate every probabilistic Turing machine by a conventional Turing machine, and, moreover, this can be done with at most an exponential loss of time. Thus, coin tossing does not extend our absolute algorithmic capabilities, but it does allow us to make better use of them. Perhaps it will eventually be possible to exploit coin tossing in rendering *provably* intractable problems solvable in practice. As of now, however, we know of no fast probabilistic algorithm for any provably intractable problem, only for ones that *might* be intractable, such as testing primality. We should add that some problems that are conjectured to be intractable are also conjectured to remain so even in the face of probabilism. Factoring numbers is one example, and we shall have occasion to return to it later.

*   *   *

Cryptography

Let us now turn to a new and exciting application area of algorithmics. It is described here because, in an indirect way, it makes use of probabilistic algorithms. Its novel feature, however, is the fact that it exploits the difficulty of solving other problems even in the presence of probabilism. This in itself is quite surprising, as we would expect negative results that establish lower bounds on the solvability of algorithmic problems to be of no practical value, except in preventing people from trying to improve on these bounds. Not so. Problems for which no good algorithms are known are crucial here.

The area in general is that of **cryptography**, and it concerns the need to communicate in secure, private, and reliable ways. Cryptography has numerous diverse applications in military, diplomatic, financial, and industrial circles. The need for good cryptographic protocols is greatly enhanced by the fast proliferation of computer-based communication systems. Increasingly, computers are becoming responsible for storing, manipulating, and transmitting anything from contracts, strategic commands, and business transactions, to ordinary confidential information such as military, medical, and personal data. This situation, in turn, makes problems of eavesdropping and tampering all the more acute.

One of the basic problems in cryptography is that of encrypting and decrypting data. How should we encode an important message in such a way that the receiver should be able to decipher it, but not an eavesdropper? Moreover, can the message be 'signed' by the sender, so that (1) the receiver can be sure that the sender alone could have sent it, (2) the sender cannot later deny having sent it, and (3) the receiver, having received the signed message, cannot sign any message in the sender's name, not even additional versions of the very message that has just been received? The signature issue is relevant to numerous applications, such as money transfer orders and electronic contracts. We could continue at length with such questions and their motivating examples, as there are many, and each raises new challenges. For some of these, elegant and useful solutions have been found, whereas for others there are none. We shall concentrate here on the encryption and signature problems.

Conventional cryptosystems are based on **keys**. These are used to translate a message M into its encrypted form, the **cipher-text** H, and then to decrypt it back into its original form. If we denote the general encryption procedure associated with the key by E, and the corresponding decryption procedure by D, we may write:

$$H = E(M) \quad \text{and} \quad M = D(H)$$

In other words, the encrypted version H is obtained by applying the E procedure to the message M, and the original M can be retrieved from H

by applying the D procedure to H. A simple example that we have all used in our childhood calls for the key K to be some number between 1 and 25, for E to be the procedure that replaces every letter with the one residing K positions further along in the alphabet, and for D to replace every letter with the one residing K positions earlier. In this way, E and D are mutually dual; D is E's inverse. (For purposes of counting letters the alphabet is considered to be cyclic; a follows z.)

This standard approach can be illustrated using the metaphor of a locked box. To exchange secret messages with a friend we should first prepare a box with a securable latch. Then we should buy a padlock with two keys, one for us and one for our friend. Thereafter, sending a message involves putting it in the box, locking the box using the key, and sending the box to its destination. No one can read the message *en route* unless they have the key, and since there are only two keys, kept by the sender and the intended receiver, the system is quite secure.

This approach has several drawbacks. First, it does not address the signature issue. Receivers can make up fake messages of their own and claim that they were sent by the sender, and the sender in turn can deny having sent authentic messages. Another major drawback concerns the need to cooperate in the selection and safe distribution of keys. In general, there are more than two parties involved in a communication network, and to enable privacy between any two there must be some secure way of distributing pairs of keys, one for each pair of parties. Given that the main applications of modern cryptography are in computerized environments, the digital keys cannot be distributed along the same (unsafe) communication channels as the encrypted messages. It would thus be necessary to resort to other far more expensive methods, such as personal delivery by a trusted courier. In applications involving hundreds of parties this is clearly not feasible.

Public-Key Cryptography

In 1976 a novel approach to the encryption, decryption, and signature problems was proposed, the **public-key cryptosystem**. It is perhaps best explained by a variant of the locked-box metaphor. The idea is to use a different kind of padlock, one that can be locked without a key, by simply clicking it shut. Opening such a lock, however, requires a key. To set up the mechanism for exchanging secret information, each potential user of the system goes out on his own and purchases such a padlock and key. He then writes his name on the padlock, and places it on the table, in public view. The key, however, is kept by the purchaser. Now, assume party B wants to send a message to party A. B puts the message into a box, goes to the table, picks up A's padlock and locks the box with it. For this, no key is needed. The box is then sent to A, who uses his key to open the lock and read the message. No one other than A has the key, and thus the message is safe. Notice that no prior communication or cooperation between A and B is needed. Once any party has decided to join the game, has bought a padlock and has made it public, that party can start receiving messages.

To understand how public-key systems can be used in digital, computerized environments, let us assume that messages are (perhaps lengthy) sequences of digits. Thus, some direct and straightforward method of translating symbols into digits has already been applied. Party A's padlock is just the encryption function E_A that transforms numbers into other numbers, and A's key is a secret way of computing the decryption function D_A. Thus, each party makes their encryption procedure public but keeps their decryption procedure private. To send a message to A, party B uses A's public encryption procedure E_A and sends A the number $E_A(M)$. Now A can decipher it using his private procedure D_A. For the method to work, both functions must be easy to compute, and the duality equation:

$$D_A(E_A(M)) = M$$

must hold for every message M. Most importantly, however, it should be impossible to deduce a method for computing the decryption function D_A from the publicly known encryption function E_A. Here 'impossible' really means 'computationally infeasible', so that what we really need is an appropriate kind of **one-way trapdoor function**; that is, a function E_A for each A, which is easy to compute, say in low-order polynomial-time, but whose inverse function D_A cannot be computed in polynomial-time unless A's secret key is known. The analogy to trapdoors is obvious: a trapdoor cannot be activated unless the existence or location of the secret lever or button is known. Later we shall discuss such functions.

As far as signatures go, it is obvious that, unlike a handwritten one, a digital signature that is to be used in a computerized cryptosystem must not only be a function of the signing party, but also of the message that is being signed. Otherwise, the receiver could make changes to the signed message before showing it to a neutral judge, or even attach the signature to a totally different message. If the message is a money-transfer order, the receiver can simply add a couple of crucial zeros to the sum and claim the new signed message to be authentic.

To use one-way trapdoor functions for signing messages too we require that the E_A and D_A functions are *mutual* inverses; that is, not only should the decryption of any encrypted message M yield M in its original form, but also the *en*cryption of a *de*crypted message has to yield the original message. Thus we require both:

$$D_A(E_A(M)) = M \quad \text{and} \quad E_A(D_A(M)) = M$$

Since a message is but a number and both E_A and D_A are functions on numbers, it makes sense, at least mathematically, to apply D_A to a message M. But what *practical* sense does it make? Why would anyone be interested in applying a decryption function to an unencrypted message? The answer is simple. In order to sign it! Here is the way it works (see Figure 11.4).

Party A   **Party B**

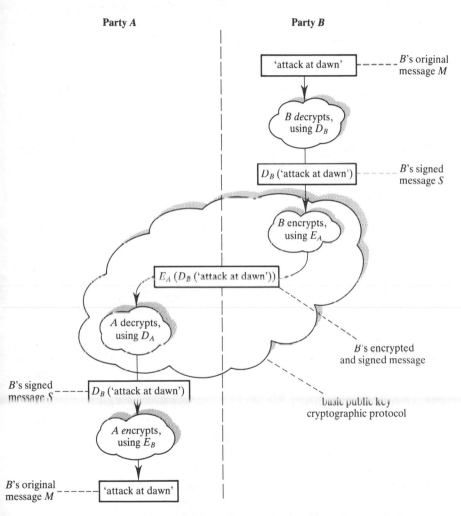

Figure 11.4   Sending signed and encrypted messages using public-key cryptography.

If party B wants to send party A a *signed* message M, B first computes his special message-dependent signature S, by applying his own private *de*cryption function D_B to M. Thus:

$$S = D_B(M)$$

He then encrypts the signature S in the usual public-key fashion, using A's public encryption function E_A, and sends the result, namely, $E_A(D_B(M))$, to A. Upon receiving this strange-looking number, A first decrypts it using his private decryption function D_A. The result is $D_A(E_A(S))$, which is really $D_A(E_A(D_B(M)))$. However, since D_A undoes anything that E_A has tied up, the result of this will be just S, or $D_B(M)$. (Notice that A cannot yet read the message M, nor is he in any way convinced that B was really the sender.) Finally, A applies B's public *en*cryption function E_B to S, yielding:

$$E_B(S) = E_B(D_B(M)) = M$$

Thus, all at once, A sees the message M and can also be quite sure that only B could have sent it. This follows from the fact that the functions are such that no number will result in M when subjected to E_B unless that number was precisely $D_B(M)$, and no one besides B could have produced $D_B(M)$, since the decryption function D_B is B's closely guarded secret. Moreover, A cannot sign any other message in B's name, as signing entails applying B's secret function D_B to the new message.

However, there is still the possibility that A will be able to send the very same message M to some other party, say C, with B's signature. The reason is that during the process A has possession of $D_B(M)$, which he can then encrypt using E_C, sending the result to C, who will think it came from B. This might be critical in case the message M is 'I, General B, hereby order you to set out on the following dangerous mission: ...' To prevent this situation, the name of the receiver in the message should always be included, as in 'I, General B, hereby order you, Major A, to set out on the following dangerous mission: ...' Such mischief on A's behalf (and at C's expense) would then become impossible. Of course, this means that it should be impossible for A to compute the function D_B without the right key, even for some slightly modified message M' which is very close to the message M for which he has access to $D_B(M)$.

The concept of public-key cryptography thus sounds very promising. To make it work, however, requires that we find appropriate definitions of the keys and the corresponding E and D procedures, which enjoy all the nice properties we have discussed. In other words, we are interested in one-way trapdoor functions, and if we want to use the signature feature they must also satisfy the mutual inverse property.

It is by no means clear that such functions exist. In fact, it could be argued that the requirements are paradoxical, almost self-contradictory. Where do we find a one-way function with a really hard-to-compute inverse? Taking square roots, for example, is not that much harder than its converse, squaring, and moving backwards in the alphabet is as easy as moving forwards. In addition, the difficult direction must become easy to compute, given the secret key. Are there such functions? We shall now see that there are, but the difficulty of computing the inverse without the key will rest on conjectured, not proven, intractability. The question of whether there are such functions with *provably* intractable inverses is still open.

The RSA Cryptosystem

About a year after the concept of public-key cryptosystems emerged, the first method to implement it was found. The resulting system, called the **RSA cryptosystem**, after the initials of its inventors, is described here. Since then, several other definitions have been suggested, some of which have consequently been shown not to be secure. The RSA approach, however, remains one of the most interesting of them all, and, as explained later, there is reason to believe that it is really unbreakable.

It is important to understand what it means for a public-key cryptosystem to be broken, or cracked. Since the integrity of a public-key system hinges on the difficulty of computing the D functions without the right keys, breaking such a system involves finding a fast algorithm for computing the D function given knowledge of the corresponding E function. If signatures are used, one might also have knowledge of several examples of messages M and their cipher-texts $D(M)$. Thus, while cracking certain kinds of conventional cryptographic methods might require lucky guesses, or sophisticated ways of finding some secret code or number, cracking public-key cryptosystems is really tantamount to finding clever polynomial-time algorithms for certain problems that are believed to be of inherent super polynomial-time behavior. And this is algorithmic work *par excellence*.

The RSA system is based on the contrast between testing primality and factoring. The first, as we have seen, can be carried out fast, using a probabilistic algorithm, but for the latter there are no known fast methods, not even probabilistic ones, and factoring is actually conjectured not to be even in RP. Each party A, secretly and at random, chooses two large prime numbers P and Q, of length, say, around 150 digits, and multiplies them, resulting in the product $N = P \times Q$. Party A keeps the primes secret, but makes their product (as well as another quantity, as explained later) public. The crucial fact is that, given the product, no one except A himself can find the two prime factors. Here are the details.

** Following the choice of P and Q, party A then chooses a large number K (say 300 digits long) which is to have no common factors with the product of $P-1$ and $Q-1$ (call that product R), except, of course, the trivial factor 1. Finally, A computes the number G to be the **multiplicative inverse** of

K modulo R, meaning that $K \times G$ yields a remainder of 1 when divided by R. Symbolically:

$$K \times G \equiv 1 \ (\text{mod} \ (P - 1) \times (Q - 1))$$

This completes A's process of going out and buying a padlock and key. The padlock is the pair $\langle G, N \rangle$, which is made public, and the secret key is K. The prime factors of N, namely, P and Q, are also kept secret. To be quite precise, we should indicate that these are all A's numbers, by writing them as P_A, Q_A, N_A, K_A, and G_A. Other parties choose their own numbers P_B, P_C, Q_B, Q_C, etc.

What do the encryption and decryption procedures look like? Well, assume B wants to send a message M to A. To encrypt it, B uses A's public pair $\langle G_A, N_A \rangle$. B first breaks M up into blocks of numbers, each between 0 and $N_A - 1$. Hereafter, we can assume that there is only one such number M, since the entire process is carried out for each of them. To obtain the cipher-text H, party B raises M to the power G_A, modulo N_A:

$$H = E_A(M) \equiv M^{G_A}(\text{mod} \ N_A)$$

That is, H is the remainder obtained when M^{G_A} is divided by N_A. This completes the definition of the encryption procedure. Notice that since all arithmetic is done modulo N_A, all numbers involved are between 0 and $N_A - 1$ so that both the message and its cipher-text are within the same range of numbers. Decryption is very similar: A, upon receiving the cipher text H, raises it to the power of his secret key K_A, also modulo N_A. Thus:

$$D_A(M) \equiv M^{K_A}(\text{mod} \ N_A)$$

It is now easy to see that:

$$D_A(E_A(M)) = E_A(D_A(M)) \equiv M^{G_A \times K_A} \ (\text{mod} \ N_A)$$

It is not so easy to see, but it is true nevertheless, that by the special way K_A and G_A were defined this last quantity is just M (mod N_A), so that decrypting the encrypted message yields the message in its original form. The fact that not only $D_A(E_A(M))$ yields M but also $E_A(D_A(M))$, and that this is true for *any* M, is what makes the RSA method fitting for signatures too.

Of course, we have to show how all the computations involved can indeed be carried out efficiently, and that $D_A(M)$ cannot be computed without knowledge of A's key K_A. The entire setting-up process starts with each party choosing two large primes, a feat that can be achieved quite painlessly using a probabilistic primality-testing algorithm repeatedly for random 150-digit numbers, as explained earlier. Of course, the chance that two parties will come up with precisely the same primes is negligible. Once P, Q, and N, their product, have been determined (we omit the A subscript here for clarity) it is easy to find an appropriate K, i.e., a large random number having no factors in common with $(P - 1) \times (Q - 1)$. Any prime that is larger than both P and Q will be fine, so that another random search for a large prime with a few more digits than the larger of P or Q will do the job.

The last step of preparation is to compute G from K, P, and Q. This, as well as the actual computations of M^G and M^K modulo N, can be carried out quite rapidly using relatively simple procedures for exponentiation modulo N and for a certain version of the greatest common divisor (gcd) algorithm. The details are omitted as they are somewhat technical in nature.   **

As far as the security of the RSA system goes, if we can factor large numbers in reasonable time the system is immediately broken, since then an adversary could take the public product N, find its factors (i.e., the two secret primes P and Q), and use them, together with the public number G, to compute the decryption key K. Dually, all the approaches suggested so far for attempting to break the RSA system have been shown to yield fast solutions to the factoring problem too. In other words, as of now, for every approach X suggested as an attack on the security of the RSA system, it has been shown that either X will not work, or that if in principle it does work, it results in a fast algorithm for factoring. However, since factoring is strongly conjectured to have no fast algorithm, not even a probabilistic one, and none of the proposed attacks on the RSA system have yielded such an algorithm, people strongly believe RSA to be safe.

There is a slightly different version of the RSA system whose security is *provably* equivalent to fast factoring. In other words, it has been shown that *any* method for cracking that particular cryptosystem will yield a fast factoring algorithm. It would be nice to be able to make this stronger statement about the original RSA system too. However, no one has been able to prove it yet.

It is worth re-emphasizing the fundamental facets of algorithmics that are involved in such ideas as the RSA cryptosystem. They include conventional sequential algorithms, apparently intractable algorithmic problems, probabilistic algorithms, and, if the method is to work reasonably fast on large numbers, then either very efficient programming or the design of special-purpose hardware.

Playing Poker Over the Phone

Public-key cryptographic functions can be used in many seemingly unrelated applications. Consider two people, A and B, who want to play poker over the phone. We can assume that each player has access to a computer, in case there are computations to be carried out during the game, and that digital information can be transmitted over the telephone line. There is no neutral referee who will deal the cards or who has global knowledge of the players' hands and/or of the cards remaining in the deck; everything must be carried out by the two players themselves. It is not too difficult to imagine less playful situations of similar nature, such as digital contract negotiations.

Obviously, each player must have some information that can be kept secret during the game, such as his hand of cards. Now, in an ordinary face-to-face game, a player cannot claim to have an ace unless he can demonstrate it by actually exposing the ace as one of the cards being held. The electronic analog of this is to wait until the game is over, and then allow each player to inspect the other's entire sequence of moves, including his private activities. This will prevent ordinary kinds of cheating.

Cheating, however, is not the only problem. A little thought reveals that dealing the cards constitutes the real challenge. We have to design a protocol that starts out with 52 (digitally represented) cards, and results in each of the two players holding a random hand of five cards, with the remaining 42 left in a pile for future use. What makes the problem far from trivial is that we must ensure that neither of the players knows the other player's hand. At first sight this sounds impossible. We can start out by somehow encrypting and shuffling the cards. However, since at least one of the players must be able to decrypt the encryption that is used, it would appear that one of them will know which of the cards has been dealt to the other, or that one of them will be able to arrange for himself to have a particularly good hand. Can we prescribe a fair and random deal? The answer is yes.

The idea is to use one-way trapdoor functions, as in public-key cryptography, but in this case we require them to have an additional property, **commutativity**, over and above the properties required for encryption and decryption. Two functions are commutative if applying both of them to any input yields the same result, regardless of the order in which they were applied. Here we require that the encryption functions are commutative; that is, for any message M we must have:

$$E_B(E_A(M)) = E_A(E_B(M))$$

This ensures that if a message is encrypted by A and then by B it can be decrypted first by A and then by B, since the double encryption will yield $E_B(E_A(M))$, which is the same as $E_A(E_B(M))$, whereby A's decryption will yield $D_A(E_A(E_B(M)))$, which is just $E_B(M)$, and finally, B's decryption will yield $D_B(E_B(M))$, which is simply the original M. The RSA functions described earlier can be shown to satisfy the commutativity requirement too (how?), hence they would appear to be adequate for the present application too.

In terms of locked boxes, commutativity means that the latch has enough room for two padlocks that can be clicked shut, side by side in any order, rather than one over the other. In this way, the first padlock to be attached need not be the last one to be removed.

As before, each player starts by selecting his own personal E and D functions. However, in contrast to public-key cryptography, none of the information is made public until the game is over, not even the encryption functions. Here is how our players A and B go about dealing themselves five cards out of a pack of 52. (Figure 11.5 illustrates the procedure, and for simplicity it shows the dealing of two cards each, out of a total of six.) First, A uses his own encryption function E_A to encrypt descriptions of the 52 cards. Recall that the entire game sequence is later checked, with both players' functions being exposed, so that A cannot encrypt an illegal set of cards, having, say, 20 aces. Using coin tossing, or any other means, A then shuffles the encrypted deck and sends the resulting list to B. Even though he knows precisely what the 52 encrypted messages look like when decrypted, B has no way of knowing which card is which, since they arrive in an order unknown to him, and E_A and D_A are A's closely kept secrets.

Now for the dealing itself. B selects ten encrypted cards, five of which he encrypts a second time using B's own function E_B. He then sends A all

Figure 11.5 Dealing cards over the phone.

ten. Thus, B now has 42 boxes locked with A's padlock, and A has ten – five locked with his own padlock and five locked with both padlocks. A now unlocks his own ten locks; that is, A decrypts the ten messages received from B using his decryption function D_A. The first five of these now become unencrypted card descriptions, and henceforth A regards them as his hand. The other five are still locked with E_B (here is where commutativity is needed – the reader should check this), and A sends them back to B. Upon receipt, B unlocks them using E_B, thus exposing his own five-card hand.

The hands are obviously disjoint, and are all different from the remaining 42 cards. Moreover, neither player knows what the other player's hand is. B does not know anything about A's hand, although B was the one who actually dealt the cards, because he selected the 10 cards from a shuffled deck that was encrypted using a function he has no way of decrypting. Similarly, A does not know anything about B's hand, although A does know how to decrypt the original encryptions, because B's five cards were encrypted a second time (by B) using a function that A has no way of decrypting. Thus the deal appears to be valid, fair, and as secure as any dealing method.

Furthermore, the reader will have no difficulty figuring out how the game continues. The only nontrivial part is when a player has to take a new card from the remaining pile, a procedure that can be carried out using precisely the same idea as in dealing the initial hands.

Despite these facts, it turns out that there are rather serious problems when it comes to implementing this dealing protocol. It has been shown, for example, that the RSA encryption functions are inadequate here. While messages encrypted using them cannot, as far as we know, be actually *deciphered* in reasonable time, certain *partial* information *can* be extracted from them. Thus, it is possible to manipulate the encrypted version of a card and figure out certain mathematical properties of its original (digital) version, such as whether it is a quadratic residue modulo an appropriate prime. This is a little like saying that one player can figure out the color (red or black) of the other's cards – clearly an unacceptable compromise in most card games.

One *ad hoc* way to overcome such problems is for party A to describe the cards prior to encryption in his own informal language, the precise form the description takes being unknown to B ahead of time, or to insert random letters and digits therein; a similar idea would be used by party B too. In this way there would appear to be no way for one player to gain anything from knowing, say, the quadratic residuity of the original descriptions of the other's cards. We should realize, however, that this approach might not be really secure, as we cannot *prove* that no relevant information about the cards leaks out. Other, more provably secure, protocols for dealing cards have indeed been discovered. They are themselves probabilistic, but are considerably more complicated than the simple and elegant one described here.

*   *   *

Research on Probabilistic Algorithms and Their Applications

Although by now it must sound repetitious, the topics discussed in this chapter are also the subject of intensive research. Probabilism in algorithmics is an exciting but relatively recent idea. Numerous new applications have been found, and many results have been established, mostly during the past ten years or so.

As with parallelism and concurrency, researchers are working in essentially two different directions. The first is the search for efficient randomized algorithms for conventional input/output-oriented algorithmic problems (this is analogous to the quest for efficient parallelized algorithms for such problems), and the second is finding ways to utilize coin tossing in the solution of problems of inherently perpetual, ongoing nature, which typically involve distributed processing. Probabilistic primality testing is an example of the former and the coin-tossing protocol for the dining philosophers is an example of the latter.

Researchers are interested in both kinds of probabilistic algorithms, Monte Carlo and Las Vegas, and in others too, and also in the relationships between them.

Some of the most difficult problems arise when concurrency and probabilism are combined. If in Chapter 10 we claimed that concurrency renders specification and verification subtle and slippery, adding coin tossing makes them doubly so. Verifying formally that the probabilistic dining philosophers protocol is deadlock free with probability 1, is a very delicate and tedious chore. Researchers are interested in finding satisfactory proof methods for probabilistic protocols and algorithms, and also in constructing probabilistic dynamic logics, which enable many different properties of such algorithms to be stated and proved in rigorous mathematical fashion.

The classification of algorithmic problems into probabilistic complexity classes is another interesting research topic. Classes such as RP, co-RP, and their intersection (sometimes called ZPP), as well as a number of additional classes, are being investigated, both from a concrete point of view and from a more abstract one. In the concrete approach, the aim is to try to find interesting problems that reside in these classes and to prove that others do not. In the abstract approach, the aim is to seek the inherent properties of these classes, and their relationship to other complexity classes, both probabilistic and nonprobabilistic ones.

** As an example, recall the Boolean networks of Chapter 10. There we claimed that every effectively computable algorithmic problem can be solved by a *uniform* set of Boolean circuits. That is, for every such problem there is an effective way of generating the circuit that solves the problem for inputs of a given size N (see Figure 10.3). It is easy to see that if the original problem is in P, that is, it is solvable in polynomial-time, then these circuits can be made to be of size polynomial in N. It has been shown that problems in RP, that is, those solvable in *random* polynomial-time, also have polynomial-sized circuits. It follows, perhaps surprisingly, that for every N there is a reasonably sized circuit for testing the primality of N-digit numbers. However, we do not know whether these circuits can be uniformly constructed in polynomial-time. If we did, we would have a proof that the primality problem is actually in P. (How?)   **

A particularly interesting direction is the connection between probabilistic algorithms and the probabilistic analysis of conventional algorithms. In Chapter 6 we briefly discussed the average-case behavior of sequential algorithms and in Chapter 7 we mentioned certain approximation approaches to NP-complete and other problems. In both cases probabilistic reasoning is involved, since certain assumptions have to be made about the probability with which certain inputs occur. The analysis addresses questions regarding the algorithm's behavior on average, or on 'almost all' inputs. In this way, probability dictates the form that the inputs will take, while the algorithm itself is totally deterministic. Here things are the other way around. Instead of worrying about the probabilistic distribution of the inputs, the algorithm itself, by tossing coins, generates the probabilities that we later reason about. It turns out that for some purposes, these two approaches are actually equivalent. In a certain technical sense, the results of the coin tossing can be regarded as additional inputs, given at the start, and conversely, generating a probabilistic distribution on the real inputs can be shifted into the algorithm itself. Thus, the probabilistic complexity of conventional algorithms and the conventional complexity of probabilistic algorithms can be viewed as two sides of the same coin, so to speak.

Applying probabilistic algorithms to cryptography, digital signatures, digital contract signing, and the security and fault tolerance of large systems, constitutes another attractive area of research. As explained earlier, besides the highly applicative nature of such work, its appeal stems from the fact that not only ideas leading to efficient solutions to some algorithmic problems can be exploited, but also *negative* results regarding the (apparent) difficulty of solving others. It is of interest that in virtually all of these applications the negative results are based on deep conjectures concerning nonpolynomial-time lower bounds on certain problems.

One issue that has not been addressed at all here is the way in which computers can be made to toss fair, unbiased coins. Allusion has repeatedly been made to this ability in the algorithms presented, but the implicit assumption that it can be done is unjustified, since a real digital computer is a totally deterministic entity, and hence, in principle, all of its actions can be predicted in advance. Therefore, a computer cannot generate truly random numbers, and hence cannot simulate the truly random tossing of fair coins. There are a number of ways of overcoming this problem. One is to appeal to a physical source. For example, our computer could be attached to a small robot hand, which in order to choose 0 or 1 at random scoops up a handful of sand from a large container, counts the sand grains contained therein, decide 0 if the number is even and 1 otherwise, and then tosses the sand back into the container. This approach has several obvious drawbacks.

Another approach involves so-called **pseudo-random** numbers. In a word, a pseudo-random sequence is one that cannot be distinguished from a truly random sequence in polynomial-time. It can be shown that if provably one-way functions exist (that is, if we could *prove* that the hard direction is really intractable), then pseudo-random number **generators** also exist. A generator is given a single number, the **seed**, as an input, and it thereafter keeps producing pseudo-random numbers forever. Thus, rather curiously, the very ability to generate the random numbers that are needed in probabilistic algorithms also hinges on conjectures regarding the intractability of other problems. If problem P is truly hard, then problem Q can be made easy by appealing to a probabilistic algorithm that uses P's hardness to generate coin tosses that are impossible to distinguish from truly random tosses.

Thus, the last word has not been said even about the most fundamental issue underlying the application of probabilism to algorithmics: the possibility of algorithmically simulating true, or almost true, randomness.

*   *   *

Theorems that Are Almost True?

At the end of Chapter 5 we discussed the four-color theorem, whose proof was carried out in part using a computer program. In a sense, this theorem cannot be claimed to have been proved in full, since no one has proved the correctness of the program, the compiler, or the operating system involved. On the other hand, if we really want to be certain that the theorem is true, we can always try to prove the correctness of these pieces of software. Thus, the proof of the theorem *is* amenable to formal verification, at least in principle.

It is interesting to imagine a different situation, which, as far as we know, has not occurred yet. What would happen if some important problem in mathematics were to be resolved with the help of a *probabilistic* algorithm, say of the Monte Carlo variety, with a diminishing probability of error? Could we then put a 'Q.E.D.' at the end of the proof? The difficulty here is that even after formally verifying program, compiler, and operating system, we will only have established rigorously that the process is error free with, say, probability $1 - 1/2^{200}$. What shall we do? Shall we claim an *almost theorem*, or a *very high probability theorem*? Will mathematicians have sufficient confidence in such a result to base further developments on it? We shall probably just have to wait and see.

Some people dismiss the whole issue by pointing out that *all* mathematical proofs have some chance of being wrong, as they are carried out by error-prone humans. And indeed, many proofs, even published ones, have been found to be flawed. This actually happened to the four-color theorem itself on a number of previous occasions. Here the situation is different, since we *do* have a rigorously verified proof of the theorem. However, one of its components, the probabilistic algorithm, is provably correct with very high probability only, a probability that can be made as high as desired by running the algorithm a little longer. As long as we use probabilistic algorithms only for petty, down-to-earth matters such as wealth, health, and survival, we can easily make do with very-likely-to-be-correct answers to our questions. The same, it seems, cannot be said for our quest for absolute mathematical truth.

And we have cast lots
Nehemiah 10: 35

for they have chosen their own ways
Isaiah 66: 3

12

Algorithmics and Intelligence

OR

Are They Better at It Than Us?

Intelligence is a wellspring of life to him who has it
Proverbs 16: 22

Son of man, can these bones live?
Ezekiel 37: 3

The question of whether computers can think, someone once said, is just like the question of whether submarines can swim. The analogy is quite apt. Although we all know more or less what submarines are capable of – and indeed they *can* do things that are akin to swimming – 'real' swimming is something we associate with entities of organic nature, such as humans and fishes, not with submarines. Similarly, although by now the reader must have a pretty good idea of what algorithmics is all about, and hence of the capabilities of computers, real thinking is associated in our minds with human beings, and perhaps also with apes and dolphins, but not with silicon-based collections of bits and bytes.

This somewhat less technical chapter is concerned with the relationship between machine-based computation and human intelligence. The issue is an emotionally loaded one, and almost anything anyone says about it causes heated controversy. For our own part, we shall try to avoid these controversies as best as we can. Instead, we shall discuss the relevance or irrelevance of the field of algorithmics as described in this book to the computer-based simulation of human intelligence. Mostly problems and difficulties will be pointed out, rather than solutions.

The area of research most relevant to this chapter is **artificial intelligence**, or AI for short. In most places, AI is carried out in computer science departments, and in others there is either a separate department for AI or an interdepartmental group connected, perhaps, to computer science, cognitive psychology, and neurobiology. The fact that this is the closing chapter should not lead the reader to conclude that the sole reason for studying algorithmics is rooted in the possibility that one day we shall be able to computerize intelligence. However intriguing this idea may sound, the task of writing this book has not been undertaken merely to report on the scientific basis for artificial intelligence. Algorithmics stands on its own merit, and a strong case for its importance, depth, and applicability can easily be made, whether the subject matter of this chapter is considered or not. In fact, the treatment of hard-core algorithmics in this book was completed at the close of the previous chapter. Here we deal with a new, 'softer' dimension. It is a fascinating and exciting one, but it is also controversial and speculative. Mainly, as we shall see, it is quite different.

In purely technical terms, it might be said that the present chapter focuses on another liberty that can be taken when designing algorithms, to be added to those of parallelism and coin tossing that were treated in Chapters 10 and 11. This liberty involves the introduction of rules of thumb, educated guesses of sorts, or, to use the accepted term, **heuristics**. The nature of this new facility and its motivating examples set it apart from virtually all of the issues discussed heretofore, and this is the reason for its being treated last. While heuristics represent the special nature of the *control* part of intelligent programs, there are also difficulties involved in representing and manipulating the *data* relevant to them, namely, **knowledge** in its various guises.

Some Robot Stories

Talking of swimming, here is what happened one day in one of the most respectable centers of American computer science. A delegation from the US navy visited the center to find out whether they could use the knowledge accumulated there to build a robot that, all on its own, would be able to dive underneath ships and carry out submerged maintenance chores. The scientists proudly showed these people the results of their latest efforts in robotics – a computerized robot arm connected to a video camera, which could read in, comprehend, and execute commands such as 'build a tower of three blocks', or 'place the red pyramid on the blue block'. Out of courtesy, the members of the delegation listened, observed, and then politely took their leave, deeply disappointed. These people had no idea of the incredible difficulty involved in achieving even such mundane behavior in an automatic computerized system. At one stage in the development of its controlling software, the robot arm would try to build three-block towers starting at the top! It was no small matter to 'teach' the robot about gravity, even within its very limited world of a few blocks and pyramids.

Another story involving the same group of researchers tells of a commercial company that claimed to have manufactured a robot that would carry out routine housekeeping tasks in response to commands given in plain English, such as 'wash the dishes,' or 'make lunch for four.' The company was to demonstrate the robot's abilities in public at one of the local department stores. The scientists of the group, knowing fully well what could be achieved with the current state of the art, were certain that this was a fraud. Thus, while the many spectators who had gathered to behold the miracle were busy up front taking in the scene, they were busy behind the scene trying to discover the trick. Surely enough, after a while they found the person who was using a radio transmitter to physically control the robot's movements, giving the impression that it was responding to the instructor's commands.

These stories seem to contradict the statement made in Chapter 1, to the effect that computers can control extremely sophisticated industrial robots that construct complex items consisting of numerous components. There is no contradiction. Those robots are programmed to carry out long and intricate sequences of operations by a carefully prepared recipe. In general, they can be reprogrammed to carry out different tasks, and sometimes they are able to adapt their behavior to accommodate changing situations. However, they are not able to take a look at their surroundings, decide what has to be done, and then make a plan and execute it to completion. For this reason no one knows how to program a robot to build a bird's nest from a pile of twigs. There have been some successes in dealing with very limited worlds of blocks and pyramids, but not with twigs of all shapes and sizes, or with a large and diverse array of machine components. Dealing with these requires levels of intelligence that are far beyond present-day capabilities. Even the ability to take in a simple scene such as a normal living room (using some visual sensory equipment) and 'understand' it, something every child can do, is far beyond current possibilities.

Another example given in Chapter 1 concerned the contrast between computerized tomography (synthesizing a cross-section of the brain from a large number of X-ray images taken from increasing angles) and the ability to deduce a person's age from an ordinary photograph. Here too there is no contradiction. While the former task is carried out with the aid of complex, but well-defined, algorithmic procedures, the second requires real intelligence. Computerizing intelligence, making it algorithmic, is something we know far too little about.

*   *   *

Algorithmic Intelligence?

What *is* intelligence? There is nothing to be gained by competing with philosophers, cognitive psychologists, and AI researchers regarding this question. However, from a layman's point of view it would appear that the very notion of artificial intelligence, or, to rename it to fit in with the rest of the book, **algorithmic intelligence**, is a contradiction in terms. We tend to view intelligence as our quintessential *non*programmable, and hence non-algorithmic, feature. To many people the very idea of an intelligent machine does not sound right.

Various arguments have been put forward to render unthinkable the concept of an intelligent thinking machine. To think, some say, necessarily involves emotions and feelings, and no computer can hate, love, or become angry. Others claim that thinking intelligently necessarily entails originality, and no computer can originate anything unless programmed ahead of time to do so, in which case it is no longer original. Suitable counter arguments can be formulated for most such arguments, but we will not discuss them here. It does appear, however, that a machine claimed to be intelligent must, at the very least, be able to exhibit human-like intellectual behavior. For this we do not require it to walk, see or talk like a human, only to reason and respond like one. Furthermore, whatever the agreed on criteria for intelligence turn out to be, *someone* ought to be able to check whether a candidate machine fulfills them. And who, if not a real, intelligent human being, is qualified to carry out such a test? This brings us to the idea that a machine ought to be labeled intelligent if it can convince an average human being that in terms of its intellect it is no different from another average human being.

The Turing Test

How can we set up things to make such a test possible? In 1950 Alan Turing[†] proposed the following method, now commonly called the **Turing test**. The test takes place in three rooms. In the first there is a human interrogator A, in the next there is another human, and in the third the candidate computer. The interrogator A knows the other two only by the names B and C, but does not know which is which. The three rooms are equipped with computer terminals, and A's terminal is connected to those of B and C (see Figure 12.1). Now, A is given, say, an hour in which to determine the correct identities of B and C. A is free to address any questions or statements whatsoever to B and/or C, and the computer has to make its best effort to deceive A, giving the impression of being human. The computer is said to pass the test if A does not know its identity after the

---

[†] This is the same Turing from the thesis and the machines.

allotted time has elapsed. (Actually, we require the computer to pass a number of one-session tests, with different interrogators, in order to minimize the possibility that A simply guesses which is which.)

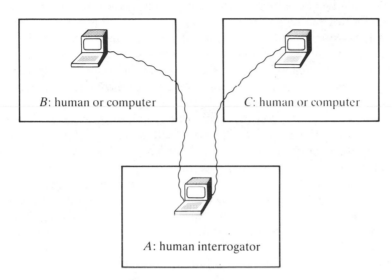

Figure 12.1   The Turing test.

Before proceeding, it should be said that no computer has ever come even marginally close to passing this test, and many researchers believe that if the interrogator tries hard enough none ever will.

Let us try to get a feel for the immense difficulty involved. Consider how an intelligent program would have to react to the following questions by A:

(1) *Are you a computer?*

(2) *What is the time?*

(3) *When was President Kennedy assassinated?*

(4) *What is 2276448 × 7896?*

(5) *Can white win in one move from the following chess position: . . . ?*

(6) *Describe your parents.*

(7) *How does the following poem strike you: . . . ?*

(8) *What do you think of Charles Dickens?*

(9) *What is your opinion on the arms race, in view of the fact that millions of people around the globe suffer from starvation?*

Notice that the programmed computer must be able to converse freely in a natural language such as English. We waive the need for it to hear and talk, and hence the electronic links. However, understanding and synthesizing language are considered to be two of the cornerstones of human intelligence, and thus they are required prerequisites here.

The first two questions are rather easy. The answer to the first should be '*no*', and for the second the program can utilize a built-in clock that is present in most computers. Question (3) requires the program to be able to access a very large pool of knowledge, comparable to the knowledge of a human being. Question (4) looks easy – computers seem to do best on such questions – but it is nevertheless subtle, since the computer must wait for a while before answering; an immediate answer would give away its identity. Question (5), of course, requires it to have some knowledge of chess, including the ability to reason about a new position. Although answers to the likes of question (6) could be prepared in advance, *A* might respond to an answer by pursuing a certain unexpected detail to which the computer might not have a ready-made answer. Questions (7), (8), and (9) are far more difficult, as they illustrate the need for exhibiting preferences, opinions, positions, and emotions, explaining them and relating them to others. In short, the competing computer must be endowed with a real personality.

One of the difficulties in programming a computer to pass the Turing test is the great diversity of areas that the conversation can lead to. There have been some apparent successes in imitating human conversation in very limited areas of discourse. A program called ELIZA, written in 1966, was able to give an impressive performance as a psychoanalyst. So impressive, in fact, that people were known to actually 'confide' in the program in ways they would never confide in a human being! Here are a couple of typical exchanges:

Person: *My wife says I am often depressed.*

ELIZA: *I'm sorry to hear you are depressed.*

Person: *The truth is I am quite unhappy.*

ELIZA: *Do you think coming here will help you not to be unhappy?*

Person: *Well, perhaps by talking to you I will find out why I hate my brother.*

ELIZA: *Tell me more about your family.*

The interesting thing about ELIZA is the fact that it cannot be said to be intelligent by any reasonable measure. In fact, despite its apparent sophistication, ELIZA is really extremely brainless, so that insofar as it gives the impression of being a thoughtful therapist, it is really a shrewd cheat. At times, it simply zeros in on a particular word or phrase that it has been taught to look out for, and responds by choosing, virtually at random, one of a small number of fixed responses. An excellent example of this is the response 'Tell me more about your family', triggered by the word 'brother'. Other times, ELIZA merely turns an incoming sentence into a question or a somewhat content-free statement, as in the exchange concerning the person's unhappiness. To do this, it utilizes a simple mechanism for figuring out the coarse structure of the input sentences.

Strange things happen on really trying to test ELIZA's intelligence, instead of just pouring out one's problems. In fact, if we said 'I was a sister in a monastery in Burma', or even 'I admire Sister Teresa', the program might very well respond with the same irrelevant response: 'Tell me more about your family'. Its response to the question about the arms race is bound to be equally amusing. ELIZA, of course, has no chance of passing the Turing test. In fact, it was not intended to. The motivation behind ELIZA was to show that it is easy to *appear* intelligent, at least for a short while, to a sympathetic observer, and within a narrow domain of discourse. To be *really* intelligent, however, is quite a different matter.

To further appreciate the difference between the genuine intelligence required to pass Turing's test, and the shallow, yet deviously deceptive nature of ELIZA's conversational abilities, here is a hypothetical exchange between the Turing test interrogator A and a really intelligent candidate, say B:

A: *What is a zupchok?*

B: *I have no idea.*

A: *A zupchok is a flying novel-writing whale. It has been carefully cultivated in a laboratory over several generations to ensure that its fins evolve into wing-like things that enable it to fly. It has also been gradually taught to read and write. It has a thorough knowledge of modern literature, and has the ability to write publishable mystery stories.*

B: *How weird!*

A: *Do you think zupchoks exist?*

B: *No way. They cannot.*

A: *Why?*

B: *For many reasons. First of all, our genetic engineering capabilities are far from adequate when it comes to turning fins into wings, not to mention our inability to cause 10-ton engineless creatures to defy gravity just by flapping those things. Secondly, the novel-writing part does not even deserve responding to, since writing a good story requires much more than the technical ability to read and write. The whole idea seems ridiculous enough. Don't you have anything more interesting to talk about?*

To carry out this conversation, B, be it the human or the computer, must display very sophisticated abilities. It must possess a large amount of *knowledge* on specific topics, such as whales, flying, novel writing, and gravity. It must be able to *learn* about a totally new concept, taking in the definitions and relating them to what it already knows. Finally, it must be able to *deduce* things from its newly acquired knowledge, such as the fact that genetic engineering is more relevant to zupchoks than, say, mathematics or Chinese philosophy. (In this particular case it must also have a sense of humor.)

* * *

Playing Games

Turing's test seems to provide a nice necessary condition for a computer to possess full human-like intelligence. However, as mentioned, computers are unlikely to pass the test, and will probably remain so in the foreseeable future, and hence we must satisfy ourselves with far more humble expectations. Most AI researchers are involved in roughly one of the following activities: (1) trying to figure out how humans learn, reason, deduce, and make plans, and (2) trying to endow computers with the ability to perform intelligently in very narrow realms. When working on the first of these they find themselves closer to psychologists and neurobiologists than to mathematicians and computer scientists. The second endeavor, however, is more relevant to our present interests.

Game playing is one of the specialized areas in which AI research has achieved significant results. It seems proper to start the discussion with a short news bulletin.

- In 1979, a computer program beat the world champion in backgammon. This did not make the program the new champion, as the game was not played in an official tournament, but the win was a win nevertheless. We must realize that a backgammon match involves many single games, so that the luck factor, introduced by the tossing of dice, is minimized, and the quality of play dominates.

- There are programs that play checkers extremely well, routinely beating their designers. Furthermore, some checkers programs are designed to learn from their mistakes, improving in time just like humans.

- Some chess-playing programs are ranked as masters. One of them has a rating of 2363 in tournament games! However, grandmasters can usually beat these programs, and we are not yet in a position to bestow the world title on a computer program. Recently, a new chess program, running on a small workstation with some special-purpose hardware, beat what was considered to be the world's best chess programs which runs on a very large super-computer.

Why can't programs play *perfect* chess or checkers, and hence beat the best human players? Why can't a computer run through all possible moves and always make the best one? The answer lies in **game trees**, which were mentioned in Chapter 2 (see Figure 12.2). In tic-tac-toe (zeros and crosses), for example, there is no difficulty. The first player has nine possible moves, to which his opponent can respond in one of eight ways, to which the first can respond in one of seven, etc. The game tree thus consists of a root with nine offspring, each of which has eight offspring, and so on. Some nodes in this tree are **terminal**, meaning that they represent either a win for one of the players or a full board with no win. In any event, any sequence of nine moves leads to a terminal node. The tree is thus of maximum depth 9, with maximum outdegree of 9 at the root. Altogether, there are no more than 9!, or 362 880, possibilities to check; hence a program can easily be written to play perfect tic-tac-toe.

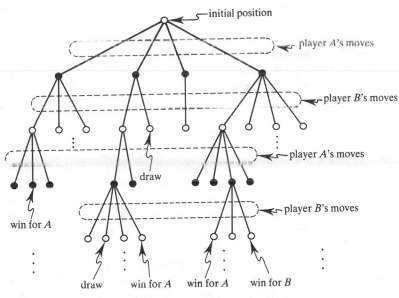

Figure 12.2   A game tree.

With chess, on the other hand, the story is quite different. White has 20 possible first moves, and the average number of possible next moves from an arbitrary chess position is around 35. Thus the tree's outdegree is about 35 on average. The depth of the tree is the number of moves (twice the number of rounds of the game), which can easily reach 80 or 100. This means that the number of possibilities to check in a typical game might be 35^{100}. In Chapter 7 we saw some such numbers, and we recall that 35^{100} is many, many orders of magnitude larger than the number of protons in the universe, or the number of microseconds since the Big Bang. Consequently, even if we ignore the bookkeeping and memory involved in a brute-force trip through all possible moves, and assume that each of them can be tested in one microsecond, no program will ever play perfect chess. The numbers for checkers are not quite as large, but perfect checkers is also out of the question.

How, then, do good chess programs operate? Well, they use **heuristics**, or rules of thumb. In the context of games, heuristics are used to help decide which parts of the game tree will be considered in an attempt to choose a good move. A typical heuristic search uses intuitive rules, incorporated into the program by the programmer, to ignore certain parts of the game tree. For example, it might be decided that, if in the last five moves nothing has changed within the four-square vicinity of a pawn, that pawn will not be moved, and hence the search can ignore all parts of the tree that are located beneath the corresponding node. Such a rule might turn out to be very insightful – it definitely results in smaller trees to be considered – but, of course, it could cost the game; Bobby Fischer might have advanced that very pawn to win in three moves. This is a very simple-minded example, and the heuristics embodied in real chess-playing programs are usually far more sophisticated. However, they are heuristics nevertheless, and by using them there is always a chance that we might miss the best move.

More About Heuristics

A nice way to explain the nature of heuristic search is to consider a person who has lost a contact lens. One possibility is to carry out a **blind search**, by bending over and feeling around for the lens at random. Another possibility is a **systematic search**, which involves continuously extending the area searched, in a methodical and organized manner (say, in ever-larger circles around a central point). This search is bound to succeed eventually, but might be very time consuming. A third possibility is an **analytic search**, whereby the precise mathematical equations governing the fall of the lens are calculated, taking into account wind, gravity, air friction, and the precise topography, tension and texture of the surface. This too, if done correctly, is guaranteed to succeed, but for obvious reasons it is impractical.

In contrast to these methods, most of us would approach the problem using a **heuristic search**. First, we would identify the approximate direction of the fall and make an educated guess as to the distance the lens could have made by falling, and then we would limit the search to the resulting area. Here, of course, the search might not be successful, but there seems to be a reasonably good chance that it will. (There is, of course, a fifth approach, the **lazy search**, which calls for searching for the closest optician and having a new lens made ...).

The main disadvantage of heuristics is in the fact that they do not guarantee success. It is always possible that a rule of thumb will fail for a particular case. As far as advantages go, besides having the potential to drastically reduce running time, heuristics are usually amenable to improvements or replacement as we become more acquainted with the problem at hand and the ways human beings tackle it. In the context of algorithmics, however, the most important characteristic of a heuristic is the fact that its performance is not subject to analysis. We can decide upon a chess heuristic, incorporate it into our chess-playing program, and from then on we will be able to assess its performance only by observation. It might play 100 excellent games before we discover that it has a serious weakness which, once known to an opponent, worsens its game dramatically.

In a sense, employing heuristics is like tossing coins. In Chapter 11 we saw how things can be improved by following the whims of random coin tosses. In other words, the search space of all possibilities was reduced, and some directions were left unexplored. Thus, we were willing to label a number 'prime' although we had not checked all possible witnesses to its non-primality. There too, success is not guaranteed; hence it is tempting to view coin tossing as a *blind* heuristic, a sort of intuitionless rule of thumb. There is a major difference, however. In the realm of probabilistic algorithms analysis replaces intuition. By employing carefully defined sets of ignorable possibilities, and using randomization to decide which to actually ignore, we are able to analyze the probability of success rigorously, making precise statements about the algorithm's performance. With heuristics we cannot.

Although the probabilistic primality-testing algorithm (and for that matter almost any algorithm, even a simple sorting routine) definitely *looks* intelligent – indeed, it does its thing much better than the average human being – we do not think of it as being truly intelligent. While its construction might have required intuitive ingenuity on the part of the designer, its performance is not based on intuition, and can be analytically accounted for. A chess-playing program, on the other hand, might be considered intelligent, as it uses nonprobabilistic rules of thumb, the results of which we cannot predict or analyze. This, then, is one possibility for interpreting our feeling that real intelligence is nonprogrammable; just replace programmable by analyzable. AI is typified by programs that are based on rules that *appear* to be helpful, but whose helpfulness has not been analyzed.

This crude attempt to define AI by some property of the resulting programs is not quite fair. Most people would prefer to define it by subject matter. Moreover, certain directions in AI research have lately become quite precise and analytic. In many cases the heuristics employed are more than just educated guesses; they are actually based on well-defined mathematical models and formulas. In computerized vision, for example, the heuristics used in detecting motion and in comprehending stereoscopic pairs of pictures are based on complicated mathematics, and strongly supported conjectures are made about the way the resulting programs behave on random inputs. The same can be said about motion planning in robotics. In such cases, the heuristic algorithms are closer to the approximation algorithms of Chapter 7 than to probabilistic ones, since the heuristics used are usually conjectured either to guarantee a good solution on average or to produce a bad one extremely rarely. We can thus call the resulting algorithms **conjectured** approximation algorithms – the only thing missing is a proof of the conjectured property. Obviously, once a proof is found we would not expect the discipline of AI to give up the algorithm just because its behavior has been precisely analyzed.

*   *   *

Evaluating and Searching

The account given of heuristics in computerized chess was also overly simplistic. In actuality there is much more going on than a few simple rules that cause the program to ignore parts of the game tree. First, there has to be a way to evaluate the quality of positions in the tree. As a simple example, consider a node for which it has been decided to ignore all but two of White's possible next moves. Assume that the first of these can lead eventually to 10 terminal nodes, three of which represent a win for White, one a win for Black, and six draws, and in the other the numbers are not 10, 3, 1, and 6, but, say, 8, 4, 3 and 1. How should the program (that plays White) compare these situations in order to choose the next move? The problem becomes much more acute when even in the directions that *are* considered we want to stop searching at a certain depth. In such a case, the most distant positions reached in the search do not give rise to definite win/lose/draw information; we only have the information that is implicit in the board configuration itself. In such a case, the evaluation function is far less obvious.

The problem of evaluating situations and assigning them numerical values to help in reaching a decision is one of the main challenges of heuristic programming, and it is not restricted only to game playing. Consider a program for carrying out medical diagnosis. Here too, there is a tree, the nodes of which represent combinations of symptomatic problems and queries to the patient, with the terminal nodes representing final diagnoses. Here too, the tree is enormous, and a heuristic search must take place, with the patient's observable symptoms and his answers to queries prescribing the directions that will be pursued. The evaluation problem here, which determines how relevant a particular set of possibilities is to the sought-after final diagnosis, is just as difficult.

Whether in chess, in medicine, or elsewhere, once an evaluation function for the search tree has been defined, there still remains the problem of exploiting the values of nodes in the tree to efficiently search through its relevant parts. Here work in AI has resulted in a number of powerful search methods that have many applications in nonheuristic algorithmics too. Many of these are based on a fundamental search strategy called the **minimax** method, which is best explained in the framework of game trees.

Figure 12.3(a) shows part of a game tree for a two-person game, like tic-tac-toe or chess, together with previously established values for each terminal node. (The terminal nodes in the figure are either real end positions of the game or intermediate positions, beyond which we have decided not to search.) The root represents a board position with player A to go, and the values represent the strength of the positions from A's point of view. Thus, 999 represents a win for A and 0 a win for B. Intermediate values reflect the relative chances of A winning from the corresponding positions, as prescribed by some heuristic evaluation function. One possible move must be chosen for A that will maximize his ability to win.

The basic idea is to repeatedly propagate values upwards in the tree, starting at the bottom. If the current parent node represents an A-move then the *maximum* of the values of the offspring nodes is attached to the parent, and if it represents a B-move then the *minimum* value is taken. The rationale for this is clear: B is assumed to play in a reasonable manner, and hence will make every effort to maximize his own chances of winning, which is to say that he will try to *minimize A*'s chances of doing so. In other words, A should make the best move (i.e., the one with maximal value) under the assumption that, following it, B will make *his* best move (i.e., the one with minimum value of A's function), following which A will make his best next move, and so on. Figure 12.3(b) shows the tree with these min–max values inserted.

This process can be shortened by observing that in some cases even partial information regarding the values of a node's second-generation offspring (i.e., its grandchildren) is sufficient for determining its final value. In Figure 12.4, for example, there is no point in evaluating the rightmost of the five second-generation subtrees, since the minimum of the three leftmost ones is 42, which is greater than 27, the known value on the right. The minimum of 27 and any possible value of the root of the rightmost tree will be no more than 27 itself, and hence the maximizing that will be carried out to determine the value at the root necessarily leads to a value of 42. A similar case occurs when the node in question represents a B-move rather than an *A*-move, but with maximum and minimum changing places. (Construct an example of this.) Methods have been found to traverse the tree during the propagation process in such a way as to take advantage of these savings. One of the better known of these, which will not be described here, is called **alpha-beta pruning**.

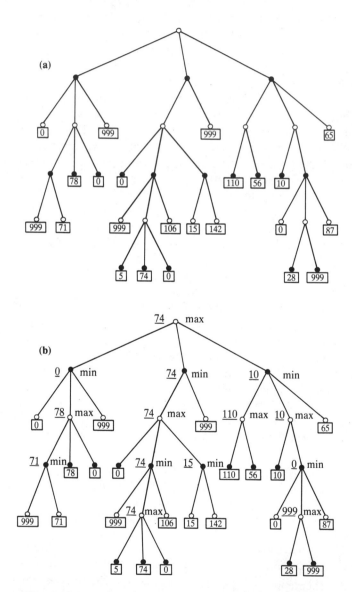

Figure 12.3 Propagating values by the minimax method.

In summary, a heuristic search consists of:

(1) heuristics embodied in a valuation function;

(2) rules as to how deep the lookahead from any given position will be (this is usually a function of the position in question); and

(3) an efficient propagation procedure for determining the values and actually making the choices.

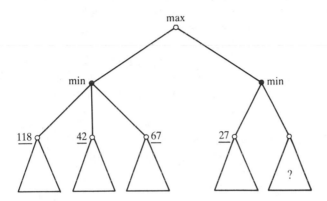

Figure 12.4   A subtree that need not be evaluated in the minimax method.

Knowledge Representation

We need more than just heuristics to achieve algorithmic intelligence. We have to find ways to represent the **knowledge** that intelligent algorithms manipulate. If the *control* parts of an AI program are special, being based upon the 'soft' notion of heuristics, then the *data* parts are also special, being based upon the 'soft' notion of knowledge.

That twice four is eight and that France is in Europe is knowledge, but so is the fact that all giraffes have long necks, that Alan Turing was brilliant, and that academics who do not publish perish. But what is 'long', and what is 'brilliant', and is 'perish' meant literally? Furthermore, how do we represent such facts in our minds or in our algorithmic knowledge bases, and how do we use them? No program can be labeled intelligent, be it one that operates in a narrow domain, such as chess or blocks and pyramids, or a general-purpose candidate for the Turing test, unless it has an appropriate mechanism for storing, retrieving, and manipulating knowledge. The problem of **knowledge representation** is indeed one of the central issues in artificial intelligence.

The difficulty is rooted in the fact that knowledge does not consist only of a large collection of facts, but also of the many intricate relationships between them. These relationships have numerous facets and attributes which, in turn, spawn other, higher level relationships with other items of knowledge. We know very little about the way we ourselves store and manipulate the immense quantities of knowledge accumulated over our life times. In fact, there is evidence that a human's knowledge base is dynamic and associative, and does not necessarily work in ways that are suggestive of the workings of digital computers.

Many models of knowledge have been suggested for use by intelligent programs. Some are based on pure computer science concepts, such as relational or hierarchical databases, and others on logical formalisms, such as the predicate calculus or modal logic. Certain programming languages, such as LISP and PROLOG, are more suitable for manipulating knowledge than others. As mentioned in Chapter 3, PROLOG, for example, seems quite apt when it comes to knowledge items involving simple relationships like 'John is Mary's father', or even 'a parent of any ancestor of Mary is also an ancestor of Mary'. However, once outside a small well-defined domain of discourse the relationships required become far more intricate, and these models become vastly inadequate. Retrieving those knowledge items that are relevant to some decision that the program has to make becomes a formidable task. The 'right' model for the algorithmic representation of knowledge is thus yet to be found.

Expert Systems

One approach to the problem is that of **production rules**. A simple production rule might state that if X is a company and Y manages that company then Y works for X. A more complex one, relevant perhaps to a scene comprehension program, would state that whenever three lines are found to meet at a single point then it is possible that they represent the corner of a three-dimensional cube, unless one of the angles is less than 45° and another more than 90°. Some of these special-purpose programs have been dubbed **expert systems**, as they are based on rules that a human expert employs in solving a particular problem. A typical expert system is constructed by questioning the expert about the ways he utilizes expertise in tackling the problem at hand. The (human) questioner attempts to discover and formulate the rules used by the expert, and the expert system then uses these rules to guide the search for a solution to a given instance of the problem. The heart of an expert system is the set of rules, given in some format, and a corresponding search mechanism for finding the rules that are applicable. The resulting systems are also called **production systems** or **rule-based systems**.

Expert systems with acceptable levels of performance have been constructed for carrying out (limited forms of) medical diagnosis, determining the structure of a molecule from its atomic formula and its mass spectrogram, finding oil-rich areas, and helping in the configuration of computer systems. We must realize, however, that besides the reliance on heuristic search, the rules that control the search are formed by questioning experts who might not always operate according to rigid rules. The chances of unexpected, perhaps catastrophic, behavior in an expert system are therefore quite high. Some people put it this way: 'Would you be willing to be taken care of by a computerized intensive care unit that was programmed according to the expert system paradigm?' Under a rare set of circumstances, the unit could administer the wrong medicine or shut a crucial valve at the wrong moment. Its behavior is governed by rules that were formulated by interviewing expert doctors who might not necessarily act in an unusual case according to any well-formed rules.

Attempts could possibly be made to subject critical expert systems to precise analytic techniques, enabling us to verify formally that certain safety properties hold for any application of the underlying rules. Since, as explained in Chapter 10, safety properties usually assert that bad things will not happen, it would appear that rule-based systems would be amenable to such an approach.

Knowledge in Learning, Planning, and Deduction

The problem of knowledge representation is indeed fundamental to the mechanization of any kind of intelligence, and it resurfaces in learning, planning, and deduction. Here are some typical examples that further illustrate the need for sophisticated representation of knowledge.

Consider a checkers program that learns. It might be supposed to know the rules and then simply to learn to avoid the mistakes it makes as it plays more games. However, even here an algorithmic point of view presents serious representational problems. Do we simply make a list of the positions and moves that turned out to be bad, and henceforth repeatedly run through them to avoid making the same mistakes again? Or do we try to remember and update more general rules of good play, which will be used to modify the program's heuristics? These questions become all the more difficult when the subject area is wider. How do children learn? How do they represent the knowledge that enables them to recognize familiar faces or synthesize new sentences they have never really heard before? How does an adult remember and retrieve the knowledge that enables him to learn how to write an essay, to organize his personal finances, or to adapt to a new environment?

Earlier we mentioned **deduction** as part of the kind of intelligence required for passing the Turing test. Programs have been written that do a reasonably good job of proving theorems in high school geometry. They are able to accumulate relevant facts and deduce new ones from them. How is it done? Do these programs simply keep a list of known theorems and a few logical inference rules (such as 'if P is true and P always implies Q, then Q is true too')? Or are they familiar with more complex chains of reasoning that are geared towards producing interesting theorems? Again, these questions become all the more difficult when the knowledge relevant to the desired deductions is not restricted to a narrow domain. How does a person's knowledge enable him to conclude that it will probably rain tomorrow, to decide upon the proper school for a child, or to prove a really deep theorem in algebraic topology?

Most of our discussion so far was related to the *internal* activities of intelligent programs. The need for them to talk, walk or see was repeatedly waived, concentrating instead on comprehension, learning, and deduction. However, a more general view of intelligent machines requires that they have also have the ability to physically imitate humans. In their most general form, they must be able to understand and synthesize human speech, as well as to perform physical tasks in the classical robot-like spirit. Here too, the problem of knowledge representation is a fundamental one. Some AI systems can understand simple views of block and pyramids using appropriate visual sensory equipment, and others can understand slowly spoken elementary English using audio equipment. How do they do so? Do the vision-based programs simply know about every possible combination of locations for the appropriate objects, or do they recognize various configurations of line junctions and utilize rules for deducing the overall arrangement from them? What happens if a new kind of object, say a cylinder, is introduced? Do the speech-recognition programs have a database consisting of the wave profiles for all possible pronunciations of each word? Or do they have built-in rules that enable them to combine spoken word segments into a whole? Again, if the domain is much broader, like those encountered by a human viewing new surroundings or listening to a rich and diverse conversation, things become far more complicated. How do human beings comprehend the variety of colors, lines, and shapes that make up the interior of a living room? How do they identify movement and distance from observing things with two eyes over some short period, and how do they understand Southern accents?

The ability to **plan** is another intelligent skill. Some robots that operate within carefully limited surroundings are capable of planning a sequence of movements that will take them to their destination. How do they do so? Do they simply carry out a search through possibilities, heuristic or otherwise? Or do they utilize more subtle knowledge that enables them to make plans with the aim of achieving more general goals? Again, wider domains make things much harder. How does a person plan a trip, outline a scheme for ending the year with a positive balance, or devise a strategy to win a war?

If intelligence is the wellspring of life (see the quotations at the start of the chapter) then knowledge representation is definitely its cornerstone.

Understanding Natural Language

To end this chapter on a lighter note, it seems worthwhile to further illustrate the difficulty of mechanizing the comprehension of ordinary natural language. The problem is really much harder than it appears.

We shall concentrate here on understanding the language, not recognizing the words, but it is instructive to first see what can happen when a speech-recognition program makes mistakes. The sentence 'His presence made all the difference' can be easily misunderstood and interpreted as 'His presents made all the difference'. Similarly, 'Any Japanese car responds well' can be heard as 'Any Japanese corresponds well', and the well-known American statement 'I pledge allegiance to the flag', when said fast, can be understood as 'I led the pigeons to the flag'. Speech-recognition programs are a pun lover's paradise.

When it comes to semantics the subtleties are much greater. A sentence cannot always be understood without the context in which it appears, and without knowing about the special nuances, phrases and slang of the language at hand. Sometimes it is also necessary to be familiar with the idiosyncrasies of the person who is speaking. A famous example involves the aphorism 'The spirit is willing but the flesh is weak'. As the story goes, this sentence was subjected first to a program that carried out a simple dictionary-based translation into Russian and then to one that translated it back into English. The result was 'The vodka is strong but the meat is rotten'. How inspiring!

Problems can arise when parts of a sentence are ambiguous. Consider the following:

Jim sat down at the table and found a large fruit salad on a plate next to the basket of bread. It took him a while, but he finally managed to eat and digest it all.

What did Jim eat? Was it the salad, the bread, or both? In some context it might be the plate, the basket, or even the table! Here grammar alone is of little help; it is the *meaning* of things that an intelligent program must be able to grasp. The following sentences are grammatically identical but they differ in the relationship between their various parts.

The lost children were found by the searchers;

The lost children were found by the mountain;

The lost children were found by nightfall.

Obviously, the correct interpretation depends on the meaning of the words 'searchers', 'mountain', and 'nightfall'. The same phenomenon occurs in the following.

The thieves stole the jewels, and some of them were subsequently sold;
The thieves stole the jewels, and some of them were subsequently caught;
The thieves stole the jewels, and some of them were subsequently found.

In this case, the word 'sold' refers to the jewels, 'caught' refers to the thieves, and 'found' can refer to either. Actually, even that much is not obvious. It is possible that the story takes place in a country where thieves are sold as slaves, rendering the first sentence ambiguous too. If the second sentence had 'threw the jewels out of the window' instead of 'stole the jewels', it would also be ambiguous.

Again, the knowledge issue appears in all its severity. We utilize an enormous amount of knowledge in disambiguating and understanding ordinary English, besides just the words and the grammar. Identifying that knowledge, and representing it in ways that capture its intricate inter-relationships, enabling useful retrieval, re-emerges as the central and fundamental problem.

Let us end our discussion with some hypothetical exchanges between a human being and a futuristic intelligent phone-answering machine.[†]

Machine: *Hello, this is Jim's phone.*

Voice: *Hello. I would like to talk to Jim.*

Machine: *Jim isn't here. Can I help you?*

Voice: *This isn't stuff I can share with a machine. When will he be here?*

Machine: *Who is this calling?*

Voice: *This is Bill Bixlot.*

Machine: *I'm sorry, Mr. Big-Slut, but Jim will not be here in the foreseeable future. Thank you for calling, Bill. (Click.)*

Voice: *Damn!*

Machine: *Hello, this is Jim's phone.*

Voice: *Oh, hello, you darling machine. I just wanted to check that we're still on for dinner and whatever.*

Machine: *Of course, Sue. I have you for Thursday at the usual spot.*

Voice: *This is Jim's fiancee, Barbara. Who is Sue?*

Machine: *Oh, Barbara, I didn't recognize your voice. I have never heard of anyone named Sue.*

Voice: *But you just said he was meeting with Sue on Thursday.*

---

† These conversations are based on those appearing in a recent essay by Robert W. Lucky. They have been modified, and are included here with permission.

Machine: *Oh* that *Sue. Are you sure you have the right number? This is Bill Finch's phone.*

Voice: *You can't pull that trick on me. Tell Jim it's all over!*

Machine: *You have reached a nonworking number. Please check your listing and redial.* (Click.)

———————

Machine: *Hello, this is Jim's phone.*

Voice: *Oh, it's you. Listen, this is his boss. I really need to get Jim right away. Can you locate him and have him call me?*

Machine: *I'm sorry, Mr. Hizboss, Jim is playing golf this afternoon and left orders not to be disturbed.*

Voice: *He is, is he? Well, look, I'm thin on patience this afternoon. This is* his boss *calling, you idiot, not Mr. Hizboss. Get Jim. Now!*

Machine: *I'm pleased to hear that you are spending time with your patients this afternoon, Dr. Thin. Business must be good. If you want to reach Jim's boss just dial 553–8861. Certainly you would never find him here in Jim's office; we have him listed in our directory under the alias of The Monster.*

Voice: *Take this message, you son of a chip, and get it straight. Tell him he is not worth the keys on your control panel. He is fired!* (Click.)

———————

Machine: *Hello, this is Jim's phone.*

Voice: *Are you satisfied with your present investments? Have you considered the advantages of tax-free municipal bonds? To hear more, please give your name and address after the beep.* (Beep.)

Machine: *Er, . . . this is Jim's phone.*

Voice: *Thank you Mr. Jimzfone. Let me tell you more about our unusual investment opportunities . . .*

*   *   *

When it comes to full artificial intelligence, the prognosis sounds rather gloomy. Essentially, we have been saying that in certain areas conventional heuristic-based AI is but a medicine that can be taken until the doctor arrives. We would hope that the doctor would eventually be able to prescribe pure analytic algorithmics. Once we have a better grip on the knowledge representation problem, we should be able to try applying non-heuristic (probably highly concurrent, and possibly also probabilistic, but analyzable) algorithmic procedures, in order to achieve acceptable intelligent performance in a wide range of application areas.

> *Such knowledge is too wonderful for me;*
> *it is high, I cannot attain unto it*
> Psalm 139: 6

> *for I am more brutish than a man,*
> *and have not the understanding of a man*
> Proverbs 30: 2

Postscript

Well, we have come a long way. Starting from the basic notion of an algorithmic problem and its solution, we have discussed the basic ways in which algorithms are constructed and written, as well as their correctness and efficiency. We have seen intractable problems and noncomputable ones, and have shown that these notions are insensitive to the choice of the model of computation and the language in which solutions are written. We have also discussed concurrency, probabilism, and heuristics.

* * *

In retrospect, we have identified three distinct kinds of complexity with which algorithmics tries to cope. In each, there remain serious obstacles that seem to require significant new ideas in order to be overcome.

The first is **computational complexity**, where we search for efficient solutions to well-defined algorithmic problems. Efficiency is based on resources such as computation time, memory space, and hardware size. New algorithmic problems pose new challenges – to find the most efficient algorithms and to prove matching lower bounds. This is particularly acute when the problem at hand is conjectured, but not known, to be intractable. From the fundamentalist's point of view, the main obstacles here are reflected in the many open questions involving complexity classes and their interrelationships. In particular, the P vs. NP and P vs. NC problems stand out as being not only very difficult but also of great interest, both theoretical and practical.

The second kind of complexity can be termed **behavioral complexity**. Here we are interested in designing extremely complex algorithmic systems, typically ones that are concurrent, distributed, and reactive in nature. Efficiency here is secondary; the main problem is in overcoming the intricacy of the system's desired behavior. Again, each new system presents a new challenge – to provide algorithms and protocols that are clear and well structured, and that yield the desired behavior under all circumstances. For the fundamentalist, the problem is to develop rigorous methods, languages, and analysis tools for the sound and painless development of such systems.

The third kind of complexity might be called **cognitive complexity**. It has to do with pseudo-algorithmic problems, which, by their very nature, are not amenable to precise definition, though we need only look around to see them continuously being solved by noncomputerized beings. They involve knowledge and intelligence, and are usually aimed at achieving human-like effects. Here too, new problems present brand new challenges – to design systems that will exhibit reasonably intelligent behavior in the appropriate realms. From a fundamentalist's point of view, the main problem is to understand how intelligent beings operate, and to represent the complex knowledge relevant to that operation in ways that are amenable to algorithmic manipulation and analysis.

These fundamental problems have not been satisfactorily solved yet. We can only hope to see a similar exposition of algorithmics in, say, 10 years; one that will be able to report on the breakthroughs needed for coping with these three types of complexity.

* * *

Even the most attentive readers will not have become either competent programmers or productive computer scientists by reading this book. It is hoped, however, that they have acquired a reasonably detailed understanding of some of the most fundamental issues in the young and exciting field of computer science. In the coming years algorithmics is expected to emerge as an influential area of interest, improving and expanding the ways computers are applied to real-world problems.

And it shall be,
when thou hast made an end of reading this book,
that thou shalt bind a stone to it,
and cast it into the midst of [the river] Perat
Jeremiah 51: 63

Bibliographic Notes

General

The purpose of these bibliographic notes is twofold. The first is to provide the reader with additional sources in which to find more detailed accounts of the topics discussed. The second is to credit the people responsible for the research reported and to point to the original publications outlining their ideas and results.

This introductory section provides information about books relevant to the entire field of algorithmics, as well as the names and publishers of periodicals and newsletters that publish papers spanning the field. The sections following provide detailed bibliographic notes for each chapter. These notes are structured so that general information about books and periodicals relevant to the subject matter of the chapter appears first. The notes are then developed, in parallel with the chapter itself, providing credits for the results mentioned, with pointers to their original published versions. Whenever appropriate, additional pointers to particularly informative, important or influential publications have been included.

Obviously, it is impossible to even come close to covering all that is relevant to algorithmics. Moreover, many profound and fundamental results do not get referred to here at all, since considerations of space and structure have prevented their inclusion in the text itself. Many of these can be found by following the references that appear in the papers and books that *are* included.

* * *

357

The Biblical quotations in this book are all taken from a translation prepared by my father, Harold Fisch:

- *Koren's Jerusalem Bible*, English Translation revised and edited by H. Fisch, Koren Publishers, Jerusalem, 1969.

As will be seen, there are excellent textbooks on almost all of the specific *sub*areas of algorithmics. However, there are precious few that attempt to provide a more general treatment. Two exceptions are:

- L. Goldshlager and A. Lister, *Computer Science: A Modern Introduction*, Prentice-Hall International, London, 1982.

- I. Pohl and A. Shaw, *The Nature of Computation: An Introduction to Computer Science*, Computer Science Press, Rockville, MD, 1981.

Both are textbooks for introductory computer science courses and contain brief but informative accounts of many of the subjects treated in this book. In addition, they discuss a number of other topics, such as operating systems and computer architecture. Additional general books, though of somewhat more elementary nature, are:

- M. S. Carberry *et al.*, *Foundations of Computer Science*, Computer Science Press, Rockville, MD, 1979.

- K. Maly and A. R. Hanson, *Fundamentals of the Computing Sciences*, Prentice-Hall, Englewood Cliffs, NJ, 1978.

Turning for a moment from the spirit of computing to its flesh and bones and the link between the three, one of the best places to read about computers and the difficulty people have in getting acquainted to them is:

- J. Shore, *The Sachertorte Algorithm and Other Antidotes to Computer Anxiety*, Viking Penguin, New York, 1985.

There are several periodicals that publish papers in virtually all areas of algorithmics:

- *Journal of the Association for Computing Machinery*, often abbreviated *J. Assoc. Comput. Mach.*, or just *J. ACM*; a quarterly published by the ACM.

- *SIAM Journal on Computing*, abbreviated *SIAM J. Comput.*, or sometimes just *SICOMP*; a quarterly published by SIAM, the Society for Industrial and Applied Mathematics.

- *Information and Computation* (formerly *Information and Control*), abbreviated *Inf. and Comput.*, or *Inf. and Cont.*; a monthly published by Academic Press.

- *Journal of Computer and System Sciences*, abbreviated *J. Comput. Syst. Sci.*, or sometimes just *JCSS*; a bimonthly published by Academic Press.

- *Theoretical Computer Science*, abbreviated *Theor. Comput. Sci.*, or sometimes just *TCS*; published in 21 issues a year by North Holland.

- *The Computer Journal*, abbreviated *Comput. J.*; a bimonthly published by the British Computer Society.

- *Fundamenta Informaticae*, abbreviated *Fund. Inf.*; a quarterly published by Elsevier North Holland.

- *Information Processing Letters*, abbreviated *Inf. Proc. Lett.*, or sometimes just *IPL*; contains short papers or communications and is published in ten issues a year by North Holland.

- *Computing Surveys*, abbreviated *Comput. Surv.*; contains lengthy survey papers and is published quarterly by the ACM.

The following journals are of somewhat more elementary nature, and occasionally contain relevant articles:

- *Communications of the Association for Computing Machinery*, abbreviated *Comm. Assoc. Comput. Mach.*, or sometimes just *CACM*; a monthly published by the ACM.

- *Computer*; a monthly published by the IEEE.

The following unrefereed newsletters contain short papers, communications and announcements relevant to many aspects of algorithmics:

- *ACM SIGACT News*; a quarterly published by ACM's Special Interest Group on Automata and Computability Theory.

- *Bulletin of the EATCS*; published by the European Association for Theoretical Computer Science.

In addition to these, the following journal publishes short reviews of books and papers in computer science, algorithmics included, and is a good place to start a search for a bibliographic item:

- *Computing Reviews*, abbreviated *Comput. Rev.*, or sometimes just *CR*; a monthly published by the ACM.

There are several annual or biannual conferences, symposia and colloquia that are devoted to algorithmics at large, and numerous others that concentrate on specific subjects. They will not be listed here, but will be referenced as the occasion arises. Nevertheless, the reader should keep in mind that many are sponsored by the various subgroups of the ACM and the IEEE, and the proceedings of many others appear in the Springer-Verlag series *Lecture Notes in Computer Science*.

Chapter 1

The following books shed light on the history of computing:

- *A Computer Perspective* (G. Fleck, ed.), Harvard University Press, Cambridge, MA, 1973.

- *A History of Computing in the Twentieth Century* (N. C. Metropolis *et al.*, eds.), Academic Press, New York, 1980.

- F. G. Ashherst, *Pioneers of Computing*, Frederick Muller, Ltd., London, 1983.

It is also worth reading the following biographies of two of the most influential pioneers of computer science:

- A. Hyman, *Charles Babbage, Pioneer of the Computer*, Princeton University Press, Princeton, NJ, 1982.

- A. Hodges, *Alan Turing: The Enigma*, Simon & Schuster, 1983.

A journal devoted entirely to the history of computation is:

- *Annals of the History of Computing*, abbreviated *Ann. Hist. Comput.*; a quarterly published by AFIPS, the American Federation of Information Processing Societies.

It often contains illuminating papers on the origins and insights of the early researchers.

*   *   *

The analogy between computer science and surgery *[p. 7]* appears in:

- E. W. Dijkstra, 'On a Cultural Gap,' *The Mathematical Intelligencer* **8** (1986), pp. 48–52.

A detailed, illustrated account of Babbage's analytical engine *[p. 8]* appears in:

- A. G. Bromley, 'Charles Babbage's Analytical Engine, 1838,' *Ann. Hist. Comput.* **4** (1982), pp. 196–217.

The latest ACM Curriculum *[p. 9]* appears in:

- 'Curriculum '78: Recommendations for the Undergraduate Program in Computer Science' (R. H. Austing *et al.*, eds.), *Comm. Assoc. Comput. Mach.* **22** (1979), pp. 147–166.

The mousse recipe *[p. 11]* is from page 73 of:

- P. C. Sinclair and R. K. Malinowski, *French Cooking*, Weathervane Books, 1978.

Chapter 2

There are numerous excellent textbooks devoted to algorithms and data structures. In the notes for Chapters 4, 5 and 6 a number of those that emphasize design methods, design through correctness proofs, and design for efficiency, respectively, are listed. Here are some that are fitting for this less specific chapter:

- A. V. Aho, J. E. Hopcroft and J. D. Ullman, *Data Structures and Algorithms*, Addison-Wesley, Reading, MA, 1983.

- E. Horowitz and S. Sahni, *Fundamentals of Data Structures*, Computer Science Press, Rockville, MD, 1976.

- D. E. Knuth, *The Art of Computer Programming*, Vol. 1: *Fundamental Algorithms* (2nd edn.), Addison-Wesley, Reading, MA, 1973.

- T. A. Standish, *Data Structure Techniques*, Addison-Wesley, Reading, MA, 1980.

- N. Wirth, *Algorithms and Data Structures*, Prentice-Hall, Englewood Cliffs, NJ, 1986.

The following early monographs have been extremely influential:

- E. W. Dijkstra, 'Notes on Structured Programming,' in *Structured Programming*, Academic Press, New York, 1972.

- C. A. R. Hoare, 'Notes on Data Structuring,' in *Structured Programming*, Academic Press, New York, 1972.

In the first three chapters of the following book there is a rather original treatment of control and data (the material is treated through a dialect of the programming language LISP):

- H. Abelson and G. J. Sussman, *Structure and Interpretation of Computer Programs*, MIT Press, Cambridge, MA, 1985.

An exposition of several of the issues treated in this chapter is:

- N. Wirth, 'Data Structures and Algorithms,' *Scientific American* **251**: 3 (1984), pp. 60–69.

Apart from the general periodicals listed earlier, here are some additional journals that publish papers on algorithms and data structures:

- *Journal of Algorithms*, abbreviated *J. Algs.*; a quarterly published by Academic Press.

- *Journal of Complexity*, abbreviated *J. Complex.*; a quarterly published by Academic Press.

- *Mathematical Systems Theory*, abbreviated *Math. Syst. Theory*; a quarterly published by Springer-Verlag.

- *Discrete & Computational Geometry*, abbreviated *Disc. Comput. Geom.*; a quarterly published by Springer-Verlag.

- *Combinatorica*; a quarterly published by North Holland.

- *Journal of Symbolic Computation*, abbreviated *J. Symb. Comput.*; a quarterly published by Academic Press.

- *Computing*; published by Springer-Verlag.

- *BIT*; a quarterly published by Data A/S, Denmark.

*   *   *

The bubblesort algorithm *[pp. 23–24]*, as well as a host of other sorting methods, is described in detail in Knuth's encyclopedic volume:

- D. E. Knuth, *The Art of Computer Programming*, Vol. 3: *Sorting and Searching*, Addison-Wesley, Reading, MA, 1973.

The controversy surrounding the 'goto' statement *[pp. 24–25]* is generally considered to have originated in the following letter to the editor:

- E. W. Dijkstra, 'Go To Statement Considered Harmful,' *Comm. Assoc. Comput. Mach.* **11** (1968), pp. 147–148.

More about this controversy, as well as the possibility of eliminating certain control structures in favor of a set of minimal ones *[p. 34]*, can be found in the following papers:

- D. E. Knuth, 'Structured Programming with **go to** Statements,' *Comput. Surv.* **6** (1974), pp. 261–301.

- D. Harel, 'On Folk Theorems,' *Comm. Assoc. Comput. Mach.* **23** (1980), pp. 379–389.

The following book is devoted to the idea (put forward by many researchers) of writing only well-structured programs that use only a few selected control constructs:

- R. C. Linger, H. D. Mills and B. I. Witt, *Structured Programming: Theory and Practice*, Addison-Wesley, Reading, MA, 1979.

A good place to read about various flowchart techniques and notations *[pp. 25–27]* is:

- T. R. G. Green, 'Pictures of Programs and Other Processes, or How To Do Things with Lines,' *Behaviour and Information Technology* **1** (1982), pp. 3–36.

There are many places to read about gradual, top-down design of large algorithms and programs, using subroutines or other similar means *[pp. 30–31]*. Apart from Dijkstra's notes on structured programming, the following have been particularly influential:

- N. Wirth, 'Program Development by Stepwise Refinement,' *Comm. Assoc. Comput. Mach.* **14** (1971), pp. 221–227.

- D. L. Parnas, 'A Technique for Software Module Specification with Examples,' *Comm. Assoc. Comput. Mach.* **15** (1972), pp. 330–336.

- E. Yourdon and L. L. Constantine, *Structured Design: Fundamentals of a Discipline of Computer Program and Systems Design*, Prentice-Hall, Englewood Cliffs, NJ, 1979

Recursion *[pp. 31–33]* is a fascinating subject and a wealth of interesting material about it can be found in:

- E. Roberts, *Thinking Recursively*, John Wiley & Sons, New York, 1986.

- D. R. Hofstadter, *Gödel, Escher, Bach: An Eternal Golden Braid*, Basic Books, New York, 1979.

To better appreciate the subtlety induced by the self-referential nature of recursion, the following book is heartily recommended, together with those of its references that are heartily recommended therein;

- D. Harel, *Algorithmics: The Spirit of Computing*, Addison-Wesley, Reading, MA, 1987.

The recursive solution to the Towers of Hanoi problem *[pp. 33–34]* appears in almost any elementary book on algorithms, including several of those already mentioned.

Treesort *[pp. 44–47]* is described in detail and is traced back to its many independent inventors in Knuth's volume on sorting and searching previously mentioned, where it is called *tree insertion sort*.

Self-adjusting data structures *[p. 47]* appear routinely in many of the algorithms described in the general books listed for this chapter. Perhaps the most well known are *balanced binary trees*, which are discussed in detail in Knuth's volume on sorting and searching.

There are a number of textbooks devoted to databases *[pp. 48–49]*. They contain a wealth of information on various database models, languages and design methods:

- C. J. Date, *An Introduction to Database Systems* (4th edn.), Addison-Wesley, Reading, MA, 1986.

- J. D. Ullman, *Principles of Database Systems* (2nd edn.), Computer Science Press, Rockville, MD, 1982.

- D. Maier, *The Theory of Relational Databases*, Computer Science Press, Rockville, MD, 1983.

- H. F. Korth and A. Silbershatz, *Database System Concepts*, McGraw-Hill, New York, 1986.

The following paper is considered to have been one of the most influential in shaping the current approaches to databases:

- E. F. Codd, 'A Relational Model for Large Shared Data Banks,' *Comm. Assoc. Comput. Mach.* **13** (1970), pp. 377–387.

The following periodical and newsletter publish papers about database systems:

- *ACM Transactions on Database Systems*, abbreviated *ACM Trans. Database Syst.*, or sometimes just *TODS*; a quarterly published by the ACM.

- *ACM SIGMOD Record*; an unrefereed newsletter published by ACM's Special Interest Group on Management of Data.

The following contain information on the possibility of defining special, self-tailored *abstract data types*:

- B. H. Liskov and J. V. Guttag, *Abstraction and Specification in Program Development*, MIT Press, Cambridge, MA, 1986.

- J. V. Guttag and J. J. Horning, 'The Algebraic Specification of Abstract Data Types,' *Acta Inf.* **10** (1978), pp. 27–52.

Chapter 3

There are a number of books on the general principles of designing programming languages. Here are four:

- H. Ledgard and M. Marcotty, *The Programming Language Landscape*, Science Research Associates, Chicago, 1981.

- J. E. Nicholls, *The Structure and Design of Programming Languages*, Addison-Wesley, Reading, MA, 1975.

- T. W. Pratt, *Programming Languages: Design and Implementation* (2nd edn.), Prentice-Hall, Englewood Cliffs, NJ, 1984.

- R. D. Tennet, *Principles of Programming Languages*, Prentice-Hall International, London, 1981.

The following one emphasizes abstract data types:

- D. M. Harland, *Polymorphic Programming Languages*, Halstead Press, New York, 1984.

In addition, the following volume contains an extensive collection of some of the central papers in the programming language area, discussing both principles and specific languages:

- *Programming Languages: A Grand Tour* (3rd edn.; E. Horowitz, ed.), Computer Science Press, Rockville, MD, 1987.

The history of programming languages is described in a paper by P. Wegner in this 'grand tour', and also in:

- *History of Programming Languages* (R. L. Wexelblat, ed.), Academic Press, New York, 1981.

- J. E. Sammet, *Programming Languages: History and Fundamentals*, Prentice-Hall, Englewood Cliffs, NJ, 1969.

An exposition of several issues related to programming languages and their structure is:

- L. G. Tesler, 'Programming Languages,' *Scientific American* **251**: 3 (1984), pp. 70–78.

Here are some periodicals that contain papers about the principles of programming languages:

- *ACM Transactions on Programming Languages and Systems*, abbreviated *ACM Trans. Prog. Lang. Syst.*, or simply *TOPLAS*; a quarterly published by the ACM.

- *Computer Languages*, abbreviated *Comput. Lang.*; a quarterly published by Pergamon Press.

- *Science of Computer Programming*, abbreviated *Sci. Comput. Prog.*; a bimonthly published by North Holland.

- *Software: Practice and Experience*, abbreviated *Softw. Pract. Exp.*; a monthly published by John Wiley & Sons.

- *IEEE Transactions on Software Engineering*, abbreviated *IEEE Trans. Soft. Eng.*; a monthly published by the IEEE.

- *ACM SIGPLAN Notices*; an unrefereed newsletter published monthly by ACM's Special Interest Group on Programming Languages.

* * *

The BNF notation for syntax definitions *[p. 52]* appears in:

- J. Backus, 'The Syntax and Semantics of the Proposed International Algebraic Language of the Zurich ACM-GAMM Conference,' *Proc. Int. Conf. on Information Processing*, UNESCO, pp. 125–132, 1959.

It was used extensively in the celebrated and extremely influential definition of the language ALGOL 60:

- P. Naur (ed.), 'Revised Report on the Algorithmic Language Algol 60,' *Comm. Assoc. Comput. Mach.* **6** (1963), pp. 1–17.

Syntax diagrams for defining the syntax of programming languages *[Fig. 3.1]* appear in:

- K. Jensen and N. Wirth, *PASCAL User Manual and Report*, Springer-Verlag, New York, 1974.

Turning to semantics *[pp. 54–56]*, the following papers have been particularly influential in research on the semantics of programming languages:

- D. S. Scott and C. Strachey, 'Towards a Mathematical Semantics for Computer Languages', *Proc. Symp. on Computers and Automata* (J. Fox, ed.), Polytechnic Inst. of Brooklyn Press, New York, pp. 19–46, 1971.

- D. S. Scott, 'Mathematical Concepts in Programming Language Semantics,' *Proc. 1972 Spring Joint Computer Conference*, AFIPS Press, Montvale, NJ, pp. 225–234, 1972.

Several books treat the semantics of programming languages in depth, among which are:

- J. E. Stoy, *Denotational Semantics: The Scott–Strachey Approach to Programming Language Theory*, MIT Press, Cambridge, MA, 1977.

- J. W. de Bakker, *Mathematical Theory of Program Correctness*, Prentice-Hall International, London, 1980.

- D. A. Schmidt, *Denotational Semantics: A Methodology for Language Development*, Allyn and Bacon, Inc., Boston, 1986.

The latter, besides being up to date, contains an extensive bibliography on programming language semantics. Good survey papers on semantics are

- R. D. Tennent, 'The Denotational Semantics of Programming Languages,' *Comm. Assoc. Comput. Mach.* **19** (1976), pp. 437–453.

- D. S. Scott, 'Logic and Programming Languages,' *Comm. Assoc. Comput. Mach.* **20** (1977), pp. 634–641.

There is really only one book that needs to be read to learn all about the compilation process *[pp. 57–59]*, including optimizing compilers:

- A. Aho, R. Sethi and J. D. Ullman, *Compilers: Principles, Techniques, and Tools*, Addison-Wesley, Reading, MA, 1986.

FORTRAN *[pp. 61–62]* was designed by J. Backus and a team of scientists from IBM in 1954. One of the many books describing it is:

- D. D. McCracken, *A Guide to FORTRAN Programming*, John Wiley & Sons, New York, 1961.

An extended and more contemporary version, FORTRAN 77, is described in:

- W. Brainerd, 'FORTRAN 77,' *Comm. Assoc. Comput. Mach.* **21**, (1978), pp. 806–820.

COBOL *[pp. 62–63]* was designed in 1959 by a technical committee sponsored by the US Department of Defense. One of the many books describing it is:

- D. D. McCracken, *A Guide to COBOL Programming*, John Wiley & Sons, New York, 1963.

PASCAL *[pp. 63–66]* was designed by N. Wirth and was first described in:

- N. Wirth, 'The Programming Language PASCAL,' *Acta Informatica* **1** (1971), pp. 35–63.

Good places to read about PASCAL are:

- D. Cooper and M. Clancy, *Oh! Pascal!*, W. W. Norton & Co., New York, 1982.

- K. Jensen and N. Wirth, *PASCAL User Manual and Report* (3rd edn.), Springer-Verlag, New York, 1984.

- D. Wood, *Paradigms and Programming in PASCAL*, Computer Science Press, Rockville, MD, 1984.

An important paper assessing the language, and written by its inventor, is:

- N. Wirth, 'An Assessment of the Programming Language PASCAL,' *IEEE Trans. Soft. Eng.* SE-1 (1975), pp. 192–198.

SNOBOL *[pp. 66–68]* was designed in 1963 by a group at Bell Telephone Laboratories headed by R. E. Griswold. A good place to read about it is:

- R. E. Griswold, J. F. Poage and I. P. Polonsky, *The SNOBOL4 Programming Language* (2nd edn.), Prentice-Hall, Englewood Cliffs, NJ, 1971.

LISP *[pp. 68–70]* was designed by J. McCarthy in 1960, based on the *lambda calculus* of A. Church and S. C. Kleene. A good reference to the lambda calculus is:

- H. P. Barendregt, *The Lambda Calculus: Its Syntax and Semantics* (2nd edn.), North Holland, 1984.

In addition to Abelson and Sussman's book, which was mentioned in the notes for Chapter 2, the LISP language is described in many places, among which are:

- J. Allen, *The Anatomy of LISP*, McGraw-Hill, New York, 1978.

- P. H. Winston and B. K. P. Horn, *LISP* (2nd edn.), Addison-Wesley, Reading, MA, 1984.

PROLOG *[pp. 70–72]* was designed by A. Colmerauer in 1970, based upon the ideas of R. Kowalski. The underlying approach is described in:

- R. Kowalski, 'Algorithm = Logic + Control,' *Comm. Assoc. Comput. Mach.* **22** (1979), pp. 424 436.

- J. W. Lloyd, *Foundations of Logic Programming*, Springer-Verlag, Berlin, 1984.

Good books for reading about the language are:

- W. F. Clocksin and C. S. Mellish, *Programming in PROLOG* (2nd edn.), Springer-Verlag, New York, 1984.

- L. Sterling and E. Shapiro, *The Art of Prolog*, MIT Press, Cambridge, MA, 1986.

- F. Giannesini, H. Kanoui, R. Pasero and M. van Caneghem, *PROLOG*, Addison-Wesley, Reading, MA, 1986.

APL *[pp. 72–73]* was designed in 1962 by K. E. Iverson at IBM and was first described in:

- K. E. Iverson, *A Programming Language*, John Wiley & Sons, New York, 1962.

Good places to read about the language are:

- L. Gilman and A. J. Rose, *APL: An Interactive Approach*, John Wiley & Sons, New York, 1984.

- R. P. Polivka and S. Pakin, *APL: The Language and its Usage*, Prentice-Hall, Englewood Cliffs, NJ, 1975.

Chapter 4

There are several excellent books on algorithms that, among other things, emphasize design paradigms and methods. Among them are:

- A. V. Aho, J. E. Hopcroft and J. D. Ullman, *The Design and Analysis of Computer Algorithms*, Addison-Wesley, Reading, MA, 1974.

- E. Horowitz and S. Sahni, *Fundamentals of Computer Algorithms*, Computer Science Press, Rockville, MD, 1978.

A more elementary book is:

- R. G. Dromey, *How to Solve it by Computer*, Prentice-Hall International, London, 1982.

Apart from these, there are many books that are organized around specific kinds of algorithms, but implicitly contain also a wealth of information about algorithmic methods. Here are some:

- S. Even, *Graph Algorithms*, Computer Science Press, Rockville, MD, 1979.

- G. H. Gonnet, *Handbook of Algorithms and Data Structures*, Addison-Wesley, Reading, MA, 1984.

- T. C. Hu, *Combinatorial Algorithms*, Addison-Wesley, Reading, MA, 1982.

- K. Melhorn, *Data Structures and Algorithms* 1: *Sorting and Searching*, Springer-Verlag, Berlin, 1984.

- K. Melhorn, *Data Structures and Algorithms* 2: *Graph Algorithms and NP-Completeness*, Springer-Verlag, Berlin, 1984.

- K. Melhorn, *Data Structures and Algorithms* 3: *Multi-Dimensional Searching and Computational Geometry*, Springer-Verlag, Berlin, 1984.

- D. E. Knuth, *The Art of Computer Programming*, Vol. 1: *Fundamental Algorithms* (2nd edn.), Addison-Wesley, Reading, MA, 1973.

- D. E. Knuth, *The Art of Computer Programming*, Vol. 2: *Seminumerical Algorithms*, Addison-Wesley, Reading, MA, 1969.

- D. E. Knuth, *The Art of Computer Programming*, Vol. 3: *Sorting and Searching*, Addison-Wesley, Reading, MA, 1973.

- E. L. Lawler, *Combinatorial Optimization: Networks and Matroids*, Holt, Rinehart & Winston, New York, 1976.

- C. H. Papadimitriou and K. Steiglitz, *Combinatorial Optimization: Algorithms and Complexity*, Prentice-Hall, Englewood Cliffs, NJ, 1982.

- E. M. Reingold, J. Nievergelt and N. Deo, *Combinatorial Algorithms: Theory and Practice*, Prentice-Hall, Englewood Cliffs, NJ, 1977.

- R. Sedgewick, *Algorithms*, Addison-Wesley, Reading, MA, 1983.

- R. E. Tarjan, *Data Structures and Network Algorithms*, CBMS-NSF Regional Conf. Series in Appl. Math., SIAM, Philadelphia, PA, 1983.

*   *   *

Two books on computational geometry *[pp. 81–83]* are Melhorn's third volume and:

- F. P. Preparata and M. I. Shamos, *Computational Geometry: An Introduction*, Springer-Verlag, New York, 1985.

The mergesort algorithm *[p. 84]* is described in many of the books listed, but (as mentioned earlier in connection with bubblesort and treesort) Knuth's 1973 volume on sorting and searching, although not absolutely up to date, is by far the most comprehensive reference.

The greedy spanning tree algorithm *[pp. 86–87]* is from:

- R. C. Prim, 'Shortest Connection Networks and Some Generalizations,' *Bell Syst. Tech. J.* **36** (1957), pp. 1389–1401.

Another important paper on minimal spanning trees is:

- J. B. Kruskal, Jr., 'On the Shortest Spanning Subtree of a Graph and the Traveling Salesman Problem,' *Proc. Amer. Math. Soc.* **7** (1956), pp. 48–50.

An early paper relevant to both spanning trees and shortest path algorithms is:

- E. W. Dijkstra, 'A Note on Two Problems in Connexion with Graphs,' *Numerische Mathematik* **1** (1959), pp. 269–271.

The history of spanning tree algorithms, which apparently starts well before Prim and Kruskal, is traced in:

- R. L. Graham and P. Hell, 'On the History of The Minimal Spanning Tree Problem,' *Ann. Hist. Comput.* **7** (1985), pp. 43–57.

Here are two books in which dynamic planning *[pp. 87–90]* (= dynamic programming) is outlined in more detail:

- R. Bellman, *Dynamic Programming*, Princeton University Press, Princeton, NJ, 1957.

- S. E. Dreyfus and A. M. Law, *The Art and Theory of Dynamic Programming*, Academic Press, New York, 1977.

Two very influential papers concerning algorithmic problems on graphs are:

- R. E. Tarjan, 'Depth First Search and Linear Graph Algorithms,' *SIAM J. Comput.* **1** (1972), pp. 146–160.

- J. E. Hopcroft and R. E. Tarjan, 'Efficient Algorithms for Graph Manipulation,' *Comm. Assoc. Comput. Mach.* **16** (1973), pp. 372–378.

Chapter 5

There are a number of books devoted to methods and tools for the verification of algorithms and programs:

- S. Alagić and M. A. Arbib, *The Design of Well-Structured and Correct Programs*, Springer-Verlag, New York, 1978.

- J. W. de Bakker, *Mathematical Theory of Program Correctness*, Prentice-Hall International, London, 1980.

- J. Loeckx and K. Seiber, *The Foundations of Program Verification*, John Wiley & Sons, New York, 1984.

- Z. Manna, *Mathematical Theory of Computation*, McGraw-Hill, New York, 1974.

In addition, the following books contain informative chapters on correctness and verification:

- R. Bird, *Programs and Machines: An Introduction to the Theory of Computation*, John Wiley & Sons, New York, 1976.

- J. M. Brady, *The Theory of Computer Science: A Programming Approach*, Chapman and Hall, London, 1977.

- S. A. Greibach, *Theory of Program Structures: Schemes, Semantics, Verification*, Springer-Verlag, Berlin, 1975.

- E. V. Krishnamurthy, *Introductory Theory of Computer Science*, Springer-Verlag, New York, 1983.

Apart from the general periodicals listed earlier, the following journals publish many papers pertaining to algorithmic correctness:

- *ACM Transactions on Programming Languages and Systems*, sometimes abbreviated *ACM Trans. Prog. Lang. Syst.*, or simply *TOPLAS*; a quarterly published by the ACM.

- *Acta Informatica*, abbreviated *Acta Inf.*; a bimonthly published by Springer-Verlag.

- *Science of Computer Programming*, abbreviated *Sci. Comput. Prog.*; a bimonthly published by North Holland.

- *Journal of Automated Reasoning*, abbreviated *J. Autom. Reas.*; published by D. Reidel Publishing Co.

- *IEEE Transactions on Software Engineering*, abbreviated *IEEE Trans. Soft. Eng.*; a monthly published by the IEEE.

*   *   *

The two stories of computer errors *[p. 91]* are among numerous ones that are reported regularly in:

- *ACM Software Engineering Notes*; an unrefereed newsletter published by ACM's Special Interest Group on Software Engineering.

The place to read about syntactic analysis and error handling *[p. 93]* in compilation is:

- A. V. Aho, R. Sethi and J. D. Ullman, *Compilers: Principles, Techniques, and Tools*, Addison-Wesley, Reading, MA, 1986.

Good places to read about testing *[pp. 96–97]* are:

- W. R. Adrion, M. A. Branstad and J. C. Cherniavsky, 'Validation, Verification and Testing of Computer Software,' *Comput. Surv.* **14** (1982), pp. 152–192.

- G. J. Myers, *The Art of Software Testing*, John Wiley & Sons, New York, 1979.

The mermaid aphorism *[p. 96]* appears on page 17 of:

- G. D. Bergland, 'A Guided Tour of Program Design Methodologies,' *IEEE Computer* **14** (1981), pp. 13–37.

The aphorism about the absence/presence of errors *[p. 97]* appears on page 6 of:

- E. W. Dijkstra, 'Notes on Structured Programming,' in *Structured Programming*, Academic Press, New York, 1972.

The notion of partial correctness *[p. 99]* appears in:

- Z. Manna, 'The Correctness of Programs,' *J. Comput. Syst. Sci.* **3** (1969), pp. 119–127.

The statement about the time software is released for use *[p. 100]* appears on page 1330 of:

- D. L. Parnas, 'Software Aspects of Strategic Defense Systems,' *Comm. Assoc. Comput. Mach.* **28** (1985), pp. 1326–1335.

A provocative but important paper on the (im)possibility of proving correctness of programs is:

- R. A. De Millo, R. J. Lipton and A. J. Perlis, 'Social Processes and Proofs of Theorems and Programs,' *Comm. Assoc. Comput. Mach.* **22** (1979), pp. 271–280.

Both the intermediate assertion (invariant) method for proving partial correctness *[pp. 100–103]*, and the convergence method (sometimes called the *well-founded sets method*) for proving termination *[p. 103]* are due to R. W. Floyd. They were first described as proof methods in the following paper, although they have their roots in much earlier work of Turing, von Neumann and others:

- R. W. Floyd, 'Assigning Meanings to Programs,' *Proc. Symp. on Applied Math.* (Vol. 19: 'Mathematical Aspects of Computer Science'), American Math. Soc., Providence, RI, pp. 19–32, 1967.

Three important and influential papers expounding upon Floyd's methods are:

- C. A. R. Hoare, 'An Axiomatic Basis for Computer Programming,' *Comm. Assoc. Comput. Mach.* **12** (1969), pp. 576–583.

- S. Cook, 'Soundness and Completeness of an Axiom System for Program Verification,' *SIAM J. Comput.* **7** (1978), pp. 70–90.

- E. M. Clarke, 'Programming Language Constructs for which it is Impossible to Obtain Good Hoare-Like Axioms,' *J. Assoc. Comput. Mach.* **26** (1979), pp. 129–147.

An excellent survey of the methods and ideas that originated in the work of Floyd, Hoare and Cook is:

- K. R. Apt, 'Ten Years of Hoare's Logic: A Survey,' *ACM Trans. Prog. Lang. Syst.* **3** (1981), pp. 431–483.

An efficient algorithm for finding a minimal set of checkpoints to which assertions can be attached for proving correctness *[p. 109]* appears in:

- A. Shamir, 'Finding Minimum Cutsets in Reducible Graphs,' Tech. Rep. MIT/LCS/TM-85, Mass. Inst. of Tech., Cambridge, MA, 1977.

That a partially correct program can, in principle, always be proved correct *[p. 109]* is established in Cook's paper. That a totally correct program can also be so proved is established in:

- D. Harel, 'Arithmetical Completeness in Logics of Programs,' *Proc. Int. Colloq. on Automata, Lang. and Prog.*, Lecture Notes in Computer Science, Vol. 62, Springer-Verlag, Berlin, pp. 268–288, 1978.

A good place to read about mathematical induction *[p. 111]* and the ways it is used in program verification is

- M. Wand, *Induction, Recursion, and Programming*, North Holland, 1980.

The simple iterative solution to the Towers of Hanoi problem *[p. 113]* appears in:

- P. Buneman and L. Levy, 'The Towers of Hanoi Problem,' *Inf. Proc. Lett.* **10** (1980), pp. 243–244.

The following books contain detailed approaches to as-you-go verification *[pp. 113–114]*, by providing methodologies for constructing well-structured and correct programs:

- E. W. Dijkstra, *A Discipline of Programming*, Prentice-Hall, Englewood Cliffs, NJ, 1976.

- D. Gries, *The Science of Programming*, Springer-Verlag, New York, 1981.

- J. C. Reynolds, *The Craft of Programming*, Prentice-Hall International, London, 1981.

Here are some pointers to work that has been done on computer-aided program verification *[pp. 114–115]*:

- R. S. Boyer and J. S. Moore, *A Computational Logic*, Academic Press, New York, 1979.

- R. L. Constable *et al.*, *Implementing Mathematics with the Nuprl Proof Development System*, Prentice-Hall, Englewood Cliffs, NJ, 1986.

- M. J. Gordon, A. J. Milner and C. P. Wadsworth, *Edinburgh LCF: A Mechanised Logic of Computation*, Lecture Notes in Computer Science, Vol. 78, Springer-Verlag, Berlin, 1979.

- W. Polak, *Compiler Specification and Verification*, Lecture Notes in Computer Science, Vol. 124, Springer-Verlag, Berlin, 1981.

Three basic papers on dynamic logics *[p. 116]* are:

- A. Salwicki, 'Formalized Algorithmic Languages,' *Bull. Acad. Polon. Sci., Ser. Sci. Math. Astron. Phys.* **18** (1970), pp. 227–232.

- V. R. Pratt, 'Semantical Considerations on Floyd-Hoare Logic,' *Proc. 17th IEEE Symp. on Foundations of Computer Science*, IEEE, New York, pp. 109–121, 1976.

- M. J. Fischer and R. E. Ladner, 'Propositional Dynamic Logic of Regular Programs,' *J. Comput. Syst. Sci.* **18** (1979), pp. 194–211.

A survey of many of the formalisms and results on the subject is:

- D. Harel, 'Dynamic Logic', in *Handbook of Philosophical Logic*, Vol. II (D. Gabbay and F. Guenthner, eds.), D. Reidel Publishing Co., Holland, pp. 497–604, 1984.

Good places to read about program synthesis *[p. 116]* are:

- N. Dershowitz, *The Evolution of Programs*, Birkhäuser, Boston, 1983.

- Z. Manna and R. Waldinger, 'A Deductive Approach to Program Synthesis,' *ACM Trans. Prog. Lang. Syst.* **2** (1980), pp. 90–121.

Two early papers on program transformations *[pp. 116–117]* are:

- J. Darlington and R. M. Burstall, 'A System which Automatically Improves Programs,' *Proc. 3rd Int. Conf. on Artificial Intelligence*, Stanford, CA, pp. 479–485, 1973.

- S. L. Gerhart, 'Proof Theory of Partial Correctness Verification Systems,' *SIAM J. Comput.* **5** (1976), pp. 355–377.

A good survey of implemented systems that aid in program testing is:

- H. Partsch and R. Steinbrüggen, 'Program Transformation Systems,' *Comput. Surv.* **15** (1983), pp. 199–236.

Building upon the work of many predecessors, the four-color problem *[pp. 117–118]* was finally solved by K. I. Appel and W. Haken, and was first announced in:

- K. I. Appel and W. Haken, 'Every Planar Map is Four Colorable,' *Bull. Amer. Math. Soc.* **82** (1976), pp. 711–712.

A detailed account of the problem and its solution can be found in:

- T. L. Saaty and P. C. Kainen, *The Four Color Problem: Assaults and Conquest*, Dover Publishers, New York, 1986.

Chapter 6

Most of the books recommended in the notes for Chapter 4 are also relevant here, since they typically spend considerable time analyzing the efficiency of the algorithms they present. Two of them are mentioned here again, as books that contain a good overview of the subject of algorithmic efficiency, with examples of a variety of algorithms:

- A. V. Aho, J. E. Hopcroft and J. D. Ullman, *The Design and Analysis of Computer Algorithms*, Addison-Wesley, Reading, MA, 1974.

- E. Horowitz and S. Sahni, *Fundamentals of Computer Algorithms*, Computer Science Press, Rockville, MD, 1978.

A useful book whose title speaks for itself is:

- J. L. Bentley, *Writing Efficient Programs*, Prentice-Hall, Englewood Cliffs, NJ, 1982.

Its author, J. L. Bentley, writes a monthly column on efficient algorithms in the *Comm. Assoc. Comput. Mach.*, called *Programming Pearls*. Another book devoted to algorithmic efficiency is:

- P. W. Purdom, Jr. and A. A. Brown, *The Analysis of Algorithms*, Holt, Rinehart & Winston, New York, 1985.

A handbook containing much of the mathematics used in typical analyses of algorithmic efficiency is:

- D. H. Greene and D. E. Knuth, *Mathematics for the Analysis of Algorithms*, Birkhäuser, Boston, 1981.

As far as periodicals are concerned, besides the ones listed in the general section of the notes, those listed in the notes for Chapter 2 are relevant here too.

*   *   *

The history of the big-O notation (which, strictly speaking, should be called the *big-Omicron* notation) *[p. 123]* and its adoption in computer science is traced in:

- D. E. Knuth, 'Big Omicron and Big Omega and Big Theta,' *SIGACT News* 8: 2 (1976), pp. 18–24.

Several variants of binary search *[pp. 124–129, 139–140]*, as well as their analysis and origins, appear in Knuth's volume on searching and sorting:

- D. E. Knuth, *The Art of Computer Programming*, Vol. 3: *Sorting and Searching*, Addison-Wesley, Reading, MA, 1973.

Treesort and mergesort *[pp. 133–135]* are also analyzed in detail in Knuth's volume, as is quicksort. Quicksort was invented by C. A. R. Hoare and first appeared in:

- C. A. R. Hoare, 'Quicksort,' *Comput. J.* 5 (1962), pp. 10–15.

The convex hull algorithm *[pp. 142–144]* appears in:

- R. L. Graham, 'An Efficient Algorithm for Determining the Convex Hull of a Finite Planar Set,' *Inf. Proc. Lett.* 1 (1972), pp. 132–133.

Two books devoted to computational geometry, which among many other topics include more efficient convex hull algorithms, are:

- F. P. Preparata and M. I. Shamos, *Computational Geometry: An Introduction*, Springer-Verlag, New York, 1985.

- K. Melhorn, *Data Structures and Algorithms* 3: *Multi-Dimensional Searching and Computational Geometry*, Springer-Verlag, Berlin, 1984.

Almost linear algorithms for the spanning tree problem *[p. 145]* appear in:

- M. L. Fredman and R. E. Tarjan, 'Fibonacci Heaps and their Uses in Improved Network Optimization Algorithms,' *Proc. 25th IEEE Symp. on Foundations of Computer Science*, IEEE, New York, pp. 338–346, 1984.

- H. Gabow, Z. Galil and T. H. Spencer, 'Efficient Implementation of Graph Algorithms Using Contraction,' *Proc. 25th IEEE Symp. on Foundations of Computer Science*, IEEE, New York, pp. 347–357, 1984.

Chapter 7

The following book is devoted in its entirety to intractability. It concentrates on the class of NP-complete problems and related issues and, in addition, contains a detailed annotated list of numerous problems that are NP-complete:

- M. R. Garey and D. S. Johnson, *Computers and Intractability: A Guide to NP-Completeness*, W. H. Freeman & Co., San Francisco, CA, 1979.

One of the authors of this book, D. S. Johnson, writes a periodical column in the *Journal of Algorithms*, called *The NP-Completeness Column: An Ongoing Guide*. Together, the book and the accumulating columns provide a list of hundreds of known NP-complete problems that, at any point in time, comes as close to being really complete as anything of its kind.

A number of books contain chapters that discuss intractable problems and NP-completeness. They include:

- M. D. Davis and E. J. Weyuker, *Computability, Complexity, and Languages: Fundamentals of Theoretical Computer Science*, Academic Press, New York, 1983.

- J. E. Hopcroft and J. D. Ullman, *Introduction to Automata Theory, Languages, and Computation*, Addison-Wesley, Reading, MA, 1979.

- E. Horowitz and S. Sahni, *Fundamentals of Computer Algorithms*, Computer Science Press, Rockville, MD, 1978.

- E. V. Krishnamurthy, *Introductory Theory of Computer Science*, Springer-Verlag, New York, 1983.

- H. R. Lewis and C. H. Papadimitriou, *Elements of the Theory of Computation*, Prentice-Hall, Englewood Cliffs, NJ, 1981.

- M. Machtey and P. Young, *An Introduction to the General Theory of Algorithms*, North Holland, Amsterdam, 1978.

- K. Melhorn, *Data Structures and Algorithms 2: Graph Algorithms and NP-Completeness*, Springer-Verlag, Berlin, 1984.

- C. H. Papadimitriou and K. Stieglitz, *Combinatorial Optimization: Algorithms and Complexity*, Prentice-Hall, Englewood Cliffs, NJ, 1982.

Two excellent expository articles on the subject of intractability, which were an inspiring source in the preparation of Chapter 7, are:

- H. R. Lewis and C. H. Papadimitriou, 'The Efficiency of Algorithms,' *Scientific American* **238**: 1 (1978), pp. 96–109.

- L. J. Stockmeyer and A. K. Chandra, 'Intrinsically Difficult Problems,' *Scientific American* **240**: 5 (1979), pp. 140–159.

The following survey papers, written by three researchers who have made fundamental contributions to the subject matter of this chapter, are very informative:

- M. O. Rabin, 'Complexity of Computations,' *Comm. Assoc. Comput. Mach.* **20** (1977), pp. 625–633.

- S. A. Cook, 'An Overview of Computational Complexity,' *Comm. Assoc. Comput. Mach.* **26** (1983), pp. 401–408.

- R. M. Karp, 'Combinatorics, Complexity, and Randomness,' *Comm. Assoc. Comput. Mach.* **29** (1986), pp. 98–109.

* * *

The table and graphs appearing in Figures 7.3, 7.4, 7.5 and 7.7 are based in part on those appearing in Garey and Johnson's book and the two *Scientific American* articles previously mentioned.

The following early papers have been most influential in laying the foundations for complexity theory and in recognizing the importance of the dichotomy between polynomial and super-polynomial-time *[pp. 155–159]*:

- M. O. Rabin, 'Degree of Difficulty of Computing a Function and a Partial Ordering of Recursive Sets,' *Technical Report No. 2*, Hebrew University, Branch of Applied Logic, Jerusalem, 1960.

- A. Cobham, 'The Intrinsic Computational Difficulty of Functions,' *Proc. 1964 Int. Congress for Logic, Methodology, and Phil. of Sci.*, (Y. Bar-Hillel, ed.), North Holland, pp. 24–30, 1965.

- J. Edmonds, 'Paths, Trees, and Flowers,' *Canad. J. Math.* **17** (1965), pp. 449–467.

- J. Hartmanis and R. E. Stearns, 'On the Computational Complexity of Algorithms,' *Trans. Amer. Math. Soc.* **117** (1965), pp. 285–306.

- M. Blum, 'A Machine Independent Theory of the Complexity of Recursive Functions,' *J. Assoc. Comput. Mach.* **14** (1967), pp. 322–336.

The identification of the class of NP-complete problems *[pp. 160–161]*, together with the landmark result (Cook's Theorem) that established the NP-completeness of the satisfiability problem *[pp. 165, 171]*, is due to S. A. Cook and appears in:

- S. A. Cook, 'The Complexity of Theorem Proving Procedures,' *Proc. 3rd ACM Symp. on Theory of Computing*, ACM, New York, pp. 151–158, 1971.

Similar results were obtained independently, but a little later, by L. A. Levin in:

- L. A. Levin, 'Universal Search Problems,' *Problemy Peredaci Informacii* **9** (1973), pp. 115–116 (in Russian). English translation in *Problems of Information Transmission* **9** (1973), pp. 265–266.

The significance of these discoveries was recognized in the following important paper, in which several other problems (including the traveling salesman problem, 3-colorability, and Hamiltonian paths *[pp. 162–166]*) were shown to be NP-complete using polynomial-time reductions:

- R. M. Karp, 'Reducibility Among Combinatorial Problems', in *Complexity of Computer Computations* (R. E. Miller and J. W. Thatcher, eds.), Plenum Press, New York, pp. 85–104, 1972.

That the traveling salesman problem remains NP-complete not only for general graphs but even for city networks with Euclidean distances is shown in:

- C. H. Papadimitriou, 'The Euclidean Traveling Salesman Problem is NP-Complete,' *Theor. Comput. Sci.* **4** (1977), pp. 237–244.

That the timetable problem is NP-complete *[p. 164]* is shown in:

- S. Even, A. Itai and A. Shamir, 'On the Complexity of Timetable and Multicommodity Flow Problems,' *SIAM J. Comput.* **5** (1976), pp. 691–703.

That the primality problem is in NP *[p. 173]* is shown in:

- V. R. Pratt, 'Every Prime has a Succint Certificate,' *SIAM J. Comput.* **4** (1975), pp. 214–220.

Approximation algorithms *[pp. 173–175]* appear in many of the books and papers mentioned above. In particular, chapters on the subject appear in the books of Garey and Johnson, Horowitz and Sahni, Melhorn, and Papadimitriou and Stieglitz.

The 1.5-times-the-optimum algorithm for the traveling salesman problem *[p. 174]* is due to N. Christofides and appears in the aforementioned books of Melhorn, and Papadimitriou and Steiglitz. The heuristic algorithm for the same problem, which is almost always good *[p. 174]*, appears in:

- R. M. Karp, 'The Probabilistic Analysis of Partitioning Algorithms for the Traveling-Salesman Problem in the Plane,' *Math. Oper. Res.* **2** (1977), pp. 209–224.

An excellent collection of up-to-date papers on the traveling salesman problem is:

- *The Traveling Salesman Problem: A Guided Tour of Combinatorial Optimization* (E. L. Lawler *et al.*, eds.), John Wiley & Sons, New York, 1985.

That a polynomial-time algorithm yielding a coloring of a graph with no more than twice the minimal number of colors cannot exist unless P = NP *[p. 174]* is proved in:

- M. R. Garey and D. S. Johnson, 'The Complexity of Near-Optimal Graph Coloring,' *J. Assoc. Comput. Mach.* **23** (1976), pp. 43–49.

The first proof that a problem of interest has an exponential-time lower bound appears in:

- A. R. Meyer and L. J. Stockmeyer, 'The Equivalence Problem for Regular Expressions with Squaring Requires Exponential Time,' *Proc. 13th Ann. Symp. on Switching and Automata Theory*, IEEE, New York, pp. 125–129, 1972.

That generalized chess and checkers are provably intractible *[p. 175]* is shown, respectively, in:

- A. S. Fraenkel and D. Lichtenstein, 'Computing a Perfect Strategy for $n \times n$ Chess Requires Time Exponential in n,' *J. Combinatorial Theory*, Series A31 (1981), pp. 199–214.

- J. M. Robson, 'N by N Checkers is Exptime Complete,' *SIAM J. Comput.* **13** (1984), pp. 252–267.

Roadblock *[pp. 175–176]* is described in the *Scientific American* paper by Stockmeyer and Chandra previously mentioned and was proved to be intractible in:

- L. J. Stockmeyer and A. K. Chandra, 'Provably Difficult Combinatorial Games,' *SIAM J. Comput.* **8** (1979), pp. 151–174.

Propositional dynamic logic *[p. 177]* was defined and shown to be intractible in:

- M. J. Fischer and R. E. Ladner, 'Propositional Dynamic Logic of Regular Programs,' *J. Comput. Syst. Sci.* **18** (1979), pp. 194–211.

That Presburger arithmetic requires double-exponential time *[p. 179]* is shown in:

- M. J. Fischer and M. O. Rabin, 'Super-Exponential Complexity of Presburger Arithmetic', in *Complexity of Computation* (R. M. Karp, ed.), Amer. Math. Soc., Providence, RI, pp. 27–41, 1974.

That WS1S requires nonelementary time *[p. 179]* is shown in:

- A. R. Meyer, 'Weak Monadic Second Order Theory of Successor is not Elementary Recursive,' in *Logic Colloquium* (R. Parikh, ed.), Lecture Notes in Mathematics, Vol. 453, Springer-Verlag, Berlin, pp. 132–154, 1975.

A good survey of many upper and lower bounds on the complexity of satisfiability problems is:

- J. Ferrante and C. W. Rackoff, *The Computational Complexity of Logical Theories*, Lecture Notes in Mathematics, Vol. 718, Springer-Verlag, Berlin, 1979.

The simplex method for linear planning *[p. 180]* was discovered in the early 1950s by G. B. Dantzig and a detailed account appears in:

- G. B. Dantzig, *Linear Programming and Extensions*, Princeton University Press, Princeton, NJ, 1963.

The first polynomial-time algorithm for the problem appeared in the influential paper:

- L. G. Khachiyan, 'A Polynomial Algorithm in Linear Programming,' *Doklady Akademiia Nauk SSSR* **244** (1979), pp. 1093–1096 (in Russian). English translation in *Soviet Mathematics Doklad* **20** (1979), pp. 191–194.

Another polynomial-time algorithm for linear planning, which is thought to perform better than Khachiyan's in practice, appears in:

- N. Karmarkar, 'A New Polynomial-Time Algorithm for Linear Programming,' *Proc. 16th ACM Symp. on Theory of Computing*, ACM, New York, pp. 302–311, 1984.

Chapter 8

Historically, the interest in noncomputability and undecidability dates back to a plan devised by the great mathematician David Hilbert. At the turn of the century, Hilbert proposed that all mathematical problems should be encoded in some suitable logical formalism, and an algorithm be found for determining truth therein. That this is essentially impossible was proved in 1931 by Kurt Gödel in the following landmark paper, which showed that truth in the first-order predicate calculus is not even partially decidable (a result sometimes referred to as *Gödel's Incompleteness Theorem*):

- K. Gödel, 'Über formal unentscheidbare Sätze der Principia Mathematica und verwandter Systeme, I,' *Monatshefte für Mathematik und Physik* **38** (1931), pp. 173–198.

An English translation of this paper, entitled 'On Formally Undecidable Propositions of Principia Mathematica and Related Systems', appears in the following book, which constitutes a collection of many of the early pioneering papers on the subject matter of this chapter:

- *The Undecidable: Basic Papers on Undecidable Propositions, Unsolvable Problems and Computable Functions* (M. Davis, ed.), Raven Press, New York, 1965.

An early and clear exposition of the subject matter of this and the next chapter is:

- B. A. Trakhtenbrot, *Algorithms and Automatic Computing Machines*, D. C. Heath & Co., Boston, 1963.

Many books contain material about undecidable and noncomputable problems. Here are some:

- R. Bird, *Programs and Machines: An Introduction to the Theory of Computation*, John Wiley & Sons, New York, 1976.

- G. Boolos and R. Jeffrey, *Computability and Logic* (2nd edn.), Cambridge University Press, Cambridge, 1980.

- W. S. Brainerd and L. H. Landweber, *Theory of Computation*, John Wiley & Sons, New York, 1974.

- J. M. Brady, *The Theory of Computer Science: A Programming Approach*, Chapman & Hall, London, 1977.

- N. J. Cutland, *Computability: An Introduction to Recursive Function Theory*, Cambridge University Press, Cambridge, 1980.

- M. D. Davis and E. J. Weyuker, *Computability, Complexity, and Languages: Fundamentals of Theoretical Computer Science*, Academic Press, New York, 1983.

- F. Hennie, *Introduction to Computability*, Addison-Wesley, Reading, MA, 1977.

- J. E. Hopcroft and J. D. Ullman, *Introduction to Automata Theory, Languages, and Computation*, Addison-Wesley, Reading, MA, 1979.

- A. J. Kfoury, R. N. Moll and M. A. Arbib, *A Programming Approach to Computability*, Springer-Verlag, New York, 1982.

- E. V. Krishnamurthy, *Introductory Theory of Computer Science*, Springer-Verlag, New York, 1983.

- H. R. Lewis and C. H. Papadimitriou, *Elements of the Theory of Computation*, Prentice-Hall, Englewood Cliffs, NJ, 1981.

- M. Machtey and P. Young, *An Introduction to the General Theory of Algorithms*, North Holland, 1978.

The most mathematically detailed and comprehensive treatment of recursive function theory, which includes noncomputability as a subarea, is:

- H. Rogers, *Theory of Recursive Functions and Effective Computability*, McGraw-Hill, New York, 1967.

Three influential early books are:

- S. C. Kleene, *Introduction to Metemathematics*, North Holland, 1952 (eighth reprint, 1980).

- M. Davis, *Computability and Unsolvability*, McGraw-Hill, New York, 1958. (Second edition published by Dover Publications, New York, in 1982).

- M. L. Minsky, *Computation: Finite and Infinite Machines*, Prentice-Hall, Englewood Cliffs, NJ, 1967.

The following book contains a somewhat unusual and entertaining account of the subject:

- D. R. Hofstadter, *Gödel, Escher, Bach: An Eternal Golden Braid*, Basic Books, New York, 1979.

In addition to the periodicals mentioned in the general section of these notes, the following journals contain papers on recursive function theory, and hence also on undecidability and noncomputability:

- *Journal of Symbolic Logic*, abbreviated *J. Symb. Logic*, or sometimes just *JSL*; a quarterly published by the Association for Symbolic Logic.

- *Zeitschrift für Mathematische Logik und Grundlagen der Mathematik*, abbreviated *Zeitschr. Math. Logik und Grundlagen Math.*, or sometimes simply *ZML*; a bimonthly published in Berlin by VEB Deutscher Verlag der Wissenschaften.

*   *   *

The quotation from *TIME [p. 184]* is by E. Baxter, managing editor of *Personal Software* magazine, and appears on pages 44–45 of the April 16, 1984 issue.

Tiling, or domino problems *[pp. 186–188]* were introduced by H. Wang in the following paper, which also contains a proof of the undecidability of a slightly restricted version:

- H. Wang, 'Proving Theorems by Pattern Recognition,' *Bell Syst. Tech. J.* **40** (1961), pp. 1–42.

The unrestricted version was proved undecidable in:

- R. Berger, 'The Undecidability of the Domino Problem,' *Memoirs Amer. Math. Soc.* **66** (1966).

A fascinating book about tilings of the plane is:

- B. Grünbaum and G. C. Shephard, *Tilings and Patterns*, W. H. Freeman & Co., New York, 1987.

The two results stating that the domino snake problem is decidable in the whole plane but becomes undecidable in the half-plane *[p. 190]* appear, respectively, in:

- D. Myers, 'Decidability of the Tiling Connectivity Problem,' Abstract 79T–E42, *Notices of the Amer. Math. Soc.* **195**: 26 (1979), A-441.

- H. -D Ebbinghaus, 'Undecidability of Some Domino Connectability Problems,' *Zeitschr. Math. Logik und Grundlagen Math.* **28** (1982), pp. 331–336.

The word correspondence problem *[pp. 191–192]*, sometimes called *Post's correspondence problem*, or simply PCP, was introduced and proven undecidable by E. L. Post in:

- E. L. Post, 'A Variant of a Recursively Unsolvable Problem,' *Bull. Amer. Math. Soc.* **52** (1946), pp. 264–268.

The problem of deciding the equivalence of syntactic definitions of programming languages *[p. 192]* is known better as the equivalence problem for *context-free grammars* and was proven undecidable in:

- Y. Bar-Hillel, M. Perles and E. Shamir, 'On Formal Properties of Simple Phrase Structure Grammars,' *Zeit. Phonetik, Sprachwiss. Kommunikationsforsch.* **14** (1961), pp. 143–172.

That program verification is noncomputable *[p. 193]* follows from the fact that truth in the first-order predicate calculus is undecidable, and is thus due, in essence, to K. Gödel, as discussed at the beginning of this section. The following paper discusses the $3x + 1$ algorithm *[p. 194]* and its variants in great detail:

- J. C. Lagarias, 'The $3x + 1$ Problem and its Generalizations,' *Amer. Math. Monthly* **92** (1985), pp. 3–23.

That the halting problem is undecidable *[pp. 194–195, 197–200]* is due, in essence, to A. Turing in his extremely important paper:

- A. Turing, 'On Computable Numbers with an Application to the Entscheidungsproblem,' *Proc. London Math. Soc.* **42** (1936), pp. 230–265. Corrections appeared in: *ibid.*, **43** (1937), pp. 544–546.

Rogers' book referenced earlier contains detailed accounts of the results on recursive enumerability *[pp. 201–204]* and hierarchies of undecidable problems, as well as the fact that the totality problem is not r.e. Many of these results are based on important early work of Stephen C. Kleene in:

- S. C. Kleene, 'Recursive Predicates and Quantifiers,' *Trans. Amer. Math. Soc.* **53** (1943), pp. 41–73.

That PDL with recursion is highly undecidable *[p. 206]* is proved in:

- D. Harel, A. Pnueli and J. Stavi, 'Propositional Dynamic Logic of Non-regular Programs,' *J. Comput. Syst. Sci.* **26** (1983), pp. 222–243.

Recurring domino problems are defined and shown to be highly undecidable *[p. 206]* in:

- D. Harel, 'Effective Transformations on Infinite Trees, with Applications to High Undecidability, Dominoes, and Fairness,' *J. Assoc. Comput. Mach.* **33** (1986), pp. 224–248.

Chapter 9

The material of this chapter is traditionally treated together with that of the previous one. Consequently, the list of books and periodicals mentioned at the beginning of the notes for Chapter 8 serves this chapter too.

*   *   *

Turing machines *[pp. 215–220]* were invented by Alan Turing and were first described in his fundamental paper:

- A. Turing, 'On Computable Numbers with an Application to the Entscheidungsproblem,' *Proc. London Math. Soc.* **42** (1936), pp. 230–265. Corrections appeared in: *ibid.*, **43** (1937), pp. 544–546.

The Church/Turing thesis *[pp. 221–222]* is named after Alonzo Church and Alan Turing. Ideas leading to it appear in Turing's paper and in the following extremely important paper:

- A. Church, 'An Unsolvable Problem of Elementary Number Theory,' *Amer. J. Math.* **58** (1936), pp. 345–363.

Fascinating historical accounts of the evolution of the lambda calculus, recursive function theory and the Church/Turing thesis are:

- S. C. Kleene, 'Origins of Recursive Function Theory,' *Ann. Hist. Comput.* **3** (1981), pp. 52–67.

- M. Davis, 'Why Gödel Didn't Have Church's Thesis,' *Inf. and Cont.* **54** (1982), pp. 3–24.

- J. B. Rosser, 'Highlights of the History of the Lambda-Calculus,' *Ann. Hist. Comput.* **6** (1984), pp. 337–349.

An interesting approach to modifying the thesis so as to capture terminating computations in real programming languages appears in:

- Y. Gurevich, 'Logic and the Challenge of Computer Science', in *Current Trends in Theoretical Computer Science* (E. Börger, ed.), Computer Science Press, Rockville, MD, 1987.

The lambda calculus *[p. 222]* was the result of work by Church and Kleene, appearing explicitly in:

- S. C. Kleene, 'A Theory of Positive Integers in Formal Logic,' *Amer. J. Math.* **57** (1935), pp. 153–173, 219–244.

It is described in great detail in:

- H. P. Barendregt, *The Lambda Calculus: Its Syntax and Semantics* (2nd edn.), North Holland, 1984.

Post's production systems *[p. 222]* appear in the following important paper:

- E. Post, 'Formal Reductions of the General Combinatorial Decision Problem,' *Amer. J. Math.* **65** (1943), pp. 197–215.

Kleene's definition of recursive functions *[p. 222]* is based on that of Gödel, and appears in:

- S. C. Kleene, 'General Recursive Functions of Natural Numbers,' *Math. Ann.* **112** (1936), pp. 727–742.

Three of the first papers to prove the equivalence of these formalisms are:

- S. C. Kleene, 'λ-Definability and Recursiveness,' *Duke Math. J.* **2** (1936), pp. 340–353.
- E. Post, 'Finite Combinatory Processes – Formulation 1,' *J. Symb. Logic* **1** (1936), pp. 103–105.
- A. M. Turing, 'Computability and λ-Definability,' *J. Symb. Logic* **2** (1937), pp. 153–163.

As mentioned earlier, the definitive reference on recursive functions and their properties is:

- H. Rogers, *Theory of Recursive Functions and Effective Computability*, McGraw-Hill, New York, 1967.

Many variants of Turing machines, in particular, nondeterministic and multi-tape machines *[pp. 223–224]*, as well as the reduction from two-way to one-way infinite tapes *[pp. 224–228]*, are described in:

- J. E. Hopcroft and J. D. Ullman, *Introduction to Automata Theory, Languages, and Computation*, Addison-Wesley, Reading, MA, 1979.

Counter programs, sometimes called *counter machines [pp. 228–229]*, are described in many of the aforementioned books, but constitute a particularly important part of:

- M. L. Minsky, *Computation: Finite and Infinite Machines*, Prentice-Hall, Englewood Cliffs, NJ, 1967.

That two counters suffice *[p. 231]* is proved in Minsky's book, and originally in:

- M. L. Minsky, 'Recursive Unsolvability of Post's Problem of 'tag' and Other Topics in the Theory of Turing Machines,' *Annals Math.* **74** (1961), pp. 437–455.

A more elegant proof (which forms the basis of the treatment herein) is given in:

- P. C. Fischer, 'Turing Machines with Restricted Memory Access,' *Inf. and Cont.* **9** (1966), pp. 364–379.

An important paper related to particularly interesting sublanguages of the language of counter programs is:

- A. R. Meyer and R. Ritchie, 'The Complexity of Loop Programs,' *Proc. ACM National Conf.*, ACM, New York, pp. 465–469, 1967.

The concept of a universal program *[pp. 232–234]* is, again, due to Alan Turing. In his 1936 paper he actually constructed a universal Turing machine and argued its importance.

The following is an exposition of Turing machines and related topics:

- J. E. Hopcroft, 'Turing Machines,' *Scientific American* **250**: 5 (1984), pp. 70–80.

The connection between Turing machines and complexity classes such as P was made in the early work on complexity theory; for example, in:

- J. Hartmanis and R. E. Stearns, 'On the Computational Complexity of Algorithms,' *Trans. Amer. Math. Soc.* **117** (1965), pp. 285–306.

The class NP has been defined using nondeterministic Turing machines *[pp. 238–239]* ever since Cook's original paper:

- S. A. Cook, 'The Complexity of Theorem Proving Procedures,' *Proc. 3rd ACM Symp. on Theory of Computing*, ACM, New York, pp. 151–158, 1971.

The reduction of the halting problem to a half-plane tiling problem *[pp. 240–244]* is based on the original proof in:

- H. Wang, 'Proving Theorems by Pattern Recognition,' *Bell Syst. Tech. J.* **40** (1961), pp. 1–42.

The idea of using diagonalization for proving exponential-time lower bounds *[pp. 243–247]* goes back to M. O. Rabin's work in the 1960s and the aforementioned paper by Hartmanis and Stearns.

Finite automata *[pp. 249–250]* seem to have originated in the following pioneering work on modeling nervous activity:

- W. S. McCulloch and W. Pitts, 'A Logical Calculus of the Ideas Immanent in Nervous Activity,' *Bull. Math. Biophysics* **5** (1943), pp. 115–133.

Two important early papers are:

- S. C. Kleene, 'Representation of Events in Nerve Nets and Finite Automata,' in *Automata Studies* (C. E. Shannon and J. McCarthy, eds.), *Ann. Math. Studies* **34** (1956), pp. 3–41. (Earlier version: RAND Research Memorandum RM-704, 1951).

- M. O. Rabin and D. Scott, 'Finite Automata and their Decision Problems,' *IBM J. Res.* **3** (1959), pp. 115–125.

Proving limitations of finite automata by the pigeon hole principle *[p. 251]* (leading to the so-called *pumping lemma*) is based upon proofs in:

- Y. Bar-Hillel, M. Perles and E. Shamir, 'On Formal Properties of Simple Phrase Structure Grammars,' *Zeit. Phonetik, Sprachwiss. Kommunikationsforsch.* **14** (1961), pp. 143–172.

Pushdown automata *[p. 253]* first appeared in explicit form in:

- A. G. Oettinger, 'Automatic Syntactic Analysis and the Pushdown Store,' *Proc. Symp. in Applied Math.* **12**, Amer. Math. Soc., Providence, RI, pp. 104–129, 1961.

Several important papers on the subject were written in the late 1950s by N. Chomsky, among which are:

- N. Chomsky, 'Three Models for the Description of Language,' *IRE Trans. Inf. Theory* **2** (1956), pp. 113–124.

- N. Chomsky, 'On Certain Formal Properties of Grammars,' *Inf. and Cont.* **2** (1959), pp. 137–167.

A detailed and insightful historical survey of the development of formal languages and automata theory is:

- S. A. Greibach, 'Formal Languages: Origins and Directions,' *Ann. Hist. Comput.* **3** (1981), pp. 14–41.

Many of the books mentioned in the notes for Chapter 8 contain thorough treatments of finite automata, pushdown automata and related formalisms. There are also many books devoted exclusively to automata and formal language theory. They include:

- S. Ginsburg, *Algebraic and Automata-Theoretic Properties of Formal Languages*, North Holland, 1975.

- M. A. Harrison, *Introduction to Formal Language Theory*, Addison-Wesley, Reading, MA, 1978.

- A. Salomaa, *Jewels of Formal Language Theory*, Computer Science Press, Rockville, MD, 1981.

The following paper proposes a definition of computable queries for databases *[p. 254]* and implicitly suggests an appropriate CT thesis for computing on such structures:

- A. K. Chandra and D. Harel, 'Computable Queries for Relational Data Bases,' *J. Comput. Syst. Sci.* **21** (1980), pp. 156–178.

Chapter 10

This chapter is really divided into two: parallelism (that is, solving algorithmic problems efficiently using parallel processes) and concurrency (that is, dealing with the design and behavior of concurrent protocols and systems.) Unfortunately, there are apparently no books that are devoted to parallel algorithms, though some are in the writing. Most research done on the subject is very new, and can be found only in technical papers. With concurrency the situation is better. Here are some books that treat the specification and design of concurrent protocols:

- M. Ben-Ari, *Principles of Concurrent Programming*, Prentice-Hall International, London, 1982.

- R. E. Filman and D. P. Friedman, *Coordinated Computing: Tools and Techniques for Distributed Software*, McGraw-Hill, New York, 1984.

- C. A. R. Hoare, *Communicating Sequential Processes*, Prentice-Hall International, London, 1985.

- F. André, D. Herman and J. -P. Verjus, *Synchronization of Parallel Programs*, MIT Press, Cambridge, MA, 1985.

The following books contain articles relevant to parallelism and concurrency:

- *Algorithms, Software and Hardware of Parallel Computers*, (V. E. Kotov and J. Miklosko, eds.), Springer-Verlag, New York, 1984.

- *Logics and Models of Concurrent Systems* (K. R. Apt, ed.), NATO ASI Series, Vol. 13, Springer-Verlag, New York, 1985.

A good book that discusses parallel computers is:

- R. W. Hockney and C. R. Jesshope, *Parallel Computers: Architecture, Programming and Algorithms*, Adam Hilger Ltd., Bristol, 1985.

Apart from the periodicals mentioned in the general section, the following journals publish papers relevant to the subjects of this chapter:

- *Journal of Parallel and Distributed Computing*, abbreviated *J. Par. Dist. Comput.*; a quarterly published by Academic Press.

- *International Journal of Parallel Programming*, abbreviated *Int. J. Parallel Prog.*; a bimonthly published by Plenum Press.

- *Distributed Computing*, abbreviated *Dist. Comput.*; a bimonthly published by Springer International.

- *ACM Transactions on Programming Languages and Systems*, abbreviated *ACM Trans. Prog. Lang. Syst.*, or sometimes simply *TOPLAS*; a quarterly published by the ACM.

- *Science of Computer Programming*, abbreviated *Sci. Comput. Prog.*; a bimonthly published by North Holland.

- *Software: Practice and Experience*, abbreviated *Softw. Pract. Exp.*; a monthly published by John Wiley & Sons.

- *Journal of Systems and Software*, abbreviated *J. Syst. Softw.*; a quarterly published by Elsevier Science Publications.

- *IEEE Transactions on Software Engineering*, abbreviated *IEEE Trans. Soft. Eng.*; a monthly published by the IEEE.

- *IEEE Transactions on Computers*, abbreviated *IEEE Trans. Comput.*; a monthly published by the IEEE.

*   *   *

The ditch-digging example *[p. 258]* is due to A. Pnueli, and the child-having one *[p. 258*: footnote] is based on a sentence appearing on page 17 of the following insightful book:

- F. P. Brooks, Jr., *The Mythical Man-Month*, Addison-Wesley, Reading, MA, 1979.

There are three places in which to read in detail about parallel sorting algorithms *[pp. 260–267]*. The first, of course, is:

- D. E. Knuth, *The Art of Computer Programming*, Vol. 3: *Sorting and Searching*, Addison-Wesley, Reading, MA, 1973.

The second is the following survey:

- D. Bitton, D. J. DeWitt, D. K. Hsaio and J. Menon, 'A Taxonomy of Parallel Sorting,' *Comput. Surv.* **16** (1984), pp. 287–318.

The third source for parallel sorting algorithms is the entire April 1985 issue (Vol. C-34, No. 4) of *IEEE Transactions on Computers*, which contains several articles on parallel sorting.

An influential paper on Boolean networks *[p. 264]* is:

- A. Borodin, 'On Relating Time and Space to Size and Depth,' *SIAM J. Comput.* **6** (1977), pp. 733–744.

The odd–even sorting network *[pp. 264–266]* was invented by K. E. Batcher and is described in:

- K. E. Batcher, 'Sorting Networks and their Applications,' *Proc. 1968 Spring Joint Comput. Conf.*, AFIPS Press, Reston, VA, pp. 307–314, 1968.

The logarithmic-time sorting network with $O(N \times \log N)$ processors *[p. 266]*, sometimes called the *AKS network*, after its inventors, appears in:

- M. Ajtai, J. Komlós and E. Szemerédi, 'An $O(n\log n)$ Sorting Network,' *Proc. 15th ACM Symp. on Theory of Computing*, ACM, New York, pp. 1–9, 1983.

The optimal sorting network *[pp. 266–267]* is based on the AKS network and appears in

- T. Leighton, 'Tight Bounds on the Complexity of Parallel Sorting,' *IEEE Trans. Comput.* **C-34** (1985), pp. 344–354.

A good survey of parallel algorithms on graphs, including ones for finding minimal spanning trees and traveling salesman paths, is:

- M. J. Quinn and N. Deo, 'Parallel Graph Algorithms,' *Comput. Surv.* **16** (1984), pp. 319–348.

Systolic networks *[pp. 267–270]* were first studied in:

- H. T. Kung, 'Let's Design Algorithms for VLSI Systems,' *Proc. Conf. Very Large Scale Integration: Architecture, Design, Fabrication*, California Inst. Tech., pp. 65–90, 1979.

- H. T. Kung and C. E. Leiserson, 'Algorithms for VLSI Processor Arrays', in *Introduction to VLSI Systems* (C. Mead and L. Conway, eds.), Addison-Wesley, Reading, MA, pp. 271–292, 1980.

A good exposition is:

- H. T. Kung, 'Why Systolic Architectures?' *Computer* **15-1** (1982), pp. 37–46.

The recent results about the limitations of parallelism when it comes to actually configuring processors in three-dimensional space *[p. 272]* appear in:

- P. M. B. Vitányi, 'Interconnects in Multiprocessor Systems: The Communication Bottleneck', Manuscript, Oct. 1986.

The parallel computation thesis *[pp. 272–273]* is discussed, and evidence for it is presented, in:

- L. M. Goldschlager, 'A Universal Interconnection Pattern for Parallel Computers,' *J. Assoc. Comput. Mach.* **29** (1982), pp. 1073–1086.

An important paper leading to this thesis is:

- V. R. Pratt and L. J. Stockmeyer, 'A Characterization of the Power of Vector Machines,' *J. Comput. Syst. Sci.* **12** (1976), pp. 198–221.

The class NC *[pp. 273–274]*, *Nick's Class*, is named after Nicholas Pippenger, who first defined and investigated it. The two relevant papers are:

- S. A. Cook, 'Towards a Complexity Theory of Synchronous Parallel Computation,' *L'Enseignement Mathématique* **27** (1981), pp. 99–124.

- N. Pippenger, 'On Simultaneous Resource Bounds (preliminary version),' *Proc. 20th IEEE Symp. on Foundations of Computer Science*, IEEE, New York, pp. 307–311, 1979.

The following is a detailed and informative survey of results and open questions concerning NC and several of its interesting subclasses:

- S. A. Cook, 'A Taxonomy of Problems with Fast Parallel Algorithms,' *Inf. and Cont.* **64** (1985), pp. 2–22.

Several solutions to mutual exclusion problems *[pp. 276–277]* are surveyed in the books by Ben-Ari, Hoare, and Filman and Friedman already mentioned. The solution presented here, both the two-processor version and the general version *[pp. 278–281]*, appears in:

- G. L. Peterson, 'Myths about the Mutual Exclusion Problem,' *Inf. Proc. Lett.* **12** (1981), pp. 115–116.

Safety and liveness *[p. 282]* are discussed in:

- L. Lamport, 'Proving the Correctness of Multiprocess Programs,' *IEEE Trans. Soft. Eng.* **SE-3** (1977), pp. 125–143.

- S. Owicki and L. Lamport, 'Proving Liveness Properties of Concurrent Programs,' *ACM Trans. Prog. Lang. Syst.* **4** (1982), pp. 455–495.

Apart from these two, here are some of the basic papers that discuss correctness proofs for concurrent protocols *[pp. 282–283]*:

- S. Owicki and D. Gries, 'Verifying Properties of Parallel Programs: An Axiomatic Approach,' *Comm. Assoc. Comput. Mach.* **19** (1976), pp. 279–285.

- K. R. Apt, N. Francez and W. P. de Roever, 'A Proof System for Communicating Sequential Processes,' *ACM Trans. Prog. Lang. Syst.* **2** (1980), pp. 359–385.

- J. Misra and K. M. Chandy, 'Proofs of Networks of Processes,' *IEEE Trans. Soft. Eng.* **SE-7** (1981), pp. 417–426.

Temporal logic *[pp. 283–285]* was suggested for use in the context of algorithmic specification and verification in:

- A. Pnueli, 'The Temporal Semantics of Concurrent Programs,' *Theor. Comput. Sci.* **13** (1981), pp. 45–60.

The following is a detailed survey of temporal logic and its uses:

- A. Pnueli, 'Applications of Temporal Logic to the Specification and

Verification of Reactive Systems: A Survey of Current Trends,' in *Current Trends in Concurrency* (J. de Bakker *et al.*, eds.), Lecture Notes in Computer Science, Vol. 224, Springer-Verlag, Berlin, pp. 510–584, 1986.

An interesting recent approach to dealing with concurrency, which is different from temporal logic, can be found in:

- V. R. Pratt, 'Modelling Concurrency with Partial Orders,' *Int. J. Parallel Prog.* **15** (1986), pp. 33–71.

A good place to read about the automatic verification of finite-state protocols *[p. 285]* is:

- E. M. Clarke, E. A. Emerson and A. P. Sistla, 'Automatic Verification of Finite-State Concurrent Systems Using Temporal Logic Specifications,' *ACM Trans. Prog. Lang. Syst.* **8** (1986), pp. 244–263.

The definitive reference on fairness in its various guises *[pp. 285–286]* is:

- N. Francez, *Fairness*, Springer-Verlag, Berlin, 1986.

The dining philosophers problem *[pp. 287–288]* was introduced by E. W. Dijkstra and is described, for example, in:

- E. W. Dijkstra, 'Hierarchical Ordering of Sequential Processes,' *Acta Inf.* **1** (1971), pp. 115–138.

Solutions to it appear in the books already mentioned. That there is no fully distributed, fully symmetric solution with no new processors *[pp. 288–289]* was observed in:

- N. A. Lynch, 'Fast Allocation of Nearby Resources in a Distributed System,' *Proc. 12th ACM Symp. on Theory of Computing*, ACM, New York, pp. 70–81, 1980.

Here are some references to the concurrent languages SIMULA 67, Concurrent PASCAL, ADA, MODULA-2, and concurrent versions of PROLOG *[p. 289]*:

- G. Lamprecht, *Introduction to SIMULA 67* (2nd edn.), Braunschweig, Germany, 1983.

- P. Brinch Hansen, *The Architecture of Concurrent Programs*, Prentice-Hall, Englewood Cliffs, NJ, 1977.

- J. G. P. Barnes, *Programming in ADA* (2nd edn.), Addison-Wesley, Reading, MA, 1984.

- N. Wirth, *Programming in MODULA-2* (3rd, corrected, edn.), Springer-Verlag, Berlin, 1985.

- K. Clark and S. Gregory, 'PARLOG: Parallel Programming in Logic,' *ACM Trans. Prog. Lang. Syst.* **8** (1986), pp. 1–49.

- E. Shapiro, 'Concurrent PROLOG: A Progress Report,' *Computer* **19**: 8 (1986), pp. 44–58.

A good survey of the features present in many concurrent programming languages *[pp. 289–294]* is:

- G. R. Andrews and F. B. Schneider, 'Concepts and Notations for Concurrent Programming,' *Comput. Surv.* **15** (1983), pp. 3–43.

As far as particular features go, the **cobegin** statement *[p. 289]*, as well as semaphores *[pp. 290–291]*, appear in:

- E. W. Dijkstra, 'Cooperating Sequential Processes,' in *Programming Languages* (F. Genuys, ed.), Academic Press, New York, 1968.

Monitors *[pp. 291–292]* appear in:

- C. A. R. Hoare, 'Monitors: An Operating System Structuring Concept,' *Comm. Assoc. Comput. Mach.* **17** (1974), pp. 549–557.

The '!' and '?' notations for communication rendezvous *[pp. 292–293]* appear in Hoare's aforementioned book and were first discussed in:

- C. A. R. Hoare, 'Communicating Sequential Processes,' *Comm. Assoc. Comput. Mach.* **21** (1978), pp. 663–677.

Data-flow diagrams and similar formalisms for the functional decomposition of large systems *[pp. 294–295]* appear in many texts on *software engineering*. Among them are:

- M. A. Jackson, *System Development*, Prentice-Hall, Englewood Cliffs, NJ, 1982.
- R. S. Pressman, *Software Engineering – A Practitioner's Approach*, McGraw-Hill, New York, 1982.
- I. Sommerville, *Software Engineering* (2nd edn.), Addison-Wesley, Reading, MA, 1985.
- E. Yourdon, *Managing the Structured Techniques*, Prentice-Hall, Englewood Cliffs, NJ, 1979.

The term *reactive systems [p. 295]* is due to A. Pnueli; see the survey of temporal logic previously mentioned.

Statecharts *[pp. 297–300]* were introduced in the following paper, which also contains (a more intricate version of) the digital watch example;

- D. Harel, 'Statecharts: A Visual Formalism for Complex Systems,' *Sci. Comput. Prog.* **8** (1987), pp. 231–274.

Some other approaches to the behavioral specification of reactive systems are Petri nets, CSP, CCS and ESTEREL. The paper and book by Hoare are good places to read about CSP, as is:

- S. D. Brookes, C. A. R. Hoare and A. D. Roscoe, 'A Theory of Communicating Sequential Processes,' *J. Assoc. Comput. Mach.* **31** (1984), pp. 560–599.

Descriptions of the other three approaches can be found, respectively, in:

- W. Reisig, *Petri Nets: An Introduction*, Springer-Verlag, Berlin, 1985.

- R. Milner, 'Calculi for Synchrony and Asynchrony,' *Theor. Comput. Sci.* **25** (1983), pp. 267–310.

- G. Berry and I. Cosserat, 'The ESTEREL Synchronous Programming Language and its Mathematical Semantics', in *Seminar on Concurrency* (S. D. Brookes and G. Winskel, eds.), Lecture Notes in Computer Science, Vol. 197, Springer-Verlag, Berlin, 1985.

Chapter 11

This is another chapter that discusses work too new to have produced good textbooks. Some of the results reported in the text of the chapter have not even appeared in final form in a journal or conference proceedings. As far as periodicals go, the ones listed in the general section and in the notes for Chapter 2 are relevant here too.

*   *   *

The probabilistic solutions to the dining philosophers problem *[pp. 303–305]*, including the argument that the first one admits lockouts *[pp. 305–306]*, appear in:

- D. Lehman and M. O. Rabin, 'The Advantages of Free Choice: A Symmetric and Fully Distributed Solution to the Dining Philosophers Problem,' *Proc. 8th ACM Symp. on Princ. Prog. Langs.*, ACM, New York, pp. 133–138, 1981.

The primality-testing algorithm that runs in polynomial-time but depends on the extended Riemann hypothesis *[p. 309]* appears in:

- G. L. Miller, 'Riemann's Hypothesis and Tests for Primality,' *J. Comput. Syst. Sci.* **13** (1976), pp. 300–317.

The $O(N^{O(\log \log N)})$ algorithm for the problem *[p. 309]* appears in:

- L. Adelman, C. Pomerance and R. S. Rumely, 'On Distinguishing Prime Numbers from Composite Numbers,' *Ann. Math.* **117** (1983), pp. 173–206.

The two first papers containing nontrivial randomized, probabilistic algorithms appear to be the following, containing the two independent algorithms for testing primality *[pp. 309–315]*.

- M. O. Rabin, 'Probabilistic Algorithm for Testing Primality,' *J. Number Theory* 12 (1980), pp. 128–138.

- R. Solovay and V. Strassen, 'A Fast Monte-Carlo Test for Primality,' *SIAM J. Comput.* 6 (1977), pp. 84–85.

The one described in more detail in the text is that of Solovay and Strassen. A preliminary version of Rabin's algorithm appeared in the following influential paper:

- M. O. Rabin, 'Probabilistic Algorithms,' in *Algorithms and Complexity: Recent Results and New Directions* (J. F. Traub, ed.), Academic Press, New York, pp. 21–40, 1976.

A good expository survey of primality-testing algorithms is:

- C. Pomerance, 'The Search for Prime Numbers,' *Scientific American* 247: 6 (1982), pp. 136–147.

An important paper on nonprobabilistic pattern matching *[p. 313]* is:

- D. E. Knuth, J. H. Morris and V. R. Pratt, 'Fast Pattern Matching in Strings,' *SIAM J. Comput.* 6 (1977), pp. 323–350.

The probabilistic fingerprinting algorithm for the problem *[pp. 314–316]* appears in:

- R. M. Karp and M. O. Rabin, 'Efficient Randomized Pattern-Matching Algorithms,' Technical Report TR–31–81, Aiken Comput. Lab., Harvard Univ., Cambridge, MA, 1981.

The following paper contains a short, but informative, survey of approaches to probabilistic algorithms:

- R. M. Karp, 'Combinatorics, Complexity, and Randomness,' *Comm. Assoc. Comput. Mach.* 29 (1986), pp. 98–109.

An influential paper on probabilistic Turing machines and probabilistic complexity classes *[pp. 316–317]* is:

- J. Gill, 'Computational Complexity of Probabilistic Turing Machines,' *SIAM J. Comput.* 6 (1977), pp. 675–695.

Here are two good places to read about these complexity classes and their interrelationships:

- S. Zachos, 'Robustness of Probabilistic Computational Complexity Classes under Definitional Perturbations,' *Inf. and Cont.* 54 (1982), pp. 143–154.

- U. Schöning, *Complexity and Structure*, Lecture Notes in Computer Science, Vol. 211, Springer-Verlag, Berlin, 1986.

Two books dealing extensively with cryptography *[pp. 318–319]* are:

- A. G. Konheim, *Cryptography: A Primer*, John Wiley & Sons, New York, 1981.

- D. E. R. Denning, *Cryptography and Data Security*, Addison-Wesley, Reading, MA, 1982.

Public-key cryptography *[pp. 319–323]*, together with the idea of using the scheme for signatures *[pp. 321–322]*, was proposed in the following important paper:

- W. Diffie and M. Hellman, 'New Directions in Cryptography,' *IEEE Trans. Inform. Theory* **IT-22** (1976), pp. 644–654.

The RSA cryptosystem *[pp. 323–325]* is named after its inventors and appears in:

- R. L. Rivest, A. Shamir and L. Adleman, 'A Method for Obtaining Digital Signatures and Public-Key Cryptosystems,' *Comm. Assoc. Comput. Mach.* **21** (1978), pp. 120–126.

The version that is provably as difficult to crack as it is to factor large numbers *[p. 325]* appears in:

- M. O. Rabin, 'Digitalized Signatures and Public-Key Functions as Intractable as Factorization,' Technical Report MIT/LCS/TR-22, Mass. Inst. of Tech., Cambridge, MA, 1979.

An expository survey of public-key cryptography is:

- M. E. Hellman, 'The Mathematics of Public-Key Cryptography,' *Scientific American* **241**: 2 (1979), pp. 146–157.

The card dealing protocol *[pp. 325–328]* appears in:

- A. Shamir, R. L. Rivest and L. Adleman, 'Mental Poker,' in *The Mathematical Gardner* (D. A. Klarner, ed.), Wadsworth International, Belmont, CA, 1981.

That information might leak when cryptographic functions, such as the RSA ones, are used naively in the card dealing protocol *[p. 328]* was shown in:

- R. J. Lipton, 'How to Cheat at Mental Poker,' *Proc. AMS Short Course on Cryptology*, American Mathematical Society, 1981.

A more complex probabilistic protocol for dealing cards, which does not suffer from these drawbacks, appears in the following paper:

- S. Goldwasser and S. Micali, 'Probabilistic Encryption,' *J. Comput. Syst. Sci.* **28** (1984), pp. 270–299.

Important work towards providing proof methods for verifying probabilistic algorithms *[p. 329]* appears in:

- D. Kozen, 'Semantics of Probabilistic Programs,' *J. Comput. Syst. Sci.* **22** (1981), pp. 328–350.

- D. Lehman and S. Shelah, 'Reasoning with Time and Chance,' *Inf. and Cont.* **53** (1982), pp. 165–198.

- S. Hart, M. Sharir and A. Pnueli, 'Termination of Probabilistic Concurrent Programs,' *ACM Trans. Prog. Lang. Syst.* **5** (1983), pp. 352–380.

That problems in RP have polynomial-sized Boolean circuits *[pp. 329–330]* is proved in:

- L. Adleman, 'Two Theorems on Random Polynomial Time,' *Proc. 19th IEEE Symp. on Foundations of Computer Science*, IEEE, New York, pp. 75–83, 1978.

An interesting paper that discusses the two approaches to probabilism in algorithmics and their relationship *[p. 330]* is:

- A. C-C. Yao, 'Probabilistic Computations: Towards a Unified Measure of Complexity,' *Proc. 18th IEEE Symp. on Foundations of Computer Science*, IEEE, New York, pp. 222–227, 1977.

Three of the many interesting 'how to' papers on cryptographic protocols, secret-keeping protocols and similar issues are:

- A. Shamir, 'How to Share a Secret,' *Comm. Assoc. Comput. Mach.* **22** (1979), pp. 612–613.

- M. Blum, 'How to Exchange (Secret) Keys,' *ACM Trans. Comput. Syst.* **1** (1983), pp. 175–193.

- A. C-C. Yao, 'How to Generate and Exchange Secrets,' *Proc. 27th IEEE Symp. on Foundations of Computer Science*, IEEE, New York, pp. 162–167, 1986.

An early and influential paper related to random and pseudo-random numbers *[pp. 330–331]* is:

- A. Kolmogorov, 'Three Approaches to the Concept of 'the Amount of Information',' *Probl. Inf. Transm.* **1** (1965), pp. 1–7.

Information about pseudo-random numbers in the polynomial-time sense discussed in the text *[p. 331]* can be found in:

- A. Shamir, 'On the Generation of Cryptographically Secure Pseudo-Random Sequences,' *Proc. 8th Int. Colloq. Automata, Lang. and Prog.*, Lecture Notes in Computer Science, Vol. 115, Springer-Verlag, Berlin, pp. 545–550, 1981.

- A. C-C. Yao, 'Theory and Applications of Trapdoor Functions,' *Proc. 23rd IEEE Symp. on Foundations of Computer Science*, IEEE, New York, pp. 80–91, 1982.

- M. Blum and S. Micali, 'How to Generate Cryptographically Strong Sequences of Pseudo-Random Bits,' *SIAM J. Comput.* **13** (1984), pp. 850–864.

A detailed account of random and pseudo-random numbers appears in:

- D. E. Knuth, *The Art of Computer Programming*, Vol. 2: *Seminumerical Algorithms*, Addison-Wesley, Reading, MA, 1969.

An interesting exposition of some of the issues is:

- G. J. Chaitin, 'Randomness and Mathematical Proof,' *Scientific American* **232**: 5 (1975), pp. 47–52.

Chapter 12

There are several textbooks on artificial intelligence (AI). Here are four:

- N. J. Nilsson, *Principles of Artificial Intelligence*, Tioga Publishing Co., Palo Alto, CA, 1980.

- P. H. Winston, *Artificial Intelligence* (2nd edn.), Addison-Wesley, Reading, MA, 1984.

- E. Rich, *Artificial Intelligence*, McGraw-Hill, New York, 1984.

- E. Charniak and D. McDermott, *Introduction to Artificial Intelligence*, Addison-Wesley, Reading, MA, 1985.

A rather extensive treatise on the subject is:

- *The Handbook of Artificial Intelligence* Vols. 1, 2, 3 (A. Barr and E. A. Feigenbaum, eds.), William Kaufmann Inc., Los Altos, CA, 1981, 1982.

A good exposition of the subject is:

- D. L. Waltz, 'Artificial Intelligence,' *Scientific American* **247**: 4 (1982), pp. 118–133.

In addition to these, there are numerous books and papers that discuss the social, philosophical and historical aspects of computerized intelligence. Some of the most interesting and provocative of these are:

- J. R. Lucas, 'Minds, Machines, and Gödel,' *Philosophy* **36** (1961), pp. 112–117.

- J. Weizenbaum, *Computer Power and Human Reason*, W. H. Freeman & Co., San Franciso, 1976.

- H. Dreyfus, *What Computers Can't Do* (revised edn.), Harper & Row, New York, 1979.

- Y. Wilks, 'Dreyfus's Disproofs,' *British J. Philos. Sci.* **27** (1976), pp. 177–185.

- D. R. Hofstadter, *Gödel, Escher, Bach: An Eternal Golden Braid*, Basic Books, New York, 1979.

- S. Turkle, *The Second Self: Computers and the Human Spirit*, Simon & Schuster, New York, 1984.

- H. Gardner, *The Mind's New Science*, Basic Books, New York, 1985.

- J. V. Grabiner, 'Computers and The Nature of Man: A Historian's

Perspective on Controversies about Artificial Intelligence,' *Bull. Amer. Math. Soc.* **15** (1986), pp. 113–126.

The following book contains some of the original papers in the field of AI, including influential papers by A. Turing, A. Newell, M. Minsky and H. A. Simon:

- *Computers and Thought* (E. A. Feigenbaum and J. Feldman, eds.), McGraw-Hill, New York, 1961.

An influential early book is:

- A. Newell and H. A. Simon, *Human Problem Solving*, Prentice-Hall, Englewood Cliffs, NJ, 1972.

An interesting account of the history of AI is:

- P. McCorduck, *Machines Who Think*, W. H. Freeman & Co., San Francisco, 1979.

The following periodicals publish papers about AI:

- *Artificial Intelligence*, abbreviated *Artif. Intel.*; published in nine issues a year by Elsevier Science Publishers.

- *Cognitive Science*, abbreviated *Cogn. Sci.*; a quarterly published by Ablex Publishing Co.

- *Computational Intelligence*, abbreviated *Comput. Intel.*; published by the National Research Council of Canada.

- *IEEE Transactions on Systems, Man and Cybernetics*, abbreviated *IEEE Trans. Syst., Man, Cybern.*; a bimonthly published by the IEEE.

- *IEEE Transactions on Pattern Analysis and Machine Intelligence*, abbreviated *IEEE Trans. Pat. Anal. Mach. Intel.*; a bimonthly published by the IEEE.

In addition, the following publish short papers, anecdotes and announcements relevant to AI:

- *ACM SIGART Newsletter*; an unrefereed newsletter published quarterly by ACM's Special Interest Group on Artificial Intelligence.

- *The AISB Quarterly*; an unrefereed newsletter published by the European Association for Artificial Intelligence.

*   *   *

The aphorism relating thinking computers to swimming submarines *[p. 333]* is due to E. W. Dijkstra. The term *artificial intelligence [p. 334]* is generally believed to have been coined by J. McCarthy in 1956. The two robot stories *[pp. 334–335]* were related by a member of the AI Laboratory at the Massachusetts Institute of Technology.

The following paper by Alan Turing is considered to be one of the most insightful and fundamental papers on AI. It outlines and then counters several standard arguments against AI *[p. 336]*, and goes on to propose the Turing test *[pp. 336–338]*:

- A. M. Turing, 'Computing Machinery and Intelligence,' *Mind* **59** (1950), pp. 433–460. (Reprinted on pp. 11–35 of the aforementioned *Computers and Thought*.)

Most of the books on AI contain discussions of the Turing test. ELIZA *[pp. 338–339]* was written by J. Weizenbaum, and is described in the following influential paper:

- J. Weizenbaum, 'ELIZA – A Computer Program for the Study of Natural Language Communication between Man and Machine,' *Comm. Assoc. Comput. Mach.* **9** (1966), pp. 36–45.

The hypothetical exchange concerning zupchoks *[pp. 339–340]* was inspired by a similar one (concerning *cyborgs*) that appears on page 317 of:

- I. Pohl and A. Shaw, *The Nature of Computation: An Introduction to Computer Science*, Computer Science Press, Rockville, MD, 1981.

The AI books listed discuss game playing and game trees *[pp. 340–342]* in detail. An interesting expository article about computerized backgammon *[p. 340]* is:

- H. Berliner, 'Computer Backgammon,' *Scientific American* **242**: 6 (1980), pp. 64–72.

An account of the program beating the world champion in backgammon *[p. 340]* appears in:

- H. Berliner, 'Backgammon Computer Program Beats World Champion,' *Artif. Intel.* **14** (1980), pp. 205–220.

Two extremely important early papers on computerized checkers *[p. 340]* describe a system that actually learns. They are:

- A. L. Samuel, 'Some Studies in Machine Learning using the Game of Checkers,' *IBM J. Res. Develop.* **3** (1959), pp. 211–229. (Reprinted on pp. 71–105 of the aforementioned *Computers and Thought*.)

- A. L. Samuel, 'Some Studies in Machine Learning using the Game of Checkers. II – Recent Progress,' *IBM J. Res. Develop.* **11** (1967), pp. 601–617.

Good places to read about computerized chess *[pp. 341–342]* are:

- M. Newborn, *Computer Chess*, Academic Press, New York, 1975.

- D. Levy and M. Newborn, *More Chess and Computers: The Microcomputer Revolution, The Challenge Match*, Computer Science Press, Rockville, MD, 1980.

- *Chess Skill in Man and Machine* (2nd edn.; P. W. Frey, ed.), Springer-Verlag, New York, 1983.

The following short paper provides some information about Hitech, the chess program considered by many to be (currently) the best:

- H. Berliner and C. Ebeling, 'The SUPREM Architecture: A New Intelligent Paradigm,' *Artif. Intel.* **28** (1986), pp. 3–8.

The story about searching for a contact lens *[pp. 342–343]* was inspired by page 318 of Pohl and Shaw's book.

Good places to read about computerized vision and robotics *[p. 344]*, respectively, are:

- R. O. Duda and P. E. Hart, *Pattern Classification and Scene Analysis*, John Wiley & Sons, New York, 1973.

- D. Marr, *Vision: A Computational Investigation into the Human Representation and Processing of Visual Information*, W. H. Freeman & Co., San Francisco, 1982.

- S. Ullman, *The Interpretation of Visual Motion*, MIT Press, Cambridge, MA, 1979.

- J. S. Albus, *Brains, Behavior, and Robotics*, Byte Books, Peterborough, NH, 1981.

- J. J. Craig, *Introduction to Robotics: Mechanics and Control*, Addison-Wesley, Reading, MA, 1985.

- R. P. Paul, *Robot Manipulators: Mathematics, Programming, and Control*, MIT Press, Cambridge, MA, 1981.

A periodical devoted to robots is:

- *Journal of Robotic Systems*, abbreviated *J. Robot. Syst.*; a bimonthly published by John Wiley & Sons.

Virtually every textbook on AI discusses the minimax idea and its corresponding algorithm, the alpha-beta procedure *[pp. 345–346]*. The term 'alpha-beta procedure' appears to be due to J. McCarthy, and the use of the minimax idea in searching goes back to Shannon's important paper:

- C. E. Shannon, 'Programming of a Computer for Playing Chess,' *Phil. Magazine* **41** (1950), pp. 256–275.

A thorough and detailed account of heuristic search procedures, including their mathematical analysis and history, is:

- J. Pearl, *Heuristics: Intelligent Search Strategies for Computer Problem Solving*, Addison-Wesley, Reading, MA, 1984.

The following book contains several recent articles on the problem of knowledge representation *[pp. 347–348]*:

- *Readings in Knowledge Representation* (R. J. Brachman and H. S. Levesque, eds.), Morgan Kaufmann Publishers, Los Altos, CA, 1985.

The following contain a wealth of material on expert systems *[pp. 348–349]*:

- R. Duda and E. Shortliffe, 'Expert Systems Research,' *Science* **220** (1983), pp. 261–268.

- *Building Expert Systems* (F. Hayes-Roth *et al.*, eds.), Addison-Wesley, Reading, MA, 1983.

The following books constitute a collection of papers on computerized learning *[pp. 349–350]*:

- *Machine Learning: An Artificial Intelligence Approach* (R. S. Michalski *et al.*, eds.), Tioga Publishing Co., Palo Alto, CA, 1983.

- *Machine Learning: An Artificial Intelligence Approach* Vol. II (R. S. Michalski *et al.*, eds.), Morgan Kaufmann Publishers, Los Altos, CA, 1986.

Two influential early papers on computerized deduction *[pp. 349–350]* are:

- A. Newell and H. A. Simon, 'The Logic Theory Machine,' *IRE Trans. Infor. Theory* **IT-2** (1956), pp. 61–79.

- H. Gelernter, 'Realization of a Geometry Theorem-Proving Machine,' *Proc. Western Joint Comput. Conf.*, WJCC, pp. 273–282, 1959.

Here are three books that describe the problems and achievements in the computerized understanding of natural language *[pp. 351–353]*:

- T. Winograd, *Languages as a Cognitive Process*, Vol. I: *Syntax*, Addison-Wesley, Reading, MA, 1983.

- R. Schank, *The Cognitive Computer: On Language, Learning, and Artificial Intelligence*, Addison-Wesley, Reading, MA, 1984.

- J. F. Sowa, *Conceptual Structures: Information Processing in Mind and Machine*, Addison-Wesley, Reading, MA, 1983.

Important early work on the subject is described in:

- T. Winograd, *Understanding Natural Language*, Academic Press, New York, 1972.

Hearing the pledge of allegiance as having to do with pigeons *[p. 351]* is an idea used by W. Safire in one of his *On Language* columns in *The New York Times* some years ago.

The discussions with Jim's phone *[pp. 352–353]* are based on those appearing in the following delightful essay:

- R. W. Lucky, 'The Phone Surrogate,' *IEEE Spectrum* **23**: 5 (1986), p. 6.

An interesting paper relevant to the closing remarks about analytic AI *[p. 353]* is:

- A. Goldberg and I. Pohl, 'Is Complexity Theory of Use to AI?' in *Artificial and Human Intelligence* (A. Elithorn and R. Banerji, eds.), Elsevier Science Publishers, 1984.

A somewhat different approach to solving some of the problems raised in the chapter, dubbed *connectionism*, is described in:

- D. E. Rumelhart, J. L. McClelland and the PDP Research Group, *Parallel Distributed Processing: Explorations in the Microstructure of Cognition*, Vol. 1: *Foundations*, MIT Press, Cambridge, MA, 1986.

of making many books there is no end
Ecclesiastes 12: 12

Index

For I am full of words
Job 32: 18

So was ended all the work
I Kings 7: 51

(Note: Index does not refer to names that appear in bibliographic notes only.)